FLOWS

Charting the Undercurrents of Social Life

Lorne Tepperman

Rock's Mills Press

PUBLISHED BY
Rock's Mills Press

Cover: iStock.

First Edition
ISBN-13: 978-0-9881293-3-7

Contents

INTRODUCTION

Why Study Flows?

Let's begin with a high-profile social problem. These days a lot of people are concerned about cyberbullying and its consequences. But despite widespread public concern, we know surprisingly little about cyberbullying. Imagine a high school student facebooks this message: "Joanie Thompson is a slut. Last weekend, she did it with three members of the basketball team." Well, we can with good reason suspect that Joanie won't be happy to have this message circulating: that's simple psychology. But what do we know about the social effects of this message? How many people will re-circulate the message online or in face-to-face gossip? How many will believe the message? How many will talk about it with Joanie? How many will post their own messages about Joanie, or about the sender of this message? How long will it take at the high school (and beyond it) for this rumour to die out?

The fact is, we don't know the answers to any of these questions. When you get to the end of this book, you will find me asserting that sociology does not have the answers to many important, obvious, and basic questions about the world we live in. This is a controversial statement, and it brings the book to a close with a bang. But throughout the book, I build up to this conclusion by pointing to one topic after another that can be viewed from a different, and I believe more fruitful, standpoint. That's because the assertion that sociology has been on the wrong track necessarily leads to other questions: for example, how did it get on the wrong track to begin with, and why? To answer those questions would take a whole other book; so consider the present book merely a promise and a tease.

Flows is about discrete, countable things that move around: for instance, ideas that move from person to person (e.g., rumours), as well as people who move from place to place. It's that quality of movement that makes such things eminently measurable. Each thing of interest is either *here* or *there*, *present* or *absent*, *one* or *zero*. And that fundamental fact makes this book easy to understand—easier to understand, that is, than a book about complicated matters like feelings and relationships that vary over time in hard-to-measure ways. In short, this book is about flows of information and flows of people, flows of inventions and flows of capital—things that flow through space and flow through time. More specifically, this book is about the flow processes known as *diffusion*, *migration*, *mobility*, and *renewal*.

The book has two premises that should be acknowledged at the outset. First, thinking in terms of flows is an intuitively appealing way of grasping a range of underlying (i.e., hidden to common sense) social processes that are fundamental.

Second, thinking about society as a set of flow processes is not merely to apply a metaphor, but rather to use a universal language that applies across sub-areas of sociology, tying them together. Hence the elegance of the flow approach. Everything important in social life can, in principle, be analyzed from a flow perspective.

In the pages ahead, I will discuss a wide range of social phenomena through the lens provided by the flows perspective. But the book also raises the possibility that using this approach will uncover new problems previously hidden from view, a few of which are considered toward the end of the book. Indeed, *Flows* proposes a different way of looking at sociology and, more broadly, of looking at the world.

Thomas Kuhn, in his classic work *The Structure of Scientific Revolutions*, says a scientific paradigm is an *exemplar*: it specifies key problems, concepts, and relationships to be investigated by researchers, as well as what method they should follow. He also says a revolutionary paradigm has appeal because it takes anomalies (i.e., inconvenient facts) overlooked by old paradigms and makes sense of them. So it would be fitting for the reader to ask at this point: Are there anomalies in previous sociological theory for which the flow approach offers an explanation? Is there a demonstrable failure—or multiple failures—in existing theory that the flows approach can hope to remedy? Can I supply some examples of these, to justify the book that follows?

The various chapters in this book are full of such examples, but let's start with two simple but general ones: the problems of *social structure* and *social class*. Social structure and social class are two of the most essential concepts in sociology. You simply can't study sociology without thinking about these concepts. Yet, after two centuries, sociologists still disagree about how to define these concepts and how to measure them. And because of these disagreements in the area of definition and measurement, we have few, if any, strong, empirically testable (and tested) theories about either concept. What we have is a huge number of suppositions, insights, guesses, and bold declarations.

That isn't much to show for two centuries of work.

The problem with both social structure and social class is that, although they are said to be significant and controlling in social life, you can't see them doing their important work: you can only see their *effects*—or supposed effects. Thus, conformity to social rules is said to be an effect of social structure; yet social deviance abounds. Exclusion, exploitation, and alienation are said to be effects of social class; yet even these effects (or supposed effects) are hard to define and hard to measure.

Now consider social class, which is more specific than social structure and therefore a more manageable idea. When we speak about the *bourgeoisie* or *ruling class*, we have in mind a set of people who live near one another, interact and intermarry, dress in similar ways, send their children to the same schools and summer camps, join the same clubs, and vote for the same political parties. (They also are said to exercise *power*, another hard-to-define concept that is important but invisible except in its supposed effects.) And sometimes, depending on how we define and measure the bourgeoisie and ruling class, we find that reality conforms to our expectations. But often it doesn't; and in any case, is this not putting the horse before the cart? Shouldn't we be defining social class in terms of shared observable behaviour: that is, by saying that people belong to the same social class if and only if they live near one another, interact and intermarry with one another, send their children to the same summer camps, and so on?

This may sound trivial, but it goes to the heart of the problem. If sociology is meant to be a social *science* with clearly defined concepts and empirically testable hypotheses, then it should focus on phenomena that are unquestionably observable: on interactions, intermarriages, associations, voting choices, uses of time and money, and so on. By that standard, what could be more observable than flows? To repeat what was said earlier, flows are discrete, countable things that move around: ideas that move from person to person, and people who move from place to place. That makes them eminently measurable. Ideas, customs, and technologies have either been adopted in a new location, or they haven't. People have either moved from place A to place B, or they haven't. People have either been born or died, or they haven't.

Now, the study of social mobility is more complicated than these other flows, because (as we will see) it sometimes relies on a shared definition of *social class*. You cannot see social mobility unless there is an agreed-on set of social positions arrayed from top to bottom. Such a hierarchy exists in many formal organizations—for example, in armies, civil services, and large business organizations; and so the flow of people "up and down" these organizations is clear and meaningful. Similarly, it is meaningful to talk about "careers" in such organizations—also, entries and retirements; we can see these things happening. Here, again, the study of flows is eminently useful. It is only when we rely on such weakly defined concepts as social class and social structure that social mobility becomes a problematic concept. So I will try to steer clear of such situations.

In the end, this book tries to make sociology more powerful by making social life clearer, through the study of flows. Flows are not only visible, they are also important—arguably, the undercurrents of social life. They are processes that affect everyone's life, but processes no one sees or thinks about unless they are pointed out. As such, they provide an appealing approach to sociology for newcomers: things (and ideas) that, once learned, can never be unlearned—a dramatic new way of looking at our lives as members of society. Everything that matters—well, almost everything—is in this book: birth, death, and all the stops in between, but viewed in a way you will never find on the Disney Channel or even HBO. If you ever wanted to know more about gossip, cyberspace, job searches, accidents, doomed marriage prospects, or flows of migrants, you've come to the right place.

This book will show you that most important social events can be understood as the results of flows. As well, the book will show how various types of flows resemble one another. Thus, flows of information and flows of people, flows of inventions and flows of capital, are not only important: they are also similar and they are related. This becomes clearer when flow processes are reduced to their simplest elements, as I will do toward the end of the book.

There are, historically, two main reasons why people have tried to build simple, explanatory pictures of social life—utility and esthetics. This book supports both rationales. First, if we humans are ever to build a better world, we must first understand the world better: that is, understand the social laws that determine our behaviour in groups, organizations, and societies. The sociological enterprise is inherently aimed at usefulness, and this book hopes to contribute to this planned utility. Second, the Western scientific enterprise, ever since the Renaissance, has been guided by a fascination with the elegant symmetry and simplicity of nature. The idea of finding natural laws and drawing deductions from them represents, for many scholars and scientists, the highest creative accomplishment.

Many sociologists, too, have been drawn forward by curiosity about the lawfulness of social life. Speaking personally, my own curiosity has focused on the study of social networks and flows of resources through networks. I owe this interest, in large part, to teachers like Harrison White, who led in the systematic study of networks, and George Homans, who led in the formal study of human groups. A third scholar, Talcott Parsons, persuaded sociology (for a time) that cultures, societies, organizations, and even small groups are all social systems with similar operating structures. That difficult, beautiful, and challenging idea is still provocative, though its meaning has changed for us repeatedly over time.

One problem we sociologists have faced is making sense of human agency: that is, the role of human actors who reflect on their lives and take action in their own best interests. Some sociologists have tended towards a psychological approach, in which actors' perceptions, values, beliefs and motivations are at the forefront, though always within a social context. In this book, I take a different approach, focusing instead on social structures and opportunities. The reader is urged to imagine that I am discussing colonies of ants, or swarms of meteorites—at the very least, units whose individual properties and trajectories are determined by, not determinants of, the flows described here. In short, this book is, in its orientation, what used to be called *sociologistic* and perhaps today is called *structuralist*.

I take this approach not because people really are colonies of ants or swarms of meteorites. The assumption is only intended to exaggerate—to throw into stark relief—the importance of structural forces in social life. This is necessary because, normally, we are bombarded on every side by countervailing *psychologistic* thinking, in the pop psychology that fills our media, the voluntaristic ideology that shapes our conversation, and the economic individualism that informs our marketplace relations. *That* style of thinking focuses inevitably on individual actors and the contents of their heads: their values, aspirations, goals, rational thoughts, and so on. *That* approach assumes that society is little more than a collection of atomized, self-interested people, and focuses on the individual without considering social influences.

There *is* something to be said for that style of thinking—after all, we are all born and die as individuals, and we all possess unique combinations of thoughts and interests that we express in uniquely combined ways—but the psychologistic picture of society has been nonetheless overstated. So this book takes a starkly different path, focusing on the nature of flows themselves, rather than the characteristics of the individuals who are part of those flows and carried along by them. As such, it represents an appreciation and synthesis of a scholarly community's work on the problem. The usual caveats about responsibility for error must be read in.

CHAPTER ONE

The Study of Diffusion

Diffusion is one of several flow processes discussed in this book. As we will see, diffusion is the flow of information, ideas, inventions, practices, and supports from one person (or one group or society) to another. In this sense, it is about the sharing of social inventions and about cooperation—thus, about the highest achievement of human societies. Diffusion does away with the primitive economic notion that society is nothing but a collection of self-interested individuals, each striving on his or her own to maximize well-being in the most rational way. Society is more than a market in which individuals compete for superiority, ignorant of or in competition with other members of society. It is a place where people learn from one another and build on the gifts and achievements of others. It is also, to be sure, a place where people, individually and in groups, spread their tentacles of control over other individuals and groups. But it is not a place of lonely, unconnected individuals.

An Overview

We can view diffusion as the informal or face-to-face spread of information through a population. This includes the flow of cultural information from one society to another, the spread of investment information, the transmission of rumours within a community, the communication of safe-cracking techniques in a prison, the telling of tall tales and nasty gossip among friends, the passing along of employment information among job candidates, and casual advice about birth control or safe sex, among many other things.

The phrase *among many other things* is important, because the amount and kind of information that diffuses informally is vast. In fact, most of the important and believable information that we receive comes through processes of diffusion. We have not acquired this information at our mother's knee, in school, in church, or in front of the television set. The things we *do* learn from our parents, our teachers, our ministers, and our media idols also raise our awareness about important topics. However, we spend a great deal of our lives informally seeking and processing information from other sources that helps us reject, modify, or trust what we have learned in other ways. And, today, our best, most credible information comes to us through diffusion.

As sociologists, we study diffusion in particular ways. So, in the sections that follow, we look at different varieties of diffusion in different settings. From a sociological point of view, we will look for answers to certain general questions about the ways societies work. These questions include, but are not limited to the following: How does that thing we call social structure influence how fast people get new information and how many people in total get that information? How does the structured flow of information create and maintain social inequality? How does social structure hamper the easy flow of information, causing socially harmful, irrational, or inefficient outcomes? How can we overcome such limitations?

Consider, for instance, the question of why, in most universities, there is a relative abundance of professors who are white, able-bodied men. What is there about the diffusion or informal flow of job information that is likely to work against the hiring of women, visible minorities, First Nations people, or physically disabled people? And how, besides enacting employment equity policies, could a society change this situation?

In answering these and other questions about diffusion, we will look at the various conditions that influence diffusion. Specifically, we will consider (1) what social *contacts* make information flow possible, and how do they form? (2) What *kinds of information* are most likely to flow through social networks, and why? (3) Under what conditions do recipients *accept* the information received? And (4) how does the information received affect people's *behaviour*?

To answer these questions, we need to know something about the underlying structure of people's relationships. Specifically, it helps if we know something about the *character* of linkages between "units," whether these units are people, positions, organizations, or countries, as well as the *strength* of these linkages and the probability that information will flow from one unit to another. We will find the type of information that flows informally will vary with the type of linkage and its strength. Some information flows only through what sociologists call "strong ties," but other information flows through "weak ties" as well.

As mentioned earlier, we will consider the rate of flow of information, the total amount of information that flows, and how characteristics of the "social structure" affect this flow. Studying the diffusion of information tells us a lot about the hidden structure of society: about who is connected to whom, which people (or organizations) are closer to each other and which are more distant or positively out of touch, and what are the strengths of the relationships between different groups in society. We will not only be interested in how social structure affects flows: we will also be interested in how flows of information affect the social structure within which they take place. For example, we will see that a limited flow of information maintains social segregation and inequality, while a more open flow of information promotes social integration and equality.

In later sections we will discuss *social networks*, *cliques*, and *social isolates*. In doing so, we will discover that, because they are unconnected to sources of information, social isolates receive the least information and they receive it last. Units that have the fewest and weakest social relationships with one another are least likely to receive information from, or about, each other. Socially dominant units are more likely to send and receive information than any other units.

We will also discover that units in open (that is, non-cliquish) networks receive a larger quantity, variety, and quality of information than units in closed, cliquish, or segregated networks. So, the diffusion of information, whether among societies, organizations, or individuals, is largely determined by the degree of clique formation and segregation in a social network. *Cliques* are groups of highly interconnected people who are only loosely connected to other groups of people. Individual people, groups, organizations, and even nations can form cliques. The defining feature of a clique is structured information flow: people inside the clique get more and different information than people outside the clique, because of differences in their social connectedness. The higher the level of shared knowledge and interaction within a group, and the lower the level of shared knowledge and interaction across groups, the more likely these groups are to remain cliques.

From this standpoint, a social unit–whether a group, community, or nation–is defined by the excess of information that flows inside its borders, compared with the information flowing across its borders. Karl Deutsch first explored this idea with empirical data sixty years ago in his classic work, *Nationalism and Social Communication* (1953). Psychologist and mathematician Anatol Rapoport (1958) likewise considered how information flow was shaped by networks "biased" by strong (i.e., close) versus weak (i.e., distant) ties. Later, Kathleen Carley (1989, 1990) extended the problem to the study of cliques, suggesting in some of her writing that the social segregation of people in a network is a direct product of restricted information flow.

This restriction of information flow causes people to stop interacting, even if they previously had high levels of interaction. (Think, for example, of what happened to social relationships in Rwanda, or the former Yugoslavia, after violent armed conflict between different ethnic groups.) As we will see, cliquishness and segregation are bad for the flow of information in society as a whole. The more segregated and cliquish two groups are, the less likely information is to diffuse between them. The result is mutual ignorance, distrust, prejudice, and what sociologists call *social distance*. As people come to share more information, distinct cliques break down or become less segregated from each other. This carries an important message for people: knowledge is not only power, as some have said. Shared knowledge is also the basis for familiarity, integration, and (to some degree) social equality.

To summarize, then, the diffusion of information is an everyday phenomenon of incredible importance. We take diffusion for granted because it is so common. Yet it regulates what we know about the world, what we think, how we vote and spend our money, whom we talk to and whom we date and marry. In the sections that follow, we examine varieties of diffusion in different settings. The purpose is to flesh out the general, abstract points made in this introduction.

We begin by examining varieties of diffusion between larger social units: cultures, societies, and organizations. We then examine varieties of diffusion between smaller social units, especially individuals in social networks. These discussions allow us to consider further, in a more systematic manner, some of the important social results of diffusion.

As we have seen, social or sociocultural diffusion is the process by which people in society come to adopt a new practice, behaviour, idea, or artifact. Since new ideas are always being diffused in a population as diverse and technologically active as our own, but patterns of adoption are time-dependent, a large portion of the population will, at any given time, be uninitiated into a new idea or practice. In other words, not everyone will be up-to-date on new ideas. In fact, in any population, most people will be either ahead of the average or behind the average when it comes to knowledge and adoption of most new ideas and technologies. This means that a general concept like "Canadian culture" is pretty meaningless because, at any given moment, widely diverse cultural beliefs and practices co-exist side by side. In fact, in any society, many subcultures co-exist at the same time: regional subcultures, ethnic subcultures, even class subcultures. Even your neighbours are ahead of you, or behind you, in regard to a vast number of ideas and opinions.

We will have occasion to think about the implications of this fact later in the book.

Flows of Information

Nowhere is diffusion more evident than in the flows of information that surround all of us. As we noted earlier, diffusion is how we get most of the information we use and trust. It is also the way we get the gossip and rumours that influence our practical judgment in everyday matters, often for the worse. We get diffused information about jobs, entertainment, political matters, shopping bargains, and new scientific theories. There is more information around us today than at any time in human history, and it is impossible for any human being, in his or her lifetime, to acquire absolutely all (or even some reasonably large fraction) of that information, whether scientific, political, cultural, or otherwise, as some individuals aspired to do in earlier centuries. The sheer volume of information that now exists explains why there's no possibility we will ever again see universally knowledgeable savants like Erasmus or Voltaire or Leonardo da Vinci. Today there's just too much to know, and it's changing all the time.

In fact, we are so surrounded by information that we are positively swamped by it. With globalization and present-day information technology, we rarely have a problem finding out about anything: the rules of a Basque game called pelota, the value of a Singaporean dollar, who Zeus was married to in ancient mythology, and so on. Our problem is making sense of this mountain of information that we can so easily access, and properly evaluating the conclusions we draw from it.

Sometimes this information problem is trivial. We can all live without knowing the rules of pelota, can't we? (If you think you can't, read Callede [1993] on the topic.) But often the problem is important. Sometimes it's even a matter of life and death. People are increasingly interested in knowing how to evaluate the risks associated with different courses of action. Where should they go on vacation? Which car repair shops rip you off? Which best-sellers are worth reading? Should they agree to chemotherapy for their cancer problem? The choice of action is theirs, and they want to make the best choice. Nevertheless, they need to know how to do that.

CANCER PATIENTS. Consider this problem: Cancer patients want more information and more reassurance than their doctors have the time to provide. Their doctors realize this but can't do much about it; they're short of time. As a result, support groups grow up to provide information and reassurance to patients and their care-giving kin. These groups vary in size, and range from expert-led to peer-led, from mainly informational to mainly morale-building, and so on. Whatever their structure, these groups all have adherents, because they provide needed emotional support, social support, and/or information. Increasingly, the Internet has emerged as a key support medium, complete with online research libraries, discussion groups, chat rooms, and experts you can email. The increasing reliance of patients and their families on online resources begs the question: How well do such resources work to inform and reassure cancer patients?

In an early attempt to answer this question, an oncologist and a team of researchers (Barry Tepperman et al., unpublished, 1995) administered a multiple-choice questionnaire through a website. The researchers designed it to compare patients and family caregivers' perceptions of cancer information they received from Internet sources with information they received from their own physicians.

The data revealed that 72% of respondents contact the Internet at least daily; by contrast, 78% speak with their doctors only once a month or less often. Respondents online gather (medical) information 59% of the time and seek support (counseling and peer validation) 41% of the time. Physicians, it turns out, refer respondents to counseling or conventional support groups only rarely, and seldom encourage, evaluate, or act on information from outside sources (such as the Internet). Sixty-one percent of respondents in the study report having brought their doctors new information from these outside sources, while 39% report having attended conventional support groups or individual counselling; these respondents are especially likely to have brought outside information to their physicians. Only 38% note that their doctors also use Internet cancer resources.

Of course, in the twenty years since this research was done, the numbers will have changed; but the fundamental problem with cyberspace remains: once we gain access to a universe of information through the Internet, how do we assess it before using it? And of course, this problem goes back fifty years to a time well before the Internet existed, when Katz and Lazarsfeld (1957) developed their theory of two-step communication flow. Where mass media are concerned, they wrote, the first step for an audience is getting the information; the second step is evaluating that information before acting on it.

The big but not-so-surprising finding of the early cancer patient survey: Respondents tell us that finding information on the Internet is easier than gaining access to physicians for information. They view physicians as being more reliable sources of information, and are more likely to base their decisions about care on the information received from physicians. However, they rate Internet sources highly as being more detailed and more supportive than their physicians, and as providing more practical advice for daily living. As a result, most respondents report relying on physicians only to resolve conflicts between other information sources. They don't feel they can rely exclusively on their doctors to provide all the information they need.

Conclusions? Cancer patients seeking information value their physician as their most reliable source of information and guidance. However, they rate online resources as more accessible, supportive, detailed, and practical than the information they receive from physicians. They rely on physicians to resolve confusion over conflicting information, though a great many physicians are reportedly averse to information from outside sources (such as the Internet). That said, physicians will likely remain inaccessible and, if only for that reason, Internet use by cancer patients is likely only to increase.

This study captures, in a nutshell, the problem most people face where information is concerned. We all want lots of information and we all want credible information, but you can't often get both from the same source. So, we need to use multiple sources of information in our social networks, then cross-check that information, source against source. This is how we make health decisions, consumer decisions, political decisions, investment decisions, marriage decisions, career decisions, and whatever other decisions we face.

Information in and of itself is not enough to bring about a change in our behaviour if the costs or risks of behaviour change are high, as they will be for cancer patients. No one whose life (or time or money) is at risk will be governed exclusively by information they get from the Internet: for example, information about what medications or treatments to take, what to eat or not eat, and so on. And this is true in all domains of life: we seek not only information but also assurance the information we receive is credible, safe, and legitimate. That's why we all evaluate the information we receive before acting on it.

Sometimes, publicly broadcast information—the information we get on TV or in the newspapers, for example—is safer, more credible, and more legitimate than other kinds of information. That's because, at least in theory, such information has to satisfy both the professional standards of broadcasters and journalists themselves as well as a variety of legal and regulatory requirements, while diffused information does not. When people "broadcast" information, it flows simultaneously from a single source to multiple recipients. When they "diffuse" information, it flows sequentially from recipient to recipient, until many have received it (and sometimes distorted it, as in the game "broken telephone"). We broadcast information impersonally through the mass media but diffuse information personally, through networks of personal relationships. Some information—for example, rumours about the death of a celebrity—flows by both methods. Rumours about less publicly known people spread only through our social networks, if they spread at all.

People who rely on the broadcast method of communication—whether politicians or commercial advertisers—often try to influence the receiving public, or audience, by putting a "spin" on the information they are disseminating. After all, they want to receive the most votes or make the most sales. However, the audience is also aware and suspicious of this motivation. Today, many people verify the broadcast claims of marketers and politicians on the Internet, a type of mechanized diffusion process. Additionally, people rely on advice from others whose opinion they respect: people perceived as having particular expertise or wisdom.

In short, when cancer patients approach their physician with questions about information they have obtained on the Internet, they are doing the same thing you do when you ask your mother to advise you on casserole preparation, having found a detailed recipe in *Good Housekeeping* but not being quite sure whether it's worth making or not. The only difference is that cancers are a matter of life and death, while casseroles (usually) are not. In both cases—in all cases—we collect information, and then we evaluate it with the help of people we know and trust.

THE CASE OF HYBRID CORN. This twinned process of collection and evaluation plays an important role in the process of social innovation. All innovations, which are adoptions of new technologies or practices, require the collection and evaluation of new information. Consider this example, one with a long history in sociology: the adoption of hybrid corn by farmers in the American Midwest.

Diffusion research in social science in fact began with the study of the adoption of new hybrid seeds in Iowa. Hybrid seeds were *not* genetically modified seeds, as we might imagine today. Rather, they were seeds cross-bred naturally to flourish under specific growing conditions. For instance, some seeds were selected and perfected to withstand harsh winter conditions and uncertain supplies of moisture. Eventually, strains of corn were created that flourished in those climatic conditions, and, gradually, farmers in those climatic zones adopted these new seeds.

After the ground-breaking study of this process, the study of diffusion exploded: since then, there have been thousands of published studies of the diffusion process. They range from qualitative to highly mathematical, and examine the spread of new crops, technologies, diseases, beliefs, and rumours, among other things. So successful and widespread was the *diffusion model* developed by its originators Ryan and Gross and modified by their successors that by the 1970s researchers had concluded there was nothing left to learn about diffusion. Research on the topic briefly ceased. However, it soon began again, as researchers found new questions, new answers, and new modes of diffusion—none more important than the Internet and social media.

Another example: the diffusion of innovation among municipal police departments in northeastern Illinois. The opportunity to adopt an innovation arose when the Chicago Police Department (CPD) opened access to elements of its new centralized data warehouse to other criminal justice agencies. Through it, the CPD's partner agencies have access to the criminal history of past arrestees, outstanding warrants, the arrest status of juveniles, mug shots, digitized fingerprints, vehicle theft records, traffic violation convictions, and firearms data. Initially, representatives were sent to learn how to use the system, and then they in turn went back and trained the rest of their departments. Through this process, this innovation diffused outward from the CPD to other criminal justice agencies that adopted the technology (Geroski, 2000).

Typically, diffusion researchers focus their attention on answering the following questions: (1) Why are some people early adopters and others late adopters? (2) What factors, such as the perceived attributes of the innovation, explain the rate of adoption (i.e., whether fast or slow, compared to other populations or other innovations)? And (3) how do different communication channels (or information sources) influence the innovation-decision process at various stages? Additionally, researchers examine the *extent* to which an innovation is adopted, as this can be just as important as whether or not the innovation is adopted at all.

The study of police departments provided a clear example of variations in the degree or extent to which an innovation is adopted, and some sense of why these variations occur. In this case, adopters of the data warehouse were much more likely to already be users of databases and data sharing arrangements. More tech-savvy departments were also more likely to make greater use of the data warehouse. Pre-existing factors were important in influencing whether or not the technology was adopted, and the extent to which departments could make use of the database. Training was also important. Not only did other policing agencies have to be made aware that the resource existed; they also had to be instructed on how to use it effectively.

In general, researchers have found that the innovation-decision process is a five-stage sequence consisting of *awareness*, *interest*, *evaluation*, *trial*, and *adoption*. The mass (or broadcast) media are important in creating early awareness, but interpersonal channels are more important at the later evaluation stage. Early adopters of an innovation are typically more cosmopolitan, socially integrated, and open to new information than are later adopters. As we will see later, other variables, such as the structure of people's social networks, also play a part.

The early research on adoption of hybrid corn resulted in one other important discovery: namely, the importance that people attach to learning by doing. Farmers are not inclined to take wild risks; after all, they can go out of business or even starve if they make the wrong decision about a new seed or cultivation technique. So they tend to innovate slowly and carefully. In adopting hybrid corn seeds, the typical corn farmer spent an average of five years from first awareness to final adoption of the new seed. During this time, the farmer tested small amounts of the seed on his own farm, under known farming conditions. Only after the seed had passed this practical test was a farmer willing to risk his entire crop, and his survival, on the innovation.

What researchers found out about diffusion fifty years ago still holds up today. Farming research in Honduras finds that two factors still affect farmers' decisions to adopt new technologies: demographic characteristics (such as education) that influence the farmer's general openness to new methods, and direct training in new methods that farmers obtain from both formal and informal sources. Farmers innovate by getting the information they need and then trying it out, under safe conditions. They "learn by doing" as well as by hearing.

DIFFUSION AS A POPULAR MANIA. Another interesting fact about diffusion is that it demonstrates a characteristic statistical pattern over time. Regardless of what is being diffused, the process tends to take on a characteristic "S-curve" shape, when researchers plot the cumulative percentage of adopters as a function of time. First, there is early experimentation by a few pioneers, who demonstrate its utility to others. This is typically followed by a span of time during which the innovation spreads wildly. The adoption line eventually flattens out with time as late adopters—the few remaining laggards—finally embrace the innovation.

To return to those hybrid seeds: In the early months, when information about the new seed has just appeared, adoptions grow slowly. After a year or two, only a few farmers will have adopted the seed. Then, adoptions begin to speed up. In the third and fourth years of the study, there are twice as many (or even more) new adopters than in the first year or two. The rate of adoption continues to accelerate until (after five or so years) nearly everyone has adopted the new seed, and then the rate of new adoptions slows dramatically. After more than (say) 90% of farmers have adopted the new seed, years may pass before additional people make adoptions. In other words, the last hold-outs may hold out a long time, and some may never adopt a new technology. (We all know people who will "never" use a mobile phone, and in various parts of North America one can find sizable communities of people who have decided, usually on religious grounds, not to use electricity, or not to allow their children to be vaccinated.)

A similar pattern governs the adoption of new technologies in business and industry: for example, the adoption of computer networking in offices, or robots in factories. Gradually, a new technology is made available to substitute for the old technology. Gradually, the new technology takes an ever-larger share of the market. First mainframe computers replace offices full of filing clerks, then standalone computers replace mainframe computers, and then computer networks replace standalone computers. Eventually, laptops replace desktops, and tablets and iPads replace laptops. In each case, there is an initial slow diffusion, followed by rapid diffusion, then market domination by the new technology, then declining domination as yet-newer technologies (both hardware and software) emerge.

As we said, if you plot this process on graph paper, with "time" along the X-axis and "percentage of farmers who have adopted the seed" (or "organizations that have adopted mainframe computers," or any other innovation) along the Y-axis, you will have drawn an S-shaped curve with a long, rapidly rising middle section. What this characteristic shape tells us is that diffusion processes always feature a slow start by the courageous, a rapid, ever faster mania of copying, and a slow finish, with belated adoptions by the fearful, the poorly informed, and, sometimes, those who object to the innovation for moral, religious, or other reasons.

THE CASE OF FERTILITY CONTROL. Many of the most important human transformations of the last millennium have followed just this pattern. Consider the so-called *demographic transition*, by which means the human race exchanged its historic pattern of high mortality and high fertility for low mortality and low fertility. The last part of the transition, fertility reduction, caught on like wildfire in the late nineteenth and early twentieth centuries, thanks to diffusion. In this case, not only information and technologies diffused, but so did social norms, as a great deal of research clearly shows (see, for example, Gutmann et al., 1990; Hsueh and Anderton, 1990; David et al., 1990; Friedlander et al., 1991).

Historical evidence shows, without a doubt, that the 1870s marked a watershed in world history. It was in that decade that western and northern Europe, as well as Canada and the United States, experienced a decisive downturn in the number of children born per family that was to continue and never reverse. This downturn marked the beginning of the end of high fertility for the human race, a pattern that has subsequently spread to southern and eastern Europe, Latin America, Asia, and Africa.

Amazingly, outside of Europe, none of the social and economic variables studied by researchers predicted this downturn as well as one might have expected (Reher, 2004; Lee, 2003). In the rest of the world as in Europe, industrialization, urbanization, literacy, and large reductions in mortality all played a part in reducing fertility to some extent. However, none of these influences was as strong as earlier theorists had expected. Indeed, in the developing world, these factors were *less* influential in reducing fertility than they were in the West. Yet fertility still declined. Surprisingly, in many places, in both Europe and elsewhere, fertility reduction was as likely to occur *without* industrialization and urbanization as with it—if, that is, birth control information, technology, and motivation were present. In short, the diffusion of information and practices from early developing countries to later developing countries dramatically speeded up the process of transition.

Diffusion even played a part in the original nineteenth-century European demographic transition. Through diffusion, fertility reduction caught on like wildfire in many regions of Europe, as a result of geographic proximity to other low fertility areas. This was true even in regions that were not, themselves, urban or industrial. And researchers have found similar diffusion patterns in the American South before 1940, in Taiwan between 1960 and 1980, and elsewhere. All of this evidence suggests that interpersonal influence enters into people's decisions to limit their childbearing. As with other important decisions, when deciding whether to have additional babies, people gather information and evaluate it. In doing so, they pay attention to the thinking of people they know and respect. Even among people traditionally committed to producing large families, the decision to produce a smaller family (by means of contraception or abstinence) is an important one. So, people take it only after consulting with kin, friends, and respected elders (Martin, 1990).

VIRAL INFORMATION. One common example of diffusion by electronic means is also one that most people are aware of, however unhappily. We refer, of course, to the chain letter (or, these days, the chain email). Chain letters are messages that encourage the recipient to pass them along to others, in an attempt to spread them to as many people as possible. These days, chain letters seldom take physical form, and instead are disseminated by email, text messaging, and postings on social network sites. As a result, the data, news, and opinions embedded in and spread by chain letters now continuously circulate on a global level, and much more quickly than in the days of "snail mail" chain letters.

By following the path of one of these chain letters, we can trace the propagation of a single piece of news and information at a person-by-person level. The results are interesting and perhaps not what common sense would predict. Rather than fanning out widely and reaching many people in a very few steps, chain letters spread in a narrow tree-like pattern that continues for several hundred steps. Social networks are highly clustered, and information can take widely varying amounts of time to reach different edges in the network. The spread of information through a social network is far more complicated than simple theoretical models may predict, and this provides opportunities for the message to be distorted and lost as it diffuses. The message can also change and adapt as it circulates from person to person. By studying the process of information diffusion through the Internet, we can gain a better understanding of the global dynamics underlying social phenomena such as opinion formation and political mobilization (Liben-Nowell and Kleinberg, 2008).

With the growth and evolution of the Internet, peer-to-peer referrals have become an increasingly important phenomenon, and marketers want to exploit this immense potential through viral marketing campaigns. Viral marketing is based on consumer-consumer communications, so the diffusion of information is no longer between the advertiser and consumer, but between consumers themselves. Researchers want to know what factors impact people's decisions to respond to ads, in order to make their own advertisements more effective. They also want to know how they can increase the chances that their message will spread through diffusion, and how effective these electronic referrals will be to create awareness, trigger interest, and generate sales or product adoptions.

A field study that attempted to identify these factors observed the reactions of 1,100 individuals after they received an unsolicited e-mail from an acquaintances inviting them to take a survey and then spread the word about it. *Social tie*—the strength of the relationship between sender and recipient—turned out to be a factor that influenced how recipients behaved; however, it produced different effects depending on the stage of the process. The strength of the social tie between the sender and recipient made the recipient more aware of the message, and the degree to which the recipient felt emotionally close to the sender increased interest in the message and its contents; but demographic similarity actually exerted a negative influence on each stage of the decision-making process as to whether or not to pass the message on (De Bruyn and Lilien, 2008).

Message dissemination—the actual act of spreading a message—can be either intentional or unintentional. Unintentional message dissemination occurs when consumers don't play an intentional or deliberate role in the process. One example of unintentional message dissemination involved the launch of Microsoft's Hotmail service. Each outgoing email sent via this free Web-based service included a line promoting the service, displayed where it would be seen by every person who then received an email from a Hotmail user. This was an effective strategy, as Hotmail, which was launched in 1996, had 12 million users sign up within two years, with a marketing budget of only $500,000 during this time period. Intentional message dissemination, on the other hand, occurs when consumers willingly promote a product to their friends. This can be done through an explicit incentive (such as that used by PayPal, which offered financial incentives to have people refer their friends) or a non-explicit incentive, such as an individual's own desire to share a fun or intriguing service with friends.

Whereas most individuals use email to communicate, marketers use it to reach potential customers. As such, advertising practitioners interested in implementing viral efforts are concerned about the motivations, attitudes, and behaviours of the people who send the email to others. They are interested in turning customers into a potential marketing force. Marketers seek to leverage the power of these interpersonal networks to promote a product or service, and transform communication networks into influence networks. They seek to try capture the attention and trigger interest of a wider audience, ultimately leading to greater adoption or sales. Messages that spark strong emotion—humor, fear, sadness, or inspiration—are likely to be forwarded. Emails about free stuff and containing helpful tips are passed along almost half of the time. The most successful messages appeal to a consumer's motivation and desire for fun, entertainment, and social connections (Phelps et al., 2004).

CONCLUDING WORDS. A telling feature of diffusion is that it is locational. We know diffusion is going on when we see clumps or geographic concentrations of a given behaviour. With diffusion, a behaviour fans out from a centre of behavioural density in gradual stages. Information that diffuses arrives at the nearest locations first and the more distant locations later. The extent of geographic spread, whether it is information, technology, or behaviour that is diffusing, is a joint function of time and distance. Locations that are the same distance from the source are likely to be influenced equally and simultaneously. The distance an innovation has travelled is mainly a function of how much time has elapsed since the process began. (Of course, the world is no longer as simple as it once was; today, distance and time have been re-configured by the spread of global communications networks, as well as such transportation innovations as intercontinental air travel, nationwide freeway networks, and, before that, national rail systems.)

Consider the diffusion of fertility reduction. It began nearly 150 years ago, before the Internet, before television and radio, before airplanes, in the very decade when the telephone was invented and when railroads were considered cutting-edge technology. In those days, telegraph wires stretched across much of Western Europe and North America, the first undersea cables had already been laid, but most information travelled as it had for thousands of years: on foot or by horseback. Nonetheless, despite what would today be considered primitive conditions, fertility reduction diffused from northern and western Europe to eastern and southern Europe, and, from there, to the Middle East and the Far East. The entire process has taken about a century and a half, though it sped up after the Second World War due to the "broadcasting" of new birth control information and technology through the developing world.

Not all cases of diffusion, however, show this same characteristic locational pattern, where distance diffused is a function of time. Consider the diffusion of technology from the long-established industrial societies to rapidly industrializing nations such as Brazil, India, China, and Nigeria. This alternate pattern shows there are conditions under which ideas, information, capital and technology can spread rapidly to non-contiguous units. In particular, non-contiguous (leap-frogging) diffusion occurs when a mobile "culture carrier" gets involved. Any one of many mobile people (and things) can be "culture carriers," including migrants, books, photographs, movies, and memories. Foreign students are one example of culture carriers: they come to Canada, spend four years getting a degree, and then return to their country of origin, carrying a variety of Canadian artifacts, customs, and values with them.

Media of communication are themselves "culture carriers." As the Canadian political economist Harold Innis showed, human history has alternated between media biased toward the conservation of information over time (e.g., stone tablets) and media biased toward transmission over distance (e.g., written pages and television images). To read information from a stone tablet is to put a different existential meaning on the information than it is to read the same information from a printed page, a television screen, or a computer monitor. Transience and speed imply disposability, even allowing for wide transmission. And today, we recognize that even books are more permanent and less transportable than digital messages and entertainment.

Another type of non-contiguous diffusion occurs when technology connects people in a virtual rather than a physical neighbourhood. So-called *invisible colleges* present us with one example of a virtual neighbourhood, and the network of diffusion-researchers itself represents just such an invisible college. Or consider the network of thinkers we associate with a *school of thought*. A school of thought does not have a geographic location or street address: rather, it is made up of a set of shared beliefs, a set of procedures for discussing these beliefs, some measure of group identification, and occasions for face-to-face interaction, however infrequent. Diffusion of ideas within this school of thought does not require geographical propinquity. But it does require communication and trust.

Geographic proximity probably increases familiarity and trust among people who share information. But how much familiarity and face-to-face contact, and therefore proximity, do people need to trust each other as credible sources of information? We don't have a general answer for that question. Research into distant and electronic communication (for example, e-mail) will gradually reveal the degree to which people can generate (or at least simulate) trust technologically. Written materials (such as books) and audio materials (such as music downloads and CDs) help diffuse ideas, norms, and innovations across space and time more quickly than would otherwise be the case. Further research and future developments will reveal whether in the age of cyberspace diffusion can, for the first time in human history, be freed from the limitations of location altogether.

Flows of Support

Like information, *social support* also diffuses through social networks. This section is about the kinds of support people receive from their social networks and the reasons this support is important.

Social support, like information, is *socially structured*, in the sense we get it from a small number of others and don't get it from the vast majority of people on earth. Chiefly, we get social support from that score of people we call family and close friends, and occasionally from other members of our social network. But taken altogether, far fewer than the 500 to 1,000 people in a typical social network, let alone the seven billion people alive on earth today, give us the practical and emotional support we need to survive. To see this, just ask yourself: Who would you phone if you were wrongfully arrested and needed help with getting a lawyer or bail? If you suddenly had a heart attack and needed help getting to the hospital? If your wallet was stolen while you were away in a strange city or foreign country? If your wife or girlfriend had just dumped you and you felt like killing yourself? The number of people you might consider calling would indeed be small, and you can name all of them without any trouble.

Let's consider in more depth the social support provided to sick people and others who care for them. Common sense suggests that people, especially sick people, will readily seek out health information. Having obtained the information, they will then use it without needing much encouragement, let alone compulsion. In fact, most of us would tend to think that, after seeing a physician, the socially isolated person would be as just as likely to follow a doctor's orders as the socially integrated person. Unfortunately, this is just not so. Like other good things in life, good health is the product of social relationships as well as information. Maintaining good health usually means interacting with other people.

To get well, sick people must play a social role: that is, they must behave like a patient. As Talcott Parsons (1951) showed in his classic paper on the medical profession sixty years ago, we expect sick people in our society to play this role, and we criticize them if they don't.

In return for being allowed to skip their everyday activities and neglect their social obligations, sick people have to appear ill, consult a doctor, and follow the doctor's advice. Failure to do so will lead others to label the person a "bad patient" or even a malingerer. A person so labeled may forfeit the privileges accorded to sick people (e.g., time off work, lying around home in pajamas, and the sympathy of friends and family). So, from a social standpoint, sickness in our society requires the successful, even long-term performance of role expectations associated with "patienthood." Patients have to play their part, doctors theirs, and the supporting cast of friends and relatives also has an important part to play in this culturally scripted drama.

It is through social interaction that people come to recognize (or acknowledge) their health problems, contact health professionals, and comply with medical advice. Three factors influence the decisions people make when they experience a health problem. One is the nature of the sick person's social network: for example, its size and type of constituent ties or relations. People with larger, more varied networks are likely to have better health, if they are permitted to discuss their health with network members (Meier et al., 1996). Related and important is the advice, material aid, and emotional support that a sick person receives. People who get more social support tend to recover faster, other things being equal. We will have more to say about the role of family supports in a later chapter.

A third factor is the sick person's attitude toward illness and medical care. It is important to remember that attitudes are not created in a vacuum, and are heavily influenced by the people around us. Sick people need support from people who are energetic and engaged. They also need help from people who are sympathetic, not passing judgment on them. Ideally, medical caregivers should be the least stigmatizing members of society, but this is often not the case. Many hold and express negative views of their patients, especially in regard to patients with mental illnesses. They may see the mentally ill as potentially volatile and dangerous, and as a result, discriminate against them. It is difficult to imagine the patient having the necessary positive outlook on treatment if his or her doctor cannot overcome such prejudice and communicate respectfully.

The same situation is all too often encountered in medical practitioners' interactions with patients with HIV/AIDS. Many doctors still tend to be hesitant to perform surgery on HIV/AIDS patients, and are sometimes uncomfortable administering even minor medical procedures. Such stigmatization is one of the many problems affecting the psychosocial well-being of people who are HIV positive (Sadoh et al., 2009). How the patient is treated will affect the patient's recovery, and an accepting attitude is hugely beneficial. This means that care networks can play a large role in determining the attitude of the patient, and his or her outlook on life during the time of illness. Community supports also play an important part in helping sufferers deal with their illness (Drucker, 1990).

In turn, supportive behaviours are shaped by the flow of information about the disease, something which is tied up with health promotion strategies (Plympton and Hibbard, 1991); and these strategies follow the characteristic geographic patterns of spread (Smallman-Raynor and Cliff, 1990). The flow of correct information through the mass media is especially important, and wrong information can be damaging (Reardon and Richardson, 1991). Network members help one another assess the credibility and trustworthiness of the health care system, and of advertised remedies.

Our personal social network, embedded in this larger national and international network, plays a huge role in achieving and sustaining good health, for it influences what we think and know about health, illness, and treatment. A key player in the patient's illness drama is his or her primary caregiver—especially the sick person's spouse, parent, or child. Caregiving is highly gendered, and the responsibility usually falls on women. Men who have a spouse visit the doctor more often, for instance, because their wives often assume responsibility for managing the calendar and booking the appointment.

But being a caregiver is often taxing. The caregiver may have a full- or part-time paid job, in addition to domestic and caregiving responsibilities. Whatever their other duties, the addition of primary caregiving drains a caregiver's time and energy. People vary widely in how well they adapt to caregiving demands; and some illnesses are more taxing than others. Yet often, the caregiver finds herself needing support. The physical, emotional, and psychosocial hardships experienced as a primary caregiver can result in *caregiver burden*, an affliction we discuss later in this chapter and elsewhere.

A COMMON EXAMPLE. Take cancer patients. Cancer patients and their caregivers have a lot of respect for doctors and especially for doctors' professional expertise. Caregivers want to tap into that expertise. They also want doctors to recognize their role in helping to manage the illness, and to provide professional support, useful information, help in learning personal coping strategies, regular updates on the patient's condition, and education about the nature of the disease itself. Most often, however, doctors are unable to provide information and encouragement to the degree that is necessary.

This unavailability (as we have all learned from experience, doctors are busy people) may have long-term effects on the relationship among patients, caregivers, and their doctors. For example, it may lead to the erosion of trust. Interpersonal trust depends on the degree to which patients see their doctors as competent, responsible, and caring. The development of a two- (or three-) way relationship encourages trust, with this being accomplished through continuity of care, time allotted for responses to patients' questions, patient instruction in the details of the disease and its treatment, and patient participation in decision-making. Many medical leaders fear that such trust is gradually eroding. They blame the commercialization of medical care, conflicts of interest, media attention to medical uncertainty and error, and the growth of managed care. All these factors add up to what, in effect, becomes a bureaucratic and industrial approach to healthcare.

Given the relative unavailability of their doctors, many patients and their caregivers look for help from other sources. Support groups are one such source; they vary widely in size, composition, and type of activity. Medical professionals lead some, social-service professionals lead others, and peers lead others still. They all share a desire to help patients and caregivers help themselves and one another. However, most people get far more of the information and encouragement they need from their personal networks than from special-purpose support groups. We tend to interact and rely on those people with whom we have many different types of (often long-term) ties. These people tend to be found in our personal social support networks, not in special-purpose or focused support groups, although at the same time we must remember that we are all members of many different groups and networks at any given time.

Empirical studies (for example, Rhodes and Jason, 1990; Hawley and DeHaan, 1996; Dumont and Provost, 1999; Patterson, 2002; and Pietrzak et al., 2009) show that the support received from one's social network is a key factor in explaining resilience in dealing with life stresses and adversity. Social relationships give people a sense that they are receiving social support, and this perceived social support is important to their well-being. Beyond that, social networks are also important for providing real emotional and instrumental sustenance, as well as regulation and control.

Strong social networks encourage people to address their medical needs and use the health care system regularly. As we will see shortly, they also increase compliance with treatment plans. It is through personal and inter-organizational networks that people seek help with their health problems. As a result, the characteristics of such networks make a crucial difference in the care a sick person receives. Network size and cohesiveness are especially important: large, cohesive networks are best for people's health. Among mental health patients, network size predicts frequency of hospital stays and the use of other services. Interestingly, as the patient's network size increases, outpatient service use increases and in-patient hospitalization rates decrease. Among older people, more resource-rich and diversified networks of friends and neighbours lead to more social support and, as a result, fewer limitations on activity and better health. Among people with HIV/AIDS, large social network sizes lead to greater longevity. Talking about one's health with network members is also key.

Typically, large, cohesive networks are also associated with higher levels of social participation, and this, in turn, leads to higher levels of well-being and life satisfaction. Thus, engaged membership in a social network predicts well-being.

Personal characteristics also make a difference: they interact with network characteristics to produce positive health outcomes. For example, a larger social network is especially important for sick people who are less trusting than average; because they are distrustful, they tend to use the resources available in their networks less efficiently. For people who are more trustful, and therefore better able to mobilize support from their networks, network size is less important.

Some evidence suggests that social networks can in certain circumstances be detrimental to health—for example, through peer pressure to smoke, drink, or to hold skeptical views of the health care system. However, these are exceptions to the rule; normally, social networks help people maintain good health. Even among people who are not currently ill, social networks can be useful in this regard. That is why some health programs encourage the formation of new self-sustaining friendship networks. People who participate in these programs improve their social networks and increase their quality of life and self-esteem. They supply as well as receive social support. This is especially important for old people who live alone or have small kinship networks, and therefore receive less support than others. Not having adult children as part of one's social network limits potential informal care.

Social workers and nurses recognize the importance of good networks. As such, a key part of all case management is the reconstruction of social support networks that eroded over time or were damaged by an inability to cope with chronic illness. Interaction with family and friends often declines after people become caregivers, likely because caregiving limits one's time and strains the health of the caregiver. The demands of caregiving may even cause depression, which further decreases the caregiver's desire for social interaction. As the caregiver draws away from friends and family, he or she receives even less of the social support that would help to alleviate the problem. The resulting feeling of hopelessness can sometimes lead to caregiver burden, the affliction mentioned above.

Caregiver burden may also cause patients to feel guilty and helpless because of their increased dependency on a caregiver. In return, the caregiver may feel overloaded and start to doubt her ability to fully and adequately care for the patient. Caregiver burden can progress to the stage of burnout, which results in irritability, depression, and incapacitating anxiety due to the strong emotional demands that caring for a chronically ill patient entails (Limpawattana et al., 2013). Unfortunately, caregiver burnout is especially common among family members. Factors that affect caregiver burden include socioeconomic background, specific causes of stress related to the severity of the patient's illness, and levels of social support available (Iecovich, 2008).

Large social networks help to lessen the risk; more people around to offer support means that one person does not have to feel as if the entire weight of the world is on her shoulders. Burnout is far more common if the patient has a small social network, as there may not be enough support for either the caregiver or the patient themselves (Iecovich, 2008). Since some caregivers cannot get the all support they need from doctors, support groups, or social networks, technology may have to play a greater role. Increasingly, researchers have paid particular attention to the possible uses of the telephone and Internet as means of delivering social support.

In one study of caregivers to people diagnosed with AIDS, researchers tried out two types of intervention. One used the telephone to create discussion groups. Four or five caregivers held regularly scheduled, supportive conversations with one another over the telephone. The other intervention delivered taped informational lectures over the telephone. After three months, caregivers in both programs showed less psychological distress, more satisfaction with the support they were receiving, and more sense that they were receiving social support. After six months, however, these gains had leveled off or declined. Caregiver burden and social conflict increased again. Neither intervention was, in the long run, sufficient.

When the two programs were compared, it was found that participants learned more by listening to the informational lectures. However, they contacted family and friends more while waiting to enter a peer conversational network.

Health professionals have also set up telephone support groups for AIDS caregivers. Use of the telephone offers people a sense of confidentiality not afforded in face-to-face groups. It also offers support to people who are isolated because of the stigma associated with HIV/AIDS and the lack of adequate support networks in their communities. In one telephone-based program, semi-structured groups of caregivers used conference calls to share information about resources and coping strategies. After eight such calls, participants report having valued the group experience highly. However, though participants expressed satisfaction with the experience, other results were mixed. Measures of social isolation and self-efficacy improved, but measures of social support and coping did not. Put another way, the caregivers felt more effective than before, but they still didn't know exactly what they were doing or who would help them do it.

Like telephone groups, online groups have helped many people who are unable or unwilling to participate in traditional face-to-face support groups. Online groups—groups of people linked and exchanging information online to a bulletin board or chat-room—offer many advantages. They eliminate barriers due to time and distance, can accommodate groups of any size, and provide for an increased variety and diversity of supports. Participation is anonymous, participants have an opportunity to express themselves in writing, and the process offers training experiences for group leaders. As a result, health professionals have adapted information technology to a variety of self-help and mutual aid groups.

In a growing number of instances, lay people have done the same, setting up their own support groups without professional encouragement. These have included online 12-step groups for problems with alcohol, narcotics, eating, gambling, compulsive sexuality, relationships, smoking, and others. Where addiction is the problem, online communication provides more access to support, a dispersal of dependency, and more attention to the needs of people with esoteric concerns. Barriers related to social status cues are lowered. Reluctant group members are more likely to participate, relational communications improve, and people with interpersonal difficulties find themselves opening up more readily. Disadvantages of going online include occasional destructive interactions and lack of clear and accountable leadership. The same elements, especially anonymity and invisibility, that promote ease of online communication sometimes promote recklessness and cruelty. At worst, this may mean for some participants social isolation, ostracism, or stigmatization. Cyberbullying is the most common version of this widespread problem.

Such worst cases are, however, only that: worst cases. In many other situations, online support groups have proved a valuable resource. For example, an early one-year study (Weinberg et al., 1996) was conducted on the merits of Internet-based depression support groups. Almost all respondents reported that talking with others over the Internet helped with their symptoms. The seeking of emotional support was the most common reason for joining the group, though many people also received information about medication. When asked to compare this experience to face-to-face treatment, roughly 40% preferred online communication, while 50% preferred in-person appointments and 10% had no preference. Many online participants even informed their doctors about the group they had joined, and asked the doctor questions about the information they had gathered there. All in all, this online support group was able to foster emotional support and supplement traditional treatment, producing high user satisfaction (see also Houston et al., 2002).

Bear in mind, these numbers are changing all the time, since Internet use is growing exponentially. More and more people around the world use the Internet for more and more purposes; so it is inevitable that attitudes about online support and care will change continuously.

Social supports help caregivers and patients, whether a doctor, group, or network delivers this support. It is still not clear which mode of delivery does best at delivering which kind of support to which kinds of people. Social support is a form of social control and a means of influencing behaviour and delivering benefits. One way it does this is by influencing sick people to comply with the treatment advice they receive from their doctors. Research leaves little doubt that social support increases the likelihood of compliance.

Many factors—among others, cultural, psychological, and demographic—influence a patient's compliance with his or her doctors' advice. However, social relations are especially important.

Of course, the perceived effectiveness of the recommended treatment strongly affects compliance. Other things being equal, people will much more readily do what they believe is good for them. This means that someone must persuade them of the value of the prescribed treatment, and that, in turn, means they must have positive relationships with their doctors and caregivers. (In this sense, a patient deciding to take his medicine is like a farmer deciding to adopt new hybrid seeds.)

A new relationship-centred medical approach, with an emphasis on communication skills, may reduce problems of patient non-compliance. Health professionals will have to understand how certain aspects of the doctor/patient relationship can increase compliance. One would suspect that medical practitioners should avoid implying that a patient has been stigmatized or degraded by diseases such as HIV/AIDS, mental illness, or in some parts of the world, by tuberculosis and cholera. In cross-cultural contexts especially, medical practitioners must not only practice medicine; they must serve as health educators and facilitators, if they are to achieve the goal of having patients comply with treatment recommendations.

Family caregivers can also play an important role in ensuring compliance. For example, behaviour related to keeping medical appointments and adhering to other recommended health-related activities among African American patients with sickle cell anemia or diabetes increased significantly with increases in social support (Belgrave and Lewis, 1994). By contrast, patients with less supportive or involved family caregivers were less compliant (Boucher et al., 1996).

Typically, men and women play different roles in providing care and health support within a family, with women supplying more continuous, emotional, practical, and intimate care. While it is generally understood that treatment for illness is of great value, the *social support* needed to enable such treatment is often overlooked. Social support includes information that diffuses through social channels, but it is more than that. To be useful, social support must give caregivers the right information and encouragement at the right time. Timeliness and a show of concern give the information its legitimacy, which leads to compliance by the patient and a reduction of the caregiver's burden. With an adherence to treatment rules, the patient can pursue his or her "illness career."

Health information gains meaning and value by passing through social channels that in turn hold meaning for the sick person. So, in the end, understanding diffusion means understanding the channels of flow as much as the resources that flow through those channels.

Flows of Practices

Like information and support, social practices flow through social networks of individuals, organizations, communities, and countries. The largely unremembered nineteenth-century sociologist Gabriel Tarde rightly suggested that there were only two master social processes that dominated all the rest. The first is *innovation*—the creation of new ideas and new technologies. The second is *imitation*—the sharing of these new ideas and technologies through simple appropriation.

Imitation is indeed a master process. We are socialized largely through imitation, by observing what we see and hear around us as infants and children, then trying out the new behaviours, attitudes, and ideas ourselves and watching for approving or disapproving reactions. Those imitations that receive approval or win rewards, we keep; the others, we ditch. In school, we study a "curriculum" and learn what we need to know to imitate the older generation intellectually and occupationally. In the mass media, we see certain kinds of behaviours modeled on the news, in dramas, and in reality TV programs and receive vicarious reward or punishment by identifying with the "celebrities" we see there. Then we go out and repeat these behaviours ourselves, dressing, speaking, and striking poses like the ones we have observed in the media.

Imitation is not limited to individuals. Organizations also imitate other organizations, and for similar reasons. Organizations, whether governments, businesses, schools, rap groups, armies, or basketball teams, compete for survival. They all need continuous infusions of new, improved information. Like the corn farmers and caregivers we have discussed, organizations receive their information in a variety of ways that include group gatherings, social networks, and the mass media. And they all, corn farmers, caregivers, and organizations alike, need to evaluate their risks. They imitate other organizations because it is cheaper and easier to imitate than to invent new ideas, technologies, and practices. Moreover, when organizations imitate, they often do so in full knowledge that the ideas, technologies, and practices they are imitating work (more or less) as expected.

Consider a small sample of innovative practices that have diffused in human history, some long ago, many quite recently: hunting technology (Roscoe, 1990), holistic nursing (Johnson, 1990), fluoride mouth rinses in schools (Scheirer, 1990), pest management practices (Thomas et al., 1990), Japanese quality circles (Hodson, 1990), urban civil conflicts (Black, 2013), urban violence (Griffiths, 2013), fertility control (Matthys, 2013), medical innovations (Blume, 2013), opiate pain reliever use (Golub et al., 2013), and generous welfare programs (Schmitt and Obinger, 2013).

Some imitation occurs at the individual level and some occurs at the organizational level, and that makes individuals and organizations similar in one respect. In many ways, though, organizations, especially large formal organizations, are very different from individual corn farmers or caregivers. That's why the study of organizations is a distinct subfield of sociology. Some distinct features of organizations relate to their size. Some organizations comprise a great many people. Large organizations also control a great deal of resources: wealth, authority, prestige, and power. They usually hold more of these resources than any one individual. Large organizations also control more of these resources than smaller organizations, but all organizations use and invest their resources to increase the amount further.

In these respects—number of members and amount of resources—large organizations are only quantitatively different from small organizations. Similarly, to varying degrees, both small and large organizations have to deal with (1) conflicts among their members, (2) competing goals and interests, and (3) conflicts between short-run and long run goals. Whenever you gather a group of people for an extended period, with the purpose of pursuing hard-to-attain goals, you will encounter interpersonal and other problems. This is a reality, whatever the size of the organization.

HOW LARGE ORGANIZATIONS ARE DIFFERENT. In several respects large organizations are also qualitatively different—different in kind—from both individual people and small organizations. First, the larger an organization is, the more complex is its mode of operation: the more roles, levels, and specialized duties there will be. Typically, large organizations are so complex that they have to become bureaucracies, which is to say they adopt detailed bodies of written rules. In this respect, armies and government ministries are different from (smaller) families and hip-hop groups. Families and musical groups often have traditions, rules, and "legends" too, but they rarely write them down, much less turn them into obligations that legally bind every member.

Second, large organizations separate management from ownership. That is, the decision-makers in a large organization typically spend other people's money. "Limited liability" protects them in law if their decisions turn out badly. By contrast, in a family or hip hop group, people spend their own money. If they make a wrong decision, they can go bust and end up in jail, or find themselves sleeping on the street. This means they are likely to adopt a different outlook on risk. Decision-makers in large organizations are likelier to take bigger risks than are decision-makers in small groups, or individual corn-farmers. They are (or at least like to think they are) "too big to fail."

Third, in large organizations there are many decision-makers at many levels and often they don't fully understand or trust one another. They are connected by complicated channels of communication, both internal and external. Usually, decisions are political compromises, or aim to protect the organization or the decision-makers' own positions at the expense of the goals of the organization. Corn farmers and rap groups–people who live close to the ground—are less likely to forget where their interests lie. They may make poor decisions but not because they have removed themselves from the "front line," or because they don't know their customers, their product, or their craft.

What is interesting, then, is that despite these differences in size and structure, all organizations, large and small, use information in (many of) the same ways as individual corn farmers.

THE SHANTYTOWN EXAMPLE. Consider social movements: these are organizations of people that vary widely in size from small to large. They typically have a political agenda: a point of view, a goal, and an audience. They want to bring about social change by exerting pressure on the authorities and gaining public attention through the media.

In recent years Occupy movement protests were held all over North America and in some other parts of the world, to draw attention to the social and economic misbehaviour of dominant financial and political institutions. The best known was the Occupy Wall Street protest in New York City. A sociologist might ask: How were these protest events organized? Were they centrally planned and coordinated? Or did they form individually, with little initial contact, and gradually imitate one another? At this point, we still don't have all the information needed to make such a judgment, though preliminary accounts suggest very loose (if any) on-the-ground organization was present and the Internet was highly useful (Hatcher, 2013; Nielsen, 2013; Tremayne, 2014; and secondarily, Schneiberg, 2013).

We may gain more insight by considering a movement that, after the passage of more than 15 years, we have come to understand better: the Toronto shantytown protest of 1999. One week in Toronto that year, dozens of social activists chose to sleep in downtown Alexandra Park, to draw attention to the plight of the homeless people who were regularly forced to sleep there and in other public places. At six o'clock one morning, hundreds of Toronto police officers gathered to evict the homeless and the activists alike. Some refused to leave, police arrested them, and the story hit the front pages of Toronto's newspapers. Momentarily, the protestors had reminded well-housed Torontonians of the problem of homelessness.

Activists have staged similar but more elaborate protests in American cities and on American college campuses, to call attention to the plight of the socially disadvantaged and other minority groups: the poor, the black, and the homeless. Because they have done this by building "shanties"—temporary, ramshackle huts—for the participants, their protests have come to be called the "shantytown protest" movement. Sociologist Sarah Soule (1997) studied shantytown protests to find out how such social movements influenced one another in the United States and abroad. She found that they do so through indirect network ties.

Shantytown protests spread rapidly among U.S. campuses between 1985 and 1990. The tactic spread among colleges and universities with similar size endowments, of the same level of prestige, and of the same institutional type, Soule reports. Specifically, high-prestige liberal arts colleges with small numbers of African American students had higher-than-average rates of shantytown protest. In other words, Harvard students imitated Columbia students (and vice versa), but neither group imitated students at Towson State College in Baltimore.

To a non-sociologist, this finding may come as a surprise. Common sense suggests that a social protest is most likely to arise where we find the most pressing need, the closest familiarity with a problem, and the most direct, personal interest in solving the problem. Thus, we expect to find shantytown protests occurring on the campuses of low-tuition inner city colleges that enrol large numbers of black and other minority students, or in public parks (like Alexandra Park) to which everyone has free access.

A non-sociologist would also expect to find little connection between the locations of these protests. All that you'd expect the locations of the protests to have in common would be the presence of many poor, unemployed, minority, and homeless people. So we would predict outbreaks of shantytown protest based on demographic similarities among cities. Cities with similar levels of poverty—such as Flint, Scranton, Spokane, and Oakland—would be equally likely to have protests occur. Cities that are alike in being well-off—Boston, New York, and San Francisco, for example—would be equally *un*likely to have protests occur.

So what have sociologists actually discovered about these movements? The first thing to note about findings of sociological research on protest movements is that political protest is *not* disorganized, nor is it the unique product of local invention. It is structured and it draws, through contact and imitation, on protest activities and experience in other locations. This was true even before the rise to significance of the Internet, as we see from research done fifteen years ago on the "contagiousness of mass-mediated terrorism" (Brosius and Weimann, 1991; more recently, Cliff and First, 2013) and the "cross-national diffusion of movement ideas" (McAdam and Rucht, 1993). And as historical research has shown, it was true in much earlier eras as well, as illustrated in work on "cycles and repertoires of popular contention in early modern Japan" (White, 1993), "contagious collectivities and the spatial diffusion of Swedish trade unions, 1890–1940" (Hedstrom, 1994), "guerrilla-movement organizing in Latin America, 1956–1990" (Wickham-Crowley, 2014), and early twentieth century "suffragette militancy" (Edwards, 2014).

Interest in the political impact of the networking is especially keen today, when Internet and other high-speed communication permit almost continuous, instantaneous dissemination of information and advice. Evidence of this comes from a variety of countries spread around the globe. For example, it is discussed in connection with the "diffusion of conflict from Chechnya to Dagestan and Ingushetia" (Campana and Ratelle, 2014), "information diffusion and collective action in China" (Huan and Sun, 2014), and the role of social media in both the 2008 (Stern and Rookey, 2013) and 2012 U.S. elections (Gulati and Williams, 2013). Current research is full of discussions about the political role of diffusion in social networks (Krinsky and Crossley, 2014), "collective action in networked cultures" (Rodriguez, 2014), and "social movements and tactical choice" (Larson, 2013). Already, developed theories are surfacing about "broadcasters and hidden influential in online protest diffusion" (Gonzalez-Ballon et al., 2013), "a new wave of global mobilization" (Tejerina et al., 2013), and "nonviolent civil resistance and social movements" (Nepstad, 2013), all via diffusion, especially using new forms of media.

The other message of the shantytown protest is that leaders innovate early. The scenes of shantytown protest were all high-prestige, high-endowment universities and liberal arts colleges. The students attending these colleges were mainly upper-middle-class white youth with no firsthand experience of poverty, discrimination, unemployment, or homelessness. Some people will conclude from these facts that shantytown protestors are playing at revolution. They may predict that, in time, the protestors will outgrow the desire to outrage their parents, teachers and other rulers. After all, their (Baby Boomer) parents, teachers and other rulers outgrew their desire for outrageous behaviour.

Sociologists draw a different conclusion from the same evidence. First, they will conclude the shantytown protests occurred exactly where they should have. Prosperous, secure people—for example, white, upper-middle-class students—are better situated than anyone else to challenge authority. They have the time to protest injustice. They are also safe from harmful repercussions. On a high-prestige college campus, policemen are unlikely to show up and crack open people's heads for doing so. (That's why the signature student massacre of the 1970s happened at low-prestige Kent State University, not at high-prestige Columbia, Harvard, or Brown.)

Second, the protestors are in touch with similarly privileged students on other, similarly privileged campuses, and they swap stories about their experiences. They study each other and learn from each other. Owing to the mobility of American young people from the upper middle class, there are probably more social links among the student bodies of Harvard, Yale, and Brown than there are links among the homeless populations of Cambridge, New Haven, and Providence. Who could be better equipped to learn the skills of protest from other protestors than people whose chief accomplishment to date has been, as students, their proven learning ability?

These days, networks of student protest have taken on a new dimension through social media. Contemporary information technologies have given rise to networked communities, which have become useful for organizing, coordinating, supporting, and maintaining activism, both online and in real life.

Consider the living wage movement among college students in the United States. In 2001, the Harvard Progressive Student Labor Movement (PSLM) initiated a highly visible campaign involving political figures, celebrities, and national media. They staged a building occupation to fight for a living wage for the institution's janitors. A key component in this movement was a networked activist community that allowed students to initiate, coordinate, and maintain massive protest movements. They were able to create a shared proximity through the Internet, regardless of actual geographic location; websites and email distribution lists filled the void in information sharing and allowed participants to link to resources, connect to non-campus organizations, communicate ideas, and formulate a collective identity that is able to endure both during times of mobilization and latency (Biddix, 2008).

In the end, then, what sociologists have discovered by studying student-led protest movements contradicts common sense. The protests occurred not where the social problem was most intense, in poor cities with large numbers of poor and homeless people, but, rather, where populations of relatively affluent students existed who were best equipped to devote their time and resources to such protests. And the protests then spread from one "pocket" of these well-off, affluent student populations to another. This is consistent with the fact that most revolutionary thinkers and leaders, including Marx, Engels, Lenin, Trostsky, Ho Chi Minh, Fidel Castro and others, have been born into comfortable middle-class families, not poor families.

Now, consider a seemingly very different example, having to do with the diffusion of pharmaceutical information and the adoption of new drugs by prescribing doctors. The similarity lies in the role of imitation: just as protestors copy other protestors, doctors copy other doctors; and some doctors (like some protestors) are more likely to lead, while others are more likely to follow.

LEADERS VERSUS FOLLOWERS. Fifty years ago, sociological researchers conducted one of the earliest industrial studies of diffusion for a large drug manufacturer, to map the adoption by prescribing physicians of the new antibiotic Tetracycline (Coleman, Katz, and Menzel, 1966). This classic study found that physicians who were first to adopt the drug held the highest status in the local medical community, and were best connected and most informed. Next in line for adoptions of the new antibiotic were highly integrated but lower-status doctors. The most isolated, least informed and lowest status doctors were last to adopt the new wonder drug. (Similar patterns characterized the adoption of computer applications by physicians, according to Anderson et al., 1990; on the resistance to innovation among physicians, see Ferraro, 1994).

This pattern of innovation continues today, perhaps even more so than fifty years ago when Tetracycline arrived on the market. Change leaders in every field—whether corn farming, medicine, protest, or management—are the most likely to use brand-new products and services that the mainstream ultimately accepts. As a general rule, they seek novelty, stimulation, and information, and they are self-confident, socially connected, and fashion-conscious. New media, such as interactive information technology, allow change leaders to access a large range of online services, to develop networks of professional and personal contacts, and to get up to speed on new ideas and products.

These characteristics—connectedness, awareness, social status, and innovativeness—link to one another in ways that are hard to disentangle. However, it is safe to say that leaders lead by going first. They are the first to adopt innovations because they hear about them first through a wider-than-average range of media consumption and they evaluate them first through larger-than-average, more credible, and more varied social networks. Additionally, their past successes and high status embolden them to take chances on new things. (These are other reasons why Harvard, Columbia, and other elite schools point the way for other schools, in shantytown protests as much as in research and scholarship.)

Again, the sociological findings make sense, but they are not what a non-sociologist would have predicted. Ask a person on the street to guess what kind of organization is most likely to adopt a new technology or management strategy. He or she will say it depends on the organization's needs and resources. The non-sociologist will reason the organization that most needs the innovation is most likely to adopt it. Presumably, organizations behave rationally and gather the information they need to make rational decisions they need to make. Organizations are not copycats, this non-sociologist imagines, because mere imitation is not rational and organizations are rational. So runs the popular mythology about organizations.

However, research on organizations shows that this is not the case. In a study of administrative practices in more than 2,700 U.S. hospitals, only the early adopters of the management system "Total Quality Management" (TQM) customized TQM to their own requirements (Westphal et al., 1997). Later adopters sought legitimacy by following the normative (i.e., standard) TQM practices others had established. They wanted to appear knowledgeable by flashing their membership cards in the "Club of TQM," but they had little understanding of how TQM could actually be usefully applied to their own situation.

In this instance, as in others, industry leaders behaved rationally, by responding to their own organizational needs. Industry followers behaved less rationally. Setting aside their own organizational needs, followers try to look like everyone else, on the mistaken assumption that this is how important organizations—leading organizations—behave. However, doing so can carry huge, unexpected costs. Not every pair of pants needs a size 32 waist, even if Bill Gates (or the president of Princeton, or the Aga Khan) wears a size 32 waist.

In any competitive industry, leading organizations rely on innovations to reduce their costs, whereas second-raters rely more on imitating the front-runners. It is through imitation that technology spreads from the leaders to the followers and brings about a convergence of technologies and products among firms, as an industry matures. In the long run, firms grow similar, through a rapid growth (or demise) of smaller firms and convergence in their practices. Those that neither innovate nor imitate experience a drop in profits, as other firms adopt new technologies. In the long run, they adopt the new technology or go out of business.

In the last twenty-five years, there has been a huge amount of research on organizational imitation and the diffusion of organizational practices among organizations. Early work in this area included an analysis provocatively titled "Rat-race Dynamics and Crazy Companies" (1991); other, more prosaically titled research dealt with diffusion through inter-firm cooperation (Rosegger, 1991), diffusion of process technology in Dutch banking (Diederen et al, 1991), the diffusion of business computing (Attewell, 1992), and the diffusion of industrial robot use (Shenkar, 1992).

In recent years, research on organizational (including government) imitation and diffusion has continued, focusing on the spread of such practices as credit ratings (Trampusch, 2014), community-oriented policing (Burrus and Giblin, 2014), the environmental regulation of innovations (McGowan, 2014), financial governance ideas (Gangrud, 2013), course management systems (Lin and Chen, 2013), welfare policy-making practices (Obinger et al., 2013), alternative dispute resolution practices (Teague et al, 2013; 2012), and prosecution of human rights violations (Sikkink and Kim, 2013.) Interesting historical studies have focused on the spread of IT from developed to less developed countries (James, 2013), and the eighteenth- and nineteenth-century spread of cricket from Britain to British colonies (Lim, 2013). The most recent development has been to connect research on innovative diffusion to research on globalization (see for example, Wejnert, 2013). Some research in this realm has examined the globalization of Coca-Cola (Barkay, 2013), the NBA (Huang, 2013), language change (Maegaard et al., 2013), the politics of austerity (Major, 2013), views about fertility decline (Chen, 2013), intimate-partner violence (Pierotti, 2013), cohabitation (Dominguez-Folgueras and Castro-Martin, 2013), same-sex union rights (Fernandez and Lutter, 2013), and intellectual property protection of AIDS drugs (Chorev, 2012).

Do workers benefit from such inter-organizational diffusion? Research that examined a variety of innovative work practices (including TQM, teams, job rotation, and quality circles) found that, in 1992, more than a third of large private sector organizations were using what were then innovative work practices (Osterman, 1993). Some factors associated with the adoption of these practices are (1) being in an internationally competitive product market, (2) having a technology that requires high levels of skill, (3) following a "high road" strategy that emphasizes variety, service, and quality rather than low cost, and (4) employing such human resource practices as high levels of training and innovative pay systems.

Said another way, organizations are most likely to adopt innovative workplace practices when getting and keeping the best workers is difficult. If the competition in a firm's market is fierce, as it will be for a leading firm in a dynamic industry (e.g., computer software, or genetic engineering), worker motivation and productivity are enormously important. You can't afford to lose your best workers to the competition, or have your workers undermine your product with half-hearted efforts. Thus, leading technical firms like Microsoft and Apple will likely be the first to pioneer in administrative innovations. Lower-ranking firms, or firms in stagnant industries (e.g., textiles or soft drinks) will do so later.

Diffusion of innovations occurs more quickly when employees themselves are willing to use a new technology, and have some understanding of its use. Employee perceptions, experiences, attitudes, and the ways they communicate with management and with each other may all influence the adoption and diffusion of new technologies. Perceived benefits, previous computer experience, exposure to the technology, and networking are important determinants of employee willingness to use new computer technology, for example. To some degree, the entry of new workers from other organizations also brings about technology adoption. These new workers serve as carriers of a new technological culture. However, in the end, it is management that determines the rate of adoption.

Often, employees and management come into unnecessary conflict over new technology. The historical point of view is that technological innovation is bad for workers because machines take their jobs. Of course, this is true in the short run, but this conclusion is open to question nonetheless (see, for example, Betcherman, 1990). Unions can play an important role in the diffusion of technology, under certain conditions (Keefe, 1991; Trachtman et al., 1991), and professional associations also play a role in this process (Newell and Clark, 1990).

Research in Great Britain studied the diffusion of microelectronics throughout the manufacturing industry and surveyed workers about the impact of the new technology on jobs. They found that fewer than half of the establishments had a change in job totals (on this, see Northcott, 1986; Northcott and Walling, 1988; Vickery and Northcottt, 1995). Overall, the average net decrease was only about two jobs per factory per year. The decreases were larger in factories using the new technology most, and in those with the most advanced applications. The jobs lost were predominantly unskilled jobs. (After all, machines can easily do unskilled jobs; it is much harder to make machines that do highly skilled jobs.)

Over the same period, however, technology non-users lost about three times as many jobs as users. The decline in jobs was below average for organizations using (more advanced) centrally integrated computer systems. In short, then, jobs increased in the plants that used robots.

Some recent studies suggest manufacturing is following the same employment curve as agriculture—that with the recent advances in automation and cybernetic control, it's possible to produce just as much stuff with a tiny fraction of the workforce once required. Though a large amount of manufacturing is still done in the United States, it's mainly high-end work that uses sophisticated equipment but relatively few workers. No wonder then, that if you visit a modern automated auto plant, you will notice that (1) there aren't a lot of people on the floor (2) all the people on the floor, including those on the assembly line, wear white lab coats, and (3) machines are doing most of the physical work.

General Motors is a case in point. In recent years, it has produced about 9.7 million vehicles worldwide with a workforce of about 220,000 people. By contrast, in 1954 it employed 576,667 people who produced 3.8 million cars. So the loss in jobs isn't because GM produces fewer cars—today's GM produces three times as many cars as it did at what many business historians regard as the zenith of its economic influence in 1954. It's because it takes so many fewer people to make a car.

Those job losses have been offset so far by gains in employment elsewhere; but with many areas of white collar employment expected to be automated through advanced artificial intelligence (AI) systems in the next decade or two, will that continue? Optimists propose that Canadian employment will continue to grow in areas that, because of their specialized nature, are too complex or too expensive to automate; and because of their service component, require face-to-face interaction (e.g., health, education, and social services).

We can only hope the optimists are right.

NETWORKS OF ORGANIZATIONS. Like corn farmers and caregivers, organizational decision-makers are embedded in networks, and their network linkages help explain changes in the ways they go about their work. Network structures largely determine the speed of adaptation and ultimate patterns of prevalence of innovations (for example, of management practices). They do this by exposing a firm to particular role models and standards of appropriateness.

In one study, researchers compared the spread of two management innovations adopted in response to the 1980s wave of hostile corporate takeovers: poison pills (i.e., debt structures that made a takeover unattractive) and golden parachutes (i.e., luxurious executive payoff schemes). They found the practice of using poison pills spread rapidly through a board-to-board diffusion process, but the practice of golden parachutes spread slowly, through geographic proximity (Davis and Greve, 1997). Golden parachutes display a location-based diffusion pattern because they are more tied to the process of recruiting and retaining executives, and, even for very senior executives, labour markets are largely locational. The interactions among different companies' boards of directors, and the process by which one company tries to acquire another, are less limited by location, which as a result played little or no part in the spread of poison pills.

Management innovations involve the implementation of new practices, processes, and structures that differ significantly from current norms. Many practices in modern business were developed by management innovators, and over time, the most valuable innovations are imitated by other organizations and diffuse across industries. Birkinshaw and Mol (2006) identify four stages of management innovation: (1) dissatisfaction with the status quo, (2) inspiration from other sources, (3) invention, and (4) internal and external validation. Management innovation occurs in a manner similar to technological innovation; individuals pull together resources in novel ways, new developments arise, and innovations gradually diffuse across to other industries. However, whereas technological innovation is discrete knowledge, management innovations are typically concerned with complex social systems and relationships.

Professional associations can also play a role in carrying innovations from one organization to another. Large firms (i.e., those with more than fifty employees), firms with developed technology strategies, and firms that participated in industry events were all more likely to adopt technological innovations than other firms (Swan and Newell, 1995).

SOCIAL POLICIES. Increasingly, states share information about global problems. For example, increased discussion and exchange of climate data among nations influences environmental policy-making.

Like new technologies and organizational practices, political and social ideas diffuse, too. How else can we explain why democratic changes simultaneously occurred in all former Soviet bloc countries; why it took nine years to begin the democratic transition in Poland but only a few weeks for democratic reforms to be announced in Bulgaria and Romania; and why the transformation from a communist to a democratic system was smoother, better prepared, and less problematic in Poland than in other East European countries?

National human rights institutions have also spread globally, far beyond liberal democratic jurisdictions. Such organizations protect and promote citizens' human rights, and have diffused across international boundaries and political systems at a striking rate in recent years. Transmission of norms from one such body to another occurs through three mechanisms: (1) coercion, (2) acculturation, and (3) persuasion. The process can be observed fairly easily, particularly as the formation of one institution in a given area increases the chances of another coming into existence within a short period of time; such human rights institutions tend to be clustered both in space and time. Through this process, innovation spreads and adapts to new political conditions, and countries change their practices regarding human rights (Pegram, 2010).

Membership in intergovernmental organizations (IGOs) is also a factor that affects states' human rights behaviour. IGOs are able to affect the behaviour of their member states through socialization, a process by which human rights innovations are able to spread to other states. IGOs with specific human rights mandates have a positive effect on the human rights practices of their members, but other IGOs not associated with human rights issues have also been found to have a powerful influence on the states' human rights practices. This sort of socialization effect resulting from being part of an IGO promotes democracy and leads to more general convergence among states' interests (Greenhill, 2010).

Such socialization can operate in a various ways. IGOs have the potential to effect change in states' human rights practices by providing opportunities for humans rights norms to be transmitted between states. IGOs such as the European Union can withhold membership offers to prospective members that have inadequate human rights records, and also impose sanctions against members whose practices fall short of and violate standards. As a result, research has found that membership in IGOs that include highly democratic states improves democracy "ratings" for other, less democratic states that are also members of the IGO (Greenhill, 2010).

Often, states change ideas, institutions, or policy innovations as they diffuse, in a process known as *reinvention*. Reinvention, as in the varied examples of laws on child abuse reporting, crime victim compensation, and political campaign funding, results from a combination of social learning, political characteristics, and contextual factors.

CONCLUDING REMARKS. Organizations that innovate most readily are organizations that lead in their respective fields. That leaves open many questions about innovation that vary from one context to another. In short, sometimes it's better for an organization to innovate through invention and other times it's better to innovate by copying someone else's invention. The advantages of invention are, chiefly, that you get there before anyone else. The advantages of copying are, chiefly, that someone else pays the costs of research and development and runs the risks of failure. The issue of paying the cost of research and development, with the possibility of not being able to recoup the costs of such development, has led to changes in patent laws throughout North America.

Likewise, some industries maintain a high degree of secrecy over research and development. Other industries share more knowledge about the results of research. Academic science is, normatively, wide open in the sense that we expect scientists to publish and share their findings. We think this promotes the growth of scientific knowledge. So, is it equally true that privately-owned industries with the least secrecy are the most competitive and, therefore, the most productive? If openness and sharing are good for productivity, what policies must governments adopt—for example, in relation to patents—to promote the greatest sharing of scientific and technical information? The question remains to be answered.

Flows of Culture

Diffusion is not only about the spread of information, support, and practices. It is also about the spread of culture, knowledge, and control.

What we today speak of as "globalization" and in earlier decades called "cultural imperialism" is about the flow of cultural values, opinions, and ideas among societies that are connected by migration, trade, or governance. Often, cultural flows are associated with colonization and colonialism, so that less developed countries receive—may even have imposed on them—the cultural values of countries that dominate them politically. In the case of culture flows, we see something very obvious that is less evident with respect to flows of information, support, and practices, but which is often present nonetheless. It is this. Ideas and innovations flow asymmetrically through social networks: that is, they are more likely to flow from A to B, than from B to A, where A is more powerful than B. Powerful individuals, organizations, and societies are more likely to innovate, while less powerful individuals, organizations, and societies are more likely to imitate.

To a great degree, the spread of information, support and practices signifies the spread of control and the exercise of power. As we will see, mapping the diffusion process reveals the hidden structure of power. Typically, ideas and practices flow from powerful to powerless, while raw resources (including people) flow from powerless to powerful.

Consider the unusual but useful example of Olmec sculpture. The display of Olmec heads always impresses visitors to major archaeological museums of Mexico. The huge carved stone heads that date back more than a thousand years and stand as high as a person, weighing many tons, astonish viewers. Their majestic size, technical virtuosity, and mysterious expressions—something like the Mona Lisa's strange smile, but more serious—place these heads among humanity's most remarkable achievements.

Until the mid-1970s, we routinely assumed that full credit for these Olmec heads went to the artists of pre-Columbian Mexico. In 1976, anthropologist Ivan Van Sertima proposed that diffusion from Africa had influenced their sculpture. The first and most important contact, he proposed, was between Nubians and Olmecs in 700 B.C., and other contacts from Malawi followed in A.D. 1300. As a result, some or even many New World accomplishments, such as the Olmec heads (which some think resembled a stereotypical Negroid), owed a large debt to the Old World of Africa. If true, this claim would diminish the achievement of the Mexican artists and increase the stature of the African artists who, allegedly, set the model.

Two decades later, anthropologists challenged Van Sertima's theory at length and showed it to be without any foundation (Haslip-Viera et al., 1997). They noted that no genuine African artifact had ever been found in a controlled archaeological excavation in the New World. The presence of plants or plant genes of African origin showed that contact had occurred between the Old World and New World. However, this botanical contact had occurred long before any human contact could have taken place and was, in any event, irrelevant to the alleged Egyptian-Olmec contact. The huge Olmec heads were carved hundreds of years before the arrival of the presumed models. Also, the Olmec heads look nothing like Nubians (who have long, high noses), who are therefore an unlikely inspiration for the Mexican heads. Finally, no support could be found for diffusion of other cultural practices, such as pyramid building and mummification, from Africa (specifically, Egypt) to the New World (Borstein, 2001).

The emotional tone of the debate on this topic tells us that an ideological war is in progress; this war, it turns out, has to do with Afrocentrism. Critics of the Van Sertima theory allege that an influential group of Afrocentrists has promoted mere supposition as fact. The Afrocentrists have put forward the idea that African visitors to the New World, arriving at key points in the centuries that preceded the European discovery of the Americas, had created civilizations there. The critics go so far as to claim that this Afrocentrist theory has harmed ethnic relations in schools, on college campuses, and in North American society as a whole.

Judging from other anthropologists' response to this debate, critics of Van Sertima appear to have touched a raw nerve. Other voices joined the attack on Van Sertima, claiming that his theory belittled the genuine cultural achievements of Native Americans and that the Afrocentrism that informs Van Sertima's thesis is the product of a much older obsession of African Americans to devise a usable black past that will include Egypt as a central image and place of origin. A desire to highlight important contributions blacks have made to world history and American culture is, in their opinion, overshadowing fact. Africa has its own great civilizations, to be sure; and they deserve the world's admiration. There is no need to deny independent creative genius to the Olmec, the ancestors of Mexico's tormented indigenous peoples. Rather than embracing extreme diffusionism, arguments are made for people to realize that many origins account for the complexity of people and culture in America.

The question remains, though: What is all the fuss about? As often happens, academic debate reflects both concerns within the scientific community and concerns in the larger society. On the academic side there are concerns expressed about evidence and proof, and about the credibility and fortunes of competing schools (or networks) of researchers. On the societal side are concerns about black-white relations in America and the general validity of Afrocentrist claims. One anthropologist's view that "Afrocentrism is Eurocentrism in blackface" implies that both types of ethnocentrism are one-sided and ideological. Both lay claim to more cultural and social importance than either blacks or whites deserve based solely on race.

Underlying these arguments is the notion that cultural diffusion—for example, the diffusion of styles of sculpting—reflects differences in cultural development and even cultural superiority. Cultural diffusion is about cultural copying. Diffusion-as-copying reflects differences in power, since the more powerful tend to innovate first. Cultural styles tend to diffuse from the most developed (and most powerful) to the least developed (and least powerful) society. To label a society the sender of cultural information is to label it more developed and powerful than the society that receives the cultural information. Thus, by laying African claim to the original "big heads," Van Sertima is asserting the superiority of African culture over Mexican culture, and of black over non-black culture.

The fact of the matter is, it may have happened. Big heads may have come from Africa to America. Let's not underestimate "primitive peoples" and their technologies. Just how mobile and how isolated were our human ancestors? Some think that they were probably more mobile people, and better sailors, than many of us in developed societies will readily admit. So, we must reject "the myth of the primitive isolate," which imagines that every cultural development is a local invention.

However, that doesn't mean that every pair of culturally similar objects—e.g., African heads and Olmec heads—is a result of cultural diffusion. It simply means that we cannot assume that pre-industrial peoples were culturally isolated from one another, even if they lived on small islands in the South Pacific. We cannot go on as though every Pacific Island is a laboratory for the study of the evolution of independent human communities. We cannot assume that every community represents a separate "trial" in the historical evolution of the human race. We need to see the evidence: the tracers of linkage and flow from one culture to another.

The evidence shows that many cultures have historically been in contact with one another, and that therefore they have not evolved separately. This existence of a network of cultures leads us to wonder how many truly independent human communities have existed throughout history. How many have evolved completely from within, and how many have developed through the influence of outside ideas, techniques, and control? The answer is that we just don't know. It is as hard to say conclusively how many separate human cultures exist as it is to say how many people exist in your, or my, personal social network. Perhaps with cultures, as with people in personal networks, we are all connected at no more than five or ten removes.

There is evidence that all cultures evolved from large-scale population ranges in pre-history. Looking at kinship systems, it is possible to match them up, at least to some degree, to linguistic and genetic patterns of similarity. As such, it is possible to reconstruct a possible set of primary and secondary cultural areas, locations where societies may have formed and flourished prior to branching out (Jones, 2003).

We have long known that cultures share many elements because of common ancestry and proximity. That makes it impossible to find fully independent cultures; so it may be better to take the bull by the horns and test cross-cultural hypotheses on groups of closely related cultures. These are probably the most informative since they eliminate (i.e., control for) the effects of shared history. To do this analysis means creating phylogenies of cultures, or sets of closely related cultures, and studying independent instances of the rise and change of cultural elements.

This is essentially what S.M. Lipset (1998) did when he set out to study "American exceptionalism" by comparing the United States—its culture and social organization as "a new nation"—with three other countries to which it was closely similar: Great Britain (its parent), Canada (its North American sister), and Australia (its sister in the South Pacific). Against this backdrop of cultural kinship, Lipset studies the effect of the American Revolution on the development of the United States, and the effect of non-revolution on Britain, Canada, and Australia.

This approach assumes that cultures are genuine and observable entities; that they persist through time; and that they occasionally produce "daughter" cultures (as Britain produced the United States, Canada, and Australia). However, it is not clear what "cultural phylogeny" means: whether a mix of cultural elements, or a population or society. Likewise, it is not clear what makes up an "event of cultural change." The American Revolution may be such an event for the United States. What are equivalent events for Canada? Unlike the U.S., Canada does not have a definitive and dramatic "founding event" that has focused Canadian culture and shaped Canadian identity.

For anthropologists, the identification of "mother" and "daughter" cultures in prehistoric eras poses an additional problem. The amount of historical, linguistic, and ethnographic information is often limited. Even if we knew what constituted "events of cultural change," we may lack the information needed to study them. Yet despite the practical difficulties of studying cultural diffusion and co-evolution, the fact remains: Not only are cultures *not* isolated, they are also not simple, homogeneous, or static. Cultures are always inventing and importing new linguistic, religious, and artistic elements. Cultures, even those of small groups and communities, are pluralistic and ever-changing.

The spread of cultural ideas and values operates in two directions. First, ideas and values are embodied in material objects, of which productive and communications technologies are important types. Second, ideas and values grow out of ideologies: ways of viewing the world that justify particular distributions of power. Thus, in the end, the spread of culture implicates not only the spread of "purely cultural" objects like values and ideas about control; it also draws in the spread of material objects and the resulting divisions of labour.

Materialization, in the form of ceremonies, symbolic objects, monuments, and writing systems, hastens the spread of ideology outside the local group and the communication of power to the larger population. The materialization of ideology is one device that stabilizes power relations within societies that otherwise threaten to fragment into smaller political units. It may aid the overwhelming of one society by another.

Thus to spread the Western idea of "progress" is to spread a demand for the material technology linked to progress and for relations of production (bureaucracy, capital, and management styles) that are associated with this technology. It is also to spread an admiration for those societies, and imperial agendas, that are most closely associated with the accomplishment of progress. Implicit in the factory, the computer, the management expert, the Disney movie, is the notion that Western (and, at its core, American) capitalism is the present embodiment of the future.

The highly effective spread of capitalism can be attributed to the skill with which it has been introduced. Global advertising firms tailor their productions to local audiences, adapting tried-and-true methods to different parts of the world. But the greatest success has come not from adaptation, but from using the interaction between cultures to develop new system of logic among other peoples. This process has been termed *knowledge translation*, rather than merely knowledge transfer, as it speaks to the idea of translating bodies of knowledge to fit local realities, rather than simply the sharing of indisputable, unchangeable facts. Tacit (or implied) knowledge especially is believed to be dependent on context, and thus on location (Hughes, 2007).

It is through the changing perspectives of people, specifically members of the workforce, that ideas spread through the global economy. In spreading its concept of progress, the Western world is creating a globalized economy in which its ideals hold true, not discovering or restoring one. As individuals from transnational companies meet and interact, networks and flows of knowledge—knowledge of capitalism and its underlying concepts and practices—reach out toward all corners of the globe, furthering the diffusion of Western culture (Hughes, 2007).

There has been a lot of research on international patterns of adoption of new products and new technologies (see, for example, Dowling and Walsh, 1990), and it is fair to say that the spread of these new products and technologies often has something to tell us about the connection and relative power of different societies. In that sense, becoming a sender and not merely a receiver of products and technologies tells us something valuable about the change from national dependency to national sovereignty (Strang, 1990). The adoption and diffusion of technology also tells us something about that "collective evolutionary process" (Silverberg, 1991) that is often called modernization (Zapf, 1991; Tominaga, 1991).

In effect, we're forced to confront a conflict that was built into diffusion theories from their very origins in nineteenth-century cultural anthropology. On the one hand, diffusion theories propose that social phenomena—ideas, practices, institutions, and so on—flow from one location to another. The discovery of pyramids or bilateral inheritance practices in Place B leads one to ask where they came from and, especially, whether and how they might have come from Place A, which is also known for pyramids or bilateral inheritance patterns. On the other hand, evolutionary or modernization theories lead us to ask how and why these phenomena arose independently in two different locations. How, for example, might pyramids have appeared in Mexico despite a lack of contact with Egypt?

A middle ground is to recognize that both processes—diffusion and evolution—go on simultaneously in any society. This leads us to recognize that social structure conditions the entry and adoption of innovations from elsewhere; as a social structure evolves, it becomes more or less open to certain kinds of innovations from elsewhere. And that is at least one of the things Strang (1991) means by "adding social structure to diffusion models." The diffusion of innovations takes place within a continuously evolving complex social structure (Kamann and Nijkamp, 1991).

Sport is another activity that has played an important part in the spread and control of world culture. With few exceptions, sports have spread from Great Britain and the United States to the rest of the world, as a type of neo-colonialism or cultural imperialism. Researchers wonder whether the motivations of donors or borrowers best explain the spread of sport as a cultural artifact. To answer this difficult question, we must pay attention to the geopolitical and economic context and to the ways in which borrowers have transformed a particular sport into an instrument of their own purposes.

To understand how sports—especially such sports as soccer, baseball, and basketball—spread from their Western roots in the United States and Great Britain to all parts of the world, we can examine the introduction of the prototypically English game of cricket into societies as culturally different as the United States and India; the arrival of soccer in Latin American and African nations; the export of baseball from the United States to Japan, Latin America, and Australia; the global expansion plans of the U.S. National Football League; the worldwide spread of basketball; and the global expansion of the Olympic games.

We also need to consider the (failed) German and Slavic attempts to fashion nationalistic alternatives to the internationalism of sports, and the efforts of anthropologists, folklorists, historians, and political activists to preserve or revive traditional sports. In the end, we will realize the diffusion of sports outward from Great Britain and United States is not, at least in any simple sense, a kind of cultural imperialism. Besides, how could we explain the spread of Australian sport, which has become a cultural product circulating in domestic and international markets and broadly following American styles of production and promotion, as Americanization or globalization?

Further, it would be a mistake to assume that the introduction of Western sports to non-Western cultures is a basic transplantation. It is not a matter of simply introducing activities and having the locals perform them in the traditionally American or British way. Even basketball and football are played differently, with different rules, in the U.S. and the rest of the world. Or take the Trobriand Islanders of Melanesia, first studied by Bronisław Malinowski in the mid-1910s. A film made in 1973 entitled *Trobriand Cricket: An Indigenous Response to Colonialism* depicted how the Trobrianders had taken the traditional game of cricket and adapted it for their purposes. The version taught by missionaries at the turn of the century had been reinvented as a political tool and a means to showcase personal status. Trobriand cricket is both an individual activity, with each player out for themselves while in formal dress and attempting to impress female spectators, and a communal one. There is a massive feast held afterwards that is equally exciting as the game, with exchange of livestock, crops, and speciality food items presented by the host village.

On the surface this interpretation of Western pastimes is solely about a game, but it serves as an example of the resilience and longevity of cultural traditions (Weiner, 1997). Though the fact may not be immediately apparent, when Western activities are introduced into other cultures, new traditions are introduced and simultaneously older ones are altered yet preserved. Stating that the Trobrianders simply introduced the game of cricket to their society would be a gross oversimplification, seeing homogeneity where none exists. They adapted cricket to their own desires and needs.

American sociologist Orlando Patterson denies that Americanization is leading to the homogenization of the world (Patterson, 1994). This view, he thinks, ignores the vigour of local cultures and ethnicities, and the complexity of global culture diffusion. It also ignores the great cultural divisions within the United States itself, and the extent to which some regions (for example, the Caribbean) contribute to American popular culture and to the world music scene. The American universe is not one cultural space, Patterson says. The country includes a traditional America, a multicultural America, and an "ecumenical" America, this last being the "world's first genuinely global culture."

Outside of America, a space commonly referred to as embodying a global culture is the Internet. The digital revolution has had enormous effects on the creation, storage, replication, and distribution of cultural materials (Poster, 2008). Individuals are now able to create, store, reproduce, and circulate what it used to take teams of professionals armed with printing presses and movie sets to accomplish. Yet the Internet is not free of government interference. The Chinese government does not allow for criticism, for example, and the American government is attempting to impose U.S. copyright laws across the entirety of the Internet. At the same time, culture is being increasingly commoditized, providing advantages to those with wealth and power (Poster, 2008).

Like other technologies, communication technology vastly increases the capacity for more powerful entities to control the direction of information flow, to censor information, and to place their own desired meanings on the information that is circulating. The flow of international news between the core and the periphery is unequal, with Western industrialized countries dominating the agenda. This inequality not only means that news from the "centre" overwhelms that from countries on the periphery, but also marginalizes the exchange of news among peripheral countries. In the end, international news-flow is influenced by a country's economic development, the language(s) its people speak, its physical location, political freedom, and population size. The phrase "knowledge is power" comes to mind, though perhaps in this case "knowledge spreads power" would be more appropriate. The news is told from the perspective of the nation with the loudest voice and greatest reach, and its underlying cultural practices are transmitted across the world.

Cultural diffusion is about capturing hearts and minds. This takes place through the flow of information—information as values, ideas, images, practices, and artifacts. Since culture is the sum of all the tools we humans use to think, interact, and manage the non-human environment, cultural diffusion is a redefinition of how we are to live. And since cultural styles typically spread from the most developed to the least developed societies, following the contours of political and economic power, cultural diffusion not only identifies but also maintains the global power structure.

The very fact of cultural diffusion can furnish the basis for a culture's claim of primacy and legitimacy A culture's "success" in spreading is the demonstration of its universal value and appeal, or so its proponents will propose. Even leaving such claims of legitimacy aside, necessity rules: for instance, people today need to learn English because it has become the language of international trade, of science and technology, of entertainment and consumerism. Most people around the world adopt American mass culture to at least some degree because it is emblematic of postmodern consumerism. It declares a commitment to a certain, America-centred way of life.

Thus we have moved from a world in which one could study cultural sharing among independent, distinct cultural islands to a world in which we must study cultural distinctiveness among dependent and similar cultural regions.

Flows of Influence

The spread of culture from one society to another is, as we have seen, an indication of dominance, whether economic, political, or social. Thus, many people view the diffusion and homogenization of world culture as a form of cultural imperialism or even Americanization. However, this is only one example of a more general phenomenon: namely, the flow of *influence* among members of a social network.

Influence is a form of *social control*: a way of getting other people, organizations, communities and societies to do what you want. Like other forms of what sociologists call informal social control, influence is the exercise of power without gunfire. We influence people in our environment in a variety of ways: by rewarding them or promising them rewards, by punishing them or threatening to punish them, or by withholding desired rewards for their failure to behave as we desired.

Generally, the flow of influence, like the flow of information, innovation, support, and practice, is asymmetrical, from the most influential down to the least influential people in the network. That is another way of saying (and knowing) that, in the social world, there are inequalities of influence, just as there are inequalities of power, wealth, authority, and prestige. And in fact, these various hierarchies are connected: people (as well as organizations and societies) with more power, wealth, authority, and prestige tend to have more influence, because they have more rewards and punishments at their disposal.

Since the end of the Second World War, evidence of global diffusion, or globalization, has been growing. It has taken many forms: as we earlier, some are purely cultural. Others are financial and organizational: currency devaluations that have global consequences, debt crises in Europe and the Third World that have a ripple effect for other economies, free-trade agreements (e.g., NAFTA), free-trade zones (e.g., the European Community), and the widening of military alliances (e.g., NATO's opening up membership to states in Eastern Europe).

The world's financial system has become structurally interlocked: through high speed international finance with a high-stakes "casino quality," a growing availability of tax havens, and many free-trade areas. The spread of new agricultural, manufacturing and information technologies has also increased global experience-sharing (Burmeister, 1990). Multinational corporations, international humanitarian organizations and a global recognition of refugee, drug, debt, environmental, and terrorist problems have all accelerated the process. Transnational (or multinational) corporations' actions and interests shape the flow, the form, and the location of investment, as well as the conduct of trade and the development of technologies.

This global spread of trade, investment, and telecommunication is at the heart of globalization. By breaking down national barriers, easy information flow has produced the largest potential scope for competition and cooperation.

Power is now, some say, a product of knowledge, information processing, and symbol manipulation—a result of the new communications technology. Easier flows of information and knowledge characterize our social life. For example, social, cultural, and political movements are meaningless today without media coverage. Borders, governments, localities, and classes cannot prevent information flows. As a result, social conflict is no longer conflict between categories or classes of people, as Marx had claimed. It is between worldwide networks, markets and "identities." The only important actors on the world stage, some say, are global entities, not traditional states.

We disagree. States are still key actors in world affairs. Here's why.

CHAOS, CRIME AND BRIBERY. The increased flow of information, capital, and influence has meant mutual global dependence, but it has not meant a single world-society. Local and regional particularities remain: the ebb and flow of dictatorship and democracy in Third World countries, the spread of ethnic movements (in the Middle East and the former Soviet States, among others), and the rise of regional crime groups all show that.

The world's seemingly chaotic and uncontrollable flows of information have caused new problems. Job security has eroded, human desires for stability have been frustrated, and communication between technology-poor and technology-rich communities has broken down. Yet, for all that, states still play a role, because capital and information still have locations. Networks that channel the flow of information and capital have to be located somewhere. Most important, the creation of social institutions and social beings takes place in particular locations. Nothing illustrates this fact better than the problem of bribery, a problem that surprises people when they do business outside North America.

Many cultures have, historically, encouraged a mutual exchange of gifts or services to obtain permissions or favour. Under many circumstances, such bribery has had no economic value, but was part of mutual obligation, hierarchical symbolism, or functional lubrication. In Japanese history, people had no rights, per se; therefore everything required permission, which was granted for a gift.

Thus, bribery is central to a system in which the state has failed to establish rights. Vestiges of this practice still exist in many countries. Practices of bribery vary from one society to another, depending on the state's commitment to establishing rights. In Indonesia, for example, a standardized amount of money is still given to an official to speed up paperwork. The small sum does not stay in the pocket of the receiving official, but is distributed through the channel of paper processing and may be called an "express fee." In some Central and South American countries, however, the money given to an official for a favour goes into the pocket of the official. The amount is large and not standardized.

Without rights come both bribery and uncertainty. This means unequal treatment or mistreatment on the individual level, and the impossibility of rational planning and secure investment on the global level. Both Japan and Indonesia, among other societies, suffered enormous shocks to their financial and industrial systems as a result of high-level bribery, corruption, and nepotism. These shocks have reverberated throughout the global capital markets, so let's not underestimate the importance of state-protected rights as basic to the successful operation of a society and an economy.

What is it that states do? For the last two centuries, states have increasingly promoted civil rights through the rule of law, upgraded human capital through the provision of public education and public health, and secured at least a minimum level of human well-being by taxing and redistributing wealth. By now, most of us in the West take these state functions for granted.

Modern states have also gone a long way towards "perfecting the market" by, to some degree, controlling it. Most have established reliable currencies, minimized barriers to the entry of goods and services (e.g., low tariffs and trade barriers), minimized transaction costs (e.g., encouraged stock markets with huge numbers of buyers and sellers), enforced laws (e.g., preventing fraud and insider trading), and improved information flow (e.g., through subsidized or protected telephone and cable systems).

It is only because we can take the market-securing functions of states for granted, and because most states have done such a good job in these areas, that globalization is possible. It is paradoxical, then, that globalization largely undermines the functioning of these same states. States have put themselves out of business by doing such a good job that global (multinational) corporations can take them for granted.

Globalization itself requires the rule of law, high-quality human capital, and certain minimum guarantees of human survival. States provide this in particular places. So states that fill these needs may merge or reform, but they will never disappear. Also, even within a global framework, states continue to moderate, modify, and censor the actions of large corporate actors. And they continue to spread their political influence over other states.

INTERNATIONAL AID. To extend their control, states tax people and redistribute wealth, whether as cash, food, technology, expertise, or information. This work is often done by nongovernmental organizations (NGOs) which contributions from nation-states maintain. The United Nations (along with its subsidiary organizations such as UNESCO) is one such organization; others include the International Monetary Fund, World Bank, and Red Cross. Often, a problematic relationship develops between the NGO and the states on which it depends for funds, as, for example, between the United Nations and the United States. The "micro" politics of these NGOs also influence the ways in which states interact with one another.

Many NGOs have a philanthropic and redistributive function, but they operate within a political, economic, and ideological context. They do, in fact, largely satisfy the interests and policies of dominant member states and the capitalist system as a whole. Thus, organizations like the World Bank try to achieve "global Keynesianism," maximizing growth and stabilizing the world system in the interest of the dominant capitalist states. As a result, global inequality remains a feature of the postcolonial world. In the coming years only ten to twelve countries in the southern hemisphere—Brazil and India, among them—are likely to approach the economic performance of the North, while the remaining 140 Southern nations slip farther behind.

IMMIGRATION POLICIES. States control the global flows of talent and skill by restricting the entry of people from other countries. In this way, they regulate the local social and skill composition of the population, raising or lowering the human capital, solving or creating problems of health, education, welfare, employment and unemployment. By extension, they influence the supply of educated and skilled labour in other countries. One concern in Canada is the skill outflow, or "brain drain," of students, academics, researchers, and professionals to the United States. States try to prevent such problems by, among other things, adjusting educational spending.

Another source of contention surrounds the global flow of refugees, who are by definition granted admission on grounds other than their social or economic utility. (They are, instead, admitted on compassionate grounds, as victims of human rights violations, or because their admission achieves a political or diplomatic purpose for the government.) The total number of refugees, displaced people, and illegal labour migrants worldwide has increased dramatically in the past twenty years. An estimated 30 million people make up this multiethnic migrant diaspora largely outside government control. The large-scale, largely unregulated movement of people within and across national borders will increasingly occupy foreign policy and national security establishments.

Geographic mobility, including migration and refugee status, can be a result of colonial, Cold War, and ethno-nationalist struggles (as, for example, in Africa). Increasingly, population flow has joined the trends that challenge national sovereignty and created global–national institutional tensions—especially in the European Union, where national economic disparities are great.

Many policy options are available to states that wish to reduce unwanted (im)migration flows by altering the internal conditions generating mass emigration (Cornelius, 2005; Martin, 1994). They include trade, foreign investment, and development assistance; guest worker policies; refugee return policies; safe havens, both external and internal; exit control policies; political strategies to reduce refugee flows; and if all else fails, military intervention. Thus, international migration and refugee movements are not simple domestic issues but matters of foreign policy. By their law making, foreign policy, and foreign aid, states influence the global flow of manpower.

COMMUNICATION POLICIES. State language policies also influence international relations. Language has often been an instrument of state policy—a means of wielding and signifying power. Today, language remains an important issue throughout the world, signifying cultural significance and therefore economic and political significance. In countries like Canada, language use (e.g., bilingualism versus unilingualism) is an important symbolic and political marker of community membership. We will say more about language use and language shifting in a later chapter.

Many powerful nations have policies concerning language diffusion. The term "politics of linguistic diffusion" designates the efforts undertaken or encouraged by the French government aimed at furthering the spread of the French language beyond the borders of the French state. The English language has not, in this century, needed explicit promotion: English is recognized worldwide as the language of science, technology and business. Like French, English continues to carry overtones of colonialism and domination throughout the developing world.

In societies like Canada, with a multicultural population and constant inflows of multicultural information, communication policies are especially important aspects of statecraft. Some societies try to balance the communication needs of different subgroups. In Canada, for example, the *Broadcasting Act* of 1932 initiated an era of government involvement in providing French and English Canadians with an equal opportunity to express their respective cultures under the aegis of a public corporation. (The coming of TV widened the gap between the respective groups.)

Often, states try to push the thinking of their audiences in particular directions. State censorship under communism (in Poland for example) regulated the flow of information so that they represented the only acceptable version of reality in the media. The censors viewed themselves as gatekeepers of information. Elsewhere, censorship takes a more benign form. In Taiwan, Hong Kong, and Singapore, government has tried to create a unified public culture and identity. Such attempts in Taiwan are explicit appeals to sacred origins and the continuity of the Chinese past by the state to distinguish itself from mainland China. In contrast, the situation in Hong Kong has moved from a preoccupation with its Chinese past to a brief assertion of an independent Hong Kong identity, to the creation of a hybrid culture composed of Western values of utilitarianism and consumerism fused with Eastern values.

The state's traditional involvement in education has also had a great indirect, and unexpected, effect on local and global information flow. The development of national scientific communities in the nineteenth century paradoxically laid the foundations for the global diffusion of scientific institutions in the twentieth century. Disciplinary differentiation—a result of national investment in education—fosters international collaboration among scientists and weakens local organizations' control over the members. Thus, unintentionally, states spread their own conception of disciplinary boundaries in the arts and sciences.

TRADE AND INVESTMENT POLICIES. The globalization of information has affected no area of economic growth more than finance. Worldwide, instantaneous, and largely uncontrollable capital flow is the hallmark of this dynamic realm of activity. Global capital does not readily submit itself to national boundaries and succeeds in organizing markets to its own advantage.

Volatile capital poses a threat to the state's ability to control its economy, and portfolio investment flows are notably more volatile than direct investment flows. That's because it is easier to buy and sell stocks than it is to buy and sell businesses. Yet, even portfolio investment grants foreign investors control over host economies. This is why states try to regulate foreign investment and, to varying degrees, succeed.

PATENT LAWS AND PROTECTIONS. States also regulate the development and spread of new technologies. The level of a country's economic development only modestly influences the adoption of innovations, while state policy, by contrast, can have a large impact on the rate at which innovations are adopted. In turn, the adoption of technological innovations increases the productivity of a nation's economy. Thus, economic productivity levels are good indicators of a nation's ability to innovate and adopt new technology, but they reflect public policy as well as technology.

Normally, economic or political unification increases the diffusion of new ideas, technologies, and products. However, local government subsidies designed to promote the development of new technologies are often at the expense of the diffusion of those same technologies. By restricting diffusion, such policies can impose substantial costs on society. Removing problems associated with government policies and fostering the diffusion of new technologies requires restricting the assignment of property rights and restructuring the awards associated with inventive activity.

Researchers estimate that patented inventions that originated in the United States, Germany, and Japan have contributed more than 50% to the growth of productivity in OECD nations (Eaton and Kortum, 1996). However, not all innovations are easily adopted: they require infrastructural supports and political will. Evidence from Singapore's electronics industry, for example, suggests that industrial development in electronics involved a gradual and systematic accumulation of industrial, education and infrastructural capabilities, many of which were associated with pre-electronic forms of manufacturing (Hobday, 1994. Thus, Singapore was not able to "leapfrog" over earlier technological paradigms to catch up in the field of electronics.

Under the right conditions, global networking strategies allow developing countries to use the knowledge and skills of established partners to create strong domestic infrastructure. And many developments favour developing countries: for example, the increased demand for complex non-standardized production, consumer demand for specialized and customized products, and the demand for highly flexible organizational structure.

However, exploiting these opportunities requires government support of training and the creation of cooperative relationships with established players in the technology market. For this to happen, government and industry must encourage flexible systems of knowledge production and transformation that link science and technology to social and organizational systems.

CLOSING REMARKS. Despite the encroachments on local power we associate with the term "globalization," states continue to promote, modify, and limit the flow of ideas and information, people, goods and services. Thus, flows between states are as important as flows between cultures: indeed, they mediate flows between cultures. The state continues to be an important sender and receiver of information and control.

As we have seen, states do this with policies that redistribute wealth, allow or prevent immigration, promote or restrict communication, trade, and investment. If we view the globe as a river of flowing people and ideas, states are dams that slow, restrict and redistribute whatever comes their way. Some of their importance lies in the ability to do this. Equally, it lies in the ability to use resources strategically to promote state interests. Increasingly, state activities are moderated by international negotiation and exchange, for every nation along the river has a growing interest in how well information and control are flowing.

CHAPTER TWO

Subtypes of Diffusion

From what has come before, it should be easy to see that the various types of diffusion are related to one another, yet different. Gossip, for example, is a flow of information; it also reveals the flow of influence and of cultural (especially, moral) values within a community. It is a means of securing and enforcing behavioural conformity, and in return for this conformity, people receive the right to demand support and respect—in effect, continued membership in a local moral community. Gossip is a form of imitation, and sometimes (though less often than in the case of rumour, which we consider next) it is a type of innovation as well.

Gossip

What is most important about the flow of gossip is that it tends to flow only through pre-existing networks of social relations. We gossip with others we know about people we know, in tight, familiar communities whose rules we know. Thus, studying the flow of gossip is a way of studying the structure of a network, a clique, or a community. That is, we do not gossip randomly, about nothing or nobody in particular. Again, this demonstrates that societies are not made of atomized individuals: rather they are made of networks of police who police one another.

We all know the term *gossip*. The word's origins in old English are "God" and "sib," suggesting that people who gossip are "related in God," or kinfolk. Dictionary definitions include "evaluative talk about absent others," or, more specifically, "conversation between two people about an absent third person with whom they are both familiar." It can also be used as a noun to refer to the people who engage in such a conversation. The targets and topics discussed vary, but the practice of gossip is present in all cultural systems.

Gossip is a form of information flow, or diffusion between acquaintances. It requires common membership in a social network; this ensures familiarity, even intimacy, between the speakers, as well as familiarity with the third person about whom they are gossiping. Gossip is widely perceived to be negative, interpreted to be idle or malicious talk about someone's behaviour, regardless of its factual accuracy. This statement is not completely unfounded.

Victims of gossip, once aware of it, feel disliked and disturbed by the breach of their privacy. This often leads to a loss of self-esteem (Cole and Scrivener, 2013). The adverse effects of gossip can also extend to people who gossip. Gossipers may experience feelings of guilt because of their sharing of private information, and this in turn can similarly result in lowered self-esteem. Even when no private information or secrets have been shared, gossipers may nonetheless feel guilty for violating social norms related to politeness (Holtgraves, 2001).

Furthermore, and regardless of the nature of the gossip, whether positive or negative, gossipers are often disliked (Turner et al., 2003; Farley et al., 2010). This is because their motives are frequently assumed to be self-serving (Wilson et al., 2002). Research has shown that people can be hurt by negative gossip, but are usually unaffected by positive gossip. In other words, the self-esteem of gossip victims does not benefit from positive gossip nearly as much as it suffers because of negative gossip (Cole and Scrivener, 2013).

At the same time, it is important to note there are positive effects of gossip. Some researchers have gone so far as to say that gossip is fundamentally responsible for the existence of human society (Dunbar, 2004). By tracing the origins of language through an evolutionary perspective, these researchers have proposed that gossip arose out of a need for early humans to form social groups to protect themselves from violent predators. As these social groups got larger, "free-riders," people who "took the benefits of sociality but decline[d] to pay all of the costs," started to appear. In such a situation, gossip about "free-riders" performed the essential function of making sure that honest "reciprocators" dominated all social gatherings, ensuring that the group stayed intact (Dunbar, 2004).

As we will see, gossip affirms a community's common moral code and the moral bond among its members. It enforces social control, and achieves moral equivalence. It also provides members with the opportunity to express themselves, reinforces group identities, and strengthens social cohesion. In all instances, gossip serves to create, maintain, and change the identities of the gossipers.

Despite appearing casual and spontaneous, gossip has an underlying structure. First, speakers negotiate and ratify the willingness to gossip before they exchange any information. Second, they report and evaluate a conspicuous action of an absent person. Third, they generalize the individual characterization to social types and explicate it by a common exchange of views. They offer and test interpretations situating the individual action within the frame of general social and moral rules.

Gossip takes many forms. Some gossip is open and straightforward, but some is veiled and roundabout in how it presents information. Several factors can influence how information is presented. The openness of expression is greater if: (1) the first response to an initial evaluative statement is supportive, (2) the peer group is a stable friendship group, (3) the speakers already had some degree of consensus about the subject matter of the gossip, and (4) the target of the gossip is not a group member.

Gossip often occurs within a community characterized by inequality and concerned with reputation. Gossip can be used to defame other people and reduce the symbolic value of their name. Most people strive to maintain their reputation and enhance the way others regard them. Gossip is an attack on prestige, and often aims to reduce it. People often gossip about others who are at the same level or higher in status than they are, and don't bother gossiping downward unless they fear that "lower" groups are challenging them for social status. This is one reason that gossip was historically, and still is, a form of gendered communication. We will discuss the gender issue later.

AN EXAMPLE: THE ACADEMIC COMMUNITY. Gossip occurs in every community, so let's consider how it works in a community with which we are especially familiar: the scientific community of university-based scholars (on this, see, for example, Becher and Trowler, 2001).

This community is based on research, doing one's own work, and the norm of open and truthful communication of research results. Good work alone is to be rewarded; office politics and the manipulation of public image are not. Lying, cheating, empty self-promotion, and plagiarism are considered morally reprehensible.

In the scientific community, power and influence rest on reputation alone. A "bad name" in the community may result in a failure to get research grants or to get work published. It may even result in dismissal from teaching or research positions. So, researchers are eager to protect their good name. Reputations in this community are highly stratified and a long social distance separates the highest from the lowest ranking scholars. The highest ranking—those with the "best names" or "top reputations"—are the most likely to get prizes and awards. Such scholars are showered with research grants, lucrative publishing contracts, and invitations to lecture or teach at prestigious institutions. The lowest ranking scholars are offered none of these benefits and, as a result, are bound to envy the top ranking scholars.

In formal organizations such as universities, gossip has two functions: promotion of group cohesion and facilitation of the struggle for organizational control. In this community, gossip may take the following form: A graduate student or junior scholar may spread the word that a senior scholar had published her findings under his own name, or that a senior scholar with whom she was working faked the results reported in a journal article. An unknown scholar may tell others that a famous scholar had used unethical methods to obtain his results, had prevented the publication of findings that would have thrown his own theory into doubt, or had spread false stories about the results of other famous scientists.

Gossip can be a sort of trial in absentia, and people in communities or small societies commonly use it to handle conflicts, especially when more authoritative modes of conflict resolution are lacking. In this situation, where the principals to conflict are equal, intimate, and similar, and where they lack an organized or triangulated authority system, gossip serves as a court of community opinion, to offer popular judgment on the contending parties. Gossip thrives in communities with a high level of mutual awareness and scrutiny, where people frequently exchange information about others in the routines of everyday life. Social control in science, therefore, resembles that found in other social systems (such as tribal societies) where reputation is closely linked to community life and the stratification system.

THE FUNCTIONS OF GOSSIP. We can analyze gossiping behaviour from at least two standpoints: that of the gossip-speaker (i.e., the "gossip"), and that of the community.

Despite what research has shown about its social benefits under certain circumstances, gossip does not always serve the interests of the group as a whole, but has been demonstrated to function in accord with the selfish interests of individuals. The gossip-speaker spreads stories because doing so shows him or her off in a good light, as the protector of community standards, and perhaps even as someone whom fate has unfairly deprived of fame and fortune. A study conducted among students at Knox College demonstrated that many people are interested in the most exploitable information that can be used to enhance personal status or to diminish the reputations of others who are perceived as having a higher status than they do. Information about dishonest or irresponsible behaviour is most likely to be used against rivals, but news about good fortune is ignored. The reverse is true about personal friends and lovers, where good news is both interesting and likely to be broadcast, to the advantage of the individual spreading the news (McAndrew, Bell, and Garcia, 2007). These outcomes provide the incentive for people to gossip.

The community benefits from gossip, too. Gossip can cause conflict and strain, but in the longer run, it strengthens traditional morality and the bonds of trust between gossipers. In any community, gossip allows people to express hard-to-control desires, anxieties, and emotions. Like jokes, nicknames, and graffiti, gossip lets people "blow off steam." This amounts to neither conformity nor rebellion, but to a grudging acceptance of reality accompanied by a symbolic refashioning of events. Thus, gossip is a form of escapism. Gossip victims can turn to gossip within *their* own circles to alleviate the stresses accrued from external gossip (Feinberg et al., 2012). Gossip may also be an especially useful form of social control by temporary employees who have no other hold over their employers.

Gossip is an important form of social communication that allows people to exchange personal opinions, values, and ideas. It is a mechanism of social learning that enables people to share information about themselves and others in the community. One theory about the purpose of gossip proposes that it helps people learn how to function effectively within the complex and ambiguous structure of human social and cultural life (Baumeister, Zhang, and Vohs, 2004). Human beings are capable of cultural life because they have the innate capacity to regulate their own behaviour and alter it to suit external guidelines and rules. However, many of these rules are not explicitly stated, and can only be understood by observation and active participation within a community. Gossip is a tool for transmitting information about these unspoken rules in society, and how people are expected to act in order to conform to them.

Gossip constitutes a form of social interaction that uses narratives to communicate rules. Rather than openly stating facts or opinions, it relies on anecdotes and stories to transmit information and culture. On the surface, they appear to be simple stories about people, but what is being communicated are the shared morals and lessons behind those stories. By discussing situations that involve other people, participants can share their interpretations about socially and culturally accepted morals and reaffirm their own beliefs by listening to the judgments and opinions of others. They can learn about the culture and how to conduct themselves within the society that they belong to. Gossip communicates principles rather than facts. It is a form of observational learning—people can learn about the successes and failures of others and apply the lessons to their own lives. This creates a communicative pool of information, which allows people to transmit discoveries, offer solutions to social issues, and strengthen internal social cohesion within a community.

In this way, gossip can also act as a form of social control. It is a method of regulating members' behavior; it communicates the rules of society and acts as a deterrent to deviance by emphasizing the consequences of actions that go against community values.

In scientific networks, a core-periphery structure separates the privileged insiders from outsiders. Different people have different stakes and opportunities in the system. For example, the contacts and opportunities are different for locals and for cosmopolitans, for high-status and for low-status researchers. "Informational," less purely personal gossip circulates in cosmopolitan networks whose members deal with uncertain and rapidly changing worlds, e.g., financial markets and cutting edge research. "Moralistic" gossip, about scandals, thrives in small and dense communities that are some distance back from the cutting edge. People who are part of different kinds of networks, therefore, gossip with different people about different things.

In this way, different gossip cultures, or conversational class cultures, emerge. Core groups exchange privileged informational gossip, but peripheral groups gossip about local events and local deviants, and sometimes also about "stars."

Gossip is a way of sharing information and enjoying sociability, but it is also a form of community politics. In the scholarly community, gossip reminds people of the accepted norms of honesty and reward for hard work. By gossiping, low-ranking scholars can criticize and in that way bring high-ranking people down to earth. They can reduce moral inequality—the inequality of reputations—in the community. Even if gossip doesn't immediately affect the hierarchy of influence and pay—although it may do so in the long run—it redresses a moral imbalance in the universe.

In the eyes of "little scientists", it would be a cosmic injustice if "big scientists" were not only great researchers and scholars and the recipients of fame, fortune, and admiration, but also fine, honest, and upstanding human beings. Discovering and revealing those failures of "big scientists" provides a measure of satisfaction by making the cosmos fairer and life worth living. Thus, gossip turns out to be a means of resisting and fighting inequality, and of redressing unfairness in the cosmic system of rewards. Also, the perception that they can redress these wrongs further strengthens the hold of traditional values and institutions over low-ranking scientists. It maintains their faith in the system of rewards and the communal norms of science.

GOSSIP IN A PUBLIC SCHOOL. Gossip is also a feature of daily social interaction between schoolchildren. Adolescent schoolgirls use gossip to clarify social relationships and social norms. Gossip in which they express a high degree of sentiment helps to strengthen the social relations of these girls and reinforce the boundaries between groups. Girl-gossip focuses on romantic relationships, appearance, conceited ("stuck-up") behaviour by other girls, and attitudes toward academic achievement. Gossip is one of several collective practices in early adolescence—others include teasing and bra snapping—which give meaning to such bodily changes as the growth of breasts and spurts of height. Gossip about each other's sex lives—about which girls go "how far" with which partners—also defines the (moving) boundaries of an evolving sexual morality.

Gossip is a powerful tool that adolescents use to carve out a meaningful identity within a mass of competing peer groups and possible identities. The pervasive and intense use of gossip leads to fights in the hallways, alters friendship patterns, and keeps crowds or cliques separate. It creates a consensus within many peer groups and increases intimacy between friends, but also pushes contending groups apart. Gossip even prompts some girls to remove themselves from most close peer relations altogether.

A study that examined characteristics of gossip among fourth-grade girls and their close friends revealed that gossip is a dominant feature of conversation among this population. Most gossip was neutral in narrative form and corresponded to information sharing. Over a quarter of the talk was about peers and used by girls as a means of understanding social relationships and the behaviour of the people they knew. They predominantly discussed female peers or family members and their actions.

The study found that friendship quality and closeness were associated with the amount of peer gossip, supporting that gossip is related to social competence. Popular girls were more likely to gossip and engage in evaluative gossip than rejected girls. Gossip frequency and valence (that is, whether the gossip is favourable or critical) also related to friendship closeness and quality (McDonald, Putallaz, Grimes, Kupersmidt, and Coie, 2007). Thus, gossip in this population did not serve a socially aggressive function; it was instead a mechanism for establishing intimacy and friendship processes.

GOSSIP IN THE LARGER COMMUNITY. In other communities where people know one another by name and appearance, gossip is still a mechanism of social control.

People still use it to stigmatize others and to construct "we" and "they" images that reinforce societal divisions.

Gossip and rumour (which we discuss in the next section) are related ways of talking in which people express their interests more intimately and personally than they may when talking only about themselves. In that sense, gossip is a form of allegory, like the telling of fables to teach a moral lesson. The "facts"—for example, whether Joanie did or did not have sex with Ricky last Tuesday—are less important than the moral debate that lies beneath: namely, under what conditions does this community consider it proper for people to have sex? In some pre-industrial societies, gossip is used, along with song, divination and other rituals, to articulate grievances when conflicts arise. It can be used to attack, resist, and disgrace too-powerful members of the community as well as negotiate agreements about "the truth."

Gossip is *not* mere talk. It influences behaviour wherever people are concerned about honour and motivated by shame. In some instances, the external pressures of gossip and a concern with "saving face" serve as strong deterrents to divorce. In other instances, parents of suicide victims are shamed by the gossip of neighbours, friends, and colleagues. As a result, siblings of the suicide victim refuse to attend school. These people become the focus of stigmatizing gossip, so it is no wonder that, in many communities, families are careful to draw informational boundaries around their private sphere (on this, see, for example, Glazer and Ras, 1994).

The practice of honour killings in some Middle Eastern countries is a poignant example of how gossip can serve as a powerful form of social control. In this instance, gossip is able to contribute to the repression of an entire group by reinforcing a culture of domination. An honour killing is retributive violence by a male against a female family member for dishonouring the family. Middle Eastern societies are patriarchal, and sexual purity is valued highly in women. If a woman is seen as having committed a sexually impure act, or even if she has had something impure forcibly done *to* her (e.g., rape), there is considerable pressure put on her family to "rectify" the situation through an honour killing (Awwad, 2001).

Gossip plays a fundamental role in the practise of honour killings. A family's honour is largely rooted in its reputation, which is built up and based on gossip (Awwad 2001). A family's honourable reputation can be ruined if knowledge of even one infraction is spread around the community through gossip. If the knowledge of an individual's dishonour is spread through gossip, the situation is only rectified in the eyes of the community when the honour killing has been carried out. Gossip is used to keep a family's shame in the front of a community's consciousness and to pressure the family to commit the killing (Awwad, 2001). An honour killing is only necessary if the dishonour has been brought to the attention of the community through the use of gossip. Thus, gossip becomes a tool of social control, reinforcing the patriarchal culture of blaming women for sexual impurity and carrying out violence against them.

Gossip, though it affirms traditional morality, social cohesion, and cultural stability, can also be an intentional act of aggression. The use of gossip in this way is no different, in intent, form, or effect, than the malicious propaganda that enemies use in wartime to rally public support to their side. However, in most instances of gossip, the flip side of exclusion is inclusion, and rejection implies acceptance for those who change their behaviour. Gossip is about setting and policing boundaries and developing group identities. Deviant behaviour results in exclusion, but conforming to societal norms results in acceptance within the group. By rejecting unacceptable identities, gossips help people learn how to construct acceptable identities.

GOSSIP AS A GENDERED ACTIVITY. A large body of literature shows that men and women use conversation differently; they talk in different ways and have different conversational goals (Crawford, 1995; Wodack, 1997; Coates, 2004; Hall and Bucholtz, 2012). Typically, men in conversation are likely to be brief and confrontational, even cutting in or talking over other people's contributions. Their goal is to transmit "facts" and solve problems.

By contrast, women take more trouble to interlink their contributions to the collective effort. Their conversational goal is the achievement of sociability and solidarity, rather than the transmission of facts. So, it is not surprising that women —the more accomplished and sociable talkers—are historically associated with gossip. Gossip has overwhelmingly been regarded as a female activity. What's more, by studying women's gossip we learn about the boundaries of female social space at work, at home, and in the community at large. We gain better insights into the unspoken rules of the community through listening to gossip than we could learn through a church sermon, school lesson, or television sitcom.

Why have women historically gossiped more than men? The answer lies in the relative power of men and women. Gossip is a tool of resistance, rebellion, and revenge that attacks reputation. It is available for use by anyone, but only people who lack other social resources (e.g., wealth and power) rely on it exclusively. The weakest members of the community, when resisting power, do so in "safe," disguised ways. These ways include gossip, folktales, millennial visions, rumours, grumbling, and humour whose fable-like form shields the subordinate groups from direct retaliation.

For most of history, women lacked wealth, authority, and other forms of influence available to men. They had to rely on gossip. Gossip was especially useful for attacking other women, since a woman's social status in a community has historically relied on her reputation as chaste, honest, and good—as a keeper of family virtue. In patriarchal societies, this was the role into which men had cast women. Therefore, this was the card women had to play if they were going to attack other women.

Gossip was used to attack reputation in communities where reputation—especially women's reputation—was considered important. Using gossip to attack a man's wife was an effective means of attacking the husband, too. Regardless of the fact that gossip was an option for all genders, additional resources for attack were available to men. As such, it was a tool historically used by women.

Even today, socially dispossessed people (for example, schoolchildren and minority women) still use gossip. Migrant Filipina domestic workers in Hong Kong use gossip and humour to respond to experiences of prejudice and discrimination (Chang and Groves, 1995; Groves and Chang, 1999; Hutchinson and Brown, 2001). In an effort to distance themselves from their image as "hospitality girls" and gain respect, migrant Filipina communities also use gossip to enforce rules about the places and people with whom their number can associate. Ironically, the rules and their enforcement reproduce many of the same labels and constraints placed on Filipina workers by the employers and the Hong Kong public.

In a similar vein, gossip can create problems for migrants from traditional cultures arriving at individualistic cultures. For instance, Mexican migrants to the U.S. often suffer from culture shock. In order to reduce the culture shock and associated stresses, they are pressured to adapt to the individualistic nature of American culture. However, their traditional, collectivistic culture opposes such adaptation. It is known that individual accomplishment is emphasized in the U.S. For women, this translates into a motivation to achieve and break from historical prescriptions of the caregiver role. By contrast, the Mexican culture is one that values family success over that of the individual, and this in turn entails placing women in supportive, caregiving role (Dreby, 2008). Following immigration, family is the only social network or support that migrants have. The influence of gossip is therefore heightened, and, for Mexican migrant women, the outcome is the reinforcement of expectations for them to fulfill traditional roles (Dreby, 2008).

GOSSIP IN PRISONS. Gossip is a dominant feature of everyday life in many prisons. In a study of female inmates in Israel, gossip was identified as an extremely prevalent and influential aspect of daily prison life. Female inmates in Israel understand gossip as an essential aspect of "women's nature" and perceive it as something they are meant to engage in. The inmates use gossip to improve their material and social conditions. Through gossip, they can curry favours with one another as well as keep the social and material standings of others in check. In one example, gossip revealed that one woman had too many clothes and as a result had them taken away (Einat and Chen, 2012). At the same time, the identification of gossip as a female activity led to a negative view of femininity within the prison environment because of the negative connotations associated with gossip.

Gossip is used as a form of control as it gives the gossiper knowledge that can be used against fellow inmates. However, because gossip is often used spitefully, it decreases solidarity among the prisoners. The inmates automatically label their counterparts as gossipers, and therefore have little trust for one another. Despite this, it is employed to relieve the hardships associated with prison life. Gossip is able to diminish some of the stress from being in prison and mitigate boredom.

Interestingly, although the vast majority of the women agree that gossip was extremely widespread and common within the prison, few admitted to engaging in it themselves (Einat and Chen, 2012).

GOSSIP ONLINE. In the digital age, gossip has taken on new and unprecedented forms. These days, anyone with access to an Internet connection can instantly broadcast his or her opinion to billions of people around the globe. This has led to virtual communities that allow people to create, exchange, and discuss user-generated content. Social networking sites such as Facebook allow people to connect with friends and acquaintances around the world, while content communities and blogging sites such as YouTube and Twitter allow content and commentary to be instantly delivered to millions of subscribers. These services have enormously changed how people communicate, and also how they gossip.

Individuals increasingly expose personal information about themselves online that can be accessed by others anywhere in the world with the click of a mouse. Anyone who wants to be heard can create a blog to voice his or her opinion. Not surprisingly, concerns have emerged privacy and cyberbullying. Victims can be identified and humiliated by having their private lives exposed online for the all the world to see. Content can quickly "go viral" as in the case of a woman in South Korea who refused to clean up after her dog defecated in a train. She quickly became the target of mass public humiliation when image of her went viral across various social media websites. Her actions became a topic of gossip—and condemnation—among millions of people she had never met. With her identity revealed, she ended up dropping out of university as a result of her public shaming and embarrassment (Solove, 2007). The rise of such acts of Internet vigilantism has become a form of social control, reminding people that their actions both on and offline are constantly being monitored and evaluated by others. It has also resulted in an increased awareness of the power of online identity. For many, participating in social media is no longer simply social sharing, but has expanded to encompass building one's reputation and bringing in career opportunities and monetary income.

Building an online reputation has become more imperative as individuals and organizations try to take advantage of the Internet's all-encompassing reach in order to market their products. This has led to the formation of new relationships between consumers and the providers of the goods and services that they purchase. Each day millions of items are listed on auction and e-commerce sites. Anybody with access to the Internet is a potential seller or buyer, and most transactions take place without any physical interaction. Because of the potential risk involved, sellers want to build up a good reputation to attract as many customers as possible.

By allowing users to leave feedback about a transaction, sites such as eBay help sellers establish themselves as trustworthy and reputable (Snijders, Zijdeman, and Kritik, 2004). Having a brand promoted by bloggers and prominent online personalities is important for the success of independent online stores. Negative feedback is likely to result in backlash and criticism from dissatisfied customers who choose to warn others online.

Gossip has taken on new forms that stretch beyond the boundaries of the past. The Internet allows people to connect and form communities with others across the globe. These virtual networks all have their own complex cultures and norms. Gossip takes on different characteristics in these networks, but still unquestionably exists, demonstrating its universality across human social systems.

CONCLUDING REMARKS. For most of us in the West, honour, shame, and "saving face" are traditional ideas. We pay less attention to the politics of reputation than we once did. Of course, gossip and "image management" still play crucial roles in Western society. Employers may look at Facebook pages to find out more about job applicants; consider too, the growth of sites like LinkedIn and Academia.edu where a constructed image is important in determining the popularity and/or value of the person's work. Gossip and saving face are still important, but what people gossip about has changed. It is considered less appropriate to gossip about a person's sexuality, but still fair to gossip about rude behavior. The fields where gossip is important have changed, too. Research indicates that in certain fields of work, gossip is more important in the hiring process than in others. This tends to be true of positions requiring "soft" skills (for instance, the often required but impossible to define "leadership ability") than in positions with technical qualifications, such as an engineer or electrician.

More people today hold at least some degree of power over their lives (the sociological term is *power resources*, which include such things as guaranteed civil and legal rights) and therefore have less need to rely on gossip. Moreover, gossip can do less harm to their foes. Money and important friends can wash clean any inconvenient embarrassment, although a major exception to this rule is to be found in the realm of electoral politics where, as the impeachment proceedings targeting U.S. President Bill Clinton showed, "saving face" still influences the distribution of power. The harmful effects of gossip cannot be entirely avoided, even if one has money and power, and especially if the Internet is involved.

A new aspect of gossip in the contemporary world is that it's not limited to people we know firsthand. The media have made us feel close to, and familiar with, a wide variety of celebrities. As a result, the market for intimate information about these celebrities has exploded. Mass circulation tabloids such as the *National Enquirer* and, increasingly, a vast array of popular websites fill this need. Gossip about celebrities often centres on a minor or mundane event—a quarrel between spouses, the beginning of a romance, or a shopping spree—rather than actual scandal. Tabloids also (though not as frequently) publish stories of ordinary people, whose inclusion results from a single extraordinary accomplishment or episode: a bizarre illness, special talent, or rare act of courage. These reports have a positive tone; while celebrities may be depicted as victims of intractable problems that end in misery, ordinary people deserve—and receive—a happy ending. In both cases, gossip functions to make the universe seem just and benevolent and morally ordered.

Rumours

Rumours, like gossip, are flows of information, influence, and cultural information that display a community's moral values—also, its deepest fears and concerns, and highest goals and aspirations. More than gossip, rumours are informational inventions. Gossip is usually "true" in the sense that Mr. A really did sleep with Mrs. B, and isn't that just awful! Gossip, thus, is a moral gloss on factual information. Rumour, on the other hand, may be completely fictional, with no basis in fact; or it may contain a small amount of fact and a huge amount of invention. In either case, rumour also contains a moral gloss. Every rumour is about at least two things: the thing it purports to be about (e.g., the plan to build a new factory or shut down an old business) and the thing people actually care about (e.g., the creation or destruction of job opportunities in the community.)

Like gossip, rumours flow through networks of connected people: people who share a common culture and common social and economic concerns. Like gossip, a rumour only spreads outward to new listeners if people receiving the rumour think it is worth remembering and talking about. What has interested sociologists most about rumours is that, first, they are a form of "improvised news"—stories people make up together to fill gaps of ignorance about what is actually going on. Second, rumours are often about people who are markedly more powerful or less powerful than oneself. In effect, they are ways of engaging informationally in warfare with other social groups. This is particularly evident in connection with the spread of rumours about other ethnic or racial groups.

THE WAR AGAINST TOMATO BARONS. Consider this interesting example. In the summer of 1986, during an intense drought, rumours spread through the Dordogne region of France. Allegedly, large agricultural enterprises—Spanish "tomato barons"—had sponsored an attempted form of weather modification called cloud-seeding in order to prevent hail; the efforts had failed and resulted in drought instead. These rumours were reminiscent of similar ones involving the tomato barons that had surfaced in earlier years (Brodu, 1990).

The rumours were almost certainly wrong. Cloud-seeding is notoriously ineffective at producing rain, and there is no evidence that it can prevent rain either. Such rumours appeal to people in a time of drought because of popular superstition and the general unreliability of techniques for controlling (or even predicting) the weather. Nevertheless, other factors enter in as well. These rumours, like others we discuss in this chapter, have a political content that is just barely hidden below the surface. There is a reason why the French rumourmongers blamed *Spanish* tomato barons. After all, the French and Spanish peoples have been rivals for over five hundred years. By studying rumours, we learn something valuable about the organization of society and, also, about the organization of people's fantasy lives.

Rumours have social origins and operate by social means, which we seek to understand in this chapter. Like gossip, rumour is a type of information flow, or diffusion, that we associate with everyday life and with our personal networks of friends and acquaintances. And like the word "gossip" the very term "rumour" carries a negative connotation. We assume that a rumour conveys information that is of poor and unreliable quality, or has a malicious intent. Both gossip and rumour travel through networks of personal acquaintance, and both of them reflect and shape public opinion.

DREAMS AND RUMOURS. Let's note at the outset that not all rumours contain false information. Rumours often contain valid information that has not (yet) been authorized for release. The "news leaks" on which journalists rely so heavily and sensibly are not far from rumours, though they often come directly from one source whereas rumours pass through many intermediaries. Rumours are "unauthorized" information and our stance on authority will shape how we feel about rumours as sources of information.

Remember, too, that rumours, at worst, are no more false than dreams. We don't rely on dreams to tell us every kind of truth about external reality, but they tell us a lot nonetheless. As well, dreams tell us much that is true about *internal* reality, about our fantasies, fears, and wishes. So, too, with rumours.

Indeed, both dreams and rumours inform us in subtle ways. The word rumour comes, through French, from a Latin word meaning "noise," "murmur" or even "hum." The very sound of the word reinforces its meaning. The word clique has a harsh sound because of the two "hard" consonants ("c" and "q"), and that reflects the nature of cliques: they are loud and often harsh and, by purveying gossip and bestowing social approval or disapproval, capture our attention. Rumour, on the other hand, connotes a quieter, less certain transmission of information. Thus its dictionary definition as "hearsay, common talk, but unproved statement, rather vague." For social scientists, a rumour is an implicit theory about how the world works, embellished by allegations or attributions based on circumstantial evidence. It is also a popular narrative emerging from a lack of complete knowledge of established—that is to say, authorized—truths. A rumour is a proposition that is unverified and in general circulation.

THE PSYCHOLOGY OF RUMOUR. The great social psychologist Gordon Allport is partly to blame for the bad reputation rumours enjoy in social science. For it was Allport who, more than sixty years ago, launched the first systematic studies of rumours and their social consequences for race relations (see, for example, Allport and Postman, 1947).

In his classic works on race and racism, Allport established what is now the conventional image of rumour among social scientists. Rumour, he said, is characterized by (1) a poor quality of information—information that, with retelling, becomes increasingly distorted, exaggerated, irrational, and inauthentic; (2) a personalized means of transmission, in a random, unstructured pattern; (3) rumourmongers who are isolated, suggestible, uncritical, and irrational; and (4) harmful social consequences which include deviance, disruption, heightened anxiety and irrational behaviour.

Viewed this way, rumours are communications that are easily started and spread, and often difficult to stop. People construct rumours around unauthenticated information. They are unreliable testimonies of events, with unknown sources, that are transmitted via interpersonal communication. Several factors explain the emergence of rumours. The most important of these include individuals experiencing a lack of information, the significance of the topic for the carriers and audiences of the rumour, and the degree of anxiety of the people transmitting rumours.

The basic law of rumours that Allport and Postman proposed in 1947 stated that "the amount of rumour in circulation will vary with the importance of the subject to the individual involved, times the ambiguity of the evidence pertaining to the topic at issue." As well, the volume of rumour is proportional to people's ignorance multiplied by their anxiety. Over time, this proposed law has come into question. Many studies suggest that subjects are more inclined to spread rumours that they do *not* consider important. Credibility is another factor thought to be involved in predicting the spread of rumours. Rumours spread more often if belief in the credibility of the rumour is high rather than low. (Thus, French farmers could more readily attribute blame to Spanish farmers than to Dutch farmers, with whom they have never had a rivalry.)

Allport focused on the irrationality of rumours because he was concerned with two kinds of issues that garnered a great deal of public attention in the 1930s and 1940s: race riots and enemy propaganda. Public susceptibility to believing racial rumours and propaganda was dangerous, discreditable, and seemingly irrational. Allport's goal was to understand why people accept and act upon certain pieces of information as though they are "true." Why, for example, do they believe in unsubstantiated rumour that a black man has raped a white woman in another part of town? Such beliefs and rumours had been the basis of lynchings in the United States since the Civil War.

THE SOCIOLOGY OF RUMOUR. Had Allport been studying the flow of information in relation to a situation such as (say) the way in which Kansas corn farmers adopted new seed stocks, he might have taken a different view how humans use information. It would have been a picture of people who are rational, cautious, and practical. Instead, he studied information flow, and people's reactions to received information, in relation to racial prejudice. Here, under conditions of ignorance and anxiety, people proved willing to think anything, no matter how terrible, about people they considered unlike themselves.

This led to a belief among social scientists that, under conditions of ignorance and anxiety, people will regularly act on poor quality information, and that they will be unable to tell the difference between good and bad information. In a panic, they may behave in unpredictable, random ways, ways that are harmful, deviant and even criminal. They will become suggestible, uncritical, and irrational.

This theory seems plausible, yet the data do not support it. First, the spread of rumour is not always a passive retelling of a story. Often it takes the form of intensified information seeking, as was shown in a study of earthquake rumours in China and the United States (Turner, 1994). This study found four stages of rumour progression: (1) reliance on expert information and media sources; (2) discussion of expert information among family, friends, and workmates, leading to both clarification and distortion; (3) attempts to abate concern through questioning of local experts and authorities, often leading to suspicion; and (4) an intensified demand for information, leading to widespread scatter of misinformation. In China, unlike California, the rumours were associated with higher levels of superstition, more extreme public reactions, and attribution to foreign sources.

As sociologist Tamotsu Shibutani (1966) suggested in her study of "improvised news," rumour may be closer to other forms of individual and collective information-seeking than it is to dreaming and escapism, as the psychological, Freudian and French research traditions have maintained. From this sociological standpoint, a rumour is a solution to an ill-defined problem. In creating a rumour, society draws on its limited stock of cognitive resources, but in a purposeful manner. This process was seen, for example, in emotional responses to the explosion of the space shuttle *Challenger* in 1986, where a great deal of news, factual and improvised, spread through interpersonal channels (Kubey and Peluso, 1990).

At the same time, rumours that convey stereotypes, or archetypal images, gain wider currency in the media and in public discourse, and are more resistant to denial, than other rumours. The most successful rumours correspond to what people hope or fear will come true, rather than what happens. The mass media amplify their effect. The power of rumour is in its making visible otherwise invisible relations (e.g., the controlling role of Jews, the misbehaviour of blacks).

Rumours don't just float through the air. Contrary to what psychologists have proposed, rumours flow not between unrelated, atomized individuals, but through people's social networks. A study of an incident in Nova Scotia serves to illustrate this fact (Scanlon et. al., 1985; see also Meichenbaum, 1995). When a child was injured during a wind storm, a rumour spread that she had been killed. Employing a questionnaire, a research team interviewed a sample of sixty people in the community; they heard the rumour four times. They traced the flow of information, person by person, from one respondent back to the original source, revealing an eight-person chain. The conclusion? Rumours pass between people who know each other and are mainly of the same socioeconomic status. There was evidence the rumour had evolved as it passed along the chain. However, except for its key error–the fact that the child was not killed–the rumour remained accurate.

RUMOURS IN A STATE OF EMERGENCY. As a form of communication, rumour plays a variety of roles in human interactions. The forms that rumour takes on depend on situational variables, which also influence whether the rumour will have a positive or negative impact on the community in which it spreads. In times of emergency, people need information, and when formal news agencies fail to deliver it, they are likely to turn to informal channels such as rumour to fill that need. This is the "improvised news" that Shibutani (1966) referred to; rumour takes on the form of "collective problem-solving" by which people in the midst of an ambiguous situation attempt to pool their intellectual resources to "construe a meaningful interpretation" of the situation.

Zhang and Zhang (2009) mathematically modeled the spread of rumours during states of emergency, to examine factors that determine whether they will have a beneficial or detrimental effect within a community. When such an event occurs, it inevitably results in rumours, public panic, and social loss. These rumours can either have a positive impact on the control of situation, or conversely lead to an accelerated deterioration of the situation.

Consider the aftermath of Hurricane Katrina, when tens of thousands of displaced residents from New Orleans were evacuated to the Baton Rouge area. The lack of official information in the days following the disaster, coupled with the sudden arrival of so many strangers, lead to widespread rumours of criminal victimization among the Baton Rougians, and provided the opportunity to study social behaviour in the midst of an unprecedented disaster (Thomas, 2007).

The loss of electricity during the disaster left thousands of people without access to channels of official information. As a result, many relied on word of mouth and the spread of rumours to gain information. People began hearing horrific stories from their friends and families about murder, rape, robbery, and looting happening in New Orleans. Soon, rumours of crime began to emerge in the Baton Rouge community. This created widespread panic and increased the fear of victimization, as more people heard these stories and feared that such acts were taking place in their own community. With refugees continuing to pour into Baton Rouge and official information lacking, a situation of ambiguity and apprehension was created; this in turn led to false rumours and misconstrued information. We can see how, in some cases, rumours cause confusion, chaos, and panic in times of emergency, because of the spread of misinformation through informal channels.

But rumours can also be beneficial in times of crisis. Rumour is not inherently false—it is merely unverified information. Even that can be of use to people. Rumours serve to make people aware of a risk that's happening, share the best available information, and serve as a mechanism for coping with a sudden shocking event.

Zhang and Zhang's model (2009) discusses the interplay between the spreading rate of rumours and the development of a state of an emergency. They found that when rumours spread at certain rate, they have a positive impact: slowly spreading rumours during the middle and late stages of an emergency can actually improve the situation's stability. When facts are unknown, rumours serve as a channel of information to help people collectively discuss their situation and also as a mechanism for coping with the disaster.

SNAKE IN THE GREENS. What other positive role does rumour play in the life of a community? Sociologist Dan Miller (1992), for his part, studied the transmission of a rumour in Dayton, Ohio. Rumour-mongers alleged that a poisonous snake had popped up in the produce section of a local supermarket and bitten an old lady, who then died. To understand the rumour process better, and to find out whether Allport's assessment was correct, Miller interviewed ninety-four rumour receivers (and transmitters) within two to three days after the "snake in the greens" rumour began.

He found the information quality was, in a sense, just fine. The event had never happened—there was no snake and no dead lady—but neither was there any apparent growth in distortion during the time of the study. The information did not become more distorted and less authentic with repeated telling and the passage of time. Second, the rumour passed through existing social networks of friends and acquaintances. It did not pass through a random pattern of contacts between strangers, as Allport would have suggested. Nor were the rumour transmitters atomized or isolated. On the contrary, they were socially integrated ordinary people. Finally, the rumour did not create conflict and deviance; on the contrary, it increased social solidarity.

Given what people told Miller, this "snakes" rumour had served a social purpose. First, it provided the basis for *playful talk*, especially joking among young men, and this increased social solidarity. Second, it provided an opportunity for *critical talk*. It allowed poor black residents to speak up against the white-owned supermarket and white society, and this, too, unified the residents. Third, the rumour stimulated *chit-chat,* especially among the elderly, who used the rumour as another topic for conversation. Finally, it offered more philosophical members of the community an opportunity for *metaphorical talk* about victimization. They spoke about haves and have-nots, recalled the snake in the Garden of Eden, and reflected on the nature of good and evil. For them, the rumour promoted a general identification with underdogs everywhere.

So, the rumour was a means of social bonding and veiled social protest. It aided in the formation or validation of communal solidarity. Through repetition, the rumour brought many people together, connecting them into a larger interrelated network of communication. By the end of the first week, however, the rumour was no longer confined to low-income neighborhoods. It had spread to talk radio, news reports, and into predominantly white neighborhoods. This transformed the rumour. Now, the rumour and rumour-mongers became objects of ridicule. Shortly afterward, the rumour was dead.

THE SOCIAL BASIS OF RUMOUR FLOW. The spread of a rumour can be used to map informal communication flow. The rumour functions as a projection of social mood, a medium for mass communication, and an instrument in defining new social situations.

If you think about it, the "snake in the greens" rumour is exactly the same as the "Spanish tomato barons" rumour. Both are about something essential: about food and survival. Both rumours have a villain of a different class and a different race or nationality—a Spanish tomato baron, a white supermarket owner—whose callous disregard and desire for profit endangers the lives of good, ordinary people. In both rumours, the "authorities" are nowhere to be seen. They cannot be relied on to protect the good, ordinary people from the crimes of the villain.

A product of ignorance and anxiety? Yes. However, rumours are also a correct reading of the society in which they arise. In France and the United States, rich people *do* take advantage of poor people and authorities often let it happen without intervening. In the United States, white business owners regularly take advantage of ghetto-dwelling black people; that is fact, not rumour. In the global economy, international cooperation between capitalists often prevails over "national interests," at the expense of jobs for working people and farmers. Thus, rumours encode information about the society and the power structure that is *essentially* correct.

By this standard, rumours are part of a "gray market" where information from nonofficial sources is more valuable, because it is more likely to reflect people's everyday concerns, than information from official sources. Official, authorized information may also be seen as the source of public ignorance, not the cure for it. Thus rumours, coming from many sources and hiding many political agendas, are part of a struggle for the ideological control of a stratified society. In this way, rumours serve to equalize the social positions of the participants, reducing them to one behavioural standard and giving them something closer to equal knowledge.

Many societies do not trust their governments; and most studies indicate that in recent decades, confidence in politicians and public institutions has been declining throughout the Western world. Wherever confidence in public authority is lacking, rumours abound. In Russia and Western Europe from the seventeenth through the mid-nineteenth centuries, widespread rumours were symptomatic of continuing social instability and the feared transition to new cultural and political systems. Political rumours and anecdotes have long been devices of political communication in closed societies. Through such means, the intelligentsia, political authorities, and "ordinary people" try to influence each other's understanding of reality, as well as each other's behaviour.

Wherever there is political and economic chaos, there is a boom in rumours and the sociological study of rumours. Rumours become more widespread and influential, especially among people of higher educational and socioeconomic levels, who know information of value can be found in the "gray market." People hear rumours at their workplace and from neighbours, through the mass media, in the streets, and on public transit. Wherever there is chaos and fear of change, people endlessly fabricate and pass along rumour.

Latin America is a region that was under dictatorial rule for decades. There, rumours were often of the "tomato baron" variety. Consider the rumour that local babies were being kidnapped and murdered for organ transplants in other countries. They first appeared in the Latin American press in between 1987 and 1989. True or not, this rumour masked an important truth and, in this way, it was a sophisticated piece of propaganda. The rumour's origins lay in the fact that underdevelopment and extreme poverty had created two circumstances: the adoption of local babies by foreigners, and the development of international organs-for-transplant commerce.

Only a monstrous image of developed countries could have permitted the popular acceptance of this "legend." Rumours which are popular follow this model by obeying dominant views of social relations. Perhaps the level of agreement with dominant culture could be another way of studying rumours and their spread or popularity. The snake-in-the-greens rumour would be a prime example of this phenomenon. In recent decades, similar rumours have circulated in other parts of the developing world—in Africa, China, and India—around adoption and organ sales.

RUMOUR, FOLKLORE, AND NEWS. Increasingly, it is difficult to separate fact from fancy. One can readily confuse rumour with actual events, strange facts, fantastic beliefs, and sheer imaginativeness. We cannot rely on the media, the experts and the "authorities" to help us. History has shown that they are sometimes responsible for planting misinformation themselves.

As for *unplanted* misinformation, there is often a dreamlike element to rumours: an element of fantasy, humour, desire, and escape. The world as portrayed by rumour is, sometimes, a world we would either love or hate to live in. Fabulous beasts, unknown or extinct species, or known species with radical abnormalities inhabit this world. It is a world of danger and seduction. Rumours, like dreams, serve the creative function of endowing reality with meaning by adapting it to a symbolic system. They capture people's attention and allow them to temporarily immerse themselves in a world other than their own. Rumours are a literary form with certain invariant formal traits. They tell a recognizable story, with a plot line and recognizable good guys and bad guys. Their local character catches the listener's attention; he may be the next victim, after all.

Although the terms "rumour" and "urban legend" are often used interchangeably, DiFonzo and Bordia (2007) make an important distinction between the two. *Urban legends* function to convey mores and values in an entertaining fashion. The contents are humorous or horrible events, told in a narrative that appeals to the local community. The particular stories and characters are not important; it is the symbolic meanings behind them that matter.

Rumours arise in situational contexts of ambiguity, result from people's need for understanding, and are used to make sense of a confusing situation. They also arise in contexts of threat or potential threat, as people try to gain a regain control and defend a threatened sense of self. Individuals respond by acting on what little information they have in order to reconstruct the events surrounding their situation, in order to lessen their own feelings of helplessness. Although rumours are comprised of unverified information, that information is relevant to their situation. Both urban legends and rumours are a form of social discourse that function to help individuals make sense of and respond to unusual circumstances.

Consider the rumour about a Dallas, Texas, woman who claimed to be intentionally infecting men with the HIV/AIDS virus. According to Bird (1996; see also Correll, 2008), the media took hold of the story and transformed it from oral folklore into news. The story was a hoax; however, it was not an instance of deliberate misinformation or media errors. As a product of an oral folk tradition, it was a cultural construction reflecting and reinforcing inherent anxieties and concerns. In this case, journalism functioned as a broker for stories already extant in the culture. The rumour reflected and revealed popular anxieties within the community about the price to be paid for sexual freedom.

A panic associated with rumours of Satanic cult practices spread in May 1988 across a 250-mile-wide area of southwestern New York and northwestern Pennsylvania (Victor, 1989). In this instance, the rumour-panic took months to evolve. Satanic cult stories first appeared after the media distorted stories from national TV talk shows to fit into local gossip. Likely, Satanic cult rumours arise from underlying socioeconomic stresses that cause a breakdown in family relationships. The rumour-stories are subversion myths; they seek out an evil internal enemy to blame for people's perceived threats to traditional values. Stories about endangered children, as with this Satanism scare, suggest an underlying anxiety about the incompatibility of families and society.

Along similar lines, a rumour alleged the contamination of children's "lick and stick tattoos" by the hallucinogenic drug LSD (Renard, 1991). This rumour circulated in France from April through December 1988, and can be related to other "new urban legends" which connected LSD to Mickey Mouse prints and popular children's tattoos. Researchers document a 1987 variant of the rumour in Quebec. From Quebec it spread to Nice and other regions of France, reaching Paris in 1988. A survey found that 58 percent of high school students admitted to having heard the rumour. Official denials by the Ministry of Education were least effective with students who had been exposed to the rumour.

CLOSING REMARKS. Rumours, like dreams, gossip, and even novels, are always about something real. However much they may reflect ignorance and anxiety, they tell us a story about something important. That story is, often, about the real world as seen through a distorted lens. Sometimes, however, rumours are not distorted at all, or are distorted only slightly. As sociologists, and unlike psychologists, we will not prejudge the issue of factuality in rumours.

Rumours don't bounce around in space like fruit flies or subatomic particles. They travel through already existing social networks. Rumours spread not because people are high-strung ignoramuses but because rumours tell us a believable story and the storyteller is someone whom we know well and have reason to trust.

Searches

A *search* is a process of looking through information to find something. Thus, a search is a diffusion process in reverse. Diffusion, as we have seen, spreads out or decentralizes information from a location where it is initially concentrated. Searches concentrate or bring together information from a variety of decentralized locations. Both processes change the concentration of information over time, though in opposite directions; and as we will see, both processes work through personal networks. Because they are mirror images of each other, we can learn a great deal about diffusion by studying searches, and vice versa.

We can also learn a great deal about the hidden social structure of a society by seeing which individuals and groups play the most important and influential role in people's searches. Whether you are searching for the perfect mate, the perfect job, or a reliably good bag of marijuana, you will do this by contacting certain people and not others. You will not randomly send out letters to the universe or post an all-purpose plea for help in cyberspace: not, that is, if you expect a useful, reliable reply. When we search for something, we need more than information: we need credible, reliable information—information we can trust. And the one way we can be sure of getting information we can trust is by seeking it from, or reviewing it with, people we know we can trust: that is, familiar members of our social network.

Admittedly, in recent decades, online searching has seemingly revolutionized searches in many important ways. It takes a person next to no time to find out who invented Jell-O, what the nighttime temperature in Bangkok is in September, and where you can find the nearest restaurant serving souvlaki to go (and whether it takes credit cards). That said, really important things are still hard to find, online or otherwise. They would include such things as the answer to the question, *Where can I find a good, steady job that would take advantage of my interest and training in (fill in the blank: sociology, philosophy, commerce, biology, early childhood education, Eastern religions, mathematics, etc.)?*

SEARCH STRATEGIES. Imagine that you are searching for three things and you have three ways of finding them. You may also use any of the three ways more than once. First, you are searching for a full-time job, a good one if possible: something related to what you studied in school, with good pay, good working conditions, and prospects for advancement. Second, you are searching for social support: a shoulder to cry on. You have broken up with your girlfriend/boyfriend, and feel depressed and lonely. Third, you are searching for something that is illegal or at least disreputable: something you don't want anyone or everyone to know about. Let's say you are looking for illegal drugs, for recreational purposes.

You can search for each of these things in any of three ways. Strategy one: you can ask your best friend for information, help, or advice. Strategy two: You can randomly pick a name out of the telephone book, phone that person, and ask him/her for information, help, or advice. Or, strategy three: you can work your request for information, help, or advice into a conversation with an acquaintance at school or work. You are on a first-name basis with this "acquaintance," but you don't consider him/her a close friend.

Strategy two, the random telephone-call, has one thing in its favour: you are likely to reach someone you have never talked to before. In ten random telephone calls, you are likely to reach people who are different from you and from one another. Random calling maximizes the variety and range of information you may receive. However, no one you reach in this way is likely to be useful. People at the other end of the phone line have no motive for helping you find a good job. After all, they don't even know you. They are likely to reject your request for help in obtaining an illegal substance; you could be an undercover police officer. Even if they expressed sympathy about the loneliness you feel after your romantic breakup, their sympathy will not mean much. It comes from people you don't know or care for. So, strategy two won't work.

Strategy one is more promising. Your best friend, like your mother, father, brother, sister (and a few other relatives), is motivated to help you: he or she likes you. Your best friend is happy to help you through a period of loneliness and depression. Your best friend will also be willing to help you find a job, maybe even to find an illegal substance. However, we tend to choose friends who are like us. Because of this similarity, our close friends often form cliques. We will discuss cliques further in the next chapter. For the time being, it is enough to say that members of cliques tend to know the same things. So, the information reaching our best friends, whether about jobs or drugs, is not much different from the information already reaching us. Close friends are motivated to help us, but they likely can't help us much if we need varied or unusual information.

THE ACQUAINTANCESHIP STRATEGY. That leaves strategy three, the use of acquaintances. We all know dozens if not hundreds of people on a first-name basis. They are people with whom we have casual conversations from time to time. Some of them know each other: they may even be kin, friends, neighbours, or acquaintances of each other. Many of our acquaintances, however, do not know each other. Thus the information reaching a dozen acquaintances is varied—not as varied as the information reaching a dozen randomly selected people, but much more varied than the information reaching our dozen closest friends.

Also, because we know our acquaintances and they know us, we are willing to ask them for information or advice and they are willing to provide it. What is more, our experience with these acquaintances provides some basis on which to evaluate the quality of the information they are providing. We may well tell an acquaintance we are searching for a job, and listen for suggestions about where to look. We may tell an acquaintance we are feeling "down" because of a romantic break-up, and put some value on the kind words of support he or she offers. We may even tell an acquaintance we are looking for drugs, and hear about possible sources we had never heard of before.

This word-of-mouth strategy works backwards, too. Imagine there is a boss who is hoping to hire someone just like you; a sympathetic person who will love to comfort a person with your problems; or a dope dealer who is looking to make a sale. For various reasons, they cannot solve their recruitment problem by advertising. Can you imagine a newspaper ad that reads "Broken-hearted? I can make it all better for you" or a television spot in which Joe, the local drug dealer, declares, "Best prices, best quality, convenient one-stop shopping—come and see me!" It's true that employers often advertise jobs, and people apply for them. Yet do people get *good* jobs that way? That's a question that sociologist Mark Granovetter (1973) tried to answer in his research on managers in the Boston area. Let's consider that research after a brief bit of background on *weak ties*.

THE STRENGTH OF WEAK TIES. In a way, our confusion about job finding goes back to ideologies connected with the Protestant work ethic. In individualistic, acquisitive societies like Canada, parents and other grown-ups teach us to think that work is a good thing, and that people who work hard will get the rewards they deserve. Largely, this belief is valid in school. The harder you work, the higher your grades will likely be. However, the belief is not always true outside school. Often, people don't know how hard-working, meritorious, or qualified you are. As well, you are likely to have a problem finding out about the best job, given your abilities, then reporting your qualifications to the right employer. In other words, outside school there is an information problem and a matching problem. Both the job applicant and the employer need to find out about each other, and they also need to evaluate each other. Otherwise, merit cannot be rewarded.

In this sense, hiring a new employee is like adopting an innovation—for example, a new hybrid corn seed. You need to become aware of the new possibility, and then you need to evaluate it and become confident of the adoption decision before you take an important action. Only then is merit rewarded by adoption, or hiring.

Yet, in our society, we like to think that people who are talented and work hard will somehow inevitably get the best jobs, and the best jobs will somehow inevitably find the best employees. There is supposedly an unfailing job market that operates with an "invisible hand" to link up job buyers and job sellers. People who get bad jobs, by this reasoning, probably deserve bad jobs. They must lack the qualifications, or even the skills of self-presentation that are important when interviewing for a job. Likewise, jobs that fail to find good candidates probably also deserve to fail. They must not have presented candidates with a positive corporate image or an attractive employee package.

These may be the reasons why *some* people don't get hired, or *some* jobs get filled by poor-quality workers. However, there are other reasons, too. They include excessive reliance on impersonal means of job selection and recruitment (e.g., answering advertisements, sending out unbidden resumes) and excessive reliance on highly personal means of job finding and recruitment (e.g., getting a job through a close relative or close friend).

Granovetter (1973) found that most managers he studied had found their job through an acquaintance: what he called a *weak tie* (to distinguish it from a close friend or relative, which will be a *strong tie*). In fact, the best jobs were found that way. This continues to be the case; for example, in Holland most top managers found their jobs through informal networks, especially if they possessed more social capital (e.g., external work contacts and memberships) (Boxman et al, 1991). Social capital, accessible through one's social network, determines the speed with which jobs are found and the quality of jobs attained.

Subsequent research on social networks has shown that the process is more complex than Granovetter imagined. More recent network research suggests that reliance on acquaintances and the openness of acquaintances in sharing job prospects depends on the state of the job market (for example, whether there are plenty of jobs or few jobs vacant), the job type (how specialized or technical the job is), and on reputational concerns (for example, whether recommending your friend will affect one's own position in the company).

Still, Granovetter's findings were on the right track, particularly if the job market is robust. Under conditions of plenty, acquaintanceships turn up the best jobs, and the best job-person matches, because they give job markets the best combination of awareness, or information quantity, and evaluation, or information quality. Networks of acquaintances are large; much more varied information flows through them than through networks of friends or relatives. Yet networks of acquaintances also provide more reliable information than you can obtain from a random selection of names, or even (to cite a situation that is similar) from a giant pile of job applications and resumes from hundreds of strangers.

Often, the same process operates at the other end of the job market. Among displaced industrial workers in western Pennsylvania, those who could *not* find other jobs over a long period had much smaller social networks than those who could (Zippay, 1991). Follow-up after ten years (in 2001) showed that short-term training did not improve employment chances, with participants still relying mainly on their social networks for job acquisition. Researchers recommended instead social service interventions that increased the development of weak ties among disadvantaged groups (Zippay, 2001).

Granovetter explains that the degree of overlap of two people's friendship networks varies directly with the strength of their tie to one another. Weakly tied people have networks that overlap less, creating a greater likelihood that each will gain new information from the other. This principle has an impact on the diffusion of influence and information, mobility opportunity, and community organization. Weak ties provide society with great cohesive power, since they permit the tying together, or "bridging," of small, strongly tied, well-defined, and otherwise separate primary groupings. Where weak ties cannot flourish, people are forced back on strong ties exclusively, or left with none at all; they experience both situations as unpleasant. In a world of weak as well as strong ties, people escape the claustrophobic oppression of having only strong ties, and the alienating isolation of having no ties.

This *bridging function* of weak ties is important in insular communities that are also highly segmented and heterogeneous, as for example Israeli kibbutzim (i.e., collective communities in Israel traditionally based on agricultural production). Weak ties connect otherwise non-communicating groups, leading in many cases to the eventual dissolution of group boundaries, and increasing societal homogeneity and social stability. Thus, people extend social interactions by breaking or bridging social barriers. They can achieve defined, stable group identities only by segmenting the social network.

Weak ties are indispensable for both individual fulfillment and social cohesion. Through weak ties, people have access to information and opportunity beyond that which their immediate circle of strong ties can provide. Weak ties are also important purveyors of support. Large, heterogeneous networks of weak ties give their members many small services, including sociable companionship. By definition, they are less likely to provide emotional closeness, the most important attribute of strong ties.

Weak ties, therefore, give a society or an organization two major benefits: freedom and cohesion. First, overlapping circles of weak ties inhibit segmentation along occupational or organizational lines. This reduces inequalities and endows people with power and freedom. Complex, overlapping social roles promote autonomy, individualism, and free choice, so weak social relations are preferable to strong, authoritarian relations. In a system founded on overlapping status sets and complex role relations, everyone is involved in establishing a strong system of checks and balances, without meddlesome interference or authoritarian supervision.

Weak ties are also a major source of personnel turnover and change in group composition. People who are weakly tied to groups readily come and go. As we will see in the second half of this book, this produces organizational renewal. It also produces tertiary groups and tertiary relations, characterized by a temporary or short-term existence, weak ties with other members, little investment of self in the group, and little importance of the quality of the relationships to the group member. An increasing proportion of interpersonal ties are of this new type of interaction, and likely the online world has increased the importance of such weak ties.

HOW THE MARKET WORKS. Imagine you are an employer trying to fill a job with someone who is at least "okay," even if not perfect. You advertise the job and receive 300 job applications from people you never heard of. Of these, 100 applicants look good on paper: their record shows a good education, relevant experience, and decent recommendations. Now, you can interview these hundred people, but this will be time consuming. Likely, you ask if anyone in the office knows anything about any of the candidates. You discover that your colleague

George knows the uncle of one candidate, Sarah knows the recommender of another candidate, and Carla used to belong to the same club as someone who may be the mother of a third candidate. Suddenly, you have the basis for a "short list" of three candidates, a manageable number to interview. The result: you soon hire someone who meets the job requirements. Someone who is satisfactory, even if not ideal, comes to fill the job. Ideology aside, that's how the system works most of the time. Given the huge cost of trying to select an "ideal" candidate, this process is perfectly rational. It is good enough for the real world.

Hiring is not *always* done through the weak ties of acquaintanceships, nor do people *never* hire friends or relatives (with strong ties), nor strangers (with no ties). In at least some job markets, however, networks of acquaintanceship may be especially important. This tells us that job seekers in these markets must create and maintain networks of acquaintanceship, and they must "network" their acquaintances when they are looking for a job. Employers must also establish ongoing relations with the potential suppliers of job candidates.

At the macro level, weak ties display an important bridging function. This allows information to travel from one distinct subgroup of job referral actors to another subgroup in the broader social system—or not, as the case may be. On the other hand, the process we are describing may promote and maintain systems of discrimination. Processes that are inclusionary for insiders are also exclusionary for outsiders. So, for example, women who use personal contacts (informal methods) to find jobs tend end up in lower-paid, female-dominated jobs (Drentea, 1998). For women, using formal channels (e.g., writing letters of application) can lead to first jobs that are far higher in level than those found using informal means. This being so, women entering the job market may be better off using formal methods of job search, such as job ads, employment agencies, and company recruiters, than relying on acquaintances. Such formalized job-finding strategies increase the representation of women, recent immigrants, and visible minorities in traditionally white, male-dominated occupations, controlling for other structural and individual characteristics. Some researchers argue that it is the so-called outsiders' inability to accumulate and use network-based social capital as well as white men that leads to their disadvantaged positions (Cross and Lin, 2008).

Along similar lines, another interesting study by Elliott (1999) showed that relatively small differences in job search strategies among residents of high- and low-poverty neighborhoods are magnified in the hiring process and that supply- and demand-side factors have qualitatively different effects on earnings within these residential contexts.

There is general agreement in the research community that access to information is far from random. However, the flow of information depends on the nature of the information as well as on the nature of the network (Kilduff and Tsai, 2003). Weak inter-unit ties in an organization help a project team find simple information—for example, dollar figures on the sales of widgets—that is the province of other subunits of the organization. However, weak ties hinder the spread of complex (i.e., non-codified and dependent) knowledge: for example, information on the peculiarities of management, the sales force, or the purchasing public. Such information often requires a strong tie between the two parties to a transfer. Weak inter-unit ties, therefore, speed up projects when the identified knowledge held by other subunits is simple, but slow them down when the knowledge to be transferred is complex.

More recent studies also show that, contrary to Granovetter's findings, strong ties do play an important role in the diffusion of job information, while weak ties may only characterize the flow of job information at lower organizational levels. That's because strong ties may be needed to access important social resources. In Germany, for example, low-status job seekers do better by using strong ties to people with whom they are intimately connected (Wegener, 1991). Only high-prestige job seekers profit from their acquaintanceships. Perhaps this is because acquaintances stand to gain more by doing a high-status person the favour of passing on job information, while acquaintances of a low status-person stand to gain less. The same applies to the movement of health information (on this, see Verhaeghe and Tampubolon, 2012).

A formal model of the search process suggests that reliance on weak ties is never associated with higher expected wages, if weak ties are mainly important for relaying many job offers. Thus, if weak ties do nothing more than increase the *variety* of job information in a person's hands, high wages will not likely result. Applying for a job under this circumstance is still like cold-calling numbers in a phone book.

However, reliance on weak ties is *occasionally* associated with a higher expected wage if weak-tie offers are drawn from a better distribution of job possibilities. Said another way, if weak ties generate job offers from a wider selection of good jobs, the resulting wage may be higher than expected. Our weak ties have beneficial results only if they persuade employers who control good jobs to make job offers. Job seekers can obtain a greater amount of job information through weak ties, but long lists of undesirable, unobtainable positions are of little interest. Likewise, bad jobs are of little interest. Finding those few openings for which one will be seriously considered, and which one will consider accepting, is critical.

As predicted by the model, in some societies strong ties are important for salary determination. In Sweden, for example, strong ties, not weak ones, affect managers' incomes most (Flap and Boxman, 1999). In Norway, getting a job through informal channels does not lead to wage advantages for lower-level employees (Hansen, 1999). Among higher-level employees, those who have been contacted informally by the employer obtain the highest wages. This is a result of head-hunting, not weak ties. Employees who get a job through weak ties do not have wage advantages compared with those who contact the employer directly or are head hunted.

In Korea, employees with family ties to the corporate owners occupy many of the top executive positions in major businesses (Shin and Chin, 1989; more recently, Campbell and Keys, 2002; Ferris et al., 2003). When hiring executives, employers also give preference to candidates from the same region of the country. In Japan, institutional embeddedness, based on the importance of ties between schools and firms, is more important in college and even high school graduates' ability to find a job than is social embeddedness, which is based on the intervention of family and friends.

In urban China, strong ties provide the interpersonal trust that is key to securing job assignments that are not strictly permitted by the formal social structure (Bian, 1994). *Guanxi*, networks of personal obligation, often based on gift-giving and related to patronage, influence authorities to assign good jobs as favours to their contacts. Job seekers are indirectly connected to people with job-assigning authority through intermediaries to whom both are strongly tied. Job seekers using these indirect ties are more likely to obtain better jobs than those using direct ties. Hanser (2002) suggests that this system, while not irrelevant today, is much less popular among young people entering the Chinese labour market than it once was, presumably because of the market's greater competitveness. But while the *guanxi* system has lost some of its traditional importance, it is unlikely this system will ever go wholly out of use.

The unauthorized activity associated with *guanxi* requires secrecy, since it may be penalized if it comes to light. Like other secret activities we discuss in a later section, it relies on strong ties secured by personal familiarity and obligation. That is why good jobs are found through strong ties more frequently than through weak ties. This is true in Singapore as well as in China, suggesting it may be a Chinese cultural tradition and not a consequence of secrecy in a controlled (non-capitalist) job market (Bian, 1997).

Another factor influencing the strength of weak ties in finding jobs is the stability of the job market and of institutions within it. Under some conditions of institutional uncertainty, strong ties may be a necessary condition for capturing network resources. Weak ties may fail to provide sufficient access, leaving actors without resources and unable to act. Under other conditions of uncertainty, the strength of ties makes little difference. Thus, in newly capitalist Slovenia, managers with a good access to resources through non-overlapping networks (i.e., weak ties) could respond most effectively to opportunities for privatizing their firms. Managers with a good access to resources through overlapping networks (i.e., strong ties) were still able to take advantage of the situation but are more restrained in their methods. Only managers with poor access to resources, whatever their network structure, were unable to respond to the opportunities of privatization.

In Russia, under conditions of institutional uncertainty, both kinds of personal connections are becoming more important for successful job seeking. In one study, only 21% of Russian survey respondents found jobs through personal connections before 1990, but 60% used such connections successfully after 1990. Job searches using employment bureaus are down; it's now the case that mainly uncompetitive populations—young people, low-skilled workers, and older people—use these bureaus. Traditional enterprises hire without consulting state-run employment bureaus. New private enterprises, when looking for highly qualified professionals, use the services of private recruitment agencies (i.e., head-hunters).

CLOSING REMARKS. People positioned at each node of a network can exert discretion over the kinds of information transmitted to other members of the network. They act as go-betweens. Incorporating the individual willingness to pass information into weak ties theory, we recognize that weak ties function as "drawbridges," not fixed bridges. Bridging ties act differently in different cultural, political, and economic settings, since withholding information may confer power in some settings but not others.

It is only in this way that we can explain the strength of informational "black markets" and "gray markets," the power of information "brokers" and go-betweens, and the role of *guanxi* and other patronage networks in the flow of information. None of these relations embodies what Granovetter meant by "weak ties." Strong ties are likely more important than weak ties in spreading credible information in organizational systems that are in danger or in transition, while weak ties are more important in spreading information that is not as dangerous or valuable, in organizational systems that are more stable. The advantage of weak ties in spreading cross-boundary information lies not in their individual efficiency but in their numbers. (Like fruit flies, weak ties have an impact because they multiply prodigiously, not because they are individually meritorious.) Overall, the best information flow grows out of the best combination of weak *and* strong ties.

Weak ties were indeed important for finding good jobs in the late 1960s when Granovetter studied managers in Boston, but they may not be as effective in today's more competitive North American job market, battered as it has been by recession and downsizing, or in a society like today's Russia, which remains a society in transition. Weak ties may be more important in finding and filling jobs, even good jobs, that are plentiful because the economy is growing. In boom times, filling a vacant position causes people more concern than finding a vacant position to fill. Under conditions of scarcity, people collect and use information (and other scarce resources) in their own interest and that of their closest friends and family, while under conditions of plenty, they give information away—even to acquaintances.

If so, the strength of weak ties depends on the ratio of vacant jobs to job candidates.

Contagion

Contagion sounds more dangerous than it really is. True, the word means an outward spread (or diffusion) of something through interpersonal contact, and we often use the word to refer to epidemic diseases which spread through face-to-face contact. The word has also been applied to the interpersonal spread of other noxious influences: not only germs, but pathological behaviours like drug use, crime, mass murder, and even suicide. And today, we mean not only the spread through face-to-face contact, we also mean the spread by means of mass communication and social media. In short, then, (social) contagion is the diffusion of thoughts and practices that society considers dangerous or even disgusting. Usually, talk about contagion indicates a moral conflict or shift in society, just like discussions about social disorganization or social disintegration.

Consider the following example. During World War I, across Great Britain, young women were seemingly so attracted to men in military uniform that they behaved in what people considered immodest and sexually dangerous ways. People called the outbreak of licentiousness "khaki fever." This wartime loss of social control caused public anxiety over young women's social and sexual behaviour. Khaki fever appeared to infect not only the morally lax poor, but also the supposedly upstanding middle class.

This fear of khaki fever was symptomatic of a transition from the secretiveness of the nineteenth century to a more open public display of female sexuality in the twentieth century. In turn, the growing openness of sexual display went along with increasing social and sexual independence for women. This supposed outbreak of female sexuality illustrates many elements of contagion that we will discuss in this chapter. A new behaviour spread rapidly. Parents feared the immorality was catching. The fear was itself contagious, producing what sociologists call a *moral panic*.

Contagion, like *contact*, comes from the Latin word for "touching." It refers to a passing on of something, whether information, behaviour, or disease, by direct contact or touch. In this respect, contagion is one form of diffusion. It is also a form of diffusion about which people have old and deep beliefs. The *magical law of contagion*, a traditional belief, holds that properties, both physical and moral, can be transferred through contact, so that some essence passes from source to recipient. Even today, some people act as though they fear that poverty or mental or physical deformity may be "catching." This helps to explain the stigmatization and marginalization of some groups.

All forms of diffusion, contagion included, have certain common features. As compared with information that is *broadcast*, information that is diffused relies on personal connection. For diffusion to occur, a relevant *exposure link* must connect the people involved. The object of diffusion—for example, a rumour—must be accepted by the person receiving it. Once an individual has received the rumour, he or she continues to possess it indefinitely. The same rumour (or other object of diffusion) cannot diffuse twice to the same person. These basic features of diffusion are also basic features of contagion, and, like diffusion, contagion is strongly locational. It spreads information spatially, from near the source to farther away. Therefore, the object of contagion shows concentrations in space. Over time, these concentrations gradually grow, spread out, and move. (On this, see, for example, Antonelli, 1990.)

HOW CONTAGION IS DIFFERENT. In other respects, contagion connotes something different from diffusion. Sometimes, when social scientists talk about contagion, they mean mere *imitation*. For example, contagion of a fad such as body-piercing represents, for students of collective behaviour, a mere imitation of the behaviour of one person by another. Fads, fashions, and what people used to call "manias" we now view as forms of mindless repetition in the adoption of an innovation or novelty.

Many view *all* contagion as the unreflective, irrational adoption of a trivial or worthless new behaviour. In this view, contagion is a down-market form of diffusion and innovation, associated with mass or popular, as opposed to elite, behaviour. Unlike other innovative behaviours, contagious behaviours are supposedly impulsive (not rational), possibly destructive (not adaptive), ambiguous (not predictable), and group-driven (not fitted to individual needs). Contagion also relies on what we may call a *snowball effect*. A mass or crowd of undifferentiated, irrational actors collects through contagion, and then behaves in mindless ways. Thus, contagion is a form of diffusion that produces group activity of a disapproved kind. This is largely how people viewed khaki fever at the time.

Contagion differs from other forms of diffusion in other ways. With forms of diffusion such as social support, gossip, or the adoption of new technology, we assume that only one sender is needed to pass on information. Let's call this the *single sender principle*. This sender, presumably, continues passing the information indefinitely. This is the *no-discouragement principle*. Finally, all listeners are eligible to receive the sender's information and they are equally likely to accept it and act on it. Call this the *equal vulnerability principle*.

Research shows that contagion depends on individual susceptibilities, the infectiousness of prior adopters, and the social proximity of prior-potential adopter pairs. Like a contagious disease (e.g., measles or the common cold) a contagious behaviour follows special rules. First, it seems to require the simultaneous actions of multiple senders, to build up a critical mass of influence on the receiver. Second, contagion recognizes that senders are likely to stop their efforts after a certain time. The message "dies out"—loses its currency—or the sender becomes discouraged and does not try to send the message.

Finally, receivers vary in their openness to the message; some are not merely indifferent, they actively resist it. This not only prevents their adoption of the information; it may even discourage the information sender from making further attempts. Negative evaluations are primary regulators of behaviour in interactive groups, since they engage people's concerns about maintaining their status positions. Said another way, people stop trying to change other people's behaviour when they feel they have made themselves look like an idiot.

A THOUGHT EXPERIMENT. An example will help us understand how contagion processes work. Imagine the world is composed of individuals, each of whom is both good and bad. (In reality, everyone is both a good person and a bad person—that is, everyone has some capacity for both good and evil.) What we mean by "good people" is that they are more good than they are bad. People of high moral standards require few good examples to motivate them to act morally. Specifically, a "good person" is someone who does good deeds and otherwise behaves morally without any prodding or influence by others. A "good person" needs a huge amount of influence by others before doing a bad thing. Conversely, what we mean by a "bad person" is someone who does bad deeds and otherwise behaves immorally without any prodding or influence by others. Conversely, a "bad person" needs a huge amount of influence before doing a good thing.

Imagine a community of 5,000 people—let's say, all the first-year Arts and Science students at the University of Toronto. Everyone in this community has a bad-good score. Sarah, a good person—the best person in her first-year class—has a 0-100 score, meaning that she automatically behaves nicely, and requires the active influence of 100 bad people before behaving badly herself. Nora, the worst person in this first-year class, has a 100-0 score, meaning that she automatically behaves in a rotten manner, and requires the active influence of 100 good people before she acts nicely. Everyone else in this community of 5,000 has a bad-good score of between 0-100 and 100-0. (Presumably the group average is 50-50!)

Now, let's introduce a new behaviour into this community. George, whose score is 30-70, is nice; today he does a good deed for Ezra. The question is, will Ezra "catch the germ" and do a good deed for Sarah? The answer, according to this model, is that it depends on (1) Ezra's history of receiving good deeds from others, (2) Ezra's own bad-good score, and (3) George's likelihood of repeating the act, to hammer in goodness. If George does Ezra another good deed, or if Ezra has already received enough good deeds already so that George's good deed pushes him "over the top" into goodness, or if Ezra's resistance to goodness is already low, then Ezra may "catch" George's goodness and do a good deed for Sarah. Whether Sarah then does a good deed for Bernie depends, again, on Sarah's history of receiving good deeds from others, her bad-good score, and Ezra's persistence.

AN EPIDEMIC OF GOOD DEEDS. You can see the potential for a chain reaction here. In short order, we may unleash an epidemic of good deeds. Conversely, the process may work in the opposite fashion: we may unleash an epidemic of bad deeds if we substitute misbehaviour for good behaviour in this model. It is also possible that no epidemic occurs. If George does a good deed for nasty Ben, whose bad-good score is 90-10, George's act won't lead anywhere. Ben won't imitate the nice act because, by definition, he is nasty and it will take a huge number of nice acts to get his kindness-engine started. If, however, George does the same good deed for good-natured Ezra, whose score is 10-90, Ezra will imitate the act with Sarah, and the behaviour will continue.

This is, presumably, how crowds form, heterogeneous behaviours become homogenized, and new group norms emerge seemingly without plan or direction. The nineteenth-century sociologist Gustave LeBon thought that emergent crowds develop a collective mind. At their worst, these crowds can produce violence, looting, panic, and disorder—or khaki fever. This notion of a collective mind is, however, an oversimplification. Research shows that people can behave the same way without necessarily having the same motives or same thoughts about what they are doing. In fact, that is what is truly remarkable about collective behaviour: different people with different motives generate the same behaviour.

The likelihood that contagion will produce an epidemic is a joint function of the (1) distribution of vulnerabilities in a population, (2) the number of initial senders and their persistence, and (3) where and when the new influence (whether information, behaviour, or germ) enters the system. Epidemics are most common in populations in which uninfected people have a high average vulnerability and a frequent rate of contact with infected (or information-bearing) people.

Contagion models are by far the most complicated kind of diffusion models we have considered so far. They make important assumptions about both the *morphology* (or structure) of the social network (e.g., its size and density of linkages) and its *history*. As we can see, historical and accidental factors, such as where the new element enters the network and how vulnerable the network members at that contact point are *at that moment*, are key determinants of whether an epidemic will break out.

That's what we meant when we said earlier that some flow processes—epidemics, protest movements, popular fads, high divorce rates—only happen if a certain minimum number of people become involved and remain involved. Below that threshold or critical mass, the new information or behaviour won't take root or catch on. If it does catch on, the spread will accelerate. There will be a turning point in the curve describing diffusion over time. If the new information or behaviour doesn't catch on, the spread will decline and die out. The question for sociologists is whether we can discover the laws that govern both morphological and historical influences on social contagion.

MORPHOLOGICAL INFLUENCES ON CONTAGION. Studies of the ways that structure, or morphology, influence contagion usually focus on the character of social linkages. *Proximity* and *contact* are important. The timing of new behaviours shows an ordered spatial pattern suggesting contagion between neighbouring areas. Participants in a collective behaviour are likely to be members of small groups, rather than isolated people. In many instances, anonymity hinders the emergence of collective behaviour. Thus, for example, a young woman who "catches" khaki fever is more likely to have friends who have caught it, than she is to be a social isolate.

Some contagion occurs through simple proximity, contact, and imitation, as when alcoholism spreads from parents to children, depression spreads from children to parents, or secondary traumatization spreads from childhood victims of sexual abuse to their partners. Self-mutilations are thought to be contagious among disturbed teenagers. A few individuals are identified as being at the centre of most of the contagion activity. Suicide is also thought to be contagious among adolescents, though some people are more likely than others to incorporate the idea and act of suicide into their concepts of self.

Voting behaviour is also contagious, with voter turnout being higher among people who live with a spouse, and spouses tending influence each other's decision whether to vote or not. Even moods are contagious. For example, laughter is highly contagious, and women are even more responsive than men to other people's moods, whether negative or positive. The most famous recent work on contagion, by Nicholas Christakis and James Fowler, shows how even health-related behaviours such as weight loss, weight gain, and smoking diffuse across social networks.

Other contagion is influenced by the mass media, which spread information to people who have little or no personal contact. Recall the diffusion of Tetracycline we discussed earlier. It involved the passage of information through a variety of means. Advertising raised physicians' awareness of the new antibiotic. Where contagion occurred at all in this adoption process, its effect was through *structural equivalence*: a perception that adopting the drug was the proper action for a doctor occupying a particular position in the social structure of colleagues. Adoption was not a result of cohesion (or personal influence) nor was it strongly determined by a doctor's personal preferences.

Proximity may also be less important for contagion if the units transmitted are stable: memes rather than moods, for example. The science of *memetics* studies the transmission of *memes*, which are cultural units of information that self-replicate by means of thought contagion, using the human mind as a host. They supposedly attach themselves to people, organizations, cultures, and societies. Memes are thought to evolve through a process of natural selection similar to that of genes in evolutionary biology.

The fittest ideas, defined as those ideas that are best at self-replication (rather than truest or most helpful), orient a contagion's carrier toward acting in ways that increase the idea's host population. The propagative profile begins in family networks, as ideas gain large host populations through the production of numbers of children, and through sexual relationships. Other memes take root in cults or religions and via the mass media. In these ways, ideas acquire people—not, as we used to think, people acquire ideas.

EMOTIONAL CONTAGION. As we just mentioned, moods, emotions, and even motivation are subject to contagion. *Emotional contagion* refers to the process by which the emotions expressed by one individual are "caught" by another. People tend to mimic the facial expressions, movements, and posture of those they interact with, which leads them to experience the emotions of the other person. Individuals who possess a rich emotional language and have expressive faces are more powerful senders of emotions and can influence people through emotional contagion. Charismatic leaders are able to use such qualities to manipulate emotions in order to motivate the people around them.

A series of studies examined the role of positive emotions in the charismatic leadership process, and found a positive link between *leader emotions* and *follower mood.* Charismatic individuals are more likely to be able to infect others with their emotions, presumably because they are more engaging and tend to be more emotionally expressive. Ratings of charisma in work settings were linked to the leader's positive emotional expressions. In other words, positive attitudes in leaders can spread to their followers. Emotional contagion plays an important role within our social networks. Emotions exist within any group: coworkers, classmates, and family members, for example. The emotions of one person are able to powerfully affect those of others around them (Bono and Ilies, 2006).

Emotional contagion affects the dynamic of people working together, and can be used by people to lead effectively. Transformational leadership has an intense emotional component. Leaders who are able to elicit emotional responses from their followers are more likely to achieve desired changes. *Positive affect*, for instance, is associated with task performance, particularly on creative tasks. Emotional arousal energizes employees and leads to increased levels of effort, and greater task performance, as those in a positive mood are more likely to believe in their efforts, and therefore set higher goals. Additionally, employee cooperation has been found to increase, group loyalty and social ties are enforced, and people are more likely to help co-workers and take on additional tasks to benefit the group.

Mood theorists propose two explanations for this phenomenon. First, when the leader makes them feel positive, individuals are likely to make positive judgements of the leader as well as others. Additionally, mood has motivational properties, and people will be more likely to engage in behaviours that result in maintaining a positive state.

Johnson's (2009) study on mood contagion reported similar findings. Charismatic leadership theory explains the connection between leaders and followers that results in exceptional performance by followers in a group. Leaders make each follower feel special, give each follower needed support, and engage each follower in a personal relationship. Their attributed charisma reflects power and confidence, and their behaviours serve as a role model for followers by stressing values and beliefs, moral behavior, and a strong sense of the collective mission. Leaders are also able to inspire their followers by adding meaning to their work, which results in an increase in follower enthusiasm. Effective leaders can do this by displaying behaviours that are aimed at encouraging followers to exhibit greater effort, satisfaction, and take on greater responsibility within their roles.

Another way that social contagion can be demonstrated is by observing how motivational orientation can spread from teachers to students. Students' inferences about motives of their peers or instructors can influence their intrinsic motivation for learning. For example, students who were taught a sport activity by a paid instructor reported less interest in learning than those who were taught by a supposed volunteer, despite receiving the same lesson. When those in the former group then taught the activity to their peers, the second generation learners also reported lower levels of interest (Radel et al., 2010). The student's intrinsic motivations for the activity were affected based on what they thought the volunteer's motivations were, and this motivation was passed on to their peers.

Similarly, when students were taught by a piano teacher who they believed was a volunteer and intrinsically motivated to teach them, they reported more enjoyment while engaging in the lesson, were more interested in further learning, and exhibited greater exploratory activity in a free-play period compared with students who believed that their instructor was extrinsically motivated by payment. This was found to be the case despite the fact that students received identical lessons and demonstrated equivalent skill acquisition levels. Once students decided whether the teacher was intrinsically or extrinsically motivated, that conclusion affected their own motivation and perceptions.

In another experiment, students read a story where a protagonist engaged in an activity either as a volunteer or a paid employee, and then answered open-ended questions about what they thought that the person's motivations were. Responses were coded with respect to intrinsic or extrinsic motivation, and participants were then asked to rate their own expectations about how interested they thought they would be in the activity. Those who read about the paid employee expected that the protagonist enjoyed the activity less, and associated it with less positive affect. Those who read about the volunteer felt that they would enjoy the activity more. In short, individuals' expectations are influenced by whether they perceive extrinsic or intrinsic motivations, and their own motivations are correspondingly affected as well. We can refer to this process as the *social contagion of motivation*; when students believe their teacher engages in an activity for intrinsic reasons, they are more likely to enjoy it themselves. Teachers can therefore either undermine or support students' interest in learning.

HISTORICAL INFLUENCES ON CONTAGION. Setting—a particular time and place—is also critical to contagion, as we have seen. The likelihood of contagion depends on the local facts at a particular moment.

Consider, for example, the problem of gun violence in the United States. It seems to have reached epidemic proportions, even among young people. The website Guns Are Cool reports that there were 365 mass shootings in 2013, one per day. Many of these mass shootings failed to gain the attention we gave to Columbine or Newtown or Aurora, because the numbers killed and wounded were "only" in the single digits.

The young people—more precisely, young men—most likely to shoot others are those who carry guns, drink, smoke (a symptom of generalized delinquency among children), and expect violence by others. Mental illness plays a part; gun availability plays a bigger part; and some would say that a brutal, emasculating male culture plays the biggest part. To reduce the likelihood of further shooting incidents, we may have to reduce the availability of guns and provide counselling to young men who are having problems with their lives. But we should also remember that, like cliques, social epidemics are peer-driven. They have their own logic and rhythm, and we can't handle this problem by simply focusing on troubled individuals.

THE MYTH OF DISORGANIZATION. It is easy to see that people may view new forms of "immoral" and violent behaviour like khaki fever with alarm. Often such behaviour is thought to betoken social disorganization and/or is considered catching. Moral panics arise when people come to believe in the existence of a threat from new forms of deviance. The expansion of social control by a new source of authority, and faulty techniques of investigating deviant behaviour employed by that new source of authority, play a part in creating a fear of contagion. Finally, moral panic, like rumour and gossip, relies on a symbolic resonance of the perceived threat with a widely held demonology. That is, people find it easier to think an extended version of something they already think.

Collective behaviour theory concedes the presence of irrationality in group phenomena. *Collective behaviour* is the spontaneous, often emotional, seemingly unstructured, and non-institutional behaviour of many people reacting to a common stimulus in an ambiguous situation. This category includes the behaviours of localized groups, such as mobs, and mechanisms of collective behaviour such as rumours, fashions, fads, public opinion, and so-called mass hysteria.

Collective behaviour occurs when several people carry out the same behaviour at the same time, especially if their actions are consciously coordinated. Some collective behaviour, however, is also characterized by transient and continually changing behaviours, dependency among actions, and a failure of people to act individually. All of this gives an impression of mindless repetition, robot-like dehumanization, and automatism. However, irrationality is not essential or primary to collective behaviour; outsiders often wrongly assume it. Nor does the removal of traditional social controls produce such behaviours. With the removal of traditional controls, people often reproduce traditional behaviours nonetheless, or organize new collective actions.

For example, when disasters occur, many people volunteer to deal with disaster-generated tasks, both in the short and long run. People closest to the impacted sites are the first to volunteer for search and rescue duties. Panic, flight behaviour, and looting behaviour are all rare. People needing shelter don't wander in a daze; they go to the homes of relatives, if they have them. Panic and irrationality may occur in situations of extreme threat, but despite danger, uncertainty, and rapid change, social structures and rationality persist. People interact creatively to make sense of things, to develop symbolic meanings of the situation, and act together.

Consider, for instance, the fact that ordinary people often respond effectively to emergencies even when people in authority fail to do so. Formal organizations and government frequently fail to mobilize as quickly as expected, because of flaws in emergency-response planning. Typically, communication deficiencies, not motivational deficiencies, undermine the efficiency and coordination of emergency response. After the emergency is over, the inevitable attempt to affix blame—to decide who in charge "messed up"—actually discourages the examination of broader organizational problems and inhibits effective planning for disasters that are likely to recur in vulnerable regions (whether earthquakes, floods, or hurricanes).

In the 1977 Beverly Hills Supper Club fire in Cincinnati, Ohio, social ties remained meaningful for most, who slowed or ceased their own exit to help or account for others. Organizational breakdown occurred in only one room in which the primary exit was blocked, the lights failed, and the search for an alternate exit was initially unsuccessful.

There are good sociological reasons for seemingly irrational behaviour. Take the crowd crush at Hillsborough Stadium in Sheffield, England, in 1989. This crush was motivated by a belief that gaining access to the soccer game was both possible and desirable, despite a shortage of space and tickets. Structural conduciveness was created through media hype, poor distribution of tickets, and a differentiated market between ticket holders and non-ticketholders. Uncertainty about the possibility of gaining access to the match promoted structural strain and contributed to the generalized belief that access could be gained by force. Media hype, poor organization, and peers all stimulated mobilization for action. Poor police and stadium security led to a lack of social control.

Another explanation of the coincidence of irrationality and catastrophe is not that normal people become beastly, but that beastly people come to appear normal. At the outbreak of wars, for example, psychopaths and other social outcasts experience happiness as the focus shifts away from their personal problems. "Wargasm" permits the expression of politically violent emotions against internal and external enemies. Likewise, disasters and emergencies of other kinds are likely to bring the beasts out of the woodwork but not turn normal people into beasts.

CLOSING REMARKS. Contagion is a process of diffusion that is especially important to sociologists because it addresses the question of how people link together and, eventually, aggregate into large groups capable of collective action. Out of pairs, through aggregation, come networks, movements, parties, and other large organizations. Sociology is, or should be, the study of this transformation from small structures to large ones. Central to this transformation is the flow of information we have been calling diffusion, and the aggregative process that is contagion.

Like other forms of diffusion, contagion passes information through networks of personal contact, although important information may also pass by broadcast means. The tendency to view contagious behaviours in a negative light tells us as much about the biases and fears of the viewer as it does about the process itself. Contagious behaviours are no more chaotic than rumours, no less valid than gossip. They tell us a great deal about ordinary people, their concerns and fears. More often than not, they herald a change in popular thinking. This change, like others we have discussed, often passes through stable networks of personal relations.

Clique Formation

Cliques are groups created and maintained by diffusion. Without diffusion, there would be no cliques. Cliques are social units that control the flows of information, support, practices, and ideas among a small group of people. When cliques form, they do so by shutting off information flow to-and-from the outside and "pumping up" information flow within the group. Thus, clique formation is the process of imagining a new social unit, then bringing it into being by regulating the in-flow or diffusion of information and practices. In turn, the resulting clique becomes an important source of gossip, rumours, and search strategies: everything that is important to its members and nothing that is very important to its non-members.

Everyone remembers cliques from their high-school days. Do today's high-school students come up against cliques called *bros*, *stoners*, *hipsters*, *ravers*, *hippies*, *athletes*, *techies*, *sluts*, *leaders*, *loners*, and so on? Are they called different things now; or have they been replaced by different kinds of groups with different names? And then there are the *losers*, who don't belong to any clique. Compared to the other students—the ones in cliques—losers are invisible, isolated and unclaimed, no matter what they are called.

Everyone reading this book has, by now, suffered the savagery of school life and, especially, the cruelty of cliques. William Golding's classic novel *Lord of the Flies* depicts schoolboys tormenting, killing, and then eating the weakest on a remote, uninhabited island. What happens, however horrific, is a mere exaggeration of children's behaviour in schoolyards. Some may imagine the cruelty the boys display in Golding's novel is a reflection of unvarnished human nature, a return to Thomas Hobbes's "state of nature"—an imagined condition of violent anarchy that would exist if there were no monarch to rule the state. In fact, their cruelty is not the result of an absence of society; it is the result of *unlimited* society. If the twentieth century taught us anything, it is that nothing ensures cruelty so much as the workings of a hierarchical society under a ruthless leader.

Cliques offer an example of this structure; they are found everywhere, in every school. No one escapes childhood without becoming a member of a clique or feeling isolated because of exclusion from one. Why do cliques exist everywhere? How do they operate and how do they persist? As we will see, the answers to these questions are tied up with the diffusion of information. Cliques accumulate and redirect information. They also distort information, generate it, and send it out as gossip and rumour. Cliques are structures created by concentrated information flow; they are also the creators of information flow.

DEFINING THE TERM CLIQUE. Everyone has some experience with cliques, but definitions of the word clique vary. One definition, from the dictionary, tells us that a clique is "a small exclusive set, faction, gang, noisy set." This meaning comes from the Old French *cliquer*, meaning to click, or to make a noise. It reminds us of the social significance of cliques and clique members. People in cliques— especially the most popular ones—make a lot of noise.

A definition of clique that comes closer to our sociological meaning is the definition we gave earlier when introducing the topic of diffusion. It defines clique as "a network subset in which each node is connected to every other one, directly or indirectly." Thus, a clique is a group of tightly interconnected people. Expanding on this meaning, we can say that a clique is "a friendship circle within which members are identical to each other sociometrically, as well as mutually connected." This points out the fact that clique members are all connected to one another, and to the outside world, in similar ways.

Similarly, we can define clique as "a group that establishes exclusive social boundaries." It is also "a group of at least three members who spend 75% of their time together; a small tightly knit collection of close friends."

Another useful definition of clique is "a well-defined, densely connected network of peers who are tied to each other by positive sentiment." This definition reminds us the attachment between clique members has an emotional element, though it may have other elements as well. A clique is also "a group of people who interact frequently, share knowledge, and therefore exhibit shared behaviour." Expanding on this notion that similarity and emotion grow out of (and nurture) social interaction, we come to the definition that cliques are "interaction-based clusters of people who spend more time with each other than with other people and have similar attitudes and behaviours."

Putting all these definitions together, cliques are groups that combine friendship, similarity, interaction, exclusion, and the flow of valuable resources: information, support, and opinions, among others. In these respects, cliques are like states, which we discussed earlier. Like states, they accumulate power and resources. They receive, censor and direct information flow; like states, cliques remain distinct to the extent that information flows more readily inside and less readily across borders to the outside. If diffusion is like the flow of a river, clique formation, like state formation, is the gradual building of a dam that slows, deepens, and redirects the water.

CLIQUES IN SCHOOL SETTINGS. Cliques form in every area of life, but they are most familiar to us as part of our childhood experience. Most research on cliques has been done on schoolchildren; that is partly because children are intense clique-formers and also because students form a captive audience for sociological study. Two of the key researchers in this area are Patricia Adler and Peter Adler (see, for example, their "Dynamics of inclusion and exclusion in preadolescent cliques," 1995).

Cliques in school settings typically have a defined membership. The members are similar to another in background and behaviour, partly because cliques form by children choosing one another. Cliques have boundaries and rituals to exclude outsiders and integrate insiders. Most important, they have a leader. The leader is the most popular member of the clique and he/she dominates the other members. The leader is also key in defining the boundaries, inventing the rituals, and defining the membership.

Popularity within a clique is hierarchical. Some clique members are much more popular than others, and some cliques are more popular than other cliques. In the single-digit years of life, a single popular clique dominates the entire population at any given grade level. Other cliques rank beneath this one. Pre-teen cliques are smaller and more socially restricted then teen cliques, probably because young children are less mobile and have smaller social networks than older children. Pre-teen cliques are also more likely to be one-dimensional, in the sense that a single feature determines popularity—say, toughness for boys and prettiness for girls.

Cliques are the place we first learn the rules and expectations of society outside our family home. Through games and play largely regulated by cliques, children internalize the beliefs, values, and attitudes prevalent in adult society. By these means, they also come to form judgments of themselves. For example, they learn what it means to be "good-looking," "sexy," and "popular," to be chosen or to be passed over. Children's activities, their friendships, and their feelings about themselves depend on their involvement in the cliques that organize their social landscape.

The ranking of their clique strongly affects children's social experiences at school. Membership in a low-ranking clique, or no clique at all, can be humiliating or painfully isolating. Exclusion from the top clique, therefore, makes a big difference. However, inclusion in the top clique—in any clique—comes at the price of unlimited conformity. By threatening exclusion, clique members shape each other's attitudes and control each other's behaviour. Over time, children in the same clique become more similar to one another. In this way, cliques teach children the dynamics of power, manipulation, and conformity. They also stifle the growth of self-awareness that is struggling for expression.

THE CREATION OF INEQUALITY. Cliques create a hierarchy of students, with top-ranking, middle-ranking, and bottom-ranking groups that garner unequal amounts of prestige and respect. Cliques teach children society's strong feelings of differentiation between an in-group and out-group. Without such differentiation, conflict and prejudice could not occur. Nevertheless, if being an outsider is awful, being an insider is wonderful. Children whom other children know to be clique members—among the elect—possess more self-confidence and have a more positive self-image. Non-members are seen as less socially attractive, something which often leads to a negative self-image and less self-confidence.

Cliques affect the learning process, either positively or negatively. At best, cliques can provide support and aid in the completion of tasks. They offer children the opportunity to form close friendships, learn about social relations, practice their interpersonal skills, develop their identities, imitate adult behaviour (e.g., smoking), and resist adult standards. Children learn about human societies by taking part in friendships. How others react toward them situates them on the peer status hierarchy. They learn what kinds of social competence and charisma they possess.

At their worst, however, cliques disrupt the completion and comprehension of tasks and leave students preoccupied with issues of unpopularity, rejection, and low self-worth.

THE STRATA OF CLIQUES. The typical school social system is composed of three or four strata. These include children we can call the *isolates*; a *middle group*; the *wannabees*; and the *popular clique*.

Isolates spend most of the time by themselves. They want acceptance into the leading crowd but can't get it. Isolates avoid other isolates because associating with them will reinforce their unpopular image both internally (by reinforcing a negative self-image) and externally. They have low self-esteem and mixed academic abilities; they often lack social skills.

The middle group is made up of various independent friendship cliques. Members of this group have a medium amount of status in the school. They have no aspirations for membership in the leading crowd, though they may feel some resentment over their exclusion by the popular clique. They are strong academically and have positive traits such as self-confidence, open mindedness, trustworthiness. These are solid, responsible, successful kids that others could admire and copy.

Wannabees, by contrast, hang around the popular clique hoping for inclusion. On the periphery of the popular clique, wannabees desperately seek acceptance. Because of their thwarted desire for acceptance by the popular students, they miss an opportunity to interact with "superiors" and cannot enjoy the prospect of interacting with others like themselves.

Members of the popular clique enjoy a larger social circle, and a superior position, than the other children. They seem to be in an enviable position. However, the children often feel anxiety about their place in the group and harbour concerns about maintaining their position. Below the surface, many clique members have low self-esteem and, for them, the clique serves as a surrogate family. The lower their self-esteem, the harder they try to exclude people of inferior status whose inclusion will make membership less special.

How to get in? For boys, athletic ability has been the major determinant of position in the social hierarchy. "Coolness" is another criterion for entry into and continued membership in the top cliques. As well, social maturity (for example, being able to talk to girls, and knowing about the practices of sex) is valued. So is defiance of adult authority: challenging rules, stirring things up, getting into trouble. At the same time, members of the top clique put a low or negative value on academic performance. Teenage boys don't consider it cool to be smart. Therefore, the highest-status students do not have the highest grades. For girls, good looks are the single most important requirement for membership in the popular clique.

Social development (for example, skilfulness in talking to boys, in gossip, and in other power tactics) is also valued. Good academic performance, while not required for membership in the popular clique, is more acceptable among popular girls than among popular boys. The family background of popular girls is often unstable, due to divorce or lack of parental support. That's one reason that girls in the most popular clique often rely on the group so much for social support.

HOW CLIQUES FORM. Cliques form when different members of the school population regularly receive different amounts of information. Shared knowledge brings people together in groups, and differential ignorance keeps groups apart. The higher the level of shared knowledge and interaction within a group, the more likely that group will remain a clique. A high rate of interaction without a high level of shared knowledge leads a group, over time, to decrease its cliquishness (or exclusiveness) in interaction. However, a high level of shared knowledge, even without a high rate of interaction by members, leads a group, over time, to increase its cliquishness in both knowledge and interaction.

The segregation of information, so that only some groups have certain kinds of information and most do not, causes people to stop interacting, despite previous high levels of interaction. As people come to share more information, the differences in interaction rates across members of a society decrease. Two distinct cliques become less segregated from each other if both groups receive the same information. However, the more cliquish two groups are, the longer it takes for information to diffuse between them.

Once formed, cliques maintain themselves by continuing to ensure that members receive the same amounts and kind of information. Cliques constrain individual behaviour by defining the behaviours that members view as appropriate.

TECHNIQUES OF INCLUSION. For teenagers and pre-teens, cliques are groups within which leaders attain and wield power over their fellows. They exercise power by playing on children's needs for support and approval, building up the clique members and tearing them down. Leaders draw some of their followers into an elite inner circle, where they can bask in the glow of popularity, then reduce them to dependence and subjection by turning the group against them.

Cliques maintain their exclusivity through careful membership screening. Memberships evolve as people move away, join the group or are ejected from it. Leaders use their popularity and power to influence membership and status within the group. Leaders and others at the centre of cliques have the most say in defining potential members as acceptable or not.

Leaders maintain their position by capitalizing on the quarrels of others: that is, by dividing and conquering. This shows their inherent grasp of the subtleties of group politics, and their ability to manipulate people. By degrading and make fun of others who are lower in the hierarchy or outside the group, leaders build their power and authority on the backs of subservient members. The rites of degradation also foster clique solidarity.

Many children actively seek entry into these cliques. The easiest way to get into a clique is by befriending the leader. Clique members closest to the leader are the most popular in the group. To get closer to the leader, clique members may even abandon previous friendships or destroy existing ones. Because of the hierarchical structure of cliques, and shifting relationships within the clique, personal loyalties in cliques are less reliable than one finds in other groups.

TECHNIQUES OF EXCLUSION. The clique gains cohesion by excluding others. By excluding others, group members increase their own popularity and prestige but also maintain the group's exclusivity and stratification. Members learn that living in a social world involves power dynamics that produce inequality and hurt feelings.

Gossip is one way that clique members turn people against others on the outside; thus, gossip solidifies the group and asserts group power. Picking on outsiders also instils fear, forcing them down to acknowledge their inferior status and discouraging them from joining together to challenge the clique's power.

Limited contact with outsiders leads clique members to imagine that outsiders are "different" or undesirable people. This can change, however. Contact under favourable conditions dissipates the hostility between different cliques, or between insiders and outsiders. Such contact is more likely when the numbers are small (e.g., in a small school or a small classroom). When the numbers are large, more cliques form and they are more specialized (e.g., segregated by race, sex, or interest).

FROM ASCRIBED TO ACHIEVED STATUSES. With the passage of time, cliques become more important to children, then less important. They also become more homogeneous with respect to achieved statuses (e.g., grades, interests), and less homogeneous with respect to ascribed statuses (e.g., race, ethnicity, gender).

As children age, they become more discriminating in their friendship choices, and take on fewer friends. As well, children become more sensitive to their reputation as they become older. The number of cross-sex friendships decreases temporarily, because rigid norms evolve governing interpersonal relationships between the sexes. In the upper grades, cliques become less stable and there is less gender consistency. This happens, typically, because as students go further in school they become more concerned about, and more admiring of, academic achievement. As well, they are more likely to be "streamed" by the school system and otherwise recognized according to level of ability.

This developmental process is itself socially structured. The social structuring of activities leads people to develop relationships with others who are similar to themselves. Most relationships originate in activities that bring together people who are similar in some respect. The more similar these people are, the more they develop relationships with one another. It is this preference, as much as the preference to be with others like themselves, that leads to the social structuring of activities by age and other structural factors. Thus, school activities which segregate or stream students, whether by sex, age, ability or interest, increase the likelihood that students will organize their social relationships around these same criteria.

Paradoxically, large classrooms provide an atmosphere more conducive to friendliness and popularity than small ones. This is true especially in schools or classrooms that emphasize good grades, academic abilities, and the enjoyment of learning and self-mastery. In such classrooms, cliques are typically smaller, less stable, more homogeneous with respect to achievement, and less homogeneous with respect to gender, race, and achievement.

Processes governing the establishment of cliques change over the school year as different features of the classroom experience become more salient to students. As the range of distribution of achievement increases, cliques become less stable. That's because clique membership is based on student ranking, and student ranking changes with each test. The higher the class average, the fewer cliques exist. The consequence is that tracking or streaming (to improve students' academic achievement) leads to fewer friendship groups for high-ability students. This may hinder their social development.

CLOSING THOUGHTS. The paradox of cliques is that everyone hates them but everyone wants to belong to them—or, at least, not be excluded. It is only later that young people come to realize that "popularity" is arbitrary, staged, and fleeting. It isn't worth losing a lot of sleep over. But adolescence is a time of self-doubt. Membership in a clique provides social support and apparent guarantees of social value, even at the expense of freedom and individuality.

Cliques and the rituals of inclusion and exclusion on which they rely are more than mere children's games. They are small-scale models for how all societies state, teach, and enforce rules: a lesson in miniature in social control. They remind us that every inclusionary action is, also, an exclusionary action. Every social comparison that gives approval to A gives disapproval to not-A. Every piece of information, every belief or fact, that is intensified by repetition within the group is a piece of information that is less likely to move outside the group. It is also a guarantee the group will not hear a piece of conflicting information.

CHAPTER THREE

Sites of Selective Diffusion

All of the types and subtypes of diffusion we have discussed in the previous chapters take place in the *sites of selective diffusion* we discuss in the present chapter. So, even if we don't remind you, remember to think about the role of imitation, information flow, flows of support, gossip, and the rest when you read this chapter. Here we single out for special attention a few important, characteristic social institutions and see how diffusion works there. These are institutions that are well-known to everyone, yet we will talk about them in a somewhat different way, to highlight the importance of diffusion in creating and maintaining these institutions.

Kinship Systems

The topic of this section, *kinship systems*, is interesting because we often think of them as something that just happens. We are born into a kin group and it provides information, support, influence, and the other things we have talked about. It is only when we compare societies that we see kinship systems are socially constructed: that is, they are designed to highlight certain relationships and downplay or ignore other relationships, always with important consequences for information, support, and (as we will see), inheritance—the flow of material resources after death. Certain societies, like the Trobrianders that Bronislaw Malinowski famously studied early in the history of anthropology, highlight the role of "mother's brother" in raising children; our society doesn't. Certain societies only allow people to trace their lineage or inherit wealth on the father's side, while our society doesn't. In short, kinship defines the channels through which information, support, and influence are most likely to flow in a given society.

In this respect, kinship systems provide an important exception to the rule this book is following: namely, to treat human groups like colonies of ants or swarms of meteorites. Neither ants nor meteorites, so far as we know, imagine relationships among one another and act on these imagined relations. But humans do. We imagine relations of obligation and non-obligation among the people we know, and act on these. Indeed, the purpose of kinships relations is to specify what we owe to whom. But we rarely take time to think about the far-reaching consequences of this social construct.

Kinship is the most ancient and basic form of social organization. In pre-industrial societies, kinship is the basis of all ownership and social inclusion. Even in modern Western societies, kinship provides the basis for many flows of information, support, and property. Selected members of the kinship group are automatically included in these flows. Non-members are excluded.

The word *kin* comes from the Anglo-Saxon word meaning "tribe," "race," or "subdivision of people." Kinship is, essentially, about blood relations, lineages, and descent. Unlike most other social networks, kinship networks are composed of named roles: "son," "daughter," "mother," "father," and so on. Like all roles, these kinship roles carry duties and channel communications.

Some scholars propose that the development of kinship relations was closely associated with the "biological evolution of human reproduction and life history"—largely because kinship relations could be "manipulated" to perform "productive functions." The fact that kinship systems are capable of assigning responsibilities to "members of a family" meant that kinship could act as a powerful mechanism for coordinating a group toward productive activity (Leonetti and Hanowell, 2011). Historically, as the amount of activity, cooperation, and coordination among kin increased, dependency among family members increased accordingly. An extensive system of rewards and punishments was instituted, to control kin dynamics and increase interdependency among individuals. As a result, individuals became less self-sufficient and developed "prosocial" or "other-regarding" behaviour toward their kin. In this way, according to Leonetti and Hanowell, the rise of kinship relations in the cultural sense was closely related to human beings' basic desire to survive.

In every culture, a set of principles that anthropologists call the *classificatory kinship system* defines one's kin and thus the boundaries of one's kinship obligations. In any culture, kinship terms can be generated from a few principles: whether the kin is male or female, younger or older, whether descent follows the mother's line, the father's line, or both, and whether marriage or adoption can fill a given position, or only a blood connection by birth can do so. The dominant North American kinship system is "bilateral," meaning that we trace descent equally through a father's and mother's line. For instance, our culture doesn't distinguish between aunts (or uncles, nieces, nephews, or cousins) to whom we are related through our mothers rather than our fathers.

Compared to other cultures, North American kinship terms are uninformative. They make no gender or generational distinctions among cousins, suggesting in this way that cousins are unimportant. They do make gender and generational distinctions between siblings and between the children of siblings. We distinguish between brothers and sisters, nephews and nieces, grandnephews and grandnieces. However, we do not distinguish terminologically between a brother's sons and a sister's sons. In societies where kinship is more important, the naming of kin is more detailed. For example, the Jewish culture has a particular name for the relationship that marriage creates between the parents of a bride and a groom. This tells us that, in Jewish culture, families joined by marriage are expected to bond at various levels.

Kinship structures a variety of processes, including *inheritance*, *mate selection*, *filial piety*, and *sibling relations*. We begin with a look at the process of inheritance.

INHERITANCE. *Inheritance* is the flow of property, through kinship networks, and from the older to the younger generation. Every society assumes that, without other instructions, close kin will have first call on the property of a deceased person. This assumption tells us that kinship produces a strong bond between family members. Inheritance has a double institutional function in maintaining this bond. First, it binds generations together in later phases of the life course, thereby guaranteeing the existence of the family. Second, it protects private property, thereby contributing to the continued inequality between families.

In light of the important social functions that inheritance plays, societies have developed complex rules to govern how inheritance occurs. Different societies have constructed widely diverging rules of inheritance that reflect different cultural predispositions. Since our society is more *universalistic* than many other societies, meaning that we think that important rules should apply equally to everyone, our rules of inheritance provide equal rights for both men and women to inherit property. Interestingly, such sex-unbiased inheritance patterns are associated in human societies with monogamy. Matrilineality also favours equality in gender relations. In matrilineal societies like Malawi, women exercise a considerable range of powers in village life, especially regarding land inheritance. The situation is not very different in modern Canada, where bilateral kinship is the norm. Women increasingly inherit and run family estates, without being discriminated against as compared to their male counterparts.

On the other hand, inheritance patterns that favour men are strongly associated with general polygyny, patriarchy, and patrilineage. Although governments in some patrilineal societies have tried to enforce unbiased inheritance rules, deeply entrenched traditions have proven difficult to uproot and many most patrilineal societies continue to operate under gender-biased inheritance rules. Unexpectedly, the privatization of land tenure that comes with economic development have been found to increase patrilineal and male control, at the expense of women.

In some cultures the dominant inheritance pattern is *primogeniture* (i.e., the eldest son gets everything). Historically, primogeniture has been a conservative strategy for ensuring the survival of the family by keeping the family's property intact. Where the family's survival is not in doubt, other types of inheritance are tried. For example, in nineteenth-century Minnesota, wealthier farmers aggressively pursued new land for their sons and often handed down the family farm to a younger child.

In rural Franche-Comte until the nineteenth century, families distributed the inheritance equally among sons, while excluding daughters. This practice kept the children together on the family farm. However, the same system of equal inheritance for men can produce a different pattern, depending on environmental and economic factors For example, the equal distribution of a large amount of fertile farmland may keep sons together. The equal distribution of a small amount of scrub land, a few grazing animals, or some fishing nets will not suffice.

Children who are unlikely to inherit often leave the family home. Thus, among nineteenth-century Japanese children governed by primogeniture, the "stayers" were children without siblings, eldest sons, or eldest daughters without brothers. The "leavers" were younger sons with elder brothers, and younger daughters. The leavers left for various destinations via marriage, adoption, service, and migration.

Throughout much of history, land transfer through inheritance has been the beginning of a child's transition to adulthood, making possible marriage and parenthood. Often, children waiting to inherit land have been forced to marry late. Many non-inheritors could never marry at all. No wonder sibling rivalry and resentment flare up when inheritances are substantial and succession rules are unclear. Life and death, sex, marriage, and procreation are all linked to inheritance in pre-industrial societies.

In pre-industrial societies, ecological constraints often operated on humans—especially those in rural areas—to limit marriage and direct migration, just as they did in the animal kingdom. In nineteenth- and twentieth-century rural Ireland, for example, marriage rates for farmers varied directly with the availability of farms. Inheriting a farm often meant becoming able to marry. Big farms were best for this purpose. The incidence of celibacy among male heirs increased as the size of farms decreased. As farms got smaller and other economic opportunities decreased, emigration increased. Emigrants improved their chances for marriage by leaving Ireland.

PATTERNS OF IN- AND OUT-MARRIAGE. Marriage is the creation of a new set of kinship links that provide privileged access to information and property. In our own society, more information, support and property flow through a marriage bond than flow through any other social bond. This makes the choice of a mate important, both for the people who are getting married and those who are related to the bride and groom. No wonder families take an interest in their members' marriage choices.

In pre-industrial societies, *conjugal bonds*—the bonds between spouses—are slightly less important than *consanguineal* or blood ties—those between parents and children, and among siblings. This has a lot to do with people's immobility and reliance on land. Agricultural societies put a premium on staying put and minding the land and animals. They discourage movement, risk-taking, change, and look askance at outsiders who may have conflicting loyalties or strange ideas. Therefore, among agriculturalists, the selection of marriage partners is clique-like: that is, limited to a small range of well-known choices. Marriage patterns among pastoralists (who graze animals) and horticulturalists (who tend gardens) emphasize *endogamy*, or marriage with kinfolk. Endogamy ensures that land and animals will stay in the family after marriage. Sometimes, marriages re-link family lines that are already intermarried. Some cultures even encourage pairs of brothers to marry pairs of sisters. Such *structural endogamy* clarifies the social boundaries between kin groups and contributes to class formation. Some kin groups or tribes also exchange women in a cycle with other kin groups, thus tying together all kin groups and guaranteeing social solidarity in the community.

Even today, endogamous marriages are more common among rural, illiterate, or less educated people, especially in less developed parts of the world like the Middle East. Despite the evidence that marriage between blood relatives increases the probability of genetic malformations, high rates of consanguineous marriage continue.

Anthropologists have found that, in practice, the most common form of endogamous marriage to occur in the Middle East is that between "patriparallel cousins" (Clarke, 2007). An individual marrying his or her "father's brother's child" would be entering into such a marriage. Clarke proposes that deeply entrenched traditions of patrilineage and the "hierarchical superiority" that men commonly enjoy over women in the Middle East are primarily responsible for the large number of marriages occurring between patriparallel cousins. Given the fact that social stability and predictability are central goals of the endogamous relationship, marriage with someone as "close" or familiar as possible is highly important. Since patriparallel cousins are understood to be "closer" than matrilateral cousins in societies where patrilineage dominates, it is not surprising that many people in the Middle East form endogamous marriages with patriparallel cousins.

With increases in educational opportunity, new patterns of kinship and marriage emerge. People meet and marry people who are educationally similar to themselves, though unrelated by kinship. Such a trend perpetuates economic and social differences in the population, leading to greater exclusivity. People tend to marry within their own social class, which corresponds in large part to their own educational level.

Mate availability plays a part in shaping marriage patterns too. Other things being equal, endogamy is greatest where "similar" mates are most available. Where such mates are unavailable, people are forced to marry outside their kin group, tribe, or ethnic group, as did the white settlers and gold miners in late nineteenth-century British Columbia, who married First Nations women. Or, they may forego marriage altogether, as Vietnamese immigrants to America did when they faced a double marriage squeeze: first a shortage of men, than a shortage of women. Or, they may have to marry ethnically similar people much older or younger than usual, as happened to California's early Spanish-Mexican colonists. Though women usually married older men, sometimes they were forced to marry *much* older men against their wishes.

As an ethnic population grows, so does the likelihood that members of the group will meet one another and marry. Since 1980, for example, high levels of migration from Asia to America have reduced the rates of marriage between Asian-Americans and whites. Part of the change is a result of increased social distance between Asian-Americans and whites. Marriages between people of different Asian ethnicities have increased, while overall out-marriage rates have declined.

FILIAL RESPONSIBILITY. By marrying, people embed themselves in a second network of family obligation. The first is *consanguineal* (by blood and descent), the second *affinal* (by marriage). If they marry their own kin, the two networks are identical, thus simplifying their lives. If they marry "out" of their kin group, they must often deal with conflicting demands originating from the two networks. If they also marry out of their ethnic or cultural group, they must deal with an even greater range of conflicting values and norms.

One source of difficulty may come from obligations of *filial responsibility*—the moral responsibility of grown children to look after their aging parents. Many cultures have religious or secular norms that insist on these filial obligations. For example, one of Judaism's Ten Commandments is to "Honour thy mother and father." Notions of filial responsibility or filial piety are even more marked in China and other societies influenced by the teachings of Confucius (especially, Korea and Japan). However, social changes associated with urbanization and industrialization have weakened these traditional norms (Ogawa and Retherford, 1993). They are especially weak in the United States, where conjugal ties take precedence over filial ties, compared with (say) Korea, where traditional filial ties take precedence over conjugal ties.

These cultural differences emerge clearly when comparing Korean and American children. Both Koreans and Americans are motivated by affection, a desire to repay kindness, and a sense of responsibility. However, for Koreans, filial respect, family harmony, and filial sacrifice are the strongest motivations. Many American children have affectionate relationships with parents for whom they care, but still show a low degree of filial responsibility; by contrast, Korean caregivers are more likely to show a sense of responsibility and respect, but less affection.

Consider the results of a national survey conducted in Korea, which asked "who is responsible for taking care of elderly": 47% of respondents reported that it is the responsibility of the eldest son, while another 36% thought that any children with the means, or other sons or daughters, should be responsible. In fact, children are required by Korean family law to support their elderly parents, if they have the means (Schwarz et al., 2006). The South Korean government provides a small pension for the elderly "who cannot be supported by their children," but only three percent of the elderly in Korea received this pension in 2002.

In China, formal services supporting families and the elderly are extremely underdeveloped. Most elderly Chinese parents live with an adult son or daughter—most commonly with an adult son. Most adult children prefer to live independently, however, and most adult offspring do *not* live with their parents. This does not mean they ignore their parents. Adult children in Korea live as close to their parents as possible, have more frequent contact, and provide more regular help to their parents than do their counterparts in the U.S. These relationships are unaffected by whether parents co-reside with another child. There is some evidence of closer relationships with sons than with daughters, but parents without a son receive as much total help as do parents with sons.

The Confucian tradition of filial piety is not the only reason for the closer and more frequent interaction that Chinese and Korean children have with their elderly parents. Both China and Korea are patrilineal societies where individuals usually trace their lineage solely through their fathers; there are strict rules of inclusion and exclusion, so that women who marry are required to leave their lineage of origin and transfer to the lineage of their husband. Where such *unilinear kinship systems* predominate, in which people are members of only one lineage at a time, there will naturally be "higher proportions of tight-knit relationships" between kin (Nauck, 2009).

This stands in stark contrast to the *bilinear kinship system* that is observed in countries like Germany, Canada, and the United States, where kin loyalties are maintained on multiple descent lines, and individuals are not required to transfer from one lineage to another after marriage. As a result, people have no need to define or identify others by their membership in a certain lineage, and it is possible for individuals to have their own "network of kindred" with whom they are particularly close (Nauck, 2009).

Thanks in part to this individualization of kin relations, the social significance of kinship is greatly diminished under such circumstances and the nuclear family becomes predominant. In short, the absence or presence of a deeply-rooted tradition of filial piety is not the only factor responsible for differing ways of supporting the elderly between the East and the West. That said, recent trends indicate that children today are less willing to assume filial obligations toward their parents compared to thirty years ago. This is especially true in China, where the degree of respect shown to elders has reportedly decreased in many communities, and the very meaning of respect has changed from obedience to courteous behavior.

The one-child program has had many social consequences, among them the disappearance of sibling-, uncle- and aunt-, and cousin-relationships. With increased longevity added to declining fertility, Chinese kinship networks will continue to evolve from the short horizontal (one- or two-generation) sibling-heavy structures of a century ago to long, narrow (three- or four-generation) structures in the next century. This means there will be fewer children in the future to care for their aging parents. Already, researchers in China find that highly educated children, especially those from single-child families, show little respect for or commitment to the value of filial piety. They are less willing than other children to commit to future parental care or to share the same household with their parents when they become older. They are also less likely (at present) to co-reside with grandparents.

Throughout the industrial world, the growing work-force participation of middle-aged women has decreased the availability of home-nursing care providers. In Japan and elsewhere, the elderly often deal with this by mortgaging their homes, thus consuming the family inheritance. This further reduces the incentive of children to care for their aging parents.

RELATIONS WITH SIBLINGS. Kinship also imposes obligations on siblings. Even today, many siblings have intense lifelong relationships with one another, remaining important sources of information and support. Unmarried, childless, or widowed women stand out as possessing especially involved sibling ties.

Even after marriage and the formation of new ties with in-laws, relationships with one's family of origin, especially one's siblings, tends to remain strong. This is true even in the case of Chinese women, who are required by China's deep-rooted patrilineal tradition to leave their own family behind to join that of their husband (Nauck, 2009).

From birth onward, people are profoundly affected by the well-being of their siblings. For example, the behavioural problems of chronically ill children often lead to behavioural problems in their siblings. Siblings older than the ill child tend to be affected most, and are at a particular risk of depression and other behavioural problems. These patterns continue into adulthood. Many adults—an estimated 50% in Australia—care for disabled siblings after the death of their parents. People are often impaired emotionally and physically by the death of a sibling, more impaired even than bereaved spouses and friends.

In childhood, siblings spend a great deal of time in each other's presence, yet often they are not close friends. At age 5, children report more positive feelings, and act in a more positive manner, toward friends than toward their younger siblings. Nonetheless, siblings exercise a lot of influence over one another. For instance, both men and women report receiving more advice from their sisters than their brothers. And among adolescents, second-born and female children report receiving more advice, being more satisfied with sibling support, and being more influenced by their siblings than first-borns and men, respectively. No wonder: in our culture, we *expect* more of older siblings than of younger ones. For example, we expect older siblings to teach, help, protect, and care for the younger siblings. As well, older, especially firstborn, siblings tend to be more eager to gain adult approval, more ambitious for adult rewards, and less rebellious. They are rule-oriented and make frequent reference to rules in conflicts with their younger siblings. Younger siblings, for their part, are expected to learn, admire, and show deference to older siblings. These are the cultural scripts that shape sibling relations in our society.

Given the importance of sibling influences, we might expect children from larger families, with many brothers and sisters, to do better in life than children from smaller families. Older siblings can be a valuable source of academic knowledge and skills for younger children, who watch and imitate them. In some ethnic groups (for example, among Vietnamese Americans) sibling cooperation is significantly associated with academic achievement.

Yet research shows that siblings in fact provide few academic benefits. Firstborn and only children tend to be more ambitious than later-born children. Among Japanese boys, the probability of dropping out of high school increases, and of completing college decreases, as the number of siblings increases. (No corresponding effect is observed, however, on Japanese girls.) In Canada, children with two or more siblings perform significantly worse on standardized math tests than children with one or no siblings.

It would seem the information, support, and skills that siblings provide are not of the kind that improves academic attainment. Siblings may also teach each other delinquent behaviours. With many children to raise, parents invest less money, time, and attention in each. In any case, later-born children tend to be rebellious, since the first-born has already seized the conformist path as a way to win parental approval, and it may be that as a result they are less likely to take advantage of the learning opportunities that their older siblings provide.

CLOSING REMARKS. As we have seen, kinship provides people with close and enduring relationships through which information, support and other resources flow. Particular kinship norms vary over time and from one society to another, in response to changes in the economic, ecological, and ideological environment. What is remarkable is that, everywhere, kinship gives people access to help, advice, and support.

As we have noted, patterns of kinship are shifting. As fertility declines and populations age, relations between parents and their children are changing. As women gain more education and participate more fully in paid work, relations between husbands and wives are changing, too. Given extensive global migration and the possibility of long-distance travel, people in many different parts of the world now maintain relations with kin living in different countries. With kinship networks that are maintained over long distances, the notion of "visiting," or travelling to meet one's kin living in a different part of the world, has come to acquire a special meaning for many. For instance, in studying people who live in England and have relatives in Pakistan, Mason (2004) found that visits to Pakistan were "something to be planned with relish, looked forward to, and remembered fondly until the next time." The same study also revealed that coordinating a "visit" often required complex and sensitive "sets of negotiations" not just about the visit's practicalities (the cost, who will visit, how often they will visit), but also about "propriety, morality, and exchange" in the maintenance of kin relations across long distances.

With increased urbanization as well as greater geographic and social mobility, all of which we discuss at length in the second half of this book, extended kinship networks play a smaller role in our lives. Yet we would be wrong to suppose that this fiercely imagined social construct, kinship, has lost its social impact.

Clientelism

The *Oxford Dictionary of Politics*, third edition, defines *clientelism* as "a type of principal-agent relationship" and goes on to note that it "involves three actors: a principal, an agent, and a 'client.' Typically, a client (say, a politician's supporter and financier) transfers resources over which he has control to the agent (the politician). The agent will then transfer resources he obtains from the principal (the electorate) back to his client." The *Dictionary* observes that resources are allocated on a *particularistic*, not *universalistic*, basis: in other words, individuals are awarded contracts or public offices not because they deserve them on the basis of merit or qualifications, but because of "prior support," or, more informally, the principle of "you scratch my back, I'll scratch yours."

This kind of relationship sometimes turns into what we would view as political corruption, but in many countries it is done in the open and it is viewed everywhere as a kind of favoritism—universal, timeless, and unavoidable. What is sociologically interesting about clientelism is that it bases the flow of information, support, and favours on personal relationships and loyalties. It is the opposite of bureaucratic organization, in that there are rarely written rules governing these proceedings, nor is there an objective or impersonal application of decision-making rules. In these respects, a political system based on clientelism is more like a kinship system than it is like an idealized modern government. Certain people are considered part of the network of flowing benefits, while the majority of people are outside this network. In this respect, the clientelist system is also like a clique.

Like kinship systems, patron-client or *clientelist systems* are old and universal. In pre-industrial agricultural societies, clientelism shapes the basis of all economic and political life. Even in industrial societies, clientelism plays important roles in shaping interactions between people and facilitating various different "flows" of information, support, and property. In large part, clientelism is based on kinship: relations of patronage connect the members of a more powerful family to members of a less powerful one. Networks of patron families and client families provide the basis for all flows of information, support, and property within the community. Members of the network are privileged by inclusion in these flows and non-members are excluded, to their disadvantage.

In these respects, clientelism is an example of a governing structure that organizes social activity. Under a clientelist system, by virtue of the hierarchical relationships that exist between patrons and clients, local bosses and their functionaries carry out government. Other societies, however, operate under different governing structures that are drastically different from the clientelist system. In stable democratic societies, for instance, government functions are carried out by a professional civil service, under instructions from elected officials who are, in turn, beholden to political parties and their supporters. In other societies, an already existing hierarchy not specifically designed for governing assumes responsibility for governmental functions: for example, the church, the military, or the party.

Social turmoil often upsets the balance of power among these hierarchies and undermines public confidence in the institutions of government. Often, clientelism, which tends to be highly localized in nature, takes control of society during periods of turmoil, before national institutions exist or after they have been shattered.

The dictionary tells us that *patron* comes from a Latin word meaning "protector." It has its roots in the Latin word *pater*, or "father." *Client* also has Latin roots. Originally, it meant a "hearer" or "person who listens to advice." Today, we often use the word *client* to mean "customer, " especially the customer or "hearer" of professional advice. However, in sociology the words patron and client have a particular meaning. They denote a relationship of unequal power, often within a pre-industrial, agricultural setting.

THE ORIGINS OF THE SYSTEM. The patron-client relationship goes back at least as far as the Middle Ages, when a social system known as *serfdom* was commonly practiced in Europe. After the fall of Rome, many who worked the land were tied to the land and landlord by bonds of service. Lords sought prestige by protecting as many serfs and dependent tenants as they could. This patronage brought the lord military and political power.

With the abolition of legal serfdom, economic and religious ties kept tenants dependent on the landlord. The client—a *peasant*—continued to farm on land the patron owned, turning over much of his crop to the patron. In return, the patron gave the peasant protection. The relationship between patron and client continued to carry life-long duties of many kinds. The patron may have lent client families money, seed, or goods, to see them through bad seasons. In return, members of the client family provided unpaid labour. As the client often found it impossible to ever pay off the debt, his family could never free itself from its obligations to the patron. Debts left the client unfree, and unable to refuse to honour the patron's requests. This system is depicted well in such Italian novels (and movies) as *The Leopard* and *1900*.

Such agricultural clientelism continued well into modern times, until the late nineteenth century in Mediterranean Europe, and even later in many Asian and Latin American countries. Feudalism flourished wherever there were plantations, estates, or other large private land-holdings. Such holdings appear to favour the rise of despotic control over peasants because they make it easy for patrons to control the water supply and irrigation system, and thus to control everyone's livelihood.

Though originally rooted in agricultural relations, clientelism came to permeate every level of the social structure. In many European countries in the fifteenth to eighteenth centuries, kings used patronage to reward tribunals, administrators, explorers, and aristocrats, thus ensuring their loyalty. They granted licenses, patents, monopolies, titles, and pensions for this purpose. Clientelism came to Canada with the Hudson's Bay Company, a royal monopoly, and the seigneurial system in Quebec. In Latin America, the conquerors and colonists retained many more of the values and legal institutions of feudal Europe.

Combined with Roman Catholicism, clientelism in Latin America produced a system called *compadrazgo*, or "god parenthood." *Compadrazgo* is a form of fictive kinship that links a poor family, through a godchild, to a wealthier, more powerful godparent. Co-parenting ties, once established, give the natural parents the right to call on the godfather for material and legal support. In return, the natural parents support the godfather's political activities, and work for him when he requires it. Being a godfather is like being a lord: it confers prestige and economic and political advantages.

Clientelism in its agricultural form began to disappear everywhere with the fall of aristocracies, the creation of nation-states, and industrialization. These changes weakened the traditional landowning classes and drew peasants into cities and industrial wage-paying jobs. In certain parts of the world, Communist revolutions destroyed the land-owning classes outright and redistributed the land among the rural peasantry.

THE PRESENT-DAY VERSION. In cities, clientelism took a different form. Instead of being based on the exchange of labour for protection, urban clientelism provided the basis for political "machines." The new *patron* was a political boss who dispensed political favours—*patronage*—such as jobs, contracts, and other benefits (for example, protection from gangsters). The new *client* was an ordinary working person who repaid the patronage with votes, "kickbacks" from payments received for work, and deference. Simply put, the patron in this setting acts a cultural broker for his clients. The client's obligations are moral and political more than economic. Eventually, this devolves into corruption and organized crime, a devolution depicted well in Francis Ford Coppola's *Godfather* movies.

In the poor neighbourhoods of Latin American cities, clientelism is still evident in all political parties. Leaders exchange favours for votes without demanding an ideological commitment from their supporters. With the help of a few ward bosses, the leaders dole out public benefits to their clients. This practice keeps the client pool large and tranquil. The system continues to work so long as it meets people's immediate needs for housing, health care, and so on.

In a study of clientelism in the context of democratic elections, Gans-Morse, Mazzuca, and Nichter (2014) outline the most common forms of clientelistic practices. From "vote buying," which rewards voters for switching their voting intentions, to "abstention buying," which persuades opposing people not to vote, political parties engage in various kinds of clientelistic practices to enhance their chances of victory. The combination of at least four different clientelistic strategies is reported to be the most effective for ensuring electoral victories. This seems to show that political parties that engage in clientelistic electoral strategies need to continuously broaden the extent of their clientelism in order to remain competitive. As engaging in only one clientelistic strategy is less effective than engaging in as many as four, there is an active incentive for political parties to expand the boundaries of their political patronage.

It is important to note, however, that clientelism does not solely occur in the poorer parts of the world. Clientelism exists today in every society, from the richest to the poorest. In the United States, what many people call the "pork barrel" is essentially a form of clientelism similar to that observed in Latin America. Legislators use the pork barrel to reward supporters by building roads, housing developments, and other major public works in their districts, thus providing jobs and contracts.

Many scholars have begun to investigate common forms of clientelism that have infiltrated the democratic electoral processes of different countries. Susan Stokes (2005), for instance, took the example of Argentina to propose that political parties often discriminate in how they hand out benefits to voters. According to Stokes, it is not the case that all poor voters receive benefits (in the form of "food bags") which encourage them to vote for a particular candidate or party. Due to resource constraints, parties must target swing voters as opposed to loyalists or opponents. Stokes' analysis of Argentinian clientelism enhances our understanding of political patronage, but she makes the problematic assumption that all political organizations will engage in clientelist practices if they have the means. Szwarcberg (2013) argues to the contrary that political candidates and party operatives have the choice of foregoing the use of clientelist strategies even when they have the means to engage in them. In a study of 137 candidates running for municipal council seats in Argentina, Szwarcberg found that less than half used clientelist strategies. Among the 74 that did not distribute any benefits, 52 had the capacity to have done so had they so chosen Szwarcberg concludes that candidates do not always willingly engage in clientelistic strategies, but that those who refuse to engage in such practices generally end up losing. Nevertheless, there is a logical explanation for refusing to engage in clientelism; "non-clientelistic candidates" were reported to believe strongly in "the importance of building relationships of mutual trust and respect between voters and candidates," with a view to strengthening healthier forms of political representation.

The use of clientelistic strategies in democratic elections is a highly complex process that involves many different considerations. What is abundantly clear is that in communities built on deeply entrenched systems of clientelism, every important person acts as a patron to many clients, and no ordinary person prospers without a patron. Information, advice, support, and material resources flow between patrons and their clients. Rarely do they flow from one patron-client network to another. Networks or cliques of patrons tie the community together and tie one community to another. The nation-state itself relies on contacts and cooperation between local patrons. Thus, the entire society is a hierarchical network of patron-client networks.

CONDITIONS PRODUCING PATRONAGE. Despite variations from one country, period, or region to another, certain common conditions favour the appearance of clientelism. Consider as an example the province of Santiago del Estero in northeast Argentina. High unemployment characterizes this province, as well as an economy heavily dependent on agriculture, low wages, little education, and low levels of labour participation. As a result, clientelism in Santiago del Estero and regions like it is largely characterized by four factors.

First, it is associated with conditions of *scarcity* and *inequality*. In poor societies with a wide range of material inequality, we expect to find extensive systems of clientelism. Where most people have to struggle to survive, a few families hold control over the means of production. Whether it is land, access to wage-paying jobs, or other kinds of material benefits (e.g., welfare, housing, health care), these families monopolize much of the wealth that exists in the community. The great majority of the people are left destitute and desperate, ready to do anything to get and keep a job, a piece of land, or a place to live. Often, control over wealth and resources passes from generation to generation. In the end, a highly stratified society is built on dynasties of powerful families and an underclass of powerless families.

Second, clientelism is highly *localized*. People cannot easily pick up and leave their homes to find work elsewhere. There may be no greater availability of land elsewhere than at home, and so no point in moving. In other cases, immobility may be due to war or civil strife that makes moving around dangerous and uncertain. Ethnic or racial disadvantage may also limit people's ability to seek better conditions elsewhere. Transportation and communication systems may be primitive. People may know little about alternative places to live and work, or may be afraid to chance a move, as they have no savings to support them if they fail to find work in the new locale.

Third, clientelism provides the *only source of protection*. In a society that lacks legal or human rights as we understand them, or lacks social safety nets such as welfare, health care, and universal education, clientelism is the only way for people to get what they need. People cannot do without clientelism if other forms of protection are lacking.

Fourth and finally, clientelism flourishes among people who lack *human capital*. Even in societies with legal rights, social safety nets, unions, and mutual benefits organizations, people with poor health and education—two forms of human capital—are at a disadvantage in the competition for jobs and housing. They, more than others, often feel they need the help of a "protector."

Clientelism weakens with an improvement in each of the aforementioned four conditions. Industrial societies, despite their inequalities, are more equal than traditional agricultural societies. People in such societies are also more mobile and more knowledgeable about other communities. Increasingly, international agreements make it easier for people to move around between countries, as well as within them. The growth of nation-states and the development of legal, political, and social rights make patronage less necessary. Finally, improvements in public health care and education mean that everyone's human capital is greater than it once was. It is true that people everywhere still compete for scarce jobs, but they are better able to do so than they were a century ago. The adoption of educational qualifications for jobs in the public sector is often a major step in civil service reform and reduces the need for, or tolerance of, patronage.

PATRONAGE AND CORRUPTION. Today, patronage offends the achievement culture of many Western societies. However, we still find it everywhere. This is in large part due to the fact that we institutionally recognize and sanction clientelism, though only on a limited scale. The fact is, clientelism plays an important social function in making good the inadequacies of many formal institutions. For example, it simplifies the filling of vacant jobs, as we saw in the section on search processes. And, for especially vulnerable people, a special relationship with someone of influence or wealth continues to provide protection in a hostile world.

Periodically, political reformers vow to sweep away corruption and patronage by voting the incumbents out of office. Rarely does this achieve the expected result. Corruption never disappears permanently, because it has a social function: to stabilize and lubricate political activities. As for the patrons, bosses, godfathers, or *nomenklatura* as they are called in Russia, they land on their feet. Often, after a change in the political order, the political brokers develop the necessary organizational, technical, and leadership skills to become consultants or technocrats. "Connections" remain influential in the background, as when leaders are needed to generate local support for projects under consideration at higher institutional levels.

Patronage and corruption both rely on control of the flow of information and other resources. However, not all patronage is corruption in a strict sense. Indeed, even the idea of political corruption is a complicated notion. What people in one society consider *corruption*—the abandonment of expected standards of behaviour by those in authority for the sake of personal advantage—people in another society may consider customary and acceptable behaviour. In some Third World countries or controlled economies, this so-called corrupt behaviour may even be essential for the achievement of socially necessary outcomes. Whenever it is impossible to find a common ideological basis for cooperation between opponents, cooperation is based on material considerations such as patronage.

Citizens' belief in the inefficiency of institutions, presence of clientelism, and fear of excessive power have, since 1973, led to an erosion of confidence in national authority and a measurable decline in nationalism in Western European countries. However, people in different countries vary in how much they tolerate the rule bending and minor rule breaking that is associated with political patronage. Political systems also vary in how much they monitor corruption. Low-level corruption is less prevalent in France than in Italy, for example, but consciousness of the problem is greater among Italians, because of different patterns of monitoring organizational behaviour.

In most cases, politicians and state leaders genuinely support efforts to "reduce corruption, improve state capacity, and deliver services more efficiently" (Goetz,

2007). But when they try to enact so-called "governance reforms," deeply entrenched systems of patronage and all of the favours and advantages that select groups enjoy over others prove to be too much to eradicate. Indeed, reformer politicians risk losing the very "patronage resources" that they themselves utilize to maintain political advantages, not to mention possible personal financial rewards as well as the votes of public-sector employees who benefit from the pork barrel (Goetz, 2007).

Nevertheless, some well-enacted reforms have the potential to pay off politically if they improve either the economy or government services. Goetz proposes that politicians will be most likely to launch "governance reforms" if two conditions are fulfilled: when they find "new sources of funds to maintain their political careers" which will not be destroyed by such reforms, and when they become confident that social groups will positively respond to reforms.

In these respects, reforms aimed at eradicating systems of patronage and clientelism involve many different factors that keep them from becoming effective. Politicians may genuinely want to see reduced corruption and improved state capacity, but many are members of traditional systems of patronage who used clientelistic practices to get elected in the first place. Also, the bureaucrats who are tasked with implementing "governance reforms" are oftentimes beneficiaries of traditional systems of patronage (Goetz, 2007).

Clientelism encourages behaviours that North Americans, at least, would tend to view as corrupt, though matters may be viewed differently in other countries. Consider, for instance, the way in which universities operate in the People's Republic of China. There, individual academic departments operate semi-autonomously. The department head behaves in what we would probably consider a totalitarian manner, feeling free to admit students outside the formal admissions procedures and operate without peer review. Much of this business takes the form of "doing favours" for personal contacts: the phenomenon of *guanxi* we discussed earlier. The decision structure, which controls communication within a department, also restricts communication between departments. This contributes to "cellularity," or departmental autonomy, within the university.

EFFECTS ON POLITICAL LIFE. Clientelism has harmful effects for political life. Yet it remains an important part of the exercise of power in most Asian countries. There, politics is often based on concentrated personal power. The civil service may be the apparent source of public policy, but the driving force behind decision-making is a small clique of powerful people. Sometimes, this decision-making clique functions simultaneously as a political party, an armed group, and a sub-government to control policy-making.

To centralize their power, the leaders of new states often try to increase their resources by co-opting the bosses and weakening the networks of clientelist distribution. They compete with patron-client networks by establishing a professional civil service and by appealing to nationalistic sentiment among the ordinary people. Often, however, this strategy backfires. The state may itself be mired in clientelism. State dominance of grassroots organizations destroys the spirit of community councils and creates public apathy.

Clientelism is only one of several ways of incorporating a diverse, far-flung population into national politics. It is especially useful for otherwise socially excluded groups: for example, Gypsy communities in Greece, who use clientelism to gain some measure of integration into society as well as access to public resources. Another way is *populism*, a form of political organization often found in the same countries in which clientelism is observed. Often, power seesaws back and forth between clientelism and populism in these countries, illustrating the relative strengths and weaknesses of the two forms.

Under populism, political leaders bid for support from dispersed individual followers, by using their charisma or appealing to nationalism. What is common to *clientelism* and *populism* is that neither assumes the existence of stable political institutions, such as a civic culture (e.g., the existence of personal rights, a belief in democracy), or obedience to abstract principles of justice. Neither has a focused socioeconomic vision of the future, nor a commitment to the working class; and neither has any use for bureaucrats or intellectuals. Under both, the military is likely to play a major role in political affairs.

Amid growing corruption, clientelist systems often come to rely on the military to maintain order. In turn, the military becomes a central social institution, a steppingstone for those who want access to top positions in business and politics. The involvement of the military in social and political life often prevents the development of a democratic government and rule of law. Despite the popular rhetoric adopted by military leaders when first in power, the regimes they install often fail to adopt socially transformative goals or create new political structures to increase participation. Violence and instability mark these regimes.

This has been true in western Africa, for example, which has suffered from various forms of corruption and human rights abuses. The military regimes there have failed to strengthen state capacities, restore military discipline, or create new social and political institutions. In large part, the cause of this failure has been the military regimes' reluctance to give up power willingly. These characteristics are due, in part, to the regimes' violent culture, the subversion of military discipline, and the decay of political and social institutions under previous regimes. Such is the vulnerability of military organization that, during the second phase of the UN intervention in Somalia in 1992, patron-client relations even developed between the UN forces and local armed groups, contributing to the failure of the intervention.

Strong civil services provide an alternative to military involvement and block the access of politicians to patronage. If, however, politicians get their hands on substantial quantities of patronage, they are likely to use it for electoral and organizational purposes. Research in Greece finds that even a formal commitment to legitimate decision-making cannot protect public agencies in discretionary administrative areas. Extra-institutional social networks based on clientelism continue to influence these operations.

Also, there are long-term effects. Easy access to patronage during the formative years of a party organization has broad consequences for the subsequent development of the party system, including electoral competition and party organization. A tradition of politics based on patronage limits the range of policy choices and favours an inefficient use of public resources. Bribery, pork-barreling, and other payoffs undermine the cohesion of parties and their collective power as organizations. People are less motivated to vote for patronage than they are for personalities or principles. As a result, parties that fall out of office have a harder time getting voted back in, since they have no patronage to dispense. Voting and political participation decline in patronage systems; and apathy and cynicism develop.

EFFECTS ON ECONOMIC LIFE. Clientelism typically also has harmful effects on economic development. It distorts the functioning of markets and states' execution of developmental projects. For example, the existence of a patronage system and a need to reduce unemployment may lead to an overabundance of low-level employees in the public sector, resulting in a disorganized system of administration. In countries like Turkey, inefficiency, corruption and the existence of patron-client networks all contribute to a failure to enforce laws against environmental degradation. Bribery is common in all of these different contexts and serves to further entrench clientelism in society.

In these respects, political clientelism undermines social and economic development. A political system consisting of patron-client networks bound together by the exchange of material benefits for political support is likely to be dominated by factionalism, politicization, high administrative corruption, and low legitimacy and autonomy. In such an environment, inappropriate development strategies result from the effort to satisfy the demands of political supporters. Even attempts to improve public housing or health care for the poor run into severe institutional obstacles.

In conducting research into the effects of clientelism on economic development, many scholars have tended to focus on "macro," or "state," level phenomena. But as Hoyt (2007) shows in his study of Suriname's economy, it is possible for smaller scale "pockets of efficiency" to exist even when the dominant structure of the state is clientelist. Suriname's state oil company Staatsolie, for instance, is a well-managed firm that has produced well over 50 million barrels of crude oil since first starting its operations in the early 1980s; in 2001, Staatsolie's production capabilities became sufficient enough to cover the energy needs of Suriname itself, and the company has developed into an exporter of fuel oil to countries like Barbados. Given such statistics, it is difficult to doubt the efficiency or reliability of Staatsolie's operations. The fact is, however, that Staatsolie stands in stark contrast to how the rest of Suriname's economy operates. Since independence from Dutch colonial rule in 1975, Suriname's per capita gross domestic product has not grown by any substantial amount. Despite being well endowed with natural resources, Suriname's exploitation of these natural resources has failed to benefit its people. In addition, the misuse of foreign aid on high-profile but not particularly beneficial projects has exacerbated economic stagnation since independence. According to Hoyt, all of these problems can be traced back to the narrow clientelistic interests advanced by dominant political groups in Suriname; instead of putting forward policies that seek to develop the whole country, many of Suriname's leading political figures instead have catered to the interests of specific ethnic groups in order to cling to power.

Clientelism and corruption existed under communism, too. In Poland, for example, the prevailing pattern was mutual corruption within the ruling clique formed by the occupants of key positions in the Communist Party, state administration, economy, and police. Every member of the clique had an opportunity to take advantage of the public resources controlled by other members. Nor did the fall of communism in Eastern Europe signal the end of clientelism. Privatization created new opportunities for patronage and corruption. It channelled wealth to those already wealthy and in power. Many suspect corruption, cronyism, clientelism, and insider dealing sidetracked the process of transitioning from decades of communist rule to a capitalist economic system, leaving citizens questioning the legitimacy of the reform process. In Russia, for instance, economic elites who operate in the private economy but retain full state privileges remain highly visible.

Economic globalization increases the openness of politics to public scrutiny and accountability by everyone, citizens and outsiders alike. The most likely reason corruption will diminish is because multinational organizations do not like it. Private business craves certainty and profitability. It opposes anything that makes doing business less certain or more difficult. In the end, clientelism will survive because it eases certain kinds of transactions. However, the opposing needs for efficiency and rationality will moderate it.

Bureaucracies

Compared to kinship and clientelist systems, bureaucracies are a new form of social organization. In industrial societies, bureaucracy is the main organizational tool for managing wealth and power, and for controlling the flow of information. As workers, students, citizens, or customers, we all rely on the workings of bureaucracies every day. Increasingly, information, support, and property flow through bureaucratic organizations, not through kinship or patron-client networks. Organizational "insiders" are automatically included in these flows, while "outsiders" are not.

In terms of our discussion of flows, we can view a *bureaucracy* as a network with hierarchical relationships: people at the top send out commands, people at the bottom obey the commands and send up information. All of the nodes in the network are defined roles or offices, so that every member of the bureaucracy has clearly specified rights and responsibilities. Everyone has a person to whom he or she reports, and people below who are reporting to him or her. None of the resources in the system—the information, power, authority, wealth, technology, or otherwise—belongs to the office-holder. The office-holder merely has the right and responsibility to use organizational resources in the long-term interest of the organization.

Like a kinship system, a bureaucracy has a set of members who are expected to communicate with and support one another, and a large number of outsiders who are not expected to receive either information or support. But in a bureaucracy, these definitions are based on impersonal selection, merit, and expertise, while in a kinship system they are based on blood and mate selection. Like a patron-client system, a bureaucracy organizes and wields power on behalf of its clients; but in the case of a bureaucracy, the clients are likely to be customers or citizens, and written, impersonal rules specify how these clients are to be treated. Because it is based on expertise, written rules, and universalistic decision-making, bureaucracy is expected to behave more rationally and impartially than patron-client systems. But as we will see, that is not always the case.

The term *bureaucracy* comes from two roots: a French word meaning "office" and a Greek word meaning "government" or "rule." Thus, bureaucracy is "rule by offices or officials." This makes bureaucracy a different form of organization from the clientelist system discussed above. Although it is true that both bureaucracy and clientelism link subordinates to superordinates, or people with less power to people with more power, the superordinate in a clientelist system holds power and controls resources *personally*. Emotional attachment and loyalty count for as much as expertise and effectiveness, or even more, in the allocation of rewards. There are no written rules to govern the relations between patron and client, patron and patron, or client and client. These unwritten relationships are based on tradition and personal history. With the departure of a patron or client, the relationship ends.

By contrast, the superordinate in a bureaucracy personally owns *none* of the resources. All resources belong to the organization, of which individuals are simply a part. Resources are meant to flow from superior to inferior based on authority or office-holding alone, not because of a personal attachment. In turn, office-holding is (ideally) based on expertise and effectiveness alone. In bureaucracies, people move through offices in the organization, based on their merit. The resources remain attached to offices. They do not follow the individual movers. Also, there are elaborate written rules to govern many of the theoretically possible relationships in the organization. Organizations construct charts to show (ideal) chains of responsibility, authority, and communication between superiors and subordinates.

THE ADVANTAGES OF BUREAUCRACY. Max Weber, the first sociologist to study bureaucracies, realized that this form of organization holds enormous potential advantages over earlier organizational forms such as clientelism, particularly in bureaucracy's potential for more rational planning and effective performance. Indeed, bureaucracies state their goals explicitly, plan and discuss strategies, hire and train the most capable people, mobilize resources, evaluate effectiveness, and take steps to improve the organization. This is what makes IBM or the University of Toronto, two representative examples of bureaucracies, different from patron-client systems such as the Mafia or the government of Louis XIV.

Considering the numerous organizational advantages that bureaucracies offer, it is not surprising that they are not entirely new. A highly developed, though imperfect, form of bureaucracy existed in medieval China. There, highly trained mandarins carried out the wishes of the emperor. To call this system a bureaucracy in the strictest sense, however, poses a number of problems. The emperor's wishes, however irrational, often interfered with the efficiency of the mandarins' efforts, and the system retained many patrimonial or clientelist features.

Bureaucracy in its true form only arose under three important historical conditions: the rise of European nation-building, capitalism, and industrialization. To understand why these historical conditions cleared the way for the establishment of bureaucracies, one has to understand that the state is essentially a bureaucratic apparatus of rule that rests on rational-legal legitimacy. It comes complete with symbolic instruments—signatures, offices, seals, and registers, for example—to establish that power is impersonal and office-holders are interchangeable.

Now, consider the first historical condition that facilitated the rise of bureaucracies: nation-building. This process, and by extension imperial conquest and colonization, created the need for effective tax collection and military capability. Kings cannot run countries, or wars, without taxes. They cannot raise taxes without the help of honest and hardworking tax collectors who are loyal to the king, not to local aristocrats. They need an honest and competent military to beat down the local aristocrats and conquer the armies of other countries.

In the eighteenth and nineteenth centuries, most European governments realized that their armies were not properly organized, provisioned, and led. As the historian Eric Hobsbawm (1962) pointed out in *The Age of Revolution, 1789–1848*, the increases in administrative and military efficiency initiated in Revolutionary and then Napoleonic France, which allowed the harnessing of a greater proportion of the resources of the state, forced Prussia, Britain, and (to a lesser degree) other states to respond in kind.

Capitalism imposed similar demands. Under capitalism, a system devoted to the pursuit of maximum profits, people quickly find that some forms of social and economic organization yield higher rates of profit on investment than others. The rationality of bureaucratic organization is well-suited to a rigorous pursuit of profits. For example, a bureaucratic structure can grow as large as necessary, through a proliferation of roles, yet remain highly controlled from the top. This is less possible, if possible at all, in kinship-based or clientelist systems. The legal idea of "limited liability" also involves a bureaucracy managing investment and profits impersonally, in a way that protects both the owners and the workers. This impersonality also makes bureaucracy different from kinship and clientelist systems.

Finally, industrialization also favoured the rise of bureaucracies. Bureaucracies are good at controlling large work forces—even highly educated and differentiated work forces. As an organization grows, typically its degree of differentiation increases. Bureaucracies must solve problems of coordination and control, by means of formalization, decentralization, and changed patterns of supervision. Often, they must re-organize. Though never easy, such change is always possible and, indeed, ongoing.

As industrial enterprises grew larger with the mechanization of work, structures of control (i.e., for management and administration) had to grow, too. Post-industrial enterprises which process information and turn out services (or other information) rather than manufactured goods are no different in this respect. The growth of professional management and administration expertise during the twentieth century reflects the enormous importance of bureaucratic organization in work life today. Organizations, embedded in diverse networks of ties to external sources, growing rapidly, and responding to continuous changes in the environment, have become continuous adopters of new technology and administrative technique.

IDEAL FLOWS OF INFORMATION. Ideally, every member of a bureaucratic organization is aware of his or her position in a network of "reporting relationships." In graphic form, the bureaucracy is a Christmas-tree shaped structure that repeatedly branches out as you move down the hierarchy. Thus, at the bottom of the hierarchy there are many people whose jobs it is to (1) carry out orders from above, and (2) report work-related information up the tree to their superiors. At the top of the hierarchy, there are a few people whose job it is to (1) issue orders, (2) interpret information received from below, and (3) maintain linkages between the organization and its (political, economic, and social) environment. Also, at the top of the structure, the heads of planning, manufacturing, logistics, communications, and other departments of the organization share information.

Working within such complex hierarchical structures, bureaucrats ideally want to leave a "paper trail" of all of their activity. This entails storing and conveying all information in writing as the basis of action, something which also affords a certain degree of legal protection. Ideally, a bureaucrat never fails to record and report information up the hierarchy. Likewise, workers ideally never leak work-related information outside the organization, to superiors other than their own, to workmates in other branches of the structure, or even to workmates with the same reporting relationship. None of these actions would be helpful, in principle, to the organization's rational decision-making structure, and sometimes they might even harm the organization. Similarly, in an "ideal" bureaucracy most employees will remain strangers to one another. Accordingly, a shop supervisor will supposedly only hear about a problem related to shipping, sales, or customer satisfaction after this information has made its way *up* the structure from the bottom to the top, and then back *down* to his factory.

In practice, organizations do not work this way, as sociologists since Max Weber have pointed out. The closest that bureaucracies ever get to operating in this "ideal" fashion is in the context of the public sector in democratic countries. The public sector involves different actors of "varying authority and power" competing for influence; a process of negotiation among multiple parties determines the final "goal" or target of any public bureaucracy (Hodson et al., 2013). With the existence of visibly negotiated goals, public bureaucracies must always stay accountable to external actors and accommodate their wishes. This gives rise to claims of inefficiency and incompetence, but the fact is that these aspects of public bureaucracies also drastically increase the cost of breaking existing laws and regulations. In these respects, public bureaucracies in democratic countries can be safely expected to operate along ideal "formal-rational" lines.

In the private sector, the situation is starkly different. The goal of most private sector bureaucracies is the "pursuit of profit," something which is inherent to private bureaucracies and not something that is visibly negotiated through a political process (Hodson et al., 2013). All sorts of "rents" or costs which prevent a private sector bureaucracy from attaining its goal will have to be avoided or "externalized," meaning that there is really no push for private bureaucracies to limit operations to ideal "formal-rational lines".

Thus, alongside the ideal or formal structure, which prescribes how a bureaucracy ought to work, there is an actual or informal structure, which largely determines how the organization *really* works.

ACTUAL FLOWS OF INFORMATION. In theory, a failure to report information up the hierarchy never happens. In practice, it happens all the time. That is because workplaces are politically "contested terrains," in which controlling the flow of information is a means of changing the balance of power between superiors and subordinates. Surprisingly, it has been reported that workers in France or Russia are much more alert to the inequality of bureaucratic relations and the power of information-control to equalize relations than workers in the United States. This is in large part due to the fact that bureaucracies work differently in different societies, a notion which was first articulated by the French sociologist Michel Crozier.

Crozier reasoned that the widely diverging definitions that different cultures put on terms like inequality, deference, openness, and secrecy would influence bureaucracies to behave differently in various cultural contexts. If one accepts Crozier's argument, it is not all that surprising that French and Russian bureaucracies operate differently from American ones. Bureaucracies also seem to function differently along gender lines. Men and women differ in the roles they adopt within bureaucracies and how they perceive the workings of the organization to which they belong. Women in managerial roles, for instance, adopt a collaborative, relational approach based on familial relations. Their managerial styles emphasize the establishment of good employer-employee relations and the sharing of information and power. By contrast, men emphasize purely economic considerations. They conduct business more like a war game or a blood sport. It is not unlikely that bureaucracies will change as more women assume the top roles.

The variance between "ideal" and "real" bureaucracies is further compounded by the fact that workers typically form friendships and acquaintanceships that stand outside of hierarchical bureaucratic structures. By virtue of these relations, workers casually share work-related information. They share much of this information orally, not in writing, to encourage civility and negotiation between work teams. Often, they share it purposefully, to help one another. Sometimes, they even leak information for personal gain or to subvert their boss or the organization as a whole. Thus, within organizations based ideally on strangers relating to other strangers following written rules, workers form what amount to secret organizations or sub-communities that obey their own rules. There is a "politics from below" that includes all actions that defy, oppose, or sidestep the formal rules and roles of the organization.

For this reason and others, there has developed in sociology a large literature on the inefficiencies and irrationalities of bureaucratic organization, as a counterweight to Weber's supposition that bureaucracies were (and would inevitably be) more rational than other forms of organization. In fact, it would not be an exaggeration to say that most sociological literature about bureaucracy is concerned with the nature of this paradox that an organization designed to be rational and predictable is, more often than not, neither rational nor predictable. Largely, this occurs because bureaucracies, like other large groups and organizations, do what they have to in order to survive, even when it means failing to achieve their original goals.

However, there are other reasons for irrationality. For example, within bureaucracies different groups may hold different (and competing) interests. Management may try to cut labour costs while employees seek higher wages. Although the interests of these competing groups can be aligned, at least partially and temporarily, these internal tensions often persist and re-emerge. It is not all that surprising that organizational leadership requires the establishment of a "vision of common purpose," a quality all too often lacking or missing in bureaucracies (Hodson et al., 2012).

The basis of any informal sub-organization within a bureaucracy is trust. It relies on friendship, acquaintanceship, and gossip about third parties to strengthen existing ties. In organizations, we all build trust gradually, maintain it continuously, and destroy it easily. When we violate trust, often the result is revenge or another disruptive response: for example, confrontation, withdrawal, and feuding. Trust is easier to generate *within* organizations than *across* organizations, since it is within organizations that managers, serving as third parties, can monitor and enforce reciprocity. The result is that organizational boundaries restrict intellectual diffusion. Within organizations, the flow of information is harder to contain.

Various factors play a role in forging friendships and trust between co-workers within a bureaucratic organization. They can be classified into three broad categories: personal factors (essentially, whether people like each other or not); "workplace" factors (including such things as organizational culture); and external factors (essentially the way in which work and world beyond work interact in the context of employees' lives) (Mao et al., 2009).

Despite the many factors that encourage the formation of trust and friendship between co-workers, it must be noted that there are also restraints that prevent such kind of relationships from being formed. In fact, research has shown that many employees actually "suppressed their wish to have a workplace friendship" in order to comply with the negative view that bureaucracies usually have of such relationships. At the same time, researchers predict that growing emphasis on teamwork and other interactive aspects of the job will "attenuate" the tendency to comply with the bureaucracy's unfavourable view on workplace friendships, thereby freeing workers to form relationships with co-workers as they deem it appropriate (Mao et al., 2009).

The discrepancies between the theoretical ideal and the actual functioning of bureaucracies have been exacerbated in recent years. With the advent of globalization and the development of a "post-capitalist society," there has been pressure on bureaucracies to transform themselves to cope with these changes in the external environment. Some scholars believe traditional bureaucracies will become obsolete, unable to cope, and that a new organizational structure will emerge: one which "liberates" employees from hierarchical "constraints" and enhances their ability to cope with a rapidly changing world order. In the end, "bureaucratic controls" will be replaced "with 'structures that develop informed consent,' where command is replaced by dialogue, persuasion, and trust." Employees will be empowered to make use of their expertise and adaptability in a "responsibly autonomous manner" (Johnson et al., 2009).

Various studies seem to support the "post-bureaucratic" thesis. Organizations do as they evolve tend to delegate more authority to their workers, at the expense of traditional bureaucratic hierarchies. These same studies find, however, that the transition into a "post-bureaucratic" structure is often uneven. And it is important to note that "traditional" bureaucracy and "post-bureaucracy" are not necessarily "mutually exclusive" concepts (Johnson et al., 2009). It is very possible that mixed model bureaucracies will emerge. Indeed, scholars like Josserand et al. (2006) posit that aspects of "traditional" bureaucracy will most certainly re-surface within the more democratic operations of "post-bureaucracy". The legitimacy derived from the "democratic" participation of employees as "autonomous" agents will sit side by side with the legitimacy that is derived from traditional "power of the office" (Johnson et al., 2009).

SOLVING THE FLOW PROBLEM. Requiring all information to flow to the top of the structure, across, and then back down is slow and ponderous. Increasingly, organizations have been adopting horizontal, plus vertical, reporting relationships. To a large extent, informal organization already permits information to flow across the idealized organizational structure. Nevertheless, bureaucracies are increasingly creating formal team structures that cut across the hierarchy. These enable workers to cooperate in solving cross-branch problems. Often, this improves organizational learning and gives the organization a competitive advantage.

Besides new organizational strategies, organizations also require more flexibility from workers. They can obtain this only if workers receive more education and training and participate in organizational planning. Participation is a way of increasing personal satisfaction, cooperation, and the internalization of organizational values. This is especially important in organizations trying to make a successful transition to new technologies or new strategies of cross-organizational linkage.

Motivating workers to cooperate is also a challenge. Sometimes, material rewards are sufficient. The most profitable corporations generally provide the most extensive employee benefits packages, especially in environments that are highly competitive and uncertain. Providing more workplace autonomy has also been reported to increase job satisfaction and worker retention. In contrast, coercing workers through the proliferation and stricter enforcement of rules often fails to increase productivity, particularly where there is a need for worker autonomy and discretion. Workers grow alienated when employers use rules to coerce compliance, despite the fact that they usually do not resist rules that help them to carry out their tasks.

The motivational problem is greatest in organizations that require professional expertise and judgment, as in universities, law firms, and technology firms. There, we find employers giving increased attention to matters of organizational culture and career development. It is only by giving these workers considerable autonomy and rewards for strong identification with the firm that employers can induce the most able workers to join, stay, and carry out their duties in conformity with organizational goals. Along with this comes a need for thorough organizational socialization, which begins at the stage of recruitment and interviewing and never ends (Alvesson, 1990).

Some organizational cultures are more effective than others in creating high rates of employee commitment and retention. These factors vary by country: in Japan, Korea, and China, workers are more receptive to a collective (or group) culture than workers in North America. What is true across cultural boundaries, however, is the fact that people form stronger attachments to other people than to "the organization" as an abstract entity. Thus, patterns of clientelism develop even within bureaucracies. In the end, bureaucracies are organizations in which two principles—rule-based careerism and person-based clientelism—contend for dominance. Neither is able to beat the other decisively, once and for all.

THE PROBLEM OF RATIONALITY. Executives think bureaucracies are rational in the ways they make and execute plans. They *are* more rational, in a limited sense, than patron-client relations. Over the long term, by making impersonal decisions and rewarding excellence, bureaucracies can pursue organizational goals by deploying huge amounts of wealth and power. They are also better at remembering their history. However, the sheer size of large bureaucracies and their long-term outlook introduces certain types of irrationality that, in the end, may undermine them. A concern with the mere survival of the organization may distract attention from improving the quality of the products and services the organization produces. Consider the fact that "red tape"—or administrative delay—by bureaucracies is never eliminated. Often, it serves positive functions for the organization, such as preventing haste and dispersing responsibility. But it is precisely this bureaucratic ideal of eliminating subjectivity and individuality that undermines productivity. By putting boundaries between the organization and its environment, the organization often loses touch with the people who are the supposed objects of its efforts.

Gajduschek (2003) has gone so far as to propose that the dominance of bureaucracy as an organizational structure in our society cannot be attributed to efficiency. Indeed, from organizational sociologists to neo-classical economists, scholars working in various different disciplines of social science have been united in criticizing bureaucracies for their lack of efficiency. Gajduschek reasons instead that bureaucracies have been able to remain dominant in our society because of their ability to reduce the level of uncertainty.

To a great extent, it is true that bureaucratic operations reduce uncertainty in favour of predictability. A heavy reliance on official records and procedures, as well as the predominance of routine, are key characteristics of bureaucracies. The fact is, however, that these characteristics pose a whole new set of problems. A tendency to keep records and procedures, in an effort to routinize action, may inhibit forgetting and, therefore, learning. As a direct consequence, rule-making and record-keeping proliferate. There is some evidence that managers who are more alienated and more pessimistic make more rules. Other research suggests that rule-making reflects a failure to gain voluntary cooperation from employees with the existing rules: that is, a motivational problem exists.

According to scholars like Hodson et al. (2012), the bureaucratic impulse to "routinize all challenges" results in the creation of "multiple layers of contradictory rules." The resulting incoherence creates a sort of "internal chaos" within bureaucratic organizations which makes it much more likely that various internal processes will interact to produce "undesired and unintended outcomes." Small mistakes may then have enormous consequences.

Another result of bureaucratization is the creation of a rigid and morally indifferent *bureaucratic personality*. This type of employee substitutes proceduralism for any moral or ethical concern with outcomes. Anonymity and distance from decision-making increase as the organization grows. "Rule by offices" undermines personal responsibility for decisions the organization may take. No member of the bureaucracy takes responsibility for collective decisions. The organization often punishes whistleblowers—employees who bring forward valid information about wrongdoing or illegal conduct—for criticizing the organization. Even organizations that publicly say they want employees to "participate" and those that pledge to uphold high ethical standards may move to discredit or dismiss the whistleblower out of fear that information about waste, fraud, or abuses of power will harm the organization or its executives.

As a result, so-called collective decisions, typically taken by the top executives of bureaucracies, are liable to be foolish, harmful, or even criminal. Corporate and government bureaucracies are unique in that systemic patterns in their organizations may cause their deviant behaviour. The deviant behaviour of big business and big government occurs because of information control, norms and rewards that encourage deviant outcomes, or actions by organizational elites. For example, it may be that no one in the organization has enough information to evaluate the decisions taken, or understand why people have taken them. Executives actively discourage or even prevent subordinates from gaining this information.

In these respects, managerial elites initiate the corporate deviance, and then make their acts part of the organizational culture. It continues unchecked until challenged from inside or outside the organization. The legal system rarely penalizes organizations themselves for deviant behaviour. Once deviant behaviour is revealed, the deviants are well positioned to evade responsibility. Managers refuse responsibility by hiding behind organizational procedures or by adopting the stance that they were following orders. As a legal person, the corporation has at its disposal many more resources than individuals seeking redress for their injuries from the corporation. The legal system may eventually provide some compensation to victims. However, it is often ineffective in punishing the corporation. The result may be fraudulent practices, dangerous commercial products or even, at an extreme as in Nazi Germany, death camps. Interestingly, what we would now call the middle managers responsible for the Holocaust reported experiencing psychological repulsion at what they were doing. But most of them justified their behaviour as part of their duty to the bureaucratic system.

RELATIONS TO THE OUTSIDE WORLD. Bureaucratic organizations look at the outside world as through one-way glass. Ideally, the outside world, composed of competitors, customers, and other bystanders, cannot see into the organization, but the organization can see out. In theory, the main contact between the organization and the outside world is by means of its top executive. In full possession of organizational intelligence, this top executive is best able to act publicly in the organization's interests.

Corporations manipulate their public image and take pains to obscure what they don't want people to know. For example, they try to improve their image by manipulating public statements about executive compensation. Researchers find a negative relationship between executive salary levels and the clarity with the 114 largest profit-making firms present information on this topic in corporate proxy statements. In other words, the higher the salary levels, the more the corporation tries to hide that fact.

The separation of decision-making authority from front-line experience often creates an "us-them" point of view within the organization. If customers criticize the organization for unresponsiveness to their concerns, the organization takes a stance of embattled resistance to change. Union-based protest, and organized citizen or customer protest, put pressure on the bureaucracy. The result may be "groupthink," a resistance within the organization to taking criticism seriously, considering many options, or conceding the need for change.

Paradoxically, it is not executives at all but, rather, the front-line workers—the people who deliver goods and services to customers—who have the most contact with the outside world and know the most about it. This fact creates an asymmetry: employees with the most knowledge about the environment have the least authority to influence relations with it, and vice versa. It also creates conflicts for front-line workers. The organization expects them to profess confidence in, and loyalty to, the decisions made by top management, even if they know these decisions are wrong. This creates stress in the workers and breeds disloyalty to the organization.

In the end, employees have to practice street-level bureaucratic discretion in their dealings with customers. Only in this way can they resolve the competition between desires to standardize and individualize decisions. Ideally, bureaucracies are perfect structures for diffusing, storing, and processing information. In practice, they are helped and hindered by informal relations within the organization, and by the politics of their relations with the outside environment.

Secret Communities

We turn now to *secret communities*: sets of people tied together by shared secrets. In these communities, information, support, and property flow through secret networks.

Secret communities are similar to bureaucracies in certain respects. For example, both have important goals, make important decisions, and aim to survive as long as they possibly can. They both also have collective identities. However, they are different in a great many other ways. Unlike bureaucracies, which exist in the open and have openly expressed, written rules, secret communities often hide their existence and also have hidden, often unwritten rules and memberships. And unlike bureaucracies, secret communities may have a less evident hierarchical and leadership structure. Secret communities are based on social networks, but they are likely to have a much less detailed division of labour (or task specialization) than bureaucracies.

Like kinship and patron-client systems, secret communities are old forms of organization. In pre-industrial societies, they often serve as the basis for elite ritual and leadership activity. In any society, secret communities, which range in size from two people to many thousands, may provide the basis for political protest and resistance. However, secret communities of two or a few people are also the site of intimacy, friendship, and intense loyalty with no political purpose.

The word *secret* comes from Latin words meaning "separate" or "set apart." Thus, secrets are information set apart from the information that is open to all. Secret information sets people apart from one another. Two worlds then exist: a minority world, where a few possess the secret information, and a majority world, where most do not. The secret flow of selected information, and the withholding of this information from most people, segregates society and builds clique-like subgroups within it.

Most people are plagued by contradictory wishes to hide and to reveal information. Sharing within a select subgroup allows for an outlet, while theoretically keeping the information protected. As an extreme example of conflicting desires, consider the drug world and how marijuana and cocaine dealers handle the challenge of secrecy. Keeping illegal activities secret should be important in this business, to ensure financial gain and physical safety. Yet competing with these rational motives are the non-rational ones so characteristic of drug dealers and users: the dealer's ego, the lure of a big reputation (bringing greater sexual and dealing opportunities), the excitement of a spontaneous, hedonistic lifestyle, and the sense of magical invulnerability created, in part, by the drug experience. These contradictions between a desire for security and a desire for exhilaration promote alternating periods of paranoid secrecy and erupting openness.

Secrecy is the process of withholding or distorting information. As the practice of concealment, secrecy requires people to manage impressions, identities, networks of knowers, and means of social control, to ensure compliance and loyalty. We all have an interest in both revelation and concealment. Secrecy is the process by which we social actors open or close ourselves to others. We let some people see more of us, or a truer version of us, than others. This raises the interesting issue of the relationship between an actor's interior and exterior identities. It directs our attention to the ways an actor "plays" different situations on the social stage, to different audiences.

We must not, however, confuse secrecy with *privacy*. They are two different ways of treating knowledge. That which is "private" always belongs to a particular individual. Typically, it is separate from other information because it is deeply personal. Privacy is consensual, while secrecy is not. We all have a "right to privacy," but no equivalent "right to secrecy." Stigmatized or disadvantaged social groups that have little access to privacy often use secrecy to conceal some of their behaviours and manage public impressions. The private family and the secret LGBT world are examples of groups that use privacy and secrecy, respectively.

Any information can be "secret" information. Its secrecy lies in the accompanying warning that this information is to go no farther. It is this warning or prohibition that creates secrecy. People often convey secrets indirectly, using body language or signals with multiple meanings. Conveying secrets in this way may prevent any accusations that they have violated the secrecy, although such accusations are unlikely to begin with. An accuser would have to state the secret as part of the accusation, thus violating the secrecy themselves.

Often, there is confusion about which people have the right to tell a secret, and who can be told. This inherent tension between communication and concealment is essential to secrecy. As well, a request for selective silence often gives recipients a secret they can exploit. After the teller reveals the secret, power shifts to the receiver. He can then sanction the teller for divulging a confidence, or choose to share the information even though it would break the rules and alliances that underlie this communication.

The sharing of secrets can benefit the social relations of the receiver. To share a secret is, in the words of Georg Simmel, to create a "second world." This second world, visible only to those who share the secret, is just as real in its consequences as the "first world" the rest of us inhabit. However, maintaining this second world is easier said than done. It is one thing when the community consists only of two people, but as the group of knowers grows, it becomes harder to contain the information. Secret societies illustrate the difficulties.

Secret societies are small groups or networks engaged in secret activities. They are characterized by their secretiveness and by the deviant or even illegal behaviour of their members. Their existence presupposes the existence of another, dominant culture within which the secret society is subordinate. The secret society can never allow its members to forget their separateness. Indeed, this sense of separation is more central to defining the group than even the normative content of the particular society. It is the separation of the secret society, and the boundaries it erects to protect itself, which validates it. Often, members of the group view themselves as a kind of embattled aristocracy, like the cliques we discussed in an earlier chapter. As in cliques, complicated processes of inclusion and exclusion, ritual, centralization, and de-individualization serve to keep the secret society together.

Maintaining secrecy is a complex task requiring strong social cohesion and coordination among insiders. The probability that a secret will be successfully contained depends largely on three factors: (1) the number of insiders, (2) the degree to which insiders are disciplined, coordinated, and motivated to maintain secrecy; and (3) the degree to which the group's environment actively seeks disclosure. The secret is most secure when only a few insiders conspire together, hiding knowledge for which there is little external demand.

An environment that actively seeks disclosure puts secret societies under great pressure to close ranks and exercise caution. The higher the degree of risk, the more likely a secret society will recruit its members from among people they already trust. Therefore, secret societies under pressure recruit through pre-existing networks of relationships (friendship and kinship, in particular). This practice, however, sets limits on the secret society's size and heterogeneity. Thus, the more hostile the environment, the smaller and more homogeneous a secret society will likely be. Often, such secret societies are organized as separate and independent "cells" with little contact among themselves.

Some secret societies involve themselves in criminal activities of a non-political kind. The Mafia falls into this category. Secret societies of this kind have historically provided protection from private violence, and from the police, to people engaged in both legal and illegal enterprises. With the formation of legal private security agencies, their relationship with legal businesses has declined. Illegal businesses are the main customers for protection. These businesses seldom use legal security services, fearing the disclosure of their activities to the government. One of the main jobs of the criminal organization is to bribe and corrupt the police. Occasionally, corrupt police collect directly from the people engaged in illegal activities. As the corrupt police become more numerous and more powerful, they come to replace secret societies. A strong honest police force, on the other hand, increases the demand for, and the strength of, secret criminal societies.

Secret non-criminal societies have played an important, radical political role throughout history. In some pre-industrial societies, as in pre-colonial Nigeria, secret societies were the politico-ritual backbone of otherwise leaderless communities. They gave peasants a political voice where they went otherwise unheard. Examples include the Mau Mau of Kenya and the late nineteenth- and early twentieth-century Chinese secret societies. Other "primitive rebels" of this type have included the Molly Maguires, an Irish secret society of miners involved in labour disputes in nineteenth-century Pennsylvania.

Some secret societies, such as the Grand Orient Masons in nineteenth-century France, were known for their liberal, agnostic, and rebellious political views. Freemasonry in Italy was, for most of the eighteenth and nineteenth centuries, nationalistic, anti-Catholic, and opposed to the existing civil power. In the eighteenth century, Masonic relationships in female lodges fostered profound, intense friendships. Consciousness-raising initiation rituals heightened the idea of friendship based on virtue. An intense spirit of independence characterized these women, as did strong dedication to charity, an interest in new ideas, and a profound loyalty to friends.

Some secret societies, like South Africa's *Broederbond,* have supported the right-wing status quo. At the other end of the political spectrum, the Antireligious Commission of the USSR defended the left-wing status quo. Its membership of about 100 militant atheists specialized in court proceedings against Orthodox and Catholic bishops.

Simmel thought the hiding of reality in a secret is a major human achievement, because it makes possible the creation of a "second world alongside the manifest world." Along with larger groups defined by political or illegal activities, the idea of the second world can describe people's personal lives. Consider the establishment of long-term intimate relationships—love affairs—between single women and married men. At first, intimacy rests only on self-disclosure. The participants maintain the relationship by building secrets together. They develop strategies for concealing their intimacy. These strategies create new, shared secrets, which further intensify the sense of intimacy. In intimate relationships, as in many others, the restriction and then the secret sharing of information gives pleasure. The intimacy, and survival, of the relationship depend on the secrecy of the information sharing. Thus, creating secrets and telling secrets can be exciting, consequential activities. This type of information flow not only communicates (or withholds) useful information, it declares the boundaries of the group.

Patterns of secret exchange give form and substance to children's social worlds. All exchange of secrets comes with the expectation of reciprocity. Reciprocity—the norm that all debts will be repaid in due course—introduces a measure of continuity and coherence into children's interpersonal lives. Secret-sharing gives children a heightened sense of self. It voluntarily establishes intimate relations by dramatizing interpersonal choices: who to tell, who not to tell.

Some secrets are about oneself, while some are about others. The exchange of secrets about others is a strategic move in the battle of social hierarchies and social groupings. People you like are people you share self-revealing secrets with, and expect self-revealing secrets from. These secrets are mechanisms of inclusion. Secrets can also be mechanisms of exclusion, when embarrassing secrets are shared about members of the out-group. In these secret-sharing games, relations of reciprocity give concrete form to interpersonal and group boundaries. These are processes that create and maintain cliques through gossip.

Secrets exist in more formally defined organizations. Many organizations exist in environments where distrust is routine and justifiable. Information may be a source of wealth and organizational survival. When it is, the result is an increasing reliance on organizational secrecy, security, and intelligence strategies.

Trade-secret law promotes secrecy and restricts the circulation of ideas, employees, and technology. Corporate secrecy often makes government regulation or taxation policies ineffective or inequitable. It can also cause conflicts between top and middle management, when information is deliberately withheld from everyone but the highest ranking.

An equally critical problem is the effect of secrecy on science. The scientific community has historically relied on norms of disinterestedness and open sharing of scientific information. However, concerns with state security and corporate interest increasingly infringe on these norms of openness. The public has an interest in an open scientific establishment, so that it can democratically discuss the values and interests that science is serving. Scholars may disagree about the extent of the problem; they agree, though, that science needs new institutional mechanisms to tackle new ethical dilemmas. As well, there is a need to clarify the ownership of intellectual property and the conditions of free intellectual flow.

Outside of laws and regulations placed on corporations, governments use secrecy to gain and protect advantages: political, economic, or both. As we have all learned, the media and educational institutions are not fully effective in discovering the truth about government and transmitting it to the public. The result is a society mired in self-deception. The use of secrecy for political and economic advantage poses many problems for the operation of an "open" or democratic society. Secrecy becomes the other side of official propaganda, another form of institutional deception.

Reconciling the public goals of "freedom of information," "right to privacy," and "official secrecy" poses difficulties. Some view Britain's *Official Secrets Act* as little more than blackmail and extortion. It forces civil servants to promise never to reveal anything deemed an official secret, without knowing what secrets they must keep. We can invoke each of these principles to support or oppose any kind of disclosure in the political realm. Each has a value in protecting a democratic society that competes with other societies for world power.

Secrets as "facts" are a currency of exchange. People, organizations and even nations hoard secrets so that they can trade in them. The belief in and quest for secret information creates elaborate structures, procedures, and mechanisms, the most familiar of which may be spy organizations like the CIA, MI5, and the KGB. They bring certainty and power to the people who seek it, who then often try to create or sustain uncertainty for those less informed. As people cannot easily crosscheck secrets, this cycle of seeking and withholding is complex and full of moral gray areas.

Secrecy, like espionage, is a mechanism for the social control of information. The two work hand in hand. People not officially permitted to know the secret may still know it, but cooperate in the secrecy by not revealing their awareness. Sometimes a false but persuasive cover story aids secrecy. Or, secrets may be used to counteract one another. Information controllers also have incentives to collaborate: for example, in remaining silent about deviance.

As spy stories show us, there are many similarities between the secret worlds of American and Russian espionage. The organizations are similar and so, in the end, are the people who work in them. The reinforcing, counteractive, and collaborative uses of these information-controlling processes expand information control to such an extent that society loses control of it. Participants in the world of secrets sometimes become more concerned with catching traitors or keeping channels of access open than with transmitting or interpreting information. Thus, secret organizations, whether aimed at penetration or security, often drift from their original goals.

An example of such shifting can be found in the changing overarching logic of police investigations in the United Kingdom. There has been a shift towards investigations that interrupt ongoing criminal activity, rather than responding after the fact. It's been theorized that the change can be traced back to the increasing availability of, and reliance on, "intelligence." Proactive policing is tellingly referred to as "intelligence-led," and involves interrupting crimes or lessening their severity from the start, rather than taking the more prosecutorial route to justice. Arguably, the rationale is that police are attempting to unearth secrets about the criminal organizations immediately and obviously, rather than attempting to elicit them during a trial or reactive investigation. Regarding police work, the interpretation of information has shifted to a preliminary activity, done before interception or penetration, rather than a reactive means of ensuring future security (Innes, 2004).

On a broader scale, the drifting of goals of intelligence agencies can result in the organizations focusing on individual people or cases rather than nations, as originally intended. Out of the state's desire to know and to control private behaviour comes the development of secret police forces. The political invention of a secret police force dates only from the French Revolution, and the establishment of the Russian secret police dates back to 1825. However, there were only 100 secret agents at that time. By 1912, the Okhrana (later known as the NKVD and the KGB) comprised more than 50,000 agents. Secret police practices everywhere have become pervasive and accepted, as cultural images of social control have changed.

With the unquestioned, all-encompassing authority of figures such as kings and emperors having fallen out of style, most of us tend to think that governments' level of control over citizens' actions has lessened. While this may be true insofar as such things as laws preventing unjust or arbitrary punishment are concerned, at the same time the state has gained powers over the everyday lives of citizens that were once beyond its purview. Surveillance activities have drastically increased, and it is now the right to privacy, rather than issues of favouritism, that is deemed a major issue. As time goes on, people are becoming more and more accepting of government interference, or at least have come to expect it. Proactive policing involves techniques of gathering information that are kept hidden, making control of them difficult.

There is a general expectation of respect of human rights, but the secrecy of policing techniques inspires a new fear in those who wish to rebel. It is as if someone is always watching, and wrongdoing will always be noticed (Gubanski, 2004). Social control has changed from overt edicts to respect the powerful to covert monitoring of secrets that can be used against those who rebel.

In addition to social control, one purpose of secrecy, already noted, is to protect and maintain people's identities. This remains true whether the identity is a country's international reputation, as in the case of spy agencies, or smaller in scale. Information control increases the likelihood that we will take people at face value, as who they say they are. This satisfies their goal to gain access to settings that would otherwise be closed to them. It helps people to escape the shame and stigma that may otherwise attach to their reputation. Accordingly, secrecy is greatest in societies like Japan that attach the greatest importance to "shame" and "losing face," and impose strict limits on social participation between certain classes of people.

It has been proposed that shame is a governing force in societies. When the norms of moral communities are violated, any sense of belonging and solidarity can be threatened, evoking this emotion termed shame. It is a force similar to that of embarrassment, though with a more serious connotation. Regardless of severity, both emotions are ones that people want to avoid, and so actions that might bring them about are avoided, too. The prospect of shame prompts self-monitoring. One considers how one would appear to outsiders, imagining the judgment of that appearance, and presuming the emotion the judgment will elicit: pride or shame. If shameful, a given action or disclosure of information may be purposefully avoided.

Theoretically, shame either prevents violations of taboos in society, or results in denial and silence as a reaction to those witnessed (Scheff, 2003). In both cases, secrecy is a tool used to maintain order. The individuals will either hide the unconventional behaviour themselves, or those around them will feign obliviousness to avoid acknowledging the shameful situation. In this way, the secrets help in managing impressions and reputations. Secrecy is greater in some areas of life than others, of course. For example, people tend to maintain secrecy about mental health issues, fearing they will be stigmatized if they are viewed as mentally ill.

Much secrecy in our society surrounds sexual matters. To take a simple example, just about everyone over the age of ten knows that women menstruate monthly and use tampons or sanitary napkins to deal with it. Yet, people still suffer embarrassment in relation to menstrual matters. They often develop shopping strategies to conceal their purchase of tampons and napkins. The same is true, to an even greater degree, of the purchase of contraceptive devices: pills, condoms, and the like. This illustrates the interesting phenomenon of an "open secret": that is, a secret kept from everyone and shared by everyone. Open secrets in this way protect the privacy of human bodily functions.

Much impression management may rely on open secrets. People tacitly agree to pretend that someone is *not* wearing a toupée, does *not* have a pimple on her face, or is appropriately dressed when the opposite is true. Harold Garfinkel's classic case study of Agnes illustrated how an intersexed person sustains her social right to be a woman by hiding that which, if revealed, will discredit her feminine performance. It is often unclear whether people observing a social or sexual performance are "in the dark" about the truth, or if they are agreeing to accept the performance at face value.

Those with alternate sexual orientations have long used secrecy and techniques of impression management to conceal their true sexual identity, in order to avoid possible stigmatization and hostility. Such *passing* or identity management conceals any deviation from heteronormativity and fosters the construction of a false perception of shared reality. Coworkers may support these efforts to pass by not searching for explanations or asking personal questions. Friends and family may practice a mutual pretense called "counterfeit secrecy" when they discuss but do not acknowledge their alternative sexual identities. Though a useful protection in the short run, passing and other forms of concealment unintentionally perpetuate the notion that homosexuality is disreputable behaviour.

It is only in the last decade or two that, through disclosure, the LGBT community has become more familiar to heterosexuals. In workplaces, for example, identity management has adopted more passive techniques. Employers are urged to not ask, employees urged to not tell. Throughout the 1950s and 1960s, mental health professionals, sociologists, and gay political activists viewed secrecy among gays more positively than they viewed overtness. In the 1970s, however, they came to define the disclosure of homosexuality as more desirable for both the gay individual and the community. Many came to view covert homosexuality as psychologically and socially problematic.

Disclosure, even to friends, family, and associates, still carries a variety of risks and outcomes. Research on "coming out"—the process of public self-identification as gay, lesbian, bisexual, or transsexual—continues to find that, often, the revelation of this secret leads to rejection, however temporary. Mothers are the most likely recipients of self-disclosure from half the men and two-thirds of the women. Few youths reveal themselves to their fathers. Minority (i.e., black, Hispanic, and Asian) men and women have an especially hard time revealing themselves to family members.

Outside the personal realm, discrimination is encountered in many areas of life. Job prospects, for example, can be affected by the bias or covert discrimination of an employer, encouraging those who identify with alternate sexualities to keep them hidden. It is often easiest to allow the assumption of heteronormativity to stand, regardless of the knowledge that it should be irrelevant to a given situation. In recent years, many anti-discrimination laws have been put into place, creating the legal infrastructure for equality. Regardless of the laws, issues surrounding LGBT rights continue to be debated politically, perpetuating the idea that they are meant to be controversial. Often seen as a contributor to political leaning, opinions on LGBT rights are sometimes seen as a personal matter, one that should only be discussed among trusted individuals who will refrain from vilifying your beliefs. In other words: secrets.

Secrets and politics are intertwined in a fashion that goes far beyond opinions on isolated issues such as gay marriage. It is a pervasive concept, with both government organizations and individual politicians withholding information for various reasons. The use of secrecy in politics is explainable in at least two ways: functionalist and otherwise. The functional analysis focuses on the costs, and benefits, of openness.

For example, an analysis of the 1983 search "in public view" for a new president of the University of Florida found that full disclosure of all aspects of the search significantly diminished the quality of the candidate pool. It also inhibited the deliberation of vital issues, altered the tone of the search process, and may have influenced the votes on candidates. Observers concluded that candidates may damage themselves professionally by participating in such a process. The open nature of the search may also heighten, rather than reduce, public cynicism about its outcome.

On the other hand, a historical analysis suggests that institutional secrecy grows out of hierarchy and demands for control. In small rural communities, social relations are characterized by a high degree of equality, openness, and reciprocity. Community members carry out the main rituals of the community publicly. The right to secrecy only gains social importance in advanced archaic civilizations. There, the preservation of secret knowledge is considered legitimate for the clergy and nobility. Only the lower classes are expected to maintain openness. Secrecy there is symbolic and protective of higher rank.

Whichever explanation is correct, secrecy diverts and dams the diffusion of information. Typically, secrecy builds on already existing social networks, further segregating people who are already segregated and homogenizing groups that are already, in their most important particulars, homogeneous.

Cyberspace

We have examined secret communities built in the "real" world, out of relationships between friends and relatives. Now we turn to secret communities built in cyberspace, out of relationships among strangers. These virtual communities are so new they don't even have names yet.

We know relatively little about the social organization of cyberspace, because it is so vast and relatively new. However, what we can safely say about cyberspace is the following. First, it is enormous in size, much larger than any kinship system, patron-client system, or bureaucracy. Second, it is not organized around either particularistic relationships (like a kinship or patron-client system) or around written rules (like a bureaucracy); as a result, it is relatively chaotic and unpredictable—perhaps not so much disorganized as organized in a way we don't yet know how to describe. Third, unlike a secret community, it is largely visible in its activities, though many parts of the cyber-world have invisible activities from which most people are excluded. Fourth, unlike a clientelist system, bureaucracy, or secret community, cyberspace appears to have no system goals: nothing it is trying to achieve or protect.

Yet, like the other sites of diffusion we discuss in this chapter, cyberspace is a place where a great deal of information flows and, as a result, is a place that exercises a great deal of influence on our behaviour.

"Cyberspace" itself is no more than forty-five years old, since it was only then that the Internet was created. Yet, in the last ten years, the numbers of people worldwide "surfing the net" have increased exponentially, as in any mature process of innovation. Accordingly, there has been a flood of research about flows in cyberspace—about online flows of information, ideas, and support.

Research on the Internet itself has been going on for at least twenty-five years. Early research compared this new technology, explicitly or implicitly, with previous technologies that had also diffused and revolutionized human communication. So, for example, we find important historical studies of telephone adoption by Claude Fischer (1992), Michele Martin (1991), and Patrice Carre (1993). An interesting early study asked about the effect of culture on IT diffusion, with respect to e-mail and faxes (Straub, 1994). More generally, we find international research on information technology (Gill and Krieger, 1992) as part of a new science that was then being called "informatics."

In recent years, we have seen a great deal more social science research on a variety of sociological topics connected to online information flow. This includes discussions of "society's (virtually) time-free transition into the digital age," (Robinson and Lee, 2014), "characteristics of emerging adults who do not use social network websites" (Bobrowski and Smith, 2013), "how youths influence their parents' digital media use" (Correa, 2014), social factors that influence digital research (Dutton, 2013), the use of social media by non-profit organizations (Nah and Saxton, 2013), the shared management of open source software (Bixler and Taylor, 2012), and most provocatively, a history of the new technology titled "The spread of TCP/IP: How the Internet became the Internet" (Townes, 2012).

The online world is a key source of information, social support, and commercial opportunity. The Internet contains somewhere between 3.32 billion and a trillion pages; in truth, it is impossible to make a precise and accurate estimate of something so new and fast-changing. What can sociology say about something so new and still in its infancy? First, we know that search processes in the real world are never random; they operate through pre-existing networks. Likely, they will be the same in cyberspace. And we know from Stanley Milgram's "small world" research that the actual number of steps needed to contact any two people in world of 7 billion is probably only six.

Beyond that, the sociology of Georg Simmel, created a century ago, offers two important insights into the virtual communities of cyberspace. First, Simmel showed how "second" or constructed worlds, like the world of secrets and secrecy we discussed in the last section, can build on, and build away from, the first "real" world of our sense experience. We will see the virtual communities of cyberspace comprise such a second world, built on and away from the world we know best. Second, Simmel described the main characteristics of "the stranger" and how the interactions between strangers that characterize a city are different from interactions between intimates. Cyberspace is chiefly a world of interactions between strangers: a world even less constrained than the contemporary city. So, to understand cyberspace, we must understand both strangers and constructed worlds.

STRANGERS. The word *stranger* comes from Latin roots related to "extraneous." It means "outsider." According to Simmel, the stranger is a person living within a community and, therefore, participating in the life of the place, but not given status by "natives" as one of the in-group. He is *within* the group but not entirely *of* the group. The stranger accepts such a lack of identification with the group and feels little compulsion to submit to prevailing forms of subtle social control (e.g., gossip, shame).

Three aspects define the social position of the stranger in sociological terms. First, the stranger is what Robert Park called "marginal": partly inside and partly outside the group. The stranger enjoys a particular combination of nearness and remoteness (or social distance) from group members. Even a stranger who is structurally central and important to the functioning of the community is a cultural outsider. Second, the stranger's origins are odd and remote. With no fixed roots in the community, the stranger has the potential for a wandering life. To some degree a person without a country, the stranger displays elements of both his former and current places of residence. Finally, because of this marginality, social distance, and mobility, the stranger is free to reject local values and conventions. Such a person, though denied the freedom of participation that is the unquestioned right of community members, at once attains certain freedoms denied to members. He can see more things than they can.

For Simmel, the stranger is a characteristic figure of life, especially life in the urban metropolis. The cosmopolitan stranger is a tolerant traveler without cultural commitment, to whom nothing is foreign. The stranger brings to interactions qualities that do not stem from the group: detachment and objectivity, freedom from habit, piety and precedent. This freedom gives the stranger creativity, a fresh outlook on the community, and an ability to resolve disputes, if necessary. He can be a middleman, a go-between, or a trader. Because he is an outsider, the stranger can also be an agent of change.

For these reasons, strangers often meet with surprising openness and confidences. This is also why social researchers, as strangers, can get the intimate information they seek about people, families and communities, if they avoid "going native." Like anthropologists, "travelers" and "tourists" are favoured categories of stranger. They receive the most acceptance because they are transient and, therefore, pose the least threat to the material basis of community.

The "stranger role" is a social construction, the result of a social process of classification. Socially, insiders consider the stranger as "not one of us," a notion which may be based on different nationality, race, or culture, among other things. Encounters with strangers are encounters across socially constructed boundaries. This means that if we are to understand social relations with strangers we must also understand the construction and maintenance of social boundaries. These are the processes that make the "otherness" of a stranger seem to be an irreducible obstacle to achieving mutual understanding. We must also know how people have defined the stranger: whether, for example, as a guest, sojourner, newcomer, intruder, inner enemy, or marginal man.

On the other hand, if we are to understand the stance taken by strangers, whether assimilatory or detached, we need to understand more about passing (discussed earlier) and institutional completeness (discussed later).

STRANGERS IN THE POSTMODERN WORLD. In pre-modern societies, the stranger does not belong to the society. He or she has no defining kinship relations in the community. Traditional societies have only primary group relations: friends and enemies, no strangers. In postmodern societies, no one has kinship links that define their relationship to the community. People have a great many secondary group relations with strangers. The state has dealt in two ways with strangers—that is, with people who did not fit prescribed social norms. Either it assimilated such people, according to liberal "melting pot" norms, or it excluded them, according to less liberal, more nationalistic or racist norms.

The postmodern attitude to strangers is largely indifference, since everyone we meet is a stranger at first. Postmodern culture is organized around the "problem" of strangers. To learn how to live in an urban, cosmopolitan society is to learn how to live among, and with, strangers. The postmodern world is characterized by the permanent condition of living with strangeness. This is a result of a high degree of social and geographic mobility, segmentation of the community into heterogeneous and independent universes, and a rapidly changing culture.

People are always part stranger in any social situation, yet they feel a continued need to mark cultural boundaries and establish their own identity. This condition has produced a pervasive uncertainty that is itself permanent and irreducible. In this postmodern world, both the Left and the Right have opted to deal with strangeness by keeping people apart, through the idea of multiculturalism. However, the genuine emancipatory thrust of the postmodern world is to recognize the rights of the stranger and abolish conceptions of strangeness. This leaves people the right to define themselves as they wish, something which, as we will see, is the essence of cyberspace.

INTERACTIONS WITH STRANGERS. We know a fair amount about how people interact socially with strangers and, thus, how they will likely interact in cyberspace, where everyone is a stranger.

First, sociability among strangers generates its own etiquette. For example, city people avoid eye contact. Styles of dress are intended to convey particular impressions. Particular public settings, like laundromats, develop subcultural behaviour norms. Specific rituals act as a form of implicit grammar governing interaction. People develop techniques of "reading" strangers that rely on a good memory, observation of clothing, physical features, manners of speech, and nonverbal communication. A display of friendliness and confidence increases the likelihood of reciprocation. By these and other means, strangers strive to manage what others know and think about them. Impression management is fantasy management. In the past, CB radio operators chose "handles" or nicknames that conveyed no clear information about the interests or personality of the transmitter. Today, people on the Internet do the same when they choose names or "avatars." Among strangers, for the moment we are nothing more or less than who and what we say we are.

Second, city people typically fear strangers more than they need to. They overreact to strangers with a combination of attraction and repulsion. Some of this is because strangers represent a "shadow self" on whom people project their own fears and fantasies. The ambiguity of strangers and "otherness" excites feelings of ambivalence. We often imagine the stranger as an enemy. A typical response includes distrust, fear, stereotyping, and refusal of empathy.

Third, city people react to strangers differently, depending on whether they belong to a common nationality, network, or other group. Their reaction is based on the perceived social and cultural distance between themselves and the stranger. White middle-aged people especially fear encounters with young black men—indeed, with any young men. Not surprisingly, prejudiced white people fear criminal victimization by a black stranger more than unprejudiced white people. Thus, fear of strangers is a product of internal perceptions as much as, or more than, external conditions. Demagogues sometimes manipulate these internal perceptions of threat, as the Nazis did in whipping up hostility toward Jews. Often, the objects of hatred are familiar people or types of individual: blacks in America, Jews in Germany, Muslims in Bosnia, and so on.

Fourth, people are less likely to seek help from a stranger than from a friend. They also reveal themselves less to strangers than to friends, and receive less disclosure in return. This tendency is independent of sex and unrelated to liking. One apparent exception to this rule is "hospitality," throwing open the household to a stranger. When we practice hospitality, we disclose ourselves to strangers. However, people who live in cities, where encounters with strangers are far more common, display much more restrained and routinized hospitality than rural people. In effect, city people use hospitality to proclaim the stranger's status as a welcomed stranger, but no less a stranger.

Another apparent exception to this rule against disclosure is the use of strangers for secret sex. In the late 1980s, most of the men who visited out-of-the-way public toilets for fast impersonal sex were in their 30s or 40s, married, mainly heterosexual, and strangers to one another. They communicated through nonverbal gestures, did not use force or coercion, and did not involve youths or children. They were discrete and cautious in their sex play, and hid their secret lives from the community while trying to maintain an image of propriety. Fear of HIV/AIDS has subsequently disrupted these and other sexual practices between strangers. However, the desire for sex play with strangers has not abated, as witness the use of cyberspace for these purposes.

Fifth, self-interested competition undermines cordial relations with strangers. Strangers can develop trust and cooperation without external social controls, under some conditions. The outcome of a computer-simulated two-person game between strangers depends on whether there is a payoff for refusing to play, and on the embeddedness of the interaction. Games between embedded players who receive no payoff for stopping the game will, eventually, generate trust and cooperation. This simulation shows that effective norms for trusting strangers emerge locally, in exchanges between neighbours. Then they diffuse through weak ties to outsiders.

Under noncompetitive conditions, a growth of familiarity lessens the social distance between strangers. Familiarity reduces fear and hostility between groups, especially when interactions between "different kinds" of people are (1) gradual, relaxed, and repeated; (2) cooperative, not competitive; (3) guided by norms of friendliness; (4) between people of equal status; and (5) supported by legitimate authorities (e.g., government officials, teachers, or ministers). Such interactions are especially beneficial when they contradict the stereotyped notions strangers hold about each other. The worst inter-group problems arise in competitive situations: for example, in work settings. People, especially young people, more easily avoid conflicts in social or educational settings.

STRANGERS IN CYBERSPACE. The role and image of the stranger, which for Simmel became a metaphor for life, has a striking analogy in the operations of cyberspace. For Simmel, the stranger represents a unity of close and far, nearness and remoteness, with all the implications that carries for social interaction. Cyberspace, in many ways, is about this unity, since communication in this medium transcends constraints of both physical and social distance.

The basis of all community is communication, not physical proximity. By enhancing communication, the Internet creates new communities based on common affiliative interests. Cyberspace is a non-situated experience: new groupings in cyberspace have no location in physical space. Communication in cyberspace results in communities of interest that may either compete with, or reinforce, localized communities. For some people, computer networks open the way to more participation in public life, though for others they reduce the commitment to local communities. Does a high degree of involvement in the life of online communities necessarily mean withdrawal from the life of the local community? We don't know. However, research on ethnic communities in Toronto show that some people participate heavily in both the dominant community and the ethnic community, but some people participate in neither. People may participate in cyberspace communities similarly.

Online communities are, for many, extremely attractive. Unlike communities based on physical presence and face-to-face interaction, they combine immediacy, asynchronicity, and anonymity. The result is a realm of hyper-reality in which time, place, and individual identity lose their connection to reality, and where personally meaningful narratives co-exist, with none dominant over the others.

People use the Internet for mundane purposes: for information sharing, commerce, and social support; to keep in contact with friends and family, participate in political debates, find jobs, gather medical information, and meet new people. For example, in a demonstration project in Halifax, researchers gave young single mothers of infants access to an online social support network concerned with parenting issues. During the six-month trial period, the forty-two women contacted the network more than 16,670 times. Ninety-eight percent of the replies to concerns posted in the public forum provided positive social support—mainly emotional support, followed (in order) by informational and tangible support. Close personal relationships and a sense of community developed in this novel social environment. The mothers who participated regularly were more likely than others to report a decrease in parenting stress after the demonstration project had ended.

Cyberspace also has the potential to create new identities. In some respects, the Internet permits a more intimate, informal, and immediate form of interpersonal communication than face-to-face modes. Using computer networks for dating, to pursue and develop relationships, reduces the importance of physical traits. It increases the significance of rapport and similarity, allows freedom from gender-role constraints, and provides a space between people that balances distance and intimacy. Transition to the use of real names, when it happens, shows closeness and opens a passage from the imaginary to the real.

The Internet makes possible the use of fake identities. The capacity to generate real or virtual identities may be considered an essential aspect of postmodern relationships, not just on the "net." New technologies also provide a context for more fluid transformations of language. These new usages are largely free of many cultural indicators (e.g., age, race, sex, or physical appearance) that have constricted women's expression. They permit participants to conjure up new sexual and political orders. Online interactions encourage greater identity fluidity and multiplicity: for example, gender switching allows participants to distance themselves from gendered identities and disrupt previously held beliefs about gender. Borders, materiality, and bodily attributes, such as sex or physical attractiveness, are irrelevant in cyberspace. Geographic limitations melt away. The result is a new sense of universal "us-ness."

FLOW OF CULTURE IN CYBERSPACE. One aspect of information flow on the Internet is the phenomenon of content going viral, and being shared and re-shared via blogs, email, and other social media sites. Traditionally, videos have been distributed to consumers by very large media organizations. With the emergence of video-sharing sites and social networking, shorter videos are readily available for viewing. Due to the sheer volume of available content, people are unlikely to sort through it themselves, and therefore rely on social networks to provide them with viewing choices. This allows certain videos become popular and go "viral" through such sharing (Broxton et al., 2013).

Viral videos have characteristic qualities. Stories and videos gain traction quickly, but also fade quickly. A video may get thousands or even hundreds of thousands of views in a week, will peak quickly, and then will unlikely remain a top draw by the following week. Highly social videos behave differently than less social videos. They undergo this sharp peak and rapid decline, whereas some videos may not be quite as overwhelmingly popular, but still circulate repeatedly over a longer amount of time (Broxton et al., 2013).

This type of sharing also leads to the creation of *memetic videos*: clips that generate extensive user engagement by way of creative derivatives. From its launch in 2005, YouTube has become an emblem and a platform for the spread of such participatory culture. As we noted earlier, memes are units of culture that spread from person to person by means of copying or imitation. Memes are a pervasive part of Internet culture, and aid in its diffusion (Shifman, 2011).

Memes can be ideas, symbols or practices, such as melodies, catchphrases, clothing fashion, or architectural styles. They can be global or culture specific, but only those suited to their socio-cultural environment will successfully spread. The Internet provides an environment for large-scale spread of memes, and this method of transmission is a mechanism of diffusion of Internet culture. The Internet's flexibility, ubiquitous presence, and accessibility allow new memes to be quickly created and modified. This leads to the creation of new genres of expression (Shifman, 2011).

We must, however, make an important distinction between *viral videos* and *memetic videos*. A viral video is defined here as a clip that spreads by digital word-of-mouth mechanisms and is shared by many people without changing form. On the other hand, a memetic video involves participation in the form of contribution, and is altered from the original in the form of parodies, mashups, imitation, remixes, and other derivative work. As such, memes highlight the Internet as a participatory culture that all members contribute to. They are just small pieces of a larger culture that diffuse among the members within a community, and that all are able to build upon and change (Shifman, 2011).

WHAT IS WRONG WITH CYBERSPACE? As noted, cyberspace has the potential to blur the distinction between reality and fantasy. In principle, "cybersubjectivity" in networked "inforstructures" can reframe many personal relationships, with all of their cultural meaning. In reality, this does not happen.

For example, the "sexpics" trade on the Internet Relay Chat provides sexual acts and identities that are conventional in relation to offline heterosexual norms and (pornographic) representations. Internet communicators still behave in traditionally gendered and even sexist manners. Internet relationships are characterized by even more control of self-information—that is, impression management—than we find in face-to-face relations. In cyberspace, people engage in short-term and easily forgotten relations, display signs of omnipotence, and try to avoid responsibility and commitment, just as in the real world, only with more impunity.

The ability to depict oneself in a variety of identities and personalities creates a "zone of confusion" between reality and common-sense notions of the imaginary. This fantasy play allows unprecedented narcissism. New ways of social interaction violate the old ways, in this way providing some people with a release from oppression, which is well and good. However, there is a danger the Internet promotes emotionally disconnected or superficially erotic contacts. Is this a new world of understandings, or digital masturbation?

Anonymous Internet communication can encourage the development of meaningful personal relationships and allow less-powerful users to challenge authority figures. However, such anonymity also allows malicious communicators to depersonalize others for amusement and more powerful users to distance themselves from responsibility. Participants online veer between a desire for involvement and real (as opposed to realistic) self-presentation, and complete cynicism—an inability to authenticate and trust "the other." Online communities develop with many free riders. Problems arise in establishing boundaries and defining membership. Guidelines for negotiating conflicts among members obstruct the expansion of news groups and other virtual communities.

The creation of the Internet once fed utopian fantasies of citizen empowerment and the revitalization of democracy. Some observers call it the "Californian ideology": a belief the use of information technologies will create a new democracy by allowing everyone free expression in cyberspace. The myth of a free market, without regulatory curbs on private enterprise, feeds this fantasy. However, dominant economic, social and political forces in society are struggling, with much success, to capture and regulate the Internet. Virtual reality has come to resemble the real world. Ordinary, everyday politics has captured cyberspace. For example, violent, white racists use the Internet to further their anti-democratic goals. In this respect, they are more effective than anti-racist blacks.

The new forms of virtual community, and the technological and cultural resources required for participating in them, have the potential to create new barriers to universal access. This means new forms of social stratification. Given society's existing social and racial polarization, only some have access to the new technologies. A reliance on unregulated market forces will create social apartheid between the "information rich" and the "information poor." Global inequalities of access to information technology will intensify Third World disadvantage and reinforce existing hierarchies and hegemonies. Cyberspace will not achieve its potential until we have addressed questions of territorial sovereignty, policing, commercialization, and unequal access, among other things.

Sociologists and others have already written a great deal on this and related topics. A recent work, concerned with "measuring trustworthiness of information diffusion in social networking services" (Jung, 2014), reminds us that all that distinguishes information from "noise" is trustworthiness or credibility.

Another hazard of cyberspace is its potential for crime. It is older adults in particular who are more likely to become targets of the dangers in cyberspace: spam, phishing, scams, and viruses. This greater risk that older adults face may be primarily due to differences in education and computer use. Although older adults use the Internet regularly, they do so less than do younger adults. As a result, they may lack knowledge and awareness of computer privacy threats (Grimes et al., 2010). To be sure, naïve or unknowledgeable users of any age are susceptible to online identity fraud; however older adults are less likely to take action to protect themselves. Older adults also may be unaware of the potential misuses of personal data (Grimes et al., 2010).

SECOND WORLDS REVISITED. Does society exist in cyberspace? If so, what kinds of social classes are there? What sociological ideas must be used to explain this society? Are new ideas needed?

We can likely apply existing knowledge to understanding some of what is going on. Imagine cyberspace as a new frontier in which strangers exchange information and practice impression management on one another. The possibilities are limited by some "givens." First, the strangers are themselves the products of certain gender, class, race, and childhood experiences. Second, these interactions are all rooted in a particular historical moment. Whatever participants may fantasize, they live at a particular time and place that provides particular opportunities and constraints. Third, and more specifically, the interests, goals and technologies of large organizations—chiefly, states and private enterprises—place bounds on their interactions. These organizations have no interest in supporting the creation of a mass democracy based on universal equality.

On the Internet, some people play the stranger role more extensively and effectively than others. Internet sociability among strangers generates its own etiquette and its own language. As we have seen, secret or virtual communities built in cyberspace, out of strangers, are similar in some respects to secret communities built in reality, out of intimates. Yet several important differences exist between them.

First, we can map the personal networks through which secrets and other information flow in the real world. We are far from being able to map the flow of information in cyberspace. Second, we can exert some control over the people to whom we have ongoing social ties. That is what makes them eligible to share our secrets. We cannot control the strangers we meet casually in cyberspace. That absence of control is a large part of what makes us, and them, attractive in the first place. However, this absence of control opens the door to problems of violated privacy and various other forms of personal abuse.

For the time being at least, a walk in cyberspace, with strangers, remains a walk on the wild side. However, it is not an experience that is entirely new to humanity. We have walked with strangers before.

CHAPTER FOUR

Migration

Migration is the second major flow process we discuss in this book. Like diffusion, migration is a social process that is central to society's continued functioning. Unlike diffusion, which involves the movement of resources (information, support, and influence, for example) from person to person, migration is the movement of people from place to place.

An Overview

We should not, however, make too severe a distinction between migration and diffusion. After all, people are carriers of information, support, practices, culture and influence; when people move from one place to another, so do the information and ideas they carry. Because of migrations, different communities are composed of different kinds of people, with different kinds of ideas, practices, and the like. And that means some communities are livelier and more prosperous than other communities of similar size and wealth. An example is the migration of gay people into gay-friendly cities, and (according to geographer Richard Florida) their reportedly beneficial effects on the cities' artistic, creative, and innovative potential. More generally, cities that receive a lot of young, ambitious, well-educated in-migrants tend to prosper more than cities that lose such people, or fail to attract them.

Migration occurs in every known society, although societies vary in the number of people who change location in a given year and the distance they move, on average, from their original location. Some of this migration is international, and some is intra-national—in Canada, between provinces, or even between localities within provinces. Some of this migration, especially intra-national or internal migration, is an uncontrollable response to differing opportunities in different parts of the country. And some of this migration, especially the international migration, is a result of national policies that seek to recruit certain kinds of people and encourage them to immigrate.

Migration comes from the Latin word meaning "to wander," and refers to any movement of people from one place to another. In this chapter of the book, we discuss varied flows of people between places that include traffic, changes of residence, rural-urban migration, and international migration. We also compare migration and diffusion. Let's begin with a brief overview of migration, to get a flavour of what we will examine in closer detail below.

Migration, we find, is determined largely by economic incentives. People use migration to improve their well-being. When they migrate, people do so in a sensible and efficient manner. Few move at all in any given period. People who do move tend to move short distances. They tend to move to the nearest, often contiguous places, providing they can get what they want there.

Migration—who moves where, and when—is determined largely by the availability of information and perception of opportunities. This is why distance, contiguity, and social networks all play a part. These factors influence people's knowledge about available opportunities. The risks and "costs" of moving to a new destination decrease when many similar migrants have already arrived there. Again, this illustrates the important of social networks for migrants, and explains chain migration, which we discuss at length later.

People migrate to places where employers pay higher wages, in hopes of improving their well-being. If they have the necessary information, people base their migration on a rational choice. Poorer places lose people to richer places. Thus, large differences in regional wage rates predict large migrations. People normally move out of less developed regions, and less developed countries, into more developed regions and more developed (i.e., industrialized and/or urbanized) countries. This accounts for the massive global migration of labour witnessed in the twentieth century.

RURAL TO URBAN MIGRATION. Twentieth-century migrations from rural to urban areas illustrate this process. In the U.S., new metropolitan areas have consistently drawn the majority of migrants from interstate exchanges with existing metropolitan territories. People have been moving from countryside to city at least since the sixteenth century, when Elizabethan Englishmen worried about the constant influx of "sturdy beggars." It is only in the last two centuries, however, that this flow process assumed massive, global proportions.

Everywhere, the income differential between agricultural and non-agricultural work determines the rate of rural out-migration. This migration slows only when incomes in the two sectors are (practically) equal. Often, foreign investors influence the rates of rural-urban migration by shifting the relative distribution of economic opportunities and wage rates in a country. Economic development produces what researchers call an "urban bias" in Third World countries. Cities develop more rapidly than rural areas, and this difference stimulates a rapid influx of rural migrants.

Much migration is circular, even daily or seasonal (Vertovec, 2006). People leave the countryside, work elsewhere, and then return. Migration is a family as well as individual strategy for survival. Rural families often combine farm production, local industry and investments, and circulating employment and remittances. Daily or seasonal migration allows rural people to participate in the urban economy without cutting their rural ties. On returning home, the rural migrants bring new capital and expertise. This benefits local development and helps to homogenize the society culturally.

Some rural to urban migration is involuntary, a forced displacement that results from land enclosures, the mechanization of agriculture, or civil war. Massive uprooting of people from the land, as, for example, in the former Yugoslavia and in Central Africa, leads to massive suffering, prolonged unrest, and conflict. Rapid rural out-migration, whatever its cause, leads to rural depopulation and rapid urbanization. The result, typically, is large-scale unemployment and underemployment in the cities, and the formation of impoverished urban ghettoes. Rural migrants without permanent residential status and/or human capital are disadvantaged in the city. Shantytowns and favelas form, and a new generation grows up in what anthropologist Oscar Lewis called a "culture of poverty." Rural migrants find it hard to integrate into city life, especially if they lack skills and social contacts. They are marginalized economically, spatially, and socially.

Migrants are highly motivated to succeed in the city, though. The threat of having to return to low wages and harsh conditions in the countryside provides them with a positive incentive. As a result, migrants tend to work harder than native workers. So, even though migrants often enter jobs at lower wage levels than native-borns, within a decade or less the wage gap is eliminated. Within six years of a move, migrants earn 30% more than if they had stayed at home. The rural-to-urban move, though difficult and risky, is usually rewarded.

OTHER INTERNAL MIGRATION. In developed societies, too, flows of people are highly patterned and aimed at maximizing well-being. However, people often conceive of their well-being in different ways. In Canada, foreign-born migrants tend to move to large cities with strong economies. Native-born migrants, especially those with little education and a low income, tend to move out of Canada's large cities to smaller places where there are few immigrants.

The poor in North America, as elsewhere, are attracted to regions with more economic opportunity. This is true of both welfare recipients and the working poor. Opportunity, not the level of welfare support, dominates the decision to migrate. The amount of welfare support available has the greatest effect on migration decisions by single mothers with small children and no recent work experience. However, higher wages, increased safety, improved housing, better economic opportunities, and family ties also influence their decision.

People tend to migrate in steps from small to large places, and from the periphery to the centre (Roseman, 1971). Suburban growth in North America is due more to rural-to-suburb than city-to-suburb migration. Typically, the growth of suburbs is not due to a "flight from blight." City-to-suburb migration is due mainly to housing affordability, as young people move to own rather than rent their homes. However, by moving to the suburbs they increase travel time to work, and see less of their friends and relatives.

Through purposeful moving, most people end up content with their residence type (see, for example, Cadwallader, 1992). Those who are not content are twice as likely to prefer lower rather than higher density settings. They eventually succeed in moving to the periphery—that is, to small towns and cities. There, they find the lifestyle changes they associate with retirement or raising a family. Young, highly educated movers, in particular, look for non-metropolitan areas with recreational facilities, other social amenities, and within easy driving distance of a city.

Locations gain and lose attractiveness over the life course. Therefore, age and income are important predictors of movement. New residents (typically young people, retired people, or tourists) and new service providers (i.e., businesses) often bring with them civic or social requirements that are new to the community. As a result, massive relocations (e.g., due to the aging of the baby boom and their consequent change in housing desires) pose problems for rapidly growing non-metropolitan areas.

Elderly migrants will continue to gain importance in the coming decades (see, for example, Golledge, 1997). Migration, seasonal and otherwise, is an important part of the life cycle of elderly migrants. Healthy elderly movers are looking for outdoor recreation, a slower pace, and warmer temperatures. Much migration is aimed at escaping extremely cold winter weather by moving south and west. Typically, migrants visit many times before deciding to move. After moving, they quickly develop social ties. The likelihood of migration to a retirement community increases as an elderly person's disability advances to moderate levels. It declines as the disability becomes severe. Elderly people who live alone, and whose children do not live nearby, are most likely to live in retirement communities. Many elderly movers (especially women) become part of their children's households, especially if they suffer a confining long-term illness.

Men typically take the lead in family migration decisions. Families move to improve husbands' opportunities, not wives' (for a Canadian example of this, see Tepperman, 1985; Tepperman and Marsden, 1985). They may move even if this reduces the income and career prospects of the employed wife, at least in the short-term. As a result, migration creates or increases inequalities between husbands and wives. Married women often experience large reductions in their personal income upon moving, because of lowered employment rates. Single women and college graduates receive positive benefits from migration. When a woman migrates with her husband she foregoes the substantial advantage she could have derived if she had moved alone, since it depresses the chances of her working. (If she does work, in the long term migration does not hinder her socio-economic attainment).

MIGRATION COMPARED TO DIFFUSION. Flow processes are similar in important respects. For example, migration is similar to diffusion. Consider some of the things we know about diffusion—for example, about gossip and rumours, discussed in the first half of this book.

First, we know that information moves mainly through existing networks of social relations. Second, information moves fastest and farthest where there are many weak social ties. Third, diffusion is limited by a lack of weak social connections. Strong ties which provide redundant, or unnecessary, connections are not as good. Fourth, as we have seen, strong, redundant connections result in the formation of cliques that trap information and create social segregation. Fifth, diffusion can create new social links by increasing the connections between people, in this way breaking down the barriers between people.

Since migration and diffusion are similar in important respects, the same principles hold if we substitute "migrants" for "information" and "locations" for "people" or "groups." First, we find that people migrate mainly through existing networks of locations. That is, some locations are tied to others, but some locations are "isolated." Second, people migrate most and fastest where there are many social connections between locations. Beyond that, migration is limited by social disconnection and segregation.

Thus, a section in this chapter discusses *chain migration*: migration that takes advantage of existing social networks. Chain migration is stimulated by the successful migration and settlement of earlier migrants from the same origin. It is the reason why migrants to Toronto from any given country (e.g., Italy) tend to come from the same few regions of that country. Chain migration strengthens old links between locations, and sometimes creates new ones.

Like the flow of information, the flow of people creates new connections and strengthens old ones. Migration results in the spread of world cultures and the creation of *ethnic diasporas*, which we discuss later in this chapter.

Migration is a result of both the attributes of movers and the locational attributes of origin and destination. Some ideas move farther and faster than others. Some locations give off more ideas than others. The same is true of migrating people and locations. Some people move farther and faster than others. Some locations project, eject, shed, or lose people faster than others. On this matter, there are two kinds of theories about migration: call them theories about *attachment* and theories about *retention* (see, for example, Brettell and Hollifield, 2000).

Theories about attachment focus on the personal characteristics that dispose people to migrate or not migrate. For example, research finds that foreign-born Canadians have higher in- and out-migration rates than native-born Canadians. Migrants also tend to be more energetic and successful than non-migrants. Prior to their move, prospective migrants enjoy a consistent advantage in annual wage and salary incomes, compared to non-migrants with similar earnings-related characteristics. Highly educated people are more likely to move than less educated people, since they have more transportable human capital. All these factors contribute to attachment.

Theories about retention focus on the characteristics of different countries and regions that explain why they draw, and keep, large numbers of migrants. For example, Ontario has a strong ability to attract and retain the foreign-born, compared with Nova Scotia and Saskatchewan. Urban areas worldwide tend to show a stronger attraction and retention of migrants than rural areas. As we have seen, all migrants—native-born and foreign-born, city-born and country-born—respond to economic variables in rational way. They go where the money and the opportunities are best.

All flow processes introduce new inputs to an existing "stock" or population. Where diffusion is concerned, new information adds to the existing stock of information, ideas, and techniques. When studying diffusion, our main concerns are the amount and rate of information spread: how much information comes in and long it takes to cover the available space. So, for example, we are interested in how long it takes for a technical innovation, or rumour, to spread through an entire population, and how many people learn about it in a month, or a year. Migration is concerned about these elements, too. In studying migration, we want to know how long it takes refugees from Rwanda, Kosovo or Vietnam to resettle in Canada, or how many immigrants arrive in Canada in an average month or year.

THE BIG EFFECTS OF MIGRATION. Another similarity between diffusion and migration is that both achieve large social changes through gradual, often small, increments. Recall that, with all flows, small things eventually add up to big things, a topic we discussed at the beginning of this book. This is true of migration as well as diffusion.

A useful concept in this case is *population churn* (see, for example, Dennett and Stillwell, 2008). Canada has always had a high "turnover" or "churn" rate, meaning a rapid change in the makeup of the national population. Historically, this has been the result of both a high rate of inflow, due to births and immigration, and a high rate of outflow, due to deaths and emigration. All of these *vital rates* have been higher in Canada, for most of the nineteenth and much of the twentieth century, than in most other industrial countries. It was this observation that led the eminent Canadian sociologist John Porter to characterize Canada as a "great railroad station." The results have been a weak national identity and a corresponding need for multicultural institutions.

As we will see in the section of this book concerned with renewal, where there is a high turnover rate, *processes* of turnover determine the *structures* (i.e., the composition and institutions) of society. Given a high rate of turnover, any society's structure will be shaped by the characteristics of its flows. Thus, for example, with a large influx of young people, an "old" society rapidly becomes young. With a large influx of different races and cultures, a single-culture society rapidly becomes multicultural. How long such a transformation will take depends on how extreme are the starting conditions, and how high are the rates of flow.

This means that we can predict the future structure of society from recent processes. As this goes on, history wipes away its traces in a society with high turnover. As a result, we cannot infer the past structure from the current structure. Even modest rates of flow have a dramatic effect on society, after a long enough time. Consider a simple model of migration between a city and its surrounding area (e.g., the former city of Toronto and the surrounding Greater Toronto Area, or "GTA"). Suppose that, at time *t*, 60% of the population within a 50 kilometre radius of Toronto City Hall lives in "the city," say 5 kilometres or less from City Hall. The other 40% lives in the surrounding towns and villages, which we will call "the countryside." This was probably true of Toronto fifty years ago. The proportions were even more skewed one hundred years ago.

Now, imagine that *each year*, a small percentage leave where they are and go to the other place: i.e., 2% of people in the countryside move to the city, and 5% of people in the city move to the countryside. These are small proportions, yet they add up. If this process continues unimpeded for *n* years, the system will reach equilibrium. At this equilibrium point, the numbers of people flowing in each direction will be equal and there will be no more change in the size of either the city or the surrounding area. (For simplicity, we are ignoring the effects of births, deaths, and in-migration from other sources.) At that point, matrix algebra tells us that 29% of the GTA population will live in the city of Toronto, and 71% will live in the surrounding area.

Note, first, that small short-term changes make big long-term changes in the population and politics of the region. This is reflected in the balance of power in Ontario, between people who live in the "416" telephone area code—traditionally, the city of Toronto—and those who live in the "905" area code, which takes in the surrounding rural and suburban area. In the 1990s, the Progressive Conservatives under leader Mike Harris received their strongest electoral support from the "905" area and the strongest opposition from the "416" area. They accordingly restructured regional government to favour the "905-ers." Small and steady demographic changes over a fifty-year period had led to the election of more Conservative candidates and served to undermine Toronto's pre-eminent position in provincial politics.

Second, note that these changes were predictable and inevitable. With the help of a simple model and the available data on migration, we could have predicted this change decades ago. In Quebec, where demographers have more influence, similar data about the language use of new immigrants long ago persuaded francophones that, slowly but inevitably, French language use would become a minority practice in the province. If each year *all* anglophones retain English, *most* allophone immigrants adopt English, and *some* francophones switch to English, inevitably Quebec will become an anglophone province. This deduction led Quebec's government to implement language laws protecting French and requiring the children of new immigrants to learn French.

DIFFERENCES BETWEEN MIGRATION AND DIFFUSION. All flow processes affect the relationship between inputs, outputs, and "stock" of a population. Where diffusion is concerned, our main concerns are the amount and rate of information spread.

In the case of migration we have other concerns as well: the total number of in- and out-migrants, the changed size and mix of the population "stock" after migration, the rate of turnover of the "stock," links that migration creates with places of origin, and links that migration creates with other destinations. So, for example, in studying migration we are interested in the number of people who move out of Canada in a given period of time, as well as the number who move in. We are interested in the resulting total size of the Canadian population, the relative mix of immigrants and native-born Canadians, the annual rate of change in the national population due to migration, the links between (say) Italian immigrants in Canada and Italians at home, and the links between Italian immigrants in Canada and Italian immigrants in (say) the United States.

These are not, typically, the kinds of questions we ask about diffusion. We are not interested in the number of rumours (or innovations) leaving Canada in a given period of time, nor even in the number of rumours (or innovations) entering Canada. We keep no census of the resulting total number of rumours that circulate in Canada, no tabulation of the relative mix of local and imported rumours, no calculation of the annual rate of change in total number of rumours circulating. We know little about the links between rumours in Canada and rumours elsewhere. The closest we come to charting changes in the "information population" is through the use of public opinion surveys that examine changes in the views of Canadians, or the numbers of supporters of particular ideas, parties, or politicians. Overall, it is odd how little systematic information we possess about the flow of information and ideas, and about the global population of information, ideas, innovations, and other things that diffuse.

In large part, we have more knowledge about migration because the flow of people is more closely regulated than the flow of information. Monitoring follows regulation. To be sure, internal migration is entirely unregulated in Canada, but it is regulated (and closely tracked) in societies like China, where housing and jobs are centrally administered. As you can see, migration is like diffusion in some respects. Overall, however, migration is much more complicated. Consider a few main examples of the difference. Migrants may be drawn (pulled) forward by opportunities that are lacking at home: that is, by a high ratio of wealth to competitors for wealth. Information is *not* drawn forward by ignorance (in other words, by a relative absence of good information). Migrants may push out other competitors. For example, unskilled workers tend to move away from areas where immigrant competition is high. Information is *not* driven forward by the arrival of competing information.

Diffusion doesn't have the same effect on social structure as migration, for several reasons. First, information doesn't make rational choices to maximize its well-being. Migrants do. That makes migrants more creative and persistent. Second, as noted, diffusion doesn't drive out old or draw in new information. Migrants, sometimes, drive out old residents and draw in new ones. Third, information doesn't reproduce itself; migrants and their descendants do. Fourth, migrants maintain ties and loyalties to their origins. Information does not. Diffusion and migration are similar, but the flows of people and of information have different effects on social structure. Typically, the effects of migration, and migrants, are much more profound. Migrants reproduce, take up space, consume resources and produce wealth; information does none of these things. (It is said that information produces wealth in an "information society." However, this occurs only through the medium of people.)

These are some of the themes we explore in the sections that follow.

Movers and Stayers

From the standpoint of flows, we want to know more about the kinds of people who move frequently or repeatedly, as opposed to the kinds of people who move infrequently. Research on this topic has suggested that there really are two different kinds of migrants: people who like to stay put for the most part, and people who are willing and able to pull up their roots and move whenever good opportunities beckon (see, for example, Finnie, 1999; Kalleberg and Maastekaassa, 2001; and Waldorf, 2009).

One approach to this question is to consider the differences between people who emigrate from a country compared to the people who remain behind. Research has shown that the answer is not simple. It has generally been thought that the people who emigrate are more talented or, at least, more dynamic than the people who remain behind. A study of thirty-two U.S. immigrant groups found that nearly all immigrants were more educated than those who remained in their home countries, but immigrants varied significantly in their degree of selectivity, depending on where they came from and when they came. As well, immigration rules in the receiving country varied over time, affecting the need for foreign-born labour. As a consequence, no simple generalization can be ventured. At the same time, this helps us understand why some immigrant groups do better than others in the receiving society, since some immigrants were selected more stringently (Feliciano, 2005).

Now, let's focus on the people who are already in a country and ask: "Who moves and who stays put?" As sociologists of flows, we might reasonably ask what difference it makes if our population is mainly composed of "movers" or "stayers." Are stayers better citizens than movers? Are movers more ambitious and economically productive than stayers? Would society be disrupted if a high proportion of stayers decided to become movers? Would this disrupt local institutions and existing social networks, in this way interfering with the normal flow of information, support, practices, culture, and influence?

In the course of our lives, most of us change places of residence and work on at least one occasion. So, *moving* is familiar to all of us. Yet there is a tradition in sociology that views moving, whether over a long distance or short, as a bad thing.

THE SOCIAL DISORGANIZATION APPROACH. One point of view on this—the *social* *disorganization approach*—began with Durkheim's research on suicide. It continued with the Chicago school of sociology's early twentieth-century studies of urban ecology and its relation to crime, mental illness, alcoholism, poor health, and other deviance. This approach holds that some people are less attached to their surroundings than others. Whether because of anomie, egoism, or defective socialization, they don't fit in, so they move away. Equally, some communities are less retentive than other communities. They command less loyalty, commitment, and involvement from their residents. For these reasons, residents leave with little provocation. Some families, for instance, leave a community because of crime, especially if they have children and they are affluent enough to afford the move.

These social disorganization theories focus on deficient attachment or retentiveness as explanations of why people move. Theorists in this tradition use the same arguments to explain why people leave communities as they do to explain why people leave jobs or marriages. In their view, leaving is bad and staying is good. Stayers—people who do not leave—are better adjusted, happier, and healthier. Moving shows not only a lack of commitment, but also a lack of satisfaction, acceptance, and adjustment. A low level of civic involvement increases turnover. Conversely, a high level of turnover reduces involvement, affecting voting and other communal participation. People whose links to the community are weak are likely to move. Among young people, weak and declining ties to parents, kin and the religious community, lack of socioeconomic opportunity, and strong educational prospects predict a declining preference for living near family and remaining in the local community. People on the periphery of social networks are more likely to leave—to "fall off the edges"—than people who are highly integrated. The same is true of jobs, marriages, and residential ties.

This theory has much to recommend it. However, it doesn't have much predictive power. For example, the nuclear accident in 1979 at Three Mile Island in Pennsylvania had little apparent effect on rates of out-migration of residents living within a five-mile radius. The same proportion of residents, two percent, moved out in the year following the accident as had done so in previous years. Of these, only 15% gave the accident as the main reason for their move. If anything was going to "shake loose" some residents, surely it would have been a nuclear accident. The fact it didn't suggests we need a different approach to understanding why people move (Goldhaber et al., 1983).

THE SUBCULTURAL APPROACH. The social disorganization approach to social relations predominated in sociology through the first half of the twentieth century. Eventually, sociologists replaced it with something we can call the *subcultural theory of migration*. Residential mobility, according to this theory, improves people's lives. Theorists of this school remind us that society fluctuates in accordance with economic and social changes. People are more rooted and less mobile in some periods than in others. If there is any trend at all in the last two centuries, it reflects either no increase or an actual decrease in residential mobility. Today, often it is the most privileged who move about. They do so by choice. People who stay behind are often the people with least choice. Often, they suffer the worst consequences.

This model understands moving not as evidence that something is wrong, but as evidence that something is right. Attachment and retentiveness are largely irrelevant. Movers, in this theory, are pulled forward by a positive image of the future. For example, elderly movers tend to be more optimistic about the future than elderly stayers. Similarly, rural people who value freedom, individualism, and equality are more likely than other rural people to move to the big city. The more flexibility, boldness, and human capital people possess, the more choices they can make and do make. Swedish immigrants to America, as one example, were encouraged in their decision to move by the claim that Swedish immigrants were hardier, more enterprising, and more self-reliant than those who remained at home.

In this model, moving is good—evidence of choice—and staying is bad. People who move are likely to be happier, healthier, and better adjusted. It is common and normal to want to change jobs, locations, or both. People who are not realizing their potential occupationally are especially likely to want to change. Also, the difficulties associated with change are not as great as some think. Even low-income urban blacks experience significant employment gains by moving to middle-class suburbs. The difficulties they encounter are less severe than people think. Incidents of harassment are minor and decrease with time.

People who stay put are likely to have negative experiences. For example, stayers in the Republic of Ireland feel grief due to their friends' departures. Those who stay admit comparing themselves unfavourably with friends who have emigrated. After such comparisons, they become more likely to emigrate themselves (Fanning, 2007). In workplaces, stayers' reactions to the departure of a coworker are based on comparisons of their own situation with that of their former colleague. Coworkers who quit for reasons that reflect negatively on the stayer's job leave the stayer feeling dissatisfied with that job.

Likewise, women in abusive relationships have a hard time coming to terms with their decision to stay (Zink et al., 2003). According to one study, a third remain with their abusive partner. To do so, they must restructure their view of the marriage to view it in a positive light. Those who do leave are faced with the difficult decision of where to go, and it would be a mistake to assume that "leaving" is synonymous with "moving." During the transition period of leaving, approximately equal numbers of women did not move, moved once, and moved multiple times. Lack of safe and affordable housing makes the decision to leave more difficult than it should be. Women who leave tend to start out in private-market housing, but transfer to socially funded housing or end up living with family and friends (Ponic et al., 2011). All in all, the act of leaving is easier said than done, and often complicated by the challenges presented by moving. While moving away is still the "good" option, it is not always a practical one.

To be able to "move on"—whether to leave a community, job, marriage, or religious cult—a person must be able to disavow the past, withdraw, and experience (if necessary) feelings of failure, disappointment, and guilt. But equally important, she must also be able to imagine a new future and begin to build toward it.

MOVERS VERSUS STAYERS. The social disorganization and subcultural models of migration differ in every particular. Indeed, they are opposites—with one exception. Both models contrast movers and stayers. Both, in their simplest formulations, view movers, whether moving in or out of a community, job, or marriage, as more similar to one another than they are to stayers.

If this is true, we can split the world into two groups: the "deep roots" and the "rolling stones." Different communities have different mixes of these two kinds of people. For example, one in four householders in Johnstown, Pennsylvania, has lived in the same house since at least 1959 (Cowgill, 1978). This is a town of deep roots. By contrast, college towns are noted for their mobile residents. Four householders of ten in Bryan-College Station, Texas, the home of Texas A&M University, have moved in the preceding fifteen months. This is a town of rolling stones.

This distinction implies there is something so fundamental about the flow of people in society that we can line up people (and communities) on opposite sides of a line. On the one side are people who, for various reasons, *do* flow. On the other are people who *do not*. Mover-stayer models of mobility assume that, for purposes of simplicity, the world breaks down into those two categories. In this simplified world, no mover fails to move, and no stayer fails to stay. Stayers aren't gradually persuaded to move. The basic assumption of this model is that mobility is the result of a single determining shock or trait, not of cumulative stresses or influences.

Those who do not leave most likely plan to age-in-place. There are advantages to such a scenario: mainly, a greater level of community involvement. Stayers tend to have greater knowledge of available home- and community-based services; additionally, staying incurs less cost and has a better psychosocial prognosis than living in a nursing home. Social-support networks must be formed, often strengthening bonds between family and friends, because the relationships are necessary to maintain a healthy lifestyle. Migration may also be a result of aging, moving closer to family members or caregivers, but it is not generally a radical departure from previous habits or ways of life. In other words: people may move houses, but generally do not change routines when aging-in-place (Tang, 2011).

Alternately, there are people who tend *not* to stay.

Putting everything together, we find that a small group of frequent movers dominates migration. For example, foreign-born people are more likely than average to be movers. Other things being equal, foreign-born people in Canada have higher in- and out-migration rates than Canadian-born people. The Canadians most likely to make job-related moves are young, well-educated people with few family responsibilities. Among American Jews, more education and white-collar employment are positively correlated with greater movement and moves of longer distance. In Russia, higher income families display distinctly more mobility. In developing countries like Turkey too, better-educated people are more likely to engage in repeat moves.

In the United States, people moving both in and out of the city resemble each other more closely than they resemble people who always lived in the city. In general, movers are more likely than stayers to be white and have a higher-than-average incomes and social status. Similar patterns are evident in relation to job-leaving. Compared with stayers, movers have a lower tenure in the organization (i.e., less time invested), more need for autonomy, and less aversion to risk. Movers are also more adaptable and more ready for change.

The meaning of migration, and its effects, depend in large part on whether a move is voluntary, planned, and resourced. Typically, migrations that are involuntary, unplanned, and unsuited to the migrant's resources have unhappy results. Migrations that are voluntary, planned, and "suitable" have happier ones.

HOW VOLUNTARY IS THE MOVE? We live in a culture that places enormous importance on free choice. In societies where people rarely if ever get to choose where they will live, what job they will do, or who they will marry, an absence of choice scarcely registers. In our society, even good things may fail to satisfy us if we ourselves do not choose them (Lu, 1998; Barcus, 2004). So, for example, a high-paying, interesting job working for one's father-in-law may appeal to many who are unaccustomed to choosing. Others may see the matter differently, preferring to make their own way and take their chances.

Consider the effects of gender and marital status on residential moving. In today's world, careers have become more transportable but families have become less so, causing new challenges to mobility. The increase in dual-career families, single-parent families, and worries about elderly parents create enormous strains for today's workers. It can no longer be assumed the mover for work is a male, the trailing spouse is a female, or the family of a relocating worker will even move at all. It is becoming more common for moves to be shelved indefinitely if both partners do not agree about the need to go. According to a British housing panel, moves are about 8% likely to proceed if only the man wishes to go, while around 20% are likely to happen if both partners want to go (Coulter, 2012).

Single women and single college graduates of both sexes receive positive returns from moving. Married women, on the other hand, suffer a large reduction in personal income. Their reduced employment rates reflect their usual status as "tied" movers. Because they often follow a spouse who is moving to take a better job, they are not freely choosing to migrate. In general, Canadian women who quit their own jobs for personal reasons (such as family migration) suffer poorer wage-gains than women who quit for non-personal (job-related) reasons. Likewise, men whose moves are constrained by familial situations—for example, separated men with children in the custody of their wives—are likely to experience reduced earnings.

Post-move employment and earnings vary for different types of movers. People who move to accept a position enjoy an immediate improvement in their job and earnings. Those who move to look for a job experience an initial decline. Over time, the incomes of voluntary job changers tend to improve, the incomes of involuntary changers change little in either direction, and the incomes of stayers tend to worsen. These results suggest that young employees must take an active attitude toward their career development. Equally, organizations must help their employees plan for job mobility.

TAKING THE INITIATIVE. Taking the initiative in moving is a good thing. For example, among people filing for divorce, spouses who see themselves to be the "leaver" are more positive in their attitude toward divorce than the mate who is "left." Leavers and left do not differ in how they view the attractions of the marriage or the number of barriers to divorce. However, leavers identify a greater number of attractive alternatives to the marriage. That is because, typically, leavers spend a considerable period of time imagining a new future, and creating the foundations for one, before they leave their past lives (Wallerstein and Kelly, 2008; Vaughan, 1983).

Just as most of us are used to making choices, we are also used to making and carrying out plans. These plans involve our most important and intimate choices: who to marry, what job to take, and where to live. Indeed, the choice of where to live is often tied up with who to marry and where to work. Mates and workplaces have physical locations. Often people have to move to be near them.

However, people do not make such choices once and for all. Adult locations depend heavily on employment and marital events. Our earlier plans matter little. For example, the migration expectations of adolescents are poor predictors of migration in the first fifteen years after adolescence. Part of the reason is that people have to take their partners' plans into account too. Contemporary couples are more likely to include two career-pursuing partners, each with their own educational and occupational priorities. As well, over the life cycle, housing interests and needs change. Young married couples often prefer to live downtown, close to work and entertainment; and gradually the process of gentrification makes this possible for ever-larger numbers who can afford to pay. However, couples with young children want more space than they can afford downtown, so they trade off proximity to work and entertainment. In this way, they get more living space per dollar. By the time they retire from work thirty-five years later, the children will have left home. Older now, they will want a new kind of housing, and often a new location: something that facilitates leisure recreation. With age-related infirmities, their needs may change again. Thus, the life cycle normally moves people through a changing variety of locational wishes. Many people plan and save for these moves; they expect and await them, often with great anticipation.

EFFECT OF THE LIFE CYCLE. One in six Americans changes residence in a given year, though most of these are short moves and about 60% of movers remain in the same county (Clark and Onaka, 1983; Cuba and Hummon, 1993). Young adults make up the largest segment of the moving population. One-third of people in their twenties change their address every year, compared to less than one-tenth of people aged 45 and older. After age 30, the likelihood that a person will move declines steadily. In all economically developed societies, residential mobility is significantly related to the progression of the life cycle, and also influenced by the availability of jobs for young people (on this see McDaniel and Gazso, 2013; Mitchell, 2006).

Almost everyone leaves his or her parental home sooner or later: this move is part of declaring adulthood. However, people vary in the ages at which they leave home. The age at which men and women leave the parental home fell from the late eighteenth century to the twentieth century, with women leaving home earlier than men before the twentieth century. In the late eighteenth and early nineteenth centuries, it was common for the first move from the parental home to occur with a spouse and children, after a period of co-residence with parents. Men were most likely to leave home for employment, and women for marriage. Historically, women have often experienced residential relocation corresponding to key stages in their life cycles. These include marriage, birth of a first child, launching a professional career, and confrontation of professional risk or professional mobility in the years immediately following the completion of their studies.

Today, the most common nest-leaving pattern has changed from leaving one's home in order to marry and have children, to leaving home while still single and remaining single for the next four or so years. People increasingly opt for flexibility. Younger and better-educated people are less likely to marry, will have fewer children, and will migrate more. They are also increasingly likely to move home again, in the face of a relationship break-up or protracted unemployment. Major "demographic" events in people's lives—for example, loss of a partner through separation, divorce, or widowhood—often have unexpected effects on housing location. Marriages and births, though planned for, are sometimes unexpected and also have effects on location. The appearance and disappearance of job opportunities, likewise, may have unplanned effects on location. Some want to move, but cannot. Others want to stay, but cannot.

THE EFFECT OF RESOURCES. In most countries, movers are typically young people. Housing affordability is the chief concern for young movers who are often shifting from parental homes to rental housing, then from rental housing to home ownership. The outcome of a move, no matter how freely chosen and planned for, will also depend on the resources the mover brings along. Said simply, people with more money, social capital (e.g., connections), human capital (e.g., education), and cultural capital (e.g., literacy and social skills) will do better after a move than people with fewer of these resources. These are the resources that make people's dreams come true.

Among movers, the possession of resources for controlling and coping with the social environment is associated with the attainment of locational preferences. For example, rural-urban movement between Paris and its suburbs is socially differentiated, with low-income classes increasingly obliged to move out to the distant suburbs, or even beyond. Movers within the major cities are found to have higher incomes and occupational status deriving from resources such as education.

Occupationally, people who begin with an advantage end up with a higher income. An external advantage, like educational credentials, raises income in moves between employers. An internal advantage, like social connectedness, raises incomes for those who stay with a single employer. The difference between stayers' and movers' incomes is greatest for people in positions with only an internal advantage; here, stayers will do best. However, where movement is possible, people with external advantages show higher levels of income and income growth over a career than those with only internal advantage.

MOVES OLDER PEOPLE MAKE. The migrations of older people illustrate many of these points. Elders with longer lengths of residence, who own their home, and who utilize more community support are less likely to relocate. Thus, retirees that move do so largely with the aim of lowering their cost of living (Choi, 1996; Chen and Wilmoth, 2004).

More than 60% of movers give their own poor health, their spouse's poor health or death, and/or desire for close kinship as reasons for moving, and 25% cite money problems. Elders with greater numbers of adult children elsewhere are more likely to relocate. Similarly, migration to retirement communities is more likely among elderly people who live alone and among those whose children do not live nearby. Blacks and women are more likely to cite a desire for close kinship than are whites and men.

Some think that moving late in life contributes to health deterioration in a small but significant degree. Others find that residential relocation, with the exception of forced, permanent relocation due to urban renewal projects, is not associated with increased mortality or morbidity. Movement to a retirement community is typically correlated with health deterioration, and the likelihood of migrating increases as disability advances to moderate levels, but declines as disability becomes severe. Some find that health service consumption is higher for movers than for non-movers. Others find that not only do movers seek more care more quickly than others, they are more likely to be characterized by health vulnerabilities.

In America, increasing disability was positively related to mobility among the elderly in only one out of six moves and a variety of other factors including affiliation, economic security, comfort, and functional independence were found to influence mobility. In Canada, however, moves by elderly people seeking social support due to declining health constitute about one-third of all moves among the elderly. Regions with slower economic growth have higher proportions of in-movers who are support movers. This is consistent with the general view that the dynamics of aging result in greater service demands in more disadvantaged areas.

The top destination states in the U.S. are western and southern states, the so-called "Sunbelt" (Hazelrigg and Hardy, 1995; Hogan and Steinnes, 1993). For example, in Arizona, a quintessential Sunbelt state, life-cycle transitions associated with retirement from the labour force are highly correlated with residential mobility. The incomes of interstate migrants are higher than for intrastate migrants. Much of the economic segregation of the elderly population appears to be caused by the movement of people between states. However, intergenerational conflicts may arise as the affluent elderly retire to communities calling for increased spending on public education.

Many elderly movers become part of their children's households, with women movers outnumbering men, and the majority of movers being widowed. The greatest amount of movement takes place in the first year of widowhood, preceded by a gradual increase in the probability of moving and followed by a gradual decline in that probability. When elderly people do join a child's household, there are as many long-distance moves as short-distance moves. Those elderly moving in with a child are much more likely to report having a confining long-term illness than are migrants moving into other kinds of households, including siblings' households.

The process of moving seems to satisfy elderly movers, at least in part because retirement is now, for many people, an increasingly planned phase of the life course. Retired movers in the western U.S. move from another western state, after having visited their new community at least five times before moving. In addition, the movers appear to be more optimistic about the future than stayers. Non-movers often appear apprehensive about the future, but many movers see positive outcomes, in terms of life satisfaction, resulting from their migration. At the same time, many of the elderly movers felt they had to move because of inadequate services where they had previously lived.

THE CONSEQUENCES FOR COMMUNITIES. Such migration can have noticeable consequences for both communities that lose members and for those that gain them. Communities can be distinguished in a variety of ways. Some are large, others small. Some are growing rapidly, some are not. Some are homogeneous, in terms of ethnicity, race, religion, and social class; others are heterogeneous.

People may have much the same experience of life in one community as in another, though the two are separated by thousands of kilometres. For example, suburbs in the United States that are popular with white movers have the following characteristics, compared with core city districts: a small population size, low density, newer housing, a small percentage of minority residents, a higher percentage of traditional family homes, and a higher percentage of owner-occupied homes. This is true regardless of where in the U.S. the community is located.

Likewise, migrants vary in many ways. Some are voluntary, others not. Some are potential long-term stayers, others not. These factors, and the migrants' stage in the life cycle, affect their degree and kind of participation in the community into which they move.

It is difficult to make a blanket rule about the effects of all migrants on all communities, but a few generalizations are in order. To the extent that people plan and choose locations on the basis of a good understanding of the lifestyles available there, migration tends to produce subcultural homogeneity within communities. Thus, increases in migration create greater similarity between residents of any given community, but increased *differences* between communities. The result is the creation of a small number of "types" of community, differentiated by education, income, density, and one or two other variables. People form psychological bonds with types of settlements that help retain continuity with places across changes of residence.

The resulting geographic or locational variation in lifestyles shows up in marketing research (Sheth et al, 2000; Kotler, 1989). Increasingly, people with goods and services to sell can find particular locations where the demand for their products is likely to be greatest. This kind of marketing has been revolutionized by a data-analysis technique called PRIZM, which, in the United States, attaches social, economic, and demographic information to each of the country's 36,000 zip codes. Using this information, marketers can find out where the largest fractions of people viewing a particular television show, eating fat-free Greek yogurt, or buying late-model used cars happen to live. In turn, companies can focus advertising, product trials, or merchandising efforts on the regions or neighbourhoods where the payoff is likely highest (Goss, 1995).

Empirical research for more than two decades has shown that national or regional differences may be less important than you would think: people living in one neighbourhood often have nothing in common in terms of values and lifestyles with people living in another neighbourhood only a few miles away, yet they may share a great deal with people living in a similar neighbourhood located a thousand miles away. As Jonathan Robbins, the founder of Claritas, the company that originally developed the system, summed things up: "You can go to sleep in Fairfield, Connecticut, and wake up in Pasadena, California, but except for the palm trees, you're in the same place."

Consider the neighbourhood type the PRIZM system labels "Two More Rungs." People who live in Two More Rungs neighbourhoods—about seven of every thousand Americans—hold particular values and live in particular ways. They frequently travel to their ancestral homelands in Europe, but they tend to take discounted chartered plane trips or cruises. At home, Two More Rungs residents read *Scientific American* and *The Atlantic* twice as often as the general populace, and they would rather host a family dinner than a cocktail party. In this tradition-bound neighbourhood type, status is still a son who grows up to be a doctor, lawyer, or college professor—junior-high teachers don't cut it.

The inhabitants of Two More Rungs and everyone else who can afford to choose where they live seek neighbours who are most like themselves. People with similar educational or ethnic backgrounds, who are at similar stages in the life cycle, and have much the same amount of money to spend have similar conceptions of the "good life" and abilities to attain that kind of life. They gather together in neighbourhoods and spend their money in similar ways. That is why they are leading similar lives.

Migration trends in the Netherlands reveal another example of increasing homogeneity. If we look specifically at ethnicity, both of individuals and of neighbourhoods collectively, the trends are apparent. While ethnicity is not overly important at the individual level, it makes a far greater impact at the community level. Ethnic minorities are more likely than native Dutch to move within the same neighbourhood rather than leave, when people from the same region were compared. Additionally, native Dutch are more likely to move away from neighbourhoods as the proportion of non-native people increases. Said differently, ethnic stratification is taking place in the Netherlands, as people are moving into areas where they are (or are becoming) the majority, and fleeing those where they are not (Schaake et al., 2010).

In the case of people with *less* income and *less* choice, neighbours resemble one another, whether they are rural sharecroppers or city people on public assistance, because they suffer similar disabilities of the kind we discussed earlier. Socially and economically, they are all disabled, excluded, and decoupled from power. Race and urban-versus-rural residence play a large part in shaping lifestyles among the poor. Ideas about the good life play little part, since they cannot act on these ideas.

Some communities have a high turnover of population—a high proportion of movers—but others have low turnover and a high proportion of stayers. Communities with a high proportion of movers are likely to be different in other ways as well. Other things being equal, mover communities like Toronto and Vancouver tend to be large, growing, and heterogeneous. By contrast, stayer communities like Quebec City and St. John's, Newfoundland, tend to be small, unchanging in size (or shrinking), and homogeneous. The province of Quebec has experienced an overall loss of population and must rely on return migration as a source of population growth.

One of the more dramatic changes in twentieth-century North America has been the often-rapid transformation of small, staid, stayer communities (like Toronto and Vancouver) into mover communities. This process carries several consequences for the organization of the city and the people who live in it. Movers flow through life, changing many facets of their lives including their community, job, or marriage. Stayers, on the other hand, help to preserve the traditions and history of a place, and get more deeply involved in that place they plan to continue calling home. Globalization and greater population transience are changing the way people view their lives, and making the flow of people around the world ever more commonplace.

Traffic

There is no form of migration more characteristic of modern urban societies than traffic flow. By *traffic flow*, we normally mean the routine, repeated movement of people around a metropolitan area in an average day, week, or year. People's journeys—to work, to school, to shops, and back home—are typically repeated many times in a given year, so that individual people have customary patterns of daily and weekly movement. They tend to go to the same places over and over, and they tend to follow the same routes. Vast numbers of people leave home in the suburbs every morning, go to work or school downtown, then return home in the late afternoon. The consequence of such routine migration is the well-known traffic jam, which hundreds of millions of city dwellers experience every weekday.

Because of the sheer volume of traffic and its congested patterning, traffic is a unique type of migration. No other kind of migration displays the same emotional intensity, except possibly the flight of refugees from a war zone. One might usefully think of daily commuters as daily refugees, lacking only the gunfire.

One other important element characterizes traffic and differentiates it from other kinds of migration and even from the flight of refugees. That is the role of expensive, dangerous technology. No other type of migration is so reliant on motorized vehicles, especially personally owned and maintained vehicles; nor so reliant on the upkeep of roadways and other channels of motorized flow. The costs of such technology and infrastructure upkeep are staggering, and so are the dangers of accidents and injuries. It is safe to guess that, with the possible exception of refugees in wartime, no other migrants put their lives more at risk in flowing from place A to place B than do daily commuters. So, when we discuss traffic, we are talking about the massive daily movement of huge numbers of concentrated people in dangerous circumstances, through the use of risky technology.

The origins of the word *traffic* are obscure. Today, we use the word in two senses, to mean the large-scale movement of people and vehicles, and secondarily, the large-scale movement of goods (as in "drug trafficking"). In both cases, we mean the flow of people and things, not information.

Traffic as a movement-of-people-in-cars is the most common form of people-flow today, and an especially concentrated and intense one. For this reason, the problems we normally associate with traffic—injury, death, environmental destruction (congestion, noise, pollution), and the enormous expense of road and vehicle upkeep—are more extreme than the problems associated with other flows of people. No wonder every society, ours included, strictly regulates traffic. Other forms of people-flow carry less extreme risks and costs, and require less regulation. In this section we discuss traffic as a flow problem for social systems. We end by considering some of the risks and costs of traffic, and the efforts made to regulate them.

The movement of people in traffic, like other movements of people, aims first and foremost at maximizing the satisfaction of movers, especially drivers. Each one is self-interested, even selfish. Yet his or her movements must be accomplished in the presence of other drivers, which means there is a problem of social organization. Traffic planners must figure out how the largest number of people can get where they are going safely in the shortest period of time. The answer, as we shall see, does not emerge automatically out of unstructured interactions. A roadway is not like the stock market, in which prices emerge through interaction. Motorists cannot negotiate the rules of traffic as they go. Rules and rule-enforcers must be there in advance. Add to this complexity the fact that some people are inclined to drive in a disordered and disorderly manner, precisely because doing so is unconventional and dangerous.

The study of traffic also introduces us to other themes relevant to migration. Like migration, traffic raises issues of congestion and crowding, queuing and waiting, parallel and competing routes of flow, communities of origin and destination. Traffic is a more concentrated and rapid flow of people than migration. As a result, planning, regulation, and accidents are more visible and more pressing where traffic is concerned.

TRAFFIC AS A SOCIAL PROCESS. Research on traffic flow has been going on for more than half-a-century in both government and industry (see for example, May, 1990; Gerlough and Huber, 1976; Haight, 1965). This research centres on mathematical models for the timing of traffic lights based on a hydrodynamic model, which views the flow of traffic as a liquid. Experiments can be conducted with sensors implanted in the pavement of main arteries providing data about the state of the "fluid." A schematic chart posted in central control rooms allows the visualization of the entire traffic pattern and its regulation through traffic lights. In future, new technology will improve the visualization of the overall picture, as well as that of particular intersections.

As is well known, people commonly break traffic rules, interfering with the smooth flow of idealized traffic. The propensity to traffic deviance, like other traits, is distributed across the population. Speeding, even extreme speeding, is a typical behaviour; the numbers of speeders and their speeds are highly predictable, when computed on a sample of millions of drivers.

Some traffic flows are relatively self-regulating. Consider pedestrian traffic. A simulation model for the dynamic behaviour of pedestrian crowds has been developed based on the following assumptions for individual pedestrian movement: each pedestrian wants to walk with a certain desired speed in the direction of his or her destination. A deviation from the desired velocity (for example, an obstacle) causes the individual to accelerate. Each pedestrian keeps some distance from borders (for example, walls) and tries to avoid other pedestrians who are in the way. If that isn't possible, the pedestrian decelerates or stops (Lovas, 1994).

These assumptions can be mathematically modelled; the simulations yield realistic results that can be compared with videos of pedestrian crowds. They show the self-organization of spatial and temporal patterns, such as the development of lanes (groups) of pedestrians walking in the same direction, oscillatory changes in the walking direction in narrow passages, and a spontaneous formation of roundabout traffic at crossings. The model can be applied to the optimization of pedestrian flow in buildings, subway stations, and other locations (Helbing, 2001).

Automobile traffic moves too quickly, however, to permit such self-organization. The ability of drivers to communicate with one another, and to adjust their behaviour based on these communications, is severely limited. To understand traffic fully, we have to understand it as a regulated social system. Sociologist Arthur Stinchcombe (1975) adopted this approach, applying Parsonian social theory to traffic accidents. He proposed that a highway system's integration will improve and accident rates decrease to the degree the paths of traffic ensure "monopoly" (used only for vehicular movement), "continuity" (little stopping, starting, slowing down, or speeding up), and "efficient switching" (capacity to get on, off, or out of the path of the system). Vehicles must be designed to maximize driver control and communication with other drivers and to minimize sudden decelerations of the human body. Inefficient vehicles must be relegated to rural roads, out of the main traffic paths. The accident rate will be decreased by (1) unambiguous signals, (2) attention-getting signals, (3) a higher proportion of violations coming to the attention of the police, (4) more severe traffic penalties, and (5) arranging that individual rights and duties are not seriously curtailed by others' rights and duties. The integration of the highway system will be increased and accidents decreased if drivers have better training, if those physically handicapped for driving are prevented from it, if drinking and narcotized people are restricted from the roads, and if reckless or accident-prone drivers are reformed.

Among the factors that influence the number of fatalities on highways are speed, speed differences, and traffic composition. From the standpoint of individual drivers, congestion and accidents are unintended and unanticipated consequences of road use. There is a parabolic relationship between density and fatal accidents on highways. When densities increase, we first have a positive relationship due to the increase in the numbers of cars in the system (more cars equals more accidents). However, when density becomes so high that speeds are reduced, the number of accidents actually decreases. Thus, traffic congestion has a negative impact (i.e., time lost) but also a positive impact (i.e., reduced fatalities). In the end, congestion has little or no impact on the frequency of highway accidents (Wang et al., 2009; Downs, 2005), compared to other factors like alcohol or poor weather conditions.

The better the information that road users receive, the more efficiently they can use the transport network. Computer models now being developed may allow planners to manage traffic in a way that shortens journey times and increases the effective capacity of a road. Even a small change in the number of cars entering an expressway can disrupt the flow of traffic for hours. The models being developed are intended to regulate such flows.

Our tendency to blame drivers for accidents and injuries, rather than examine problems with the system as a whole, reflects the dominance of market ideology in North American political culture. Auto-centred systems have created a material and social infrastructure with major social impacts: high energy consumption, traffic congestion, and environmental degradation. Political processes, especially blaming individuals rather than analyzing overall systemic faults, can stand in the way of creating more effective traffic management systems.

Driving behaviour emulates other social behaviour. Thus, the car, a technical object, becomes a social and cultural object. Its widespread use has led to a restructuring of the social organization of work and leisure. Socialization, social distinction, and individualization also became associated with individual mobility as cars are equated with lifestyles. More expensive, powerful cars tend to appropriate the high-speed lanes and to respond aggressively to lane blockages. Motorists interact with one another in traffic on the basis of vehicle appearance, driving style (e.g., aggressiveness), prestige or age of vehicle, and appearance of the motorist, if he or she is visible.

Adolescents everywhere are reckless, but American adolescents are more reckless than many (Arnett et al., 1994; 1997). For example, they are more likely to drive too quickly, drive drunk, and engage in unprotected sex than Danish adolescents, due to more individualistic (or less socially responsible) socialization. We will return to this idea below.

Social behaviour in traffic is like other social behaviour: it partakes of the culture within which it is located. Road traffic is a communicative system based on verbal and nonverbal signs. Traffic participants are not only traffic-sign recipients but also producers of "traffic semiotics." Drivers use signs (e.g., the all-too-familiar "giving someone the finger") to express their anger and displeasure with fellow drivers. In Germany, there is a penalty for offensive behaviour in road traffic and fines vary for different nonverbal insults.

Traffic can also be considered part of a broader social context because it has consequences that reach father than the sphere of transportation. Traffic has an effect on the health and well-being of urban populations. An increase in perceived traffic stress, for example, leads to lower overall well-being and higher rates of depression. In addition to obvious worries such as unintentional injuries, pollution, and "road rage," indirect side effects must be considered. Displacement of city residents for highway construction forces people to move homes, and often contributes to racial segregation. Traffic noise, and limited access to medical care in heavy traffic, have an especially adverse effect on the elderly population, while safety concerns around children walking to school along heavily travelled streets negatively impact the exercise levels of many youths. Regardless of age group, there is a correlation between health and stress related to traffic and transportation issues (Gee, 2004). Such concerns demand attention on the part of both affected citizens and government.

Bad though traffic is in North America and western Europe, it is worse elsewhere. The low level of traffic regulation and consequent overreliance on drivers' self-regulation in many less-developed countries leads to epidemics of auto deaths (Soderlund and Zwi, 1995; Hazen and Ehiri, 2006). In many cities in the developing world—for example, Cairo—traffic is chaotic and not nearly as well organized as in European and American cities. Comparisons of Seattle, Washington, and Hyderabad, India, show that traffic moves in the most orderly fashion where, as in Seattle, public space is controlled and the number of transactions between drivers is reduced. Traffic-control infrastructure (e.g., stop lights, speed bumps, one-way streets, and roundabouts) and law-enforcers mediate the social order in traffic. Nothing suggests that social order evolves automatically out of driver transactions as the complexity of the arena increases. In other words, traffic isn't a problem that solves itself.

Whether in developed or developing nations, cities in general promote high-speed lifestyles that favour the car over the pedestrian. The view of cars as being essential causes people to take road accidents for granted; they are too common to draw much attention, unless especially horrific. Safety regulations are hugely important in making sure things don't get even worse than they are already. The number of accidents is declining in developed countries, yet rising in developing countries. The discrepancy can be explained by the rapid rise in automobile traffic without corresponding safety improvements. Pedestrians are particularly vulnerable as their infrastructure often takes a back seat if not previously established, another factor helping to explain why 90% of traffic fatalities occur in developing countries (Short, 2010). Globally, it is crucial that regulations and infrastructure catch up to the current situation on the streets.

Consider two developments that impact driving: mobile phones and teleworking. In-car use of mobile phones increases the risk of a collision by between four and sixteen times. Analysis of 699 drivers in Toronto who were involved in motor vehicle collisions that resulted in substantial property damage but no personal injury found that 24% had used a cellular telephone during the ten-minute period before the collision. Age and driving experience were not significantly associated with relative risk (Redelmeier and Tibshirani, 1997).

On the other hand, teleworking, or working from home while connected to the office by advanced digital technologies, reduces the number of accidents, by decreasing the amount of commuter travel and introducing flexibility into the timing of traffic flow. Telecommunications can never entirely take the place of physical transportation and face-to-face urban life. Therefore, we cannot rely on a simple substitution of new communication methods to reduce transportation and eradicate traffic congestion and pollution. The answer will have to come from somewhere else.

ACCIDENTS AND YOUNG PEOPLE. Sociologists have learned that accidents rarely happen by chance and, at least in the aggregate, accidents are highly predictable. Some kinds of situations and some kinds of people are most likely to "produce" accidents (on this, see Tepperman and Meredith, 2015). This is as true of automobile accidents as it is of nuclear accidents. People at a high risk of automobile accidents have a particular demographic profile, drinking profile, and personality profile.

Young men, of all drivers, are at the highest risk of automobile accidents. As a result, automobile accidents are, along with homicides and suicides, among the most common cause of death for young men. Compared to old men, young men have less driving experience, are more likely to drive at night, and are more likely to drive while intoxicated or drive with someone else who is intoxicated. Young drivers (especially men) are more likely to take risks on the road, and they are more often preoccupied with talking or music while driving. These aspects of youth subculture partly explain the accident-proneness of young drivers.

In addition, young people are among the "socially marginal" who tend to have an excess of driving accidents. Other socially marginal people include divorced and separated men, who are also at an above-average risk of death from traffic accidents. Single, divorced, and separated men are more likely than married men to be convicted of driving while intoxicated. In part, the risk of arrests and accidents is high because these men are more likely to drink outside the home. Men, especially divorced and separated men, people with prior criminal records, and intoxicated people are especially likely to cause fatal traffic accidents. These are the same kinds of people who are commonly found guilty of crimes of violence. This and other evidence suggests that traffic accidents are symptomatic of antisocial tendencies.

Unlike young people, old people rarely cause accidents and fatalities (for example, see Massie et al., 1995). Partly, that's because they are less inclined to take risks, or to be influenced by the behaviour of passengers or other drivers. Mainly, though, it's because they drive less than young and middle-aged people (Ryan et al., 1998). As drivers get older, they gradually forsake driving in difficult conditions, especially at night, in winter, on difficult roads, in heavy traffic, and in inclement weather. Particularly careful elderly drivers, with accident-free driving records over the previous three years, drive even less than elderly people with poorer driving records. And elderly women are even more cautious drivers than elderly men.

Not only are old people more cautious drivers. They are also more cautious pedestrians than younger people, checking for oncoming traffic before crossing at signal-controlled intersections on a downtown street.

ACCIDENTS AND DRINKING. Texting is a new and dangerous form of behavior when combined with driving. Even worse than texting-and-driving is drinking-and-driving. Alcohol and drugs are the cause of a vast number of traffic accidents, fatalities, and associated property damage (Zador et al., 2000).

Young people are the riskiest drinkers, in general. Young, single people who drink frequently are more likely to drink and drive than older, married people. In a study of students in grades 10 through 12, 13% admitted to personally driving under the influence ("DUI") of alcohol, and 31% reported having driven in the last month with someone who was DUI. Among young drivers (aged 18 to 25), even a modest .05% blood alcohol level has a significant effect on perceptions of risk. Intoxicated young drivers are likely to misjudge driving hazards and are the slowest to respond to them, even when sober. Young drivers are also more likely than older ones to run into drinking-related problems, including alcohol dependence, drunk driving, and problems at work (Hingson et al., 2002).

Among students in grades 10 to 12, men are more likely than women to drink underage, drive after drinking, and ride with drunk drivers (Williams et al., 1986; Escobedo et al., 1995; Eaton et al., 2002). Teens give men more approval than women for driving after drinking, though DUI is considered less acceptable than getting drunk at a party. This gender differentiation continues throughout adulthood. Men are more tolerant than women of drinking in bars and drinking (but not drunkenness) before driving, though the trend is toward reduced acceptance and gender equalization.

Binge-drinking drivers are at especially high risk of traffic fatalities (Wechsler et al., 1998). These men drink more often, consume more per drinking episode, and are more likely to think they can drive safely after binge drinking. They are less likely to make plans to avoid drinking-driving and more likely to have been in an alcohol-related accident. They also report deviant drinking and drinking-driving behaviour, and possess casual attitudes towards drinking-driving.

ACCIDENTS AND RISK-TAKING. Identified personality and demographic characteristics account for a large part of the connection between drinking and driving. Thus, drunk driving is part of a broader lifestyle that includes problem-driving behaviour, psychosocial unconventionality, risk-taking, hostility and aggression, sensation-seeking, and non-religiosity. Consider the issue as a health problem: high school boys who drive while drinking are also more likely to smoke cigarettes and marijuana, carry a knife, fight, and engage in sexual intercourse. They are less likely to eat nutritious foods, wear a seat belt, get enough sleep, and brush after every meal. Among high school students, a tendency towards risky driving is related not only to drinking but also to other types of sensation seeking: smoking, a variety of sexual activities, and an avoidance of homework. High school students who drive dangerously spend a lot of time "hanging out" in unstructured social activities and engaging in criminal behaviour, heavy drinking, and drug use. Boys in our society are socialized to engage in more externalized risky behaviours than girls; these behaviours include excessive alcohol consumption and dangerous driving (Donovan, 1993; Turrisi et al., 2000; Hemenway and Solnick, 1993).

Youth who participate in these kinds of multiple health-risk behaviours—all of the above, plus violence, casual and unprotected sex with multiple partners, and unintended pregnancy—are characterized by a rejection of social norms, danger seeking, impulsivity, a low threshold for anger and tension, and little capacity to relate to others. Bad driving is related not only to unhealthy behaviour but also to deviant and criminal behaviour. There is a strong positive relationship between traffic offences and a history of criminal aggression, and there is believed to be a common factor underlying both risky driving and criminal behaviour, stemming from a general disregard for long-term consequences and an affinity for risk-taking and impulsiveness. In this way, specific situations, such as those caused by irresponsible drivers, can be explained by general traits and behaviours. It should be noted that the correlation between risky behaviour and crime is weaker among young people. Whether this is because young people are more inclined to be stupid on the road yet not break the law, or because they have not had the time to build up a criminal record, is unclear (Junger et al., 2001).

Even among tenth graders, auto thieves and traffic offenders are likely to be involved in other delinquent activities as well. Post-secondary students who, by their own report, have parked illegally in handicapped parking spaces are more likely to be male, and to report smoking, drinking frequently, and driving after drinking.

Between age 18 and 25, there is a gradual decline in risky driving, as a result of the entry into conventional adult social roles and increased psychosocial and behavioural conventionality. As young people assume conventional adult social roles and learn to conform to them, their risky driving behaviours virtually disappear.

PROBLEMS RESULTING FROM TRAFFIC. The Atlanta-based Centers for Disease Control (CDC) report that "every day, almost thirty people in the United States die in motor vehicle crashes that involve an alcohol-impaired driver. This amounts to one death every forty-eight minutes. The annual cost of alcohol-related crashes totals more than $51 billion." In Third World countries the numbers are more dramatic still. In Nigeria, traffic accidents constitute the leading cause of death among Nigerian adults aged 30 to 40. Traffic accidents are the major cause of death in Ireland. In North America, pedestrian injuries are a leading cause of childhood mortality (Odero et al., 1997; Sharma et al., 2001). In fact, traffic accidents are a far greater but far less publicized cause of injury and death than many other preventable (dietary and lifestyle-related) causes of death (Danaei, 2009).

Other factors besides the ones we have discussed affect traffic accident rates. They include a population's demographic (age) structure and density. Many accidents are caused by our increased dependence on autos and the hegemony of the automobile over social space. Under conditions of dense auto traffic, accidents are bound to occur. Further, as long as there is poverty, there will be poor people driving vehicles in poor repair. Finally, the popularity of larger, heavier vehicles—SUVs and other light trucks—seems likely to increase dangers for people who are struck by these vehicles.

Congestion is yet another traffic problem (on dangers to quality of life generally, see Garling and Steg, 2007; Dratva et al., 2010). More and more people commute to work over considerable distances. The cost of traffic congestion, including lost time, wasted fuel, and higher insurance rates, is significant and mounting fast. Related to the growth of congestion is the increase in air pollution, noise, and lack of green space in and around cities. Highways today carry more and heavier trucks than they were originally designed to accommodate. One fully weighted 18-wheel tractor-trailer has an impact on a highway comparable to that of 10,000 cars. Such a dramatic increase in heavy traffic results in faster road deterioration, at greater cost to taxpayers.

Finally, traffic interferes with people's enjoyment of their neighbourhoods. It complicates crossing the street, visiting neighbours, and walking outdoors, and minimizes desire to settle in an area. In short, traffic has a negative effect on neighbourhood cohesion and community integration. The growth of street traffic increases fearfulness among people who are less socially integrated, by increasing the proportion of strangers as opposed to acquaintances on the street. By contrast, residential street closing or similar traffic modifications designed to reduce vehicular traffic also reduce the rate of growth in crime, and reduce the fear of crime even more.

These effects are especially obvious in areas that are heavily travelled by tourists. Tourism-related traffic congestion, noise and pollution are evident even in the rural communities of Ohio where people come to see the old-fashioned Amish. There, automobile traffic increasing at a rate of 13% per year since 1993 has led to a five-fold increase in the cost of farmland and a growing economic dependency on tourism. Resulting changes in ecology and environment due to tourism, including deforestation in and around cities, construction of concrete structures, traffic congestion, scarce housing, inadequate supplies of safe drinking water and health services, and garbage and waste disposal problems, represent the very opposite of those qualities that attracted tourists in the first place (Hovinen, 1995).

SOLUTIONS TO TRAFFIC-RELATED PROBLEMS. Since the problems caused by traffic are many and varied, so are the proposed solutions.

Behavioural change, rather than technology, holds the greatest promise of reducing auto crashes. People use a variety of ways to regulate their own drunk driving, including limiting how much they drink, arranging rides, using taxis, and delaying or avoiding driving. People who limit their consumption of alcohol are less likely to drive drunk than those who use other self-regulatory techniques.

Informal deterrence through peer intervention has been developed as an alternative in lowering DUI rates (Collins and Frey, 1992). Increasingly, people intervene to prevent others from driving while intoxicated. An estimated one-third to one-half of all the people faced with a potential drunk-driving situation will intervene. Techniques used include threatening to drive, taking the keys, and driving the person home. Most of these interventions are successful. Decisions to intervene are motivated mainly by concern for the immediate physical well-being of the drinking driver, and secondarily for the physical well-being of others, as well as by friendship with the drinking driver. Willingness to accept help is influenced by the quality of relationship between the intervenee and intervenor, and some characteristics of the situation (for example, whether in public or private) in which the offer is made.

Educational programs to reduce alcohol and marijuana use, and thus improve driving behaviours, report good immediate success but no effects after one year. This may be because the problem-driving behaviours are part of a larger pattern that is untouched by the educational intervention. Some report that reducing the amount of youthful driving, by raising the minimum legal driving age and imposing curfews on young people—or, alternatively, raising the minimum legal *drinking* age—significantly reduces traffic fatalities. Others report that doing so merely shifts fatal crashes from a lower to a higher age group, without any substantial reduction overall.

Risky, accident-prone drivers are different from other kinds of drivers, demographically and psychologically, so they may be affected differently by measures designed to limit drinking and driving. Alcoholics will not be deterred by anything that does not deal directly with their drinking problem. High-risk drivers will not be deterred by anything that does not deal directly with their psychological immaturity.

Law enforcement plays an important part in reducing the harm associated with traffic. Increased policing is key to increasing arrests for drunk driving. Many think that more certain and severe penalties will reduce drunk driving. For example, a long-term decline in fatalities followed the implementation of New York laws that increased the minimum drinking age (1981) and made seatbelt use mandatory (1985). Others put their faith in health-warning labels on alcoholic beverage containers, though there is little evidence yet that they change behaviour. Little success has been reported, as yet, in efforts to reduce traffic accidents by making public drink-servers responsible for the drunkenness of their patrons, though significant decline in injurious traffic crashes followed the filing of two major liability suits against servers in 1983 and 1984 (Wagenaar and Toomey, 2002; Whetten-Goldstein et al., 2000).

A change in public attitudes is important, too. For example, though a majority support mandatory seatbelt use, many continue to flout the law and will ignore any law forcing them to comply. Public service announcements create awareness about the dangers of drunk driving, often using celebrities to hammer home the message.

The development of environment- and urban-friendly transportation systems depends on institutionalized public behavior: on making people more willing to leave their cars at home and use public transit. People disagree about how to do this. Some favour imposing tolls on roads, to make drivers pay more directly and fully for the cost of road upkeep and environmental damage, lost productivity, health problems, and wasted fuel. Others propose an increase in fuel taxes, a suspension of road-building, and an increased investment in public transport.

Many of those resigned to continued high levels of car traffic put their faith in online traffic control through reprogramming traffic lights and other control devices (Mackett and Edwards, 1998). Such systems use digital technology both in vehicles and at the sides of the road to improve traffic flow and safety. Dallas's centralized system, for example, uses 4,000 detectors and twenty-seven operator-stations to manage its traffic flow. Smart highways reduce delays, enhance speed and safety, and streamline response to accidents and emergencies. Dallas decision-makers have judged that the benefits of "smart" traffic flow will more than offset its considerable costs.

Increasingly, alongside the growth of "smart" highways, we will see the development of "smart" cars. Other techniques of urban traffic control include congestion charges (tolls imposed on vehicles entering inner cities at certain times of day) and heavy purchase or licensing taxes on new vehicles. Rationally, motorists must bear the full external costs of each car journey. Using the tax system together with market forces will restrict the growth of car travel and encourage motorists to act in a more environmentally friendly manner.

Regardless of opinions on the best specific solution, there is a general societal agreement that traffic is a problem. As well as defining a movement of people, traffic impedes the flow of people getting to and from places in their day-to-day lives. While there is no consensus on how to make the system both more efficient and less dangerous, there is a growing sense of urgency to champion *something*, and a realization that the global transportation system is not, in fact, okay as it is.

Chain Migration

On a visit to Istanbul many years ago, the author got to talking with a local merchant. Yes, the merchant said, he had heard of Canada but not Toronto. "Now, Hamilton, Ontario; that's another matter. Hamilton is a wonderful place!" It turns out he had many relatives and friends there. How did he happen to know so much about Hamilton, though little about Canada and nothing about Toronto? The answer is *chain migration*. As the name suggests, chain migration is sequential migration by interconnected people, one (or a few) at a time. The successful migration of one family member creates a chain of opportunities for the whole kin network. It appears the Turkish merchant's kin had migrated as a chain to Hamilton, not Toronto. Hamilton is what "Canada" meant to them.

From a sociological standpoint, what is interesting about chain migration is that, like other topics discussed in this book, it lays to rest the assertion that society is composed of a large number of atomized individuals each labouring rationally to maximize his or her own well-being. In fact, sociologists know that most people are *not* atomized, not rational, and not aiming to maximize their well-being, at least not in some overly simplistic financial sense. Chain migration makes this fact clear. From a purely financial standpoint, it might make sense for Turkish people to migrate to Toronto, not Hamilton, let alone smaller centers like Kenora, Medicine Hat, or Kelowna. Nonetheless, immigrants come to these smaller centers all the time—if they know people there, and if they know there is a good job possibility for them there (often, in connection with knowing people there).

Typically, chain migration is based on something we discussed earlier: namely, kinship systems. People tend to migrate to places where they believe they can rely on kin (and sometimes kin-like friends) to help them get settled in with housing, schools, and most important, with jobs. These "sponsors" might go so far as to provide new immigrants with a place to live for the first little while, and may even lend them money, not to mention emotional and other practical support (e.g., help with childcare). Chain migration is clear evidence that networks of kin and friends are increasingly large and internationally dispersed; perhaps the reader of this book has kin in other countries and other continents—kin who could be called on to supply temporary lodging, help in finding a job, or at least hospitality and encouragement.

The growth of research on chain migration marks a break with traditional theories of migration, which were mainly economic and geographic. The earliest *laws of migration*, formulated by E. G. Ravenstein (1885, 1889), built on the observation that the vast majority of migrants move short distances. Ravenstein's laws are often stated as follows:

> Most migration is over a short distance; migration occurs in steps; long-range migrants usually move to urban areas; each migration produces a movement in the opposite direction (although not necessarily of the same volume); rural dwellers are more migratory than urban dwellers; within their own country females are more migratory than males, but males are more migratory over long distances; most migrants are adults; large towns grow more by migration than by natural increase; migration increases with economic development; and migration is mostly due to economic causes.

Underlying this theory or set of laws is a supposition of what early twentieth-century theorist George Kingsley Zipf (1946, 1949) called the *principle of least effort*: namely, that social processes take the easiest possible path. Migrating a short distance is much less effort, and therefore more cost-efficient, than migrating a long distance, other things being equal. Similarly, people with low moving costs such as young men tend to migrate first.

Yet other things are rarely equal: a more distant destination, C, may be much more rewarding than B. With this in mind, researchers modified Ravenstein's law, as follows: the number of migrants coming from Source A to Destination B varies *both* as (1) the inverse of the distance between A and B, and (2) directly as the difference in economic opportunities at A and B. Thus, holding distance constant, migrants will choose destinations with many and better opportunities—for example, many good jobs and a high wage rate—over destinations with fewer, poorer opportunities. This is an economic theory, in the sense that it assumes migrants are rational people who seek to maximize their well-being by migrating.

Motives for illegal (as well as legal) migration are indeed mainly economic. Most illegal migrants have unstable histories of paid employment, mostly in horticulture, sewing workshops, and the service industry. Long hours, night work, low wages, and exploitation by employers are common. Most illegal immigrants are glum about their future prospects but feel unable to return home. Such migrants and many legal migrants may form part of an underclass. They are discriminated against in markets for employment, work, and housing. Therefore they cannot be assimilated into the indigenous class structure. The arrival of large numbers of such immigrants may create a "reserve army of labour," driving down wages and dividing the working class.

We need better to understand the role of information in producing this relationship between migration, opportunities, and distance. Research on chain migration provides the insight we need.

THE ROLE OF NETWORKS. When we include information flow in our considerations, we realize that migration relies on processes of social and cultural diffusion. The intensity of migratory flow is determined by societal mediators—not only by distance and economic factors, but also by the network characteristics of potential migrants. For example, transnational linkages are more important than population growth or economic conditions when migrating to the U.S. Transnational linkages include geographic proximity, migrant networks, and U.S. political involvement. Social networks channel migrants into particular areas; they link people to particular distant communities. They may be especially important when credible information is otherwise lacking. Also, networks or chains of personal contact provide access to particular types of employment within geographically defined settlement areas. They direct people to particular destinations (on this, see, for example, Angeles, 2011).

This chain effect—the social part of the process of migration—turns out to be as important to migration as economic factors. In fact, some evidence suggests that, as immigration systems mature, as with the migration of guest workers to Germany since 1970, the effect of network variables increases and the effect of economic factors decreases. One geographer proposes that, contrary to Ravenstein's laws, future regional and local flows of migrants are more likely to be dominated by network flows than by employment opportunities. Thus, even where wage differentials between areas have closed, migration may continue because of the migrant networks already in place. In the end, the *social network*, an important concept in economic sociology, turns out to be related to key ideas in the sociology of immigration, such as the informal economy, ethnic enclaves, middleman groups, and modes of incorporation.

As we will see later, migration rates are also affected by variations in the immigration law, as well as by economic and relational variables. For now, however, note that the reason for the growing importance of networks is simple. Since migrant networks reduce the "cost" of migrating by reducing the risk, the cost drops rapidly over time, as the migrant community at a given destination gets larger. If the community is growing exponentially through births as well as immigration, the costs will drop exponentially: hence, the rapid rise in the relative importance of networks.

To summarize, the likelihood of migration is a function of costs and benefits.

Migrants want the largest possible benefits (in salaries and other life amenities) at the lowest possible cost (in terms of distance and risk). Kin and friends who live in the destination can, at least, provide reliable information and, in that way, reduce risk. Better still, they can act as sponsors, provide temporary housing, and find employment for the prospective migrant.

This is how migration has always worked. Social networks affected the northward mass migration of African Americans in the early twentieth century. Family chain migration produced the trans-Atlantic mass migration from nineteenth-century Ireland, Britain, and Germany, as living conditions there worsened. Network migration was crucial to those from the former German Democratic Republic who left to live permanently in West Germany, and for ethnic Germans who moved from countries in eastern Europe to West Germany. Mexicans with ties to migrant family members and those who live in communities where U.S. migration is prevalent are far more likely to migrate illegally than people without those resources. Even political refugees use their networks to take information about their possible asylum countries into account when fleeing. Their decisions are influenced by ethnicity and the desire to join with ethnic kin. Distance, economic considerations, and admission policies prove to be less important.

THE OUTCOMES OF CHAIN MIGRATION. Chain migration, like diffusion, has certain telltale signs (MacDonald and MacDonald, 1964; Bocker, 1994; Perez and McDonough, 2008). First, when chain migration is occurring, people at the place of origin, like the Istanbul merchant we mentioned, have uneven information about the outside world. They know nothing about almost everywhere and everything about a few places. Second, immigrants at the place of destination (e.g., Turkish migrants to Hamilton) have come from the same few villages, towns, or regions. Third, these immigrants are often related to one another by kinship, or at least by patron-client relations. Fourth, these migrants often lack money, urban skills, and social capital. This is because they have come largely by means of family unification, not because they have especially valuable skills or a high education. Chain migrants need less cash than other migrants to accomplish their migration goals.

Chain migrants are a heterogeneous mix of people in terms of education and occupational skills. Economic motives, whether owing to hardship and turbulence or pessimism about the future, are the main reason for migrating. However, often the reason for migration most commonly stated on visa applications is family reunification. The process of chain migration often begins in a family with the movement of the oldest sibling, either male or female. The immigration policy of the U.S., for example, gives priority to family reunification. As such, immigration occurs in chains linking family members.

Migration, once begun, has a snowballing effect, adding new movers within a family and creating the potential for movement in other families that may be attached to it through blood ties. The majority of chain migrants receive assistance from relatives and/or co-villagers. People from different socioeconomic classes mobilize different types of personal networks for emigration, and they use their networks in different ways. Typically, working-class people depend on kin to arrange for jobs that will enable migration. Lower-middle-class people rely on kin to provide information that will facilitate migration. Middle-class people combine links with kin and colleagues to arrange their migration. The networks of wealthier, more educated people are larger, more heterogeneous, and connect with better opportunities in the place of destination.

New settlers maintain their extended family ties over distances and establish new network relations, based on reciprocity, at the destination. Small farmers, for example, seek access to land, water, and labour via patron-client relationships with influential community members. A case study of the history of migration in the southwestern U.S. reveals that migrants maintained extended family ties and depended upon those ties for access to scarce political, economic and cultural resources.

Upon arrival, many migrants have difficulty assimilating into the urban environment. They are concentrated in specific occupations or establishments, with skills that may not be in much demand. Many find jobs through their kin and friends. Or, they may enter highly specialized jobs that are, at that moment, much in need of workers. Particular groups are called on, at particular historical moments in the life of the host society, to contribute their labour to particular enterprises. For example, some come from Italy to the Netherlands to be chimney-sweepers, mosaic- and tile-makers, makers of statuettes, and ice-cream vendors (Reyneri, 1998; Sciortino, 2004). Chain migrants to Dublin from the commune of Casalattico in the province of Frosinone, Italy, worked mainly in the fish-and-chips trade. Their social integration was minimal because working hours were long and did not promote sociability with non-Casalatticesi. These emigrants remained in close contact with their families in the commune. Many returned and the native economy was heavily subsidized by the returnees' money (De Tona, 2004; Walton, 1994).

Recall from earlier sections that dense, clique-like networks tend to limit the diffusion of information. Since chain migration is based on diffusion, densely tied communities are less likely to sponsor out-migration. Rather, they deter out-migration and try to provide alternative opportunities within the community. As a result, weak and heterogeneous ties are more important for promoting chain migration out of a community. At the receiving end, networks provide migrants with information, financial or psychological support, and help in daily life, obscuring the boundaries of the class system. These networks tend to be more effective where family connections are looser.

This sort of dynamic can be readily observed among North American immigrants to Israel. Amit and Riss (2007) show that North American Jews planning to immigrate to Israel often encounter opposition and little active support from close family members in North America. And though the great majority of North American immigrants to Israel profess religion to be their primary motive for immigrating, religious organizations, synagogues, and rabbis in North America apparently exercise little influence on the decision to immigrate.

The social networks that most prominently induce North Americans Jews to immigrate are non-personal, made up of weak ties. Specifically, Amit and Riss (2007) find that many North American Jews collect information from official government agencies like the Jewish Agency and the Ministry of Absorption when deciding to immigrate. As well, many potential immigrants seek the help of voluntary organizations like *Tehila* and *Nefesh B'Nefesh*, non-governmental entities active in promoting religious Aliyah (i.e., the immigration of Jews home to Israel from the diaspora). Weak ties offer the migrants information and potential job opportunities that induce many North American Jews to immigrate to Israel. Strong ties, on the other hand, tend to act as obstacles to migration.

THE CHAIN PROCESS. In an "ideal-type" chain migration process, one migrant comes to a destination, gets a job and housing, and saves up money to send for another family member. The second member comes over, often through a family unification program, and repeats the process, bringing over a third family member, and so on.

Research on Mexican immigrants shows that five network principles underlie the chain migration process (Wilson, 1998). First, networks are multi-local, with many geographical destinations whose importance changes over time. Second, labour market conditions structure where immigrants go and where they stay. Canada's programs for temporary foreign workers, especially the Live-in Caregiver Program, entice workers to come to Canada from less-developed countries. Though these jobs are precarious, because of inadequate labour regulation, they are more attractive than the opportunities available back home.

Third, weak ties often help people access geographical locations. In time, these ties may be converted to strong ties through marriage or *compadrazgo*, or, effectively, co-parenthood. Fourth, both dense networks and diffuse, weak-tie or acquaintance networks constitute useful social capital for their members. Fifth, the clustering in a particular occupation by immigrants from a particular source community is best explained by job recruitment through dense networks, especially close relatives.

The people best informed about possible opportunities at the destination are most likely to emigrate. A destination tends to attract new immigrants from an origin in direct proportion to the previously established amount of immigration from that origin to that destination. Thus, migration between points A and B is a contagion process whose probability is a function of past migration and "vulnerability" owing to economic conditions and distance.

The key to the process is sponsorship. Especially when the migrants are poor and/or are migrating from the countryside to the city, they rely on sponsors who will not only provide information but also a place to stay and help with employment and finances. Each link in the family chain that joins an origin with a destination—say, San Danielle del Friuli, Italy, with Buenos Aires, Argentina—has a network in the native country that can be influenced to migrate to the new setting.

Some have expressed concern over the possible "explosiveness" of chain migration, owing to what they call an "immigration multiplier" (Fawcett, 1989; Teitelbaum, 1989; Yu, 2008). This is a number that shows how many additional immigrants a single immigrant is likely to bring over, under the family reunification provisions of immigration laws. If the multiplier is a large number, the immigrant population will increase exponentially. The process will be like diffusion, where each information receiver tells something to five, ten, or twenty other people. The process of chain migration is self-perpetuating.

Migrant networks have the potential to be explosive because moving costs decrease with the number of migrants already settled in the destination area. There are a variety of reasons for this. First, migrants often send job and housing information to friends and family in the original locale. Second, settled migrants frequently help later migrants once in the new destination find jobs, residence, obtain credit, and even give them temporary lodging. Third, interaction with previous migrants eases the process of adapting to an alien environment, culture, and language. As a result, once migration starts it develops momentum, and migratory flow may increase even when economic opportunities are not as great.

Networks vary in their effectiveness, depending on the politico-economic framework existing in the receiving context. On the whole, however, immigrant social networks provide better and more varied information about economic opportunities than most other alternatives. These networks, based on kinship and a common locality, tend to cut across class lines. Compared to native-born workers, this gives immigrants an advantage in pursuing economic activity.

INSTITUTIONAL COMPLETENESS. Chain migration draws new immigrants and facilitates the newcomers' acclimation. Community social institutions preserve the social structure of the place of origin and provide personal and employment contacts and recreational outlets for the second generation. They may use extended family traditions to make the often heterogeneous immigrants socially cohesive and economically viable. As a result, chain migration produces a better integration of migrants into the host society than impersonal or commercially organized arrangements. It also increases the likelihood of upward social and economic mobility.

In large part, the integration of these newcomers is due to *institutional completeness*, the degree to which an ethnic community provides its members with the services they require through their own institutions (Breton, 1964; Rosenberg and Jedwab, 1992). These organizations include places of worship, schools, banks, and media that are distinct from those of the larger society. In a group with strong institutional completeness, members do not need to depend on the services of ethnic "outsiders." Social contact comes to be concentrated within the ethnic group. For example, the immigrant associations or *landsmanschaftn* of eastern European Jewish immigrants to the U.S. helped others members of migrant networks adjust to American culture (Schiff, 1994; Chambre, 2001). The *landsmanschaftn* counter the conventional image that American culture is imposed on vulnerable immigrants.

The Jewish community in Montreal provides an interesting case study in which to explore relations between integration and institutional completeness. Most Jews in Montreal are highly concentrated residentially, living in an area historically known as the Main. Jews also make up a sizable proportion of the suburban communities of Côte-Saint-Luc, Hampstead, Montréal-Ouest, and Westmount, as well as Outremont, Côte-des-Neiges/Notre-Dame-de-Grâce, and Saint-Laurent within Montreal. Perhaps because of this high level of residential concentration, greater than that found in any other Canadian Jewish community, the network of Jewish community organizations and support groups in Montreal is characterized by a great deal of institutional completeness (Anctil, 2011).

However, rather than helping Montreal Jews integrate into Canadian society, this institutional completeness actually separates Montreal Jewry from the larger community. Montreal Jews, for example, are more likely than any other ethnic group to have fellow group members as spouses, close friends, and business associates. Close to half of Montreal Jews participating in a survey said that their Jewish identity was a conscious and important part of their lives. Some have suggested that Montreal's uniquely bilingual environment was largely responsible for this separation. In an environment where francophone Catholics and anglophone Protestants have purposefully remained separate, institutionally and socially, Montreal Jews have built separation and segregation into their own civic lives (Anctil, 2011).

Some immigrant groups find no social networks to welcome them on their arrival. Kinship support networks are not automatically reproduced at the destination. Poverty and marginalization may weaken and break down such networks, which then can provide no support to newcomers. Whether an ethnic group can develop a community with a complete range of institutions depends on many factors. These include the size of the ethnic group, its assets, and the ties of friendship, family, and work among group members. They reveal the influence of immigration policies, the local economy, and government support (or lack thereof) in the receiving society. Sometimes, governments help out the immigrants. For example, the German government has provided aid to encourage ethnic Germans living in Kazakhstan to remain there, but this policy has largely failed because of the attractiveness of state benefits in Germany as well as family ties (Brubaker, 1998; Brown, 2005). Ethnic harmony and loyalty are also critical.

Not least, community completeness depends on the range of jobs that are available in the ethnic community. In turn, a community's degree of completeness influences the number of members who carry out most of their activities within the ethnic group. Ethnic organizations—schools, daycare centres, camps, churches, business groups, social clubs, mutual aid societies, and credit unions—all give people a chance to meet other group members. They also promote group goals and make people more aware of their ethnicity. Older immigrants, in particular, benefit from living in ethnic enclaves that largely reproduce the culture of origin.

In offering migrants support and security, networks of friends and relatives anchor the migrants and free them from having to rely on their own luck and initiative. They may provide good credit terms that enable ethnic exporters to competitively price their merchandise, increasing the probability of economic success. At the same time, ethnic networks also restrict the migrants and homogenize them culturally.

In time, institutional completeness reduces the need for specific sponsorship. Immigrants hear about the destination in various ways and are attracted by the low-risk environment. After a while, the best predictor of new immigration to the destination is the number of immigrants already there.

THE ROLE OF IMMIGRATION LAWS. Immigration, from the standpoint of the host society, satisfies several goals. Through the family unification program, it satisfies immigrant and ethnic voters. Through the refugee program, it satisfies humanitarian aspirations. Otherwise, immigration is a process for supplying local labour needs. The state, therefore, organizes immigration by political and legal measures designed to adjust labour markets to the immediate needs of capitalism.

In turn, immigration laws influence the degree to which new immigrants integrate into their adopted homelands. In a study of Filipina immigrant women in Rome and Toronto, Cristaldi and Darden (2011) found that the different immigration policies enacted by the Italian and Canadian governments influenced how new immigrants settled into their new homes. Canadian government policies, on the one hand, enabled immigrants to enjoy better opportunities for social mobility, incorporation into wider society, and eventual citizenship. On the other hand, Italian immigration policies discouraged immigrants from integrating into the wider Italian society. Italian immigration laws did not encourage or promote language competency; in turn, the inability to speak Italian severely limited the job opportunities and social mobility of immigrants. Likewise, it was hard for immigrants to gain Italian citizenship. Many immigrants, especially those living in Rome, were faced with a ten-year required residency period before being allowed to apply for citizenship; by contrast, the required residency period in Canada was just three years. As a result, many Filipinas decided to stay in Canada for good, while immigrants to Italy always planned to return to the Philippines at some point in their lives (Cristaldi and Darden, 2011).

Over time, societies adjust the balance between the numbers of immigrants who are admitted under family reunification provisions and those who are admitted for economic reasons. As the emphasis on family reunification increases, education and occupation become less important determinants of immigration.

The inflow of immigrants becomes more heterogeneous educationally and occupationally, and the overall skill level is lower. Equally, as the educational or occupational requirements rise for admission on economic criteria, more migrants from poorer countries rely on the family reunification provisions.

Thus, chain migration becomes more important for many aspiring migrants as the economic and educational standards for admission rise. That is why, for example, a majority of Latino migrants to Chicago join relatives or friends already in Chicago. Most stay with family members when they first arrive. And legal immigrants consistently report higher education, employment, and income levels than do illegal immigrants (Waters and Jimenez, 2005).

MIGRATION AS A GENDERED ACTIVITY. Migration is a family concern, but women and men often play different roles in it. A Mexican woman, for example, often resists her husband's migration, and the decision to migrate is rarely arrived at in a harmonious fashion. After the husband's departure, his wife may follow against her husband's wishes, often traveling without male kin, while pregnant, or accompanied by young children. Unmarried Mexican women also migrate, typically receiving assistance from single women who previously migrated and non-migrant women at home.

Women play an especially important role in the chain migration process. Women are more engaged as "kin-keepers": people who keep kin aware of one another's existence and get them together every now and then (Gerstel, 1988). Everywhere, women are more involved than men in maintaining kin and friendship networks. For example, most migrants from Portugal to southern New England used an intermediary who served as a link in making the connection. Research shows that thirty-seven of forty-one contacts within a single network were women. Thus, both at origins and destinations, women play a larger role in maintaining and mobilizing the networks that are used for chain migration (Simon and Brettell, 1986; Feldman-Bianco, 1992). Transnational women's networks link both immigrant women and those remaining in sending communities to resources and information: for example, childcare and employment information. Thus, women do much of the coordinating work of finding a home, managing and supervising moving, and setting up their new home as part of the process of housing their families.

Women play a part in pre-migration decision-making, as migrants themselves, and as links in the continuing interaction between migrants and non-migrants after migration. As daughters, women, especially those who are single, play particularly important roles in the migration process. They are key participants in the creation and maintenance of ties that lead to continuing flows of people, goods, and money, resulting in active social networks that span rural and urban areas.

As already noted, women also sponsor other women migrants. Consider the immigration of young women over a period of eight months from Montserrat in the West Indies to Canada (Turrittin, 1976). This pattern of immigration has depended largely on the availability of domestic work as an occupation for West Indian women. Women who take up this occupation typically sponsor other women's doing so. Friendships with Canadians, including employers, and contacts with other West Indians offer opportunities for these women to eventually leave domestic work and enter blue-collar employment, the school system, or both (Momsen, 1983).

The guarantee of domestic employment draws increasing numbers of migrant women from Africa and Asia. The main "sending" countries of migrant women are Indonesia, the Philippines, Sri Lanka, and Thailand, and the main "receiving" countries in Asia are Saudi Arabia, Kuwait, Hong Kong, Japan, Taiwan, and Singapore. The reasons cited for the large number of emigrating women include the rise in male unemployment and overseas social networks that facilitate migration. In addition, numerous studies show that employers actually prefer hiring immigrant women, perceiving them to be more "exploitable" than males or native-born females (Nawyn, 2010). Problems encountered by women migrants include the inability to migrate with their families, and prohibitions on changing jobs, marrying local citizens, or even becoming pregnant.

People often immigrate to Canada because of "push" factors in countries of origin (this is particularly true of the Philippines). At the same time, programs like the Live-in Caregiver Program "pull" people from countries in poverty to come to provide services that Canadians really do not want to do themselves, such as working as nannies or, in some instances, agricultural labourers. At the same time, economic changes in the countries of origin, sometimes imposed by international financial institutions such as the IMF or World Bank in order to deal with government debts and deficits, have resulted in cutbacks there in wages and social services, making it difficult for women to earn a living wage. As a result, mothers often immigrate to Canada using these sponsored programs, and leave their children behind in the Philippines. This could have interesting consequences when these mothers return to their country of origin, or when they become eligible to have their children come to Canada after working for three years (on this, see Parennas, 2001, 2005, 2007).

Although policy initiatives like the Live-in Caregiver Program provide the opportunity for relatively unskilled female workers to obtain permanent residency in Canada, numerous problems leave caregivers vulnerable to abuse. In a survey of caregivers conducted at McGill University, only 22.7% of respondents said their employers followed the contract they had signed together. Nearly half of the caregivers reported not being paid for overtime, and over one-third had to buy work-related items with their own money. Others reported that "living in" with one's employer entailed being on call all day and working extremely long hours. It also meant a lack of privacy and sometimes even accusations of theft and "husband stealing" (Brickner and Straehle, 2010). Given that many of the women who participate in the program are university-trained registered nurses, such jobs may represent a significant decline in social and socioeconomic status.

Nevertheless, the chance to gain permanent residency in a desirable foreign country induces many women to participate in such programs. Many of these immigrant domestic workers, in turn, initiate chain migration of families and connections. Filipina migrant domestic workers in Hong Kong sometimes develop a quasi-familial relationship with their employer. This relationship facilitates the development of migration networks by duplicating itself through the kinship networks of both employer and employee (Chang and Ling, 2000). Women also protect other migrants, especially those who work in occupations with a substantial risk of violence—for example, in the entertainment and domestic service industries. The presence of well-established networks helps keep down the levels of violence against migrant women. Sometimes, expatriate women even build an international network of contacts that facilitates geographical mobility for those who want to move incognito, for example from conflict-torn Somalia to Italy, Europe, and the United States.

Note, finally, that immigration may have a significant impact on gender relations. Traditional kin structures are gradually replaced by new solidarity structures in the city. After migration, households are often smaller and less traditional, extended families are less important and, conversely, social (friendship) networks are larger and more important. For south Asian women, migration from rural to urban areas breaks caste and gender bonds. Migration from Puerto Rico to the mainland U.S. also reduces gender oppression for women (Vega, 1990; Acosta-Belén, 2006). Puerto Rican women used migration to gain independence as single women and to counter limited marriage opportunities. Similarly, circular migration in China has affected gender relations within Chinese society. Young women who return to live in their home villages after several years of earning high wages in urban areas may face particular problems of adjustment in the areas of child care, sexual division of labour, and fertility.

Such changes, however, vary in degree from one ethnic group to another. For example, migrant Muslim women in Tunis (in Tunisia) do not go so far as to adopt Euro-American ideals of conjugal isolation. They continue to live in a world dominated by visits and daily interaction with near and extended kin (Holmes-Eber, 1997).

Return Migration

We normally think of migration—especially, international migration—as a one-way trip, from the country of origin to Canada, the country of destination. Yet nothing could be further from the truth. What actually happens has a lot to do with economic possibilities here and back home (Dustmann, 2003).

A large fraction of migrants come to Canada and other countries of destination in the western, developed world, with intentions of eventually returning to their country of origin. Often, their purpose in coming, if they have not come as refugees, is to make enough money in Canada so they can return to their country of origin and retire in comfort. In many other cases, immigrants come not only with the intention of returning, but also with the intention of sending home remittances to support their parents and children while they are abroad in Canada. The result is that billions of dollars leave Canada as remittances to China, India, and the Philippines, to name only the most common countries of origin.

Of course, many other immigrants come to Canada in hopes of finding a job and settling here permanently. For many, their goal is to ensure their children get a good education and good health care, then eventually get a good job in the Canadian labour force. These people do not intend to return to their country of origin, though in their old age some do so nonetheless.

Learning the extent and reasons for return migration would have practical importance for policy makers. There is also sociological interest in this topic. For example, we might view return migrants as being something like the movers we discussed earlier: people who are less inclined to put down permanent roots in a particular community, because they intend to move on in the foreseeable future. In this case, we could think of return migrants as movers whose eventual country of destination is also their country of origin. In effect, we might be inclined to view return migrants, and other movers, as people of the kind John Porter was thinking about when he compared Canada to a vast train station in which people are constantly arriving and departing. Certainly, in Porter's mind, such transience was likely to undermine the formation of a strong Canadian identity.

Immigration is viewed as much more of a problem in the United States than it is in Canada, because there are much higher numbers of illegal immigrants in the U.S. The assumption most people make is that these illegal immigrants, largely from Mexico and Central America, are coming to stay permanently and, once here, will draw heavily on jobs, housing, health, and social services that are also in demand by native-born citizens and legal immigrants. The problem is serious, if we assume this motivation and pay attention only to the numbers. According to the most recent reliable data, almost 12 million illegal immigrants were to be found in the United States in March 2012, and that year border patrol officials apprehended more than 600,000 individuals illegally trying to enter the country, virtually all of them along the southern border with Mexico. Yet consider that, at the same time, for every immigrant that stayed, several returned to Mexico (Lindstrom, 1996; Massey and Espinosa, 1997). It is easy to account economically for the migrants staying. But how do we explain the high rates of return migration? Was returning a rational behaviour? Most social scientists assume that people act to improve their well-being and interact with one another for purposes of exchange. It is through this exchange that people unwittingly produce social structures. So, for social science, the study of social structures starts with an examination of choices. That said, what if it becomes more rational to return to Mexico, if jobs become available there, rather than stay in a strange, hostile environment?

True, people migrate to maximize their well-being, broadly defined. Social networks help them do that, by improving the flow of information and reducing the risks associated with migration. It must follow, logically, that *return migration*—the return of migrants to their place of origin—works similarly. People go back where they came from because of a shift in the balance of benefits associated with origin and destination.

Social networks play only a small role in this, because return migrants already have plenty of information about the place of origin. Their dominant concern is, therefore, economic. Migrants will return if and when economic conditions are better in the place of origin than they are in the place of destination. And, in fact, often this *is* the reason why migrants return. But it does not account for (to pick just one example) the return to Mexico of Mexican immigrants to the United States, suggesting there are major exceptions to this "rule of rationality" that we will have to investigate. One has to do with *refugee repatriation*, the other with *sentimental return*. Refugee repatriation is the return of migrants who never freely chose to leave the origin. As their leaving was forced, often so is their return. Sentimental return is the return of migrants that we cannot explain on simple economic grounds.

REFUGEE REPATRIATION. It would be grotesque to suggest that refugees control the exit from their homeland. They are sometimes able to choose one destination over another. However, refugees are rarely able to systematically maximize their objectives or use the most efficient means of achieving them. Nor are they often able to assess the risks associated with different courses of action. Refugees are often, for uncertain periods of time, plunged into the riskiest situations imaginable. Often, luck determines how long the trip from an origin to destination will last and who will survive it. The twentieth century saw one horrible forced march of migrants after another. Rational choice never entered the picture.

Alongside the numbers of willing international migrants and unwilling refugees are another estimated twenty to twenty-five million people who have been forced out of their homes but remain under their government's jurisdiction. Increasingly, global homelessness is tied to problems of refuge and migration. Today, homelessness is a problem of worldwide access to the most basic provisions: housing, passports, visas, welfare arrangements, and health care.

With the rise of ethnic nationalism, some involuntary migration is due to the return of ethnic groups from countries where they are a minority. An example is the involuntary migration of ethnic Russians from the non-Russian republics of the former USSR (Brubaker, 1998; Kolsto, 1996). Another is the massive out-migration from the Russian North to the western and southern portions of the country. Both are a result of earlier forced migrations. Stalin had forced the original migration into Siberia and other Soviet republics. Hitler had forced migration out of the Soviet Union. By the end of the Second World War, over ten million Soviet citizens were living in occupied territory. Of these, 5.6 million were civilians in labour camps and 4.6 million were captive soldiers. Of five million citizens living outside the USSR, 1.7 million were prisoners of war. Most of the rest were slave labourers who had been deported to Germany.

After the war, large numbers of Russian workers and their families were urged to take up residence in Estonia and other Soviet republics whose loyalty was suspect. There, the Russians enjoyed wages, benefits, and preferential treatment unavailable to the indigenous population. Renewed independence in Estonia, however, changed the social and political order. Russians there had to decide whether to remain as a cultural and political minority or migrate back to Russia. Many of the Russians would prefer to return but economic uncertainties prevent them from making the move. Simultaneously, Estonian laws are forcing Russians into at least temporary second-class citizenship.

Before the collapse of the USSR, the 1989 census showed that more than one in six ethnic Russians lived in other constituent republics, such as Estonia. In 1990, about 500,000 returned to Russia, followed by 1,000,000 in 1991 (Pilkington, 1998; Zevelev, 1996).

Refugees and other forced migrants are sometimes attached to their homeland and want to return to it. Sometimes, they do not. Their willingness to return depends on past experiences and the relationship with their country of origin. Consider the likely differences in experience between expatriate Iraqi Arabs, who belong to the mainstream population in Iraq, and Iraqi Assyrians, who are a Christian minority. Or, consider the differences between Croatian (Christian) and Bosnian (Muslim) refugees from the civil war in the former Yugoslavia (Sells, 1996; Ali-Al et al., 2001). Of the two, the Muslims were treated worse by Serbian (Christian) attackers. Ironically, they were also more intent on returning to their homes than the Croatians.

Often, the international community is ignorant about political processes among refugees. A well-intentioned desire to effect reconciliation, mass repatriation, and social reconstruction may fail to take into account the extent of the ill will between the refugees and the society from which they fled. Consider the few thousand Jewish men and women who returned to Germany immediately after 1945 (Brubaker, 2001; Safran, 1991).

At first, they found it ideologically possible to settle in East Germany (GDR). There, anti-fascist credentials made one a full citizen and anti-Semites had to deny their anti-Semitism, to the point that Jews could work with them. Even so, Jews returning to Germany wavered between full integration and a temporary negation of Jewish identity. In due course, the Cold War opened a division between mere "victims of fascism" (Jews) and "fighters against fascism" (Communists). Anti-Semitic campaigns directed from Moscow began, once again, to displace the German Jews.

Or consider the Muslim Rohyingas, who fled Burma in 1990 because their pro-democracy beliefs conflicted with those of the prevailing military regime (Ekeh and Smith, 2007; Kausikan, 1993). Brutalization of the Muslims, including forced labour, rape, and property confiscation led to their exile. Neighbouring Bangladesh, with poverty and refugee problems of its own, was reluctant to accept and care for these refugees. Negotiations involving Burma, Bangladesh, and the UN finally resulted in the repatriation of all 200,000 refugees. We have no indication they were better off after their return.

RESULTS OF REPATRIATION. Of the three solutions advanced to alleviate refugee problems in the twenty-first century—repatriation, resettlement, and integration—people tend to see repatriation as most desirable. However, before promoting a return of refugees, we must ensure the conflict has been brought under control. No refugees must be forced to return to a country where they face persecution, any more than battered wives must be forced to return to abusive husbands.

The situation in countries like Afghanistan, Iraq, and Syria, for example, may not be appropriate for massive repatriation. Refugees, mostly women and children, continue to leave their homes, fleeing human rights violations, hunger, exposure, violence, ecological destruction, and land mines. Women in these three countries are under constant threat of sexual violence in the ongoing war between rival sectarian groups. They are subjected to sale and forced prostitution. A major obstacle to repatriation is the lack of any real government. The refugees wait, in Iran, Jordan, and Pakistan, for a change.

Or consider the Georgian Turkish Muslims. For two centuries, Russian governments have discriminated against them repeatedly, out of sheer prejudice. In 1944, 150,000 Georgian Turks were deported to Uzbekistan by Stalin's regime (Ray, 2000). A return to Georgia began in the mid-1970s, despite strong resistance from Georgians. Now, the independent government of Georgia is faced with the mass repatriation of these Turks. Most of them want to return. Without legislation that legalizes their return, they are in limbo. However, the Georgian government is in no hurry to further complicate a complex multi-ethnic situation in the new country by letting them back in (see also Pentikainen and Trier, 2004).

Political exiles who returned to Chile after (sometimes) decades spent outside the country faced employment problems, language difficulties, legal problems, and problems of recognition of professional experience and training (Llambias-Wolff, 1993). They also suffered material, emotional and social difficulties. Political exiles who returned to South Africa after the fall of Apartheid had similar re-entry problems.

Sometimes the society to which refugees return also faces difficulties. For example, a civil war in Liberia forced many native Ghanaians to return to their country, to the care of their relatives. Little or no government support was available. People returning to Portugal from Angola and Mozambique in the 1970s, after Portugal's loss of its African colonies, depressed Portuguese wages (Carrington and De Lima, 1996). Likewise, during the Persian Gulf crisis in 1990, the Republic of Yemen had to accommodate 800,000 of its nationals forced to leave Saudi Arabia, Kuwait, and other states in the region. A poor country already under considerable political and economic pressure, Yemen struggled to meet the needs of the mostly unskilled and uneducated returning migrants in an already stagnant economy.

ECONOMIC REASONS FOR RETURN. As we noted earlier, some return migration is the result of dramatic economic improvements in the place of origin. Some is due to a dramatic worsening in the place of destination. Economic push-pull factors explain, for example, the return migration of Greeks to the islands of the eastern Aegean. Differences in income and employment opportunities at the place of origin—say, Athens—and place of destination—say, Rhodes—were primary economic determinants of return migration (Robolis and Xideas, 1996).

Similarly, a growing number of Chinese who went abroad for study and work are being drawn back to work in Shanghai. Foreign investment and the rapid expansion of financial, legal, and other services have created an enormous demand for skilled English-speaking professionals. Hoping to lure back even more immigrants, the Chinese government and Shanghai authorities have developed generous incentive schemes. They include grants, better housing, and higher salaries. Likewise, Taiwanese expatriates are returning to jobs in electronics and telecommunications, and many are even starting their own businesses. Incentives are provided to help more entrepreneurial returnees raise capital and make the adjustment from a comfortable middle-class life in the U.S.

Between 1966 and 1990, Korea pursued an aggressive policy aimed at reversing the brain drain (Yoon, 1992). Scientists and engineers returned in large numbers, with strong, lasting effects on the research and development sector. Likewise, people who left the Philippines to escape the dictator Ferdinand Marcos and the economic ruin he caused later returned, hoping that democracy would speed economic development.

Similar processes have been noted in the United States. There, the return migration of Latinos to the Southwest is related to favourable economic conditions, notably, good wages and growth in employment, especially for younger and more educated people. Likewise, the return of blacks to the South is related to a poor business climate and lack of jobs in many northern cities. Return migration rates are higher for black migrants than for whites overall.

Many of the return migrants who are lured back by economic incentives have high educational and occupational qualifications. Migrants are most likely to return to the United States from Israel, for example, if they are well-educated. However, this is not always the case. Often the least qualified are most likely to return. Among foreign-born people in host societies such as Canada, return migrants tend to be less educated and less economically motivated. The propensity to leave Canada for a foreign home is greatest among men whose English and French are poor.

Return migrants typically have more education and better occupational prospects than non-migrants from the same homeland, especially those living in rural areas. However, their occupational experience at home has failed to prepare them adequately for work in the place of destination. Therefore, many return migrants have poorer qualifications than natives of the place of destination. Young unemployed workers are the most likely return migrants. A failure to find permanent jobs or housing also raises the likelihood of return migration. The departure of these return migrants raises the average occupational status of immigrants who remain in the place of destination.

Not all return migration is driven by simple economic variables. Some returns are sentimental returns (Massey, 1987). Returns to reservations by Native Americans are mainly due to a desire to be with family and friends, and to return to where they were born and raised. Similarly, in the U.S., a large number of blacks originally from the South return to their state of birth after retirement, though few blacks *not* born in the South move there after retiring (Longino and Biggar, 1981). This suggests that, in the absence of economic incentives, social and emotional reasons explain the return migration. "Counter-urbanization," the desire to live in a more rural residential environment, may be an important part of this phenomenon (Champion, 1998).

Sentiment likely interacts with economic factors in a decision to stay or return to one's place of origin. For example, Mexican immigrants to the U.S. with good opportunities for employment and small capital investment have a greater incentive to stay longer in the U.S. and withstand the psychic costs of separation from family and friends.

Gender issues are also important. Women coming from patriarchal societies such as Puerto Rico use migration to improve their occupational and marriage chances. Unmarried women are less likely than married women to return to Puerto Rico. They are also more likely to change their marital status if they stay in the United States than if they return to Puerto Rico.

Other things being equal, length of residence abroad has an effect on return migration (Dustmann et al., 1996). Some return migrants are, in effect, sojourners who never emotionally left their homeland. Some migrants keep "feet in two worlds" and remain oriented toward their places of origin as well as the communities they enter. From this transnational perspective, migration is not a journey between two separate communities and sets of social relationships, but along one transnational migration circuit. Some Israeli expatriates live for extended periods still expecting to return to their homeland, never doing so yet never giving up the idea. They retain strong ties to their homeland and a firm Israeli identity. Yet, the longer they stay away, the less likely they are to return. Duration of work abroad, as well as residential and job satisfaction, affects the willingness of guest workers in Germany to return to their homes in southern and southeastern Europe. Among Hong Kong-born doctors working overseas, the length of residence abroad and previous overseas training, among other things, determines the propensity to return to Hong Kong.

CONSEQUENCES OF RETURN MIGRATION. If the economic theory is valid, migrants must be better off after they return home than if they remain abroad. The home community may also be better off if, like Korea and China, it is able to make new use of its highly educated returnees. It may be worse off if it cannot make use of them because of economic stagnation or political instability, or if the returnees are inappropriately skilled.

The literature shows a variety of outcomes to return migration. Sometimes the results are strongly positive. For example, members of the Patidar community in India who return home after spending time in East Africa can enter a higher caste status. By migrating and returning to India, they literally remake themselves socially (Chandra, 1997).

Return migrants with savings often return to birthplace regions that are lagging or less developed regions of the country. Without these savings, their rate of return to less developed regions is low. Migrants who reintegrate into their regions of origin can revitalize economically disadvantaged and demographically unbalanced regions, by bringing in new skills and experience.

In the United States and elsewhere, retirees are a good source of funds for economic development. Older return migrants have high recession-proof incomes (largely discretionary) and substantial financial assets that they transfer to their community of relocation. Their demand for goods and services stimulates a variety of economic activities, including real estate, health-care and recreational services, utilities, and retail. The economic impact of these in-migrants on the community is extremely positive.

The province of Galicia in Spain experienced large changes in the first third of the twentieth century, due to migration to and from the Americas, mainly Argentina, Uruguay, and Cuba. An active group of those returning from the Americas was politically liberal and opposed the traditional political elites in Galicia (Rhoades, 1978). Money from the Americas was used in Galicia to set up schooling in progressive social ideas: for example, to promote organized unionism. In Italy, the Northeast and South have been most affected by return migration. Remittances, savings, and pensions of return migrants are all commonly cited benefits. Return migration also promotes the social mobility of families and migrants (King, 1993).

On the negative side, returnees to China with advanced Western degrees find living in China tough, materially and psychologically, after having spent years in the West. Many had become involved there in highly visible, important work that is unavailable in China, where the money-driven climate limits pure academic research. Political restrictions are also tighter on campuses than in China's business world. Therefore, Chinese scholars are returning in smaller numbers than lawyers and business people.

Returnees to Suriname from the Netherlands also occupy an ambiguous social position. Returnees serve as a cultural bridge from the primitive parts of the Surinamese jungle to the cultural circles of the Netherlands. Most see themselves as citizens of the world. However, Suriname is still a developing country. In hard economic times, they live off their savings from the Netherlands. At best, their professional skills and familiarity with Dutch ways make them more employable, despite a lack of local political connections (Bovenkerk, 1981).

The return of migrants from the U.S. to Puerto Rico is often followed by spells of unemployment. The skills that return migrants have accumulated in the U.S. are redundant. Returnees do not receive a premium for U.S. experience there, and in this sense they are no better off than those who stayed at home. Likewise, the lessons that Polish migrants learned in American industrial cities give them no practical advantage after they return to rural Polish villages.

The return of African Americans to the South sometimes leads to unpleasant reflections about the present policy on poverty and race. In response to poverty, the returnees are creating networks of mutual support and institutions for community action. However, these activities have brought them into conflict with the established white hierarchies, which have done their utmost to block the creation of grassroots organizations by the poor.

Return migration has a mixed effect on gender relations. Mostly, women feel frustrated when they return. Women returning to Barbados, Ireland, and Newfoundland, for example, are less satisfied than men to be "home." The greater dissatisfaction of women returnees stems from their limited employment opportunities and a range of social factors (Gmelch and Gmelch, 1995). Likewise, in China, young women who return to live in their home villages after several years of earning high wages in urban areas face similar problems of adjustment in the areas of child care, sexual division of labour, and fertility.

CIRCULAR MIGRATION. Conventional views suggest that migration decisions are "either-or": either migrate or don't. Such a view is static in that it gives no consideration to linkages between subsequent mobility decisions. In fact, *circular migration* may be the way of the future (Vertovec, 2006).

For example, an analysis of Salvadorean refugees reveals the existence of circular migration: a pattern of culturally sanctioned movement during which the migrant maintains social and economic ties both with the home country and another country (Miyares et al., 2003). A large portion of the Salvadorean refugee population returns to El Salvador. However, the reasons for their original migration, coupled with their positive experiences outside of El Salvador, compel them to leave again. So the circular movement continues.

In the United States, too, rates of circular migration are high. The continued migration of working class blacks between North and South is a collective response to social conditions of poverty, race, and class relations. Unlike the relocation of middle class blacks, this migration is often short-term and circular. Family members relocate back and forth between northern and southern cities as a strategy that maximizes the benefits and minimizes the disadvantages that both the North and the South are perceived to offer. By moving between the two locales, family members trade off the positive and negative features of race relations, educational and employment opportunities and family life. Such back and forth movement is the latest stage in American migration patterns.

Such circular behaviour is typical of people who originate in a rural area. Some temporary or circular migration is even daily. Data for Quito, Ecuador, and the surrounding rural areas show that daily migration contributed much more to the informal urban sector than has previously been thought (Brown et al., 1988).

In China, farmers have inadvertently formed a new social group of transient workers that is neither urban nor rural. A large proportion of the rural-urban population movement is temporary movement. Estimated at over 100 million, the country's migrant workers are peasants who come from the hinterland. Often, the residents of the eastern cities and the country's leadership look down on them. However, Sichuan officials regard migration, both inside and outside the vast province, largely as a blessing. Annual remittances from Sichuanese migrants to their home farms are now 30 billion yuan, amounting to one-fifth of all farmers' income. Also, returned migrants are creating a new entrepreneurial class, bringing capital and expertise from the coast. This makes attention to such movement essential to any assessment of social, economic, and political development. Transient workers need to be given the same rights and privileges as city dwellers in order to combat their feeling of isolation and exclusion from urban cultural life due their low income and social status (Fan, 2004).

Circular migration makes sense because it takes advantage of both the origin and destination and leavens the disadvantages of each. Since the 1960s, large waves of emigrants have left Italy for France. Immigrants still have strong bonds to their native village, and often go back and forth between Paris and home. They are not well-integrated into French life (Attias-Donfut, 2013). Sometimes, as with Puerto Rican women, they partly survive the race oppression and disadvantaged class conditions they experience in the host societies by maintaining links with the homeland. At the same time, they are aware of the gender oppression found at "home."

Another group of repeated migrants are elderly seasonal migrants. Research on older (age 60+) people in Minnesota and Arizona show that "sunbird" migration out of summer heat is more prevalent than "snowbird" migration from winter cold. Sunbirds are older as a group, and their migratory activity is linked with previous permanent migration from northern states (Hogan and Steinnes, 1996). These repeat migrants fall into three main patterns: still rooted in home place (circular), suspended between dual homes (pendular), and footloose (linear).

Yet another pattern of return migration is the "astronaut pattern" exemplified by immigrants from Hong Kong. In an astronaut family, one spouse, typically the husband, leaves the family in the country of immigration (for example, Canada) and returns to Hong Kong to continue with business activities or work. There, thanks to economic growth and labour shortages, Hong Kong workers enjoy job security and excellent financial remuneration. Periodically, the astronaut visits family still in Canada (Waters, 2005; Waters, 2002).

CONSEQUENCES OF REPEAT MIGRATION. Some of the effects of repeat migration are good and others not. Consider, for example, Mexican women whose husbands migrate to work in the U.S. About one-third felt at risk for contracting HIV/AIDS, mostly because they doubted their husbands' fidelity or had donated blood, received a blood transfusion, or received an intramuscular or intravenous injection in the last five years.

Wives of Indian men working in the Persian Gulf benefited from their husbands' absence (Weiner, 1982). Fifty percent remained independent and the majority enjoyed the support of extended kinship networks. Women were called on to make decisions, take on responsibilities, and interact with the outside world in a way that transcended their former roles and experiences. They gained self-confidence and self-esteem, and improved their status within the family during the male absence. Some of these gains were lost on the return of their partners, but it is concluded that male absence improved the long-term independence and decision-making authority of these respondents. Likewise, in China, during spousal separation, women often become heads of household. At times, they retain that role after the return of the husband. This phenomenon is most pronounced in cities.

Frequent back-and-forth travel and multidirectional exchanges of resources spread people's lives across national borders and generate a transnational outlook. Instead of being a social equalizer, transnational migration tends to reproduce and even exacerbate class, gender, and regional inequalities. It also forms a single system connecting the origin and the destination. We will discuss this further in the next section on diasporas.

CONCLUDING REMARKS. If we examine Mexico-U.S. migrations, the probabilities of, first, repeat and, second, return migration are more closely linked to the forces identified by social capital theory and the new economics of migration than to the cost-benefit calculations assumed by neoclassical economics. Rationality and choice play a part in migration, but we must not exaggerate their role. They play an even smaller part in return migration.

Diasporas

With each passing century, more people than ever before are living in countries to which they migrated; likewise, more people than ever before are children of immigrants. Today, over 20% of all Canadians were born elsewhere, and the fraction is even higher in Canada's largest cities.

But what is equally impressive is that, today, more people have kin in a larger number of foreign countries than ever before. This fact, though not thoroughly documented, is evident in statistics showing the amount of international travel and communication that is directed at linking up with kin. And this dispersion of kin is particularly marked among certain immigrant or national-origin groups: especially the Jews, Chinese, and South Asians. These are groups with kin group members not only in the original homeland but also in Canada, the United States, and often Australia, the UK, Western Europe, and even South America. Thus, we can rightly view the twenty-first century as a time of ethnic exile or, as it is often called, diaspora formation.

Diaspora comes from the Greek word meaning "a scattering" or "dispersion." Today, we use the term to mean the spread of migrants and the spread of cultures by means of these migrants. Until recently, the word was used only to describe the Jews. Today, it is used to describe the global dispersion of any historically *victimized minorities*—for example, Gypsies and Armenians, or blacks in America—or *visible and potentially victimized minorities*—for example, Arabs in Africa, East Indians in the West Indies, and Chinese people in Indonesia. Any migrant community, but especially a community comprised mainly of refugees, deportees or former slaves, is referred to as *diasporic*.

THE DIASPORIC COMMUNITY AND ITS NEW HOME. Traditionally, sociologists approached immigration and ethnicity in terms of social disorganization. As (mainly) urban dwellers, immigrants were supposedly subject to the same disorganizing forces as native-born city people. Liberation from what Karl Marx had called the "idiocy of rural life" came at a cost. Ferdinand Tonnies, an early sociologist, toted up the cost by highlighting the cultural differences between city life, which he termed *gesellschaft*, and rural life, or *gemeinschaft*.

On farms and in small towns, Tonnies observed, community life was stable, predictable, and enduring. Everyone was connected to everyone else through kinship, friendship, neighbouring, and work. Social relations were intimate and deeply meaningful. By contrast, city life was fluid, unpredictable, and temporary. City people knew few others and had few connections to them. Many exchanged goods and services for money. The social connections they had were few and limited. Most relationships were narrow and superficial, shallow and meaningless outside the realm of profit making and taking.

As we saw earlier, sociologist Georg Simmel pointed out that cities are places that put us in close range of people we've never met, making "the stranger" a central urban figure. Early American sociology considered cities dangerous and enslaving. Fast-changing urban industrial life was riddled with social pathologies and social disorganization. The most important theorist in this tradition was Chicago sociologist Louis Wirth. In his article "Urbanism as a way of life," Wirth posited three reasons that cities have less social cohesion than smaller communities: a large population, high population density, and population heterogeneity.

First, a large population ensures that most people won't know one another. Because they are strangers they do not feel tied to one another in ways that control deviance and support cooperation in a smaller community. As a result, city people are less willing to help one another, especially when helping carries a personal cost. A dense population means that city people will have many interactions and communications. It is virtually impossible to escape other people's notice or influence. The potential for too many interactions in turn leads people to develop strategies for avoiding strangers or keeping them emotionally at a distance. It also encourages them to develop institutions, like police forces and subway advertising, that control or pacify strangers in public places.

Population heterogeneity—the presence of people with widely varying values, norms, and interests—is a third problem people have to solve in the city. Confusion, if not outright conflict, is bound to arise between strangers who see the world differently and compete with one another for jobs, housing and political influence. Under these conditions, cross-cultural contacts with strangers produce a general negative feeling toward others.

Immigrants were supposed to also suffer from the breakdown of their traditional culture and social organization in the adopted homeland. This, at least, was the message of the early studies of immigration and ethnic relations, dominated by Robert Park and the Chicago school of sociology. It emphasized the pathologies of immigration, in terms like minority, ghetto, stranger, marginal man, and rootless cosmopolitan. Thomas and Znaniecki first developed this theme in their classic work, *The Polish Peasant in Europe and America*. They found that migration disturbed traditional relationships between men and women, parents and children. It upset religious faith, cultural identity, and personal aspirations, and set the individual against the community. Social and personal disorganization resulted, taking the forms of crime and delinquency, divorce, suicide, excessive drinking, and otherwise. This approach assumed the immigrant goal was assimilation and acculturation, to overcome a prevailing homelessness, placelessness, and statelessness.

Later studies, however, led to other conclusions. What had seemed to be long-term disorganization turned out to be short-term disorganization or even adaptation, if viewed from the standpoint of the future. Change proved to be for the best, even if it was often unexpected. Individualism and deviance proved to be signs of assimilation, not disorganization. Ethnic communities grew larger and stronger, and their members did not feel like strangers or second-class citizens.

Whether we focus on Germans, Italians, Japanese, Chinese, Jews, Indians, or another group, we find similar economic and cultural adaptive patterns within the same migratory groups in different countries and also similar patterns within different groups in the same countries. The transfer of knowledge, skills, and attitudes that occurs when Jews migrate from Eastern Europe to Canada occurs in much the same way as when Germans migrate to Brazil, Japanese to Peru, or Indians to the U.S. Every migrant group can be viewed simultaneously as an *enclave*—a group within a host society—a *national group* with a distant homeland, and a *transnational community* with branches around the world. Thus, far from being disorganized, the immigrant today is a participant in three connected social structures. We discuss each in turn.

When forming enclaves, immigrants tend to congregate in particular areas to preserve their lifestyles. Here, they regulate the pace of acculturation, control the young, and gain access to wider community networks for moral and economic support. The new immigrants' success owes a great deal to international political factors and prior immigrant patterns. Because members of the host society approach immigrants according to their ethnicity rather than their class, new immigrants are often forced to assert their ethnic pride as a matter of economic and cultural survival. However, the vast majority of immigrants to the U.S. and Canada experience a rapid transition to English and mainstream North American attitudes and beliefs.

Probably no group demonstrates these principles better than the Jews. As a people they have rooted themselves successfully in North America after early twentieth-century migrations, mainly from Europe. Paradoxically, the successful Jewish diaspora in North America has also been the world's most significant Zionist movement, supporting a Jewish homeland in Israel from outside Israel.

Some have proposed that everything that is new in Jewish thinking and spirituality derives from the diaspora rather from Israel. Israel is where Jews go to explore their past while America is where they go to create their future. Most of the major periods of artistic growth in Hebrew, for example, occurred under the rule of powerful empires with leading cultures that were highly attractive to substantial numbers of Jews: ancient Mesopotamia, Rome, medieval Islam, and czarist Russia. The process of assimilation was arrested by an imperial crisis in each empire. Social instability repeatedly brought violence against the Jews, causing major upheavals in Jewish demography and a psychological turn inward, away from the dominant culture. The result was a body of Hebrew literature that was influenced by the dominant culture but that asserted Jewish separatism and, to varying degrees, nationalism.

During the period between the First and Second World Wars, the Jews in North America and Europe faced the dilemma of negotiating new social roles in the context of new citizenship rights and freedoms, a desire to maintain historical identity and tradition, and the persistent environment of anti-Semitism. In the United States, the Jews achieved unprecedented political power as a result of their participation in the labour movement and the Democratic Party.

Today, the Jewish diaspora in the U.S., Europe and the former USSR is steadily decreasing because of assimilation, low birthrates, and emigration to Israel. Mass migrations of Jews from Eastern Europe are less a result of the spread of anti-Semitism than a revived memory of its past manifestations, typical of economic crises and political instability. Jewish migrants to the United States from Israel are reluctant to accept a U.S. identity and speak frequently about their plans to return. They are *Yordim*, a stigmatized Hebrew term meaning those who "go down" from the Holy Land to the diaspora (Sheffer, 1998; Safran, 2005).

By contrast, Jewish migrants to the United States from the former USSR have positive feelings about their U.S. identity. They often refer to themselves with the name given to them by Jewish resettlement agencies: "New Americans." It is precisely this openness and acceptance toward Jews, and their willingness to assimilate, that poses a problem. When there is no pressure on the "tribe," the need to defend and protect its identity is weakened.

The African American community presents a different picture. Brought to the Americas from Africa in chains, African Americans have struggled for centuries to achieve freedom, equality, and acceptance. Like the Jews, they have achieved this by forming communal and national associations. A variety of urban self-help organizations helped blacks moving from rural to urban areas. The black churches were especially important as a source of identity, cohesion, and leadership. Evolving forms of traditional African culture—for example, music and dance—contributed to black community cohesion in the United States and influenced white American culture. Music and entertainment, along with sports, provided African Americans with their best opportunity for celebrity.

For centuries, African Americans have suffered unequal treatment at the hands of white Americans. However, the diaspora may have had two beneficial effects on African Americans. First, it may have given black women in America more equality in relation to men than they enjoy in Africa. Second, white Americans, by ignoring the ethnic and tribal differences of black Americans, may have helped to eliminate in America the sources of antipathy that historically led to bloodshed in Africa. One result was the creation of a common language, Black English. In fact, Ebonics is perceived by some as a created language developed by Africans in response to their environment. It is spoken wherever African-descended people are found, alongside the language of the particular society. Thus, Ebonics is a continuum of contact languages that have developed throughout the African diaspora.

Today, structural racism against black people continues in America, Britain, and non-African communities. Africans of a mixed origin descent comprise a large but hardly advantaged portion of the population in the diaspora. At the same time, immigration from Africa continues, though more freely than in the past. Five factors feed that immigration: integration and globalization of the world economy, failures of economic and political development in Africa, immigration and refugee policies in Europe and the United States, the anglophone background of many African societies, and the historic ties of "sending" countries to the United States.

A third notable group is the diasporic Chinese. Like the Jews and Africans, people of Chinese origin people are found around the world. Like the Jews, they are often "middle-man" minorities engaged in trade or the professions. And, like the Jews, they have tended to retain a consciousness of native place of origin, through the formation of regional associations. These associations have acted to bond together members of the Chinese diaspora even in Hong Kong: they maintain the connections among people who come from the same region, and also maintain a connection with that region.

The first Chinese in North America were "sojourners" who planned to stay abroad only temporarily before returning to China. Unlike the Jews, who were violently displaced, and Africans, who were forcibly enslaved, many Chinese took the decision to relocate voluntarily. Although many of the earliest Chinese immigrants looked forward to the new lives they were starting abroad, harsh working conditions and a series of discriminatory laws limited their potential for advancement in North America. These early Chinese immigrants often related their experiences back to a clearly defined notion of home. There was a well-established tradition among the Chinese that viewed the homeland as a central, cultural core; in this regard, the Chinese did not feel the threat of the loss of their homeland, in marked contrast to the experiences of Jews or Africans. They were simply sojourners, fully intending to return home in the end (Pendery, 2008).

Over time, however, like the Jews and Africans, the Chinese in North America came to develop new identities which transcended the localized ones based on ethnicity, clan, and place of origin. Though linked to China and elsewhere in the Chinese diaspora, this identity developed out of the ongoing political response of elite merchants to the conditions of their lives in North America, and their efforts to maintain their class and gendered interests. For example, among Chinese in British Columbia between 1871 and 1911, this included exclusion from certain activities because of white-supremacist attitudes in society at large, participation in a trans-Pacific economy, and the organization of schools to educate members of the rising generation. Responding to conditions specific to British Columbia, this "Chinese" nationalism was as Canadian as it was Chinese.

Other diasporas—for example, the Russians in Baltic States (Estonia, Latvia, Lithuania) and other non-Russian parts of the former Soviet Union, the Irish in North America, and the Iranians in Europe and America—pose other problems.

THE DIASPORIC GROUP AND ITS OLD HOMELAND. As we saw earlier, kinship and other social networks maintain a flow of people and resources between the origin (old home) and destination (new home). Migration and urban experience redefine the meaning and context of kinship relations. Informal networks based on origin operate selectively, as power relations (i.e., patron-client networks). Kinship relations are strongest within the groups who have already managed to survive in the city, or who are beginning to succeed. These networks tend to isolate the poor, handicapped, disadvantaged, unsuccessful migrants, and newcomers. A dual origin-destination commitment is fostered often by the lack of economic and political security of the immigrants in their new home, and by loyalty to the old homeland.

However, the connections between old home and new home are often practical. Strong social networks emerge, involving sizable remittances from the emigrant community together with programs to enhance employment opportunities in the homeland. Remittances are used mainly to pay debts, purchase consumer goods, improve housing, and for social purposes.

In the case of the Zimbabwean diaspora in Great Britain, monetary remittances are estimated to be bigger than the total amount of British state aid to Zimbabwe. The sending of remittances is just one way in which members of the diaspora maintain financial ties with their homelands. Through investments, donations, support for political parties, financial contributions to social causes, or the payment of taxes, members of the diaspora can maintain a wide variety of different financial contacts with their homelands.

Studying these different kinds of relationships, scholars have generally understood money to be simply a resource; they have assumed that members of the diaspora maintain financial ties to their homelands because of an already existing attachment to them. By contrast, Lainer-Vos (2010) argues that money can also be understood as a way by which members of the diaspora construct new and different views of the homeland—a mechanism by which diasporas re-frame and re-negotiate those ties of attachment.

Consider the different types of relationships that varying types of financial ties gives rise to. When a flow of money is considered to be an investment, one expects notions of equality, exchange, and profit to dominate whatever transactions that take place; a certain distance and accountability between the relevant parties is required. In the case of a donation, the diasporic provider is empowered as a generous patron while those in the homeland are reduced to being "needy" receivers of aid (Lainer-Vos, 2010). In these different contexts, different sorts of ties are negotiated between the diaspora and their homelands. In each case, the exchange of money does not indicate the existence of prior identification or attachment. Instead, financial transactions work to negotiate and construct views of the "homeland" among the diaspora. Despite the material advantages emigrants may enjoy in their new home, the migrants often feel needs and aspirations that can only be satisfied in their home country, a factor which keeps their vision focused on their return. Many, for this reason, construct a house in the home village. However, the reinsertion of returned emigrants often presents problems, including competition with the local population, whose prosperity was often based on money sent back by the emigrants.

The most successful diasporic groups walk a fine line between assimilating economically and socially while maintaining a loyalty to their ethnic origin and old homeland. As a result of this loyalty, diaspora activists involved in their adopted country's politics may get caught up in conflicting allegiances: they must justify their actions in terms of their new home's values and national interests, answer to their ethnic compatriots in the new home, yet prove their loyalty to their "old home." This has proved problematic for Jewish Americans involved in Israeli issues, Irish Americans involved in Irish issues, and African Americans involved in African struggles for self-determination in South Africa and elsewhere.

Diasporas create global linkages within ethnic groups and transnational groupings based on ancestry. Political events in the home country often have effects on the migrants and their politics in the new homeland. Often, these distant events unify the immigrants and strengthen their ethnic identity and loyalty to the homeland. They may politicize the group and mobilize support for local (ethnic) institutions. They may also change relationships between the immigrant group and the host society, or between two immigrant groups.

This fact raises new questions, such as: (1) Under what conditions will diasporic groups seek influence in international affairs? (2) Under what conditions will diasporic groups succeed in influencing international affairs? (3) Does diasporic loyalty and identity offer an alternative to nation-state loyalty? And (4) is global conflict the reason why local ethnic identities are remaining strong?

Ethnic involvement in U.S. foreign affairs is an important way for disenfranchised groups to gain entry into American society and politics. In order to achieve such a role, ethnic officials must first show that they advocate principles of pluralism, democracy, and human rights outside the U.S. Ethnic lobbies may then be used by U.S. policy-makers to export and safeguard American values abroad, and are expected to become the moral conscience of new democracies or newly established states in their homelands. This further legitimates the ethnic voice in U.S. external affairs. The "Israel lobby" is arguably one of the most powerful and influential ethnic lobbies to operate in the United States. It is neither an established organization nor a recognized entity, but a loose grouping of like-minded organizations seeking to move U.S. foreign policy in a pro-Israel direction. During the last two decades, the Israel lobby is known to have influenced some of the biggest foreign policy decisions of the United States. Consider, for instance, the active role that many members of the Israel lobby took in the lead-up to the American invasion of Iraq. Mearsheimer and Walt (2006) go so far as to say that the United States would not have invaded Iraq without the efforts of pro-Israel, anti-Saddam Hussein activists. Consider, too, the active role that many members of the Israel lobby advocate the United States take in regard to Iran's nuclear program. Pro-Israel activists are among the most ardent supporters of a military strike on Iran's nuclear facilities, and seek to shape U.S. foreign policy to fit their preferences.

In part because of the activities of the Israel lobby, Israel now enjoys an extremely close relationship with the United States. Although Israel is as wealthy a nation as Spain or South Korea, it continues to receive approximately $3 billion in aid from the United States annually. Israeli companies enjoy special arrangements and access in the United States, while the Israeli government can be certain of the United States' full diplomatic support. Mearsheimer and Walt argue that this "special relationship" has had adverse effects on the pursuit of American national interests in the Middle East. Specifically, they claim that the United States' close relationship with Israel is undermining the "war on terror" and broad efforts to deal with rogue states internationally.

The argument made by Mearsheimer and Walt has been dismissed by many as being "uncivilized" and "irrational." Aaron Friedberg, for instance, argues that it is only right that the United States support Israel because it is the sole functioning democracy in the Middle East. Dennis Ross similarly argues that it is ludicrous to claim, as Mearsheimer and Walt did, that the American invasion of Iraq would not have taken place without the Israel lobby. The terrorist attacks of September 11, 2001, were the main driving force behind the invasion of Iraq, not the lobbying activities of pro-Israel activists.

The discussion surrounding the Israel lobby's influence suggests that diasporic or ethnic lobbying is very controversial, especially when it becomes successful. To a great extent, the success of the Israel lobby can be attributed to a mixture of strong connections with Israel—the "homeland" of Jewry, in Zionist thinking—yet strong assimilation into American society. Zionism as an ideology merged ancient myths about a common religion and ancestry into a successful nationalist movement, uniting diasporic Jews throughout the world and resulting, finally, in the establishment of the state of Israel in 1948. The combination of myths and political action allowed Zionism to create a single nation out of a heterogeneous and geographically scattered people.

The goals of the early Zionist program in Israel included the absorption of immigrants, integration of the diaspora, and settlement of the land. Continuing political problems with displaced Palestinians have since rendered these goals problematic, especially because of new sociopolitical divisions based on religious differences. The African and Asian Jews who migrated to Israel were typically less educated and more orthodox than the European and American Jews who immigrated earlier.

Today, many diasporic Jews are concerned about the tight connection between religion and state in Israel. Fundraising remains a powerful bond between Israel and the 8.8 million Jews who live outside of Israel. Jews who might otherwise be more involved with Judaism or with Israel are alienated by aggressive solicitation for funds. As well, many are unhappy with some of the political and foreign policy positions Israel has taken. Reform and agnostic Jews are especially concerned about the dominant position of orthodox Jewish thinking in the Israeli state: they are no more sympathetic to orthodox Judaism than to fundamentalist Islam or Christianity. Many are also critical of a militant, uncompromising approach to dealing with Palestinian rights and claims. They are disheartened by what appears to them to be an intolerant blend of religious extremism and exclusivist nationalism that refuses to contemplate meaningful measures to even partially integrate the Arab minority. They prefer to advance values such as religious pluralism, democracy, and improved Jewish-Arab relations.

Many Jewish groups are redirecting their concern and resources to local problems of religious education and social welfare. As religious pluralism, revival, and renewal catch hold in the diaspora, Israel seems more deeply caught in a sharp dichotomy between the religious and the secular. Maintaining a Jewish identity in America is a constant struggle, as is maintaining a humanist, cosmopolitan identity in Israel. There is a need, in the view of many diasporic Jews, for Israel to move toward a post-Zionist state. Such a post-Zionist Israel, although retaining its Jewish character, will safeguard and advance the interests of its citizens regardless of ethnicity. The status of non-Jewish Israelis will be enhanced and the status of non-Israeli Jews reduced. Further, Israel will be integrated into the region and engage in normal relations with its neighbours. Whether such an outcome is likely is another matter.

The situation of diasporic African Americans is different, for a variety of reasons. First, most African Americans are so many generations removed from their African homeland that they may not even be able to identify it, much less identify with it. Second, there is such a difference between America and virtually any African country—economically, culturally, socially, climatically, and otherwise—that a "return" to the homeland would constitute a major leap in the dark. There is far less difference between the urban United States (or Russia) and urban Israel than there is between the urban United States and urban (let alone rural) Ghana or Nigeria.

Having said that, the twentieth-century movement of diasporic Africans back to Africa constitutes a response to the forced diasporization of African slaves to all corners of the globe. African Americans and people of African descent from the Caribbean and South America have been returning to Africa since the eighteenth century. Research on diasporic Africans who have settled in Ghana in the past forty years find a majority expressing a strong allegiance to their national (place of birth) identities along with a sense of belonging to a larger African community.

The return of African Americans as tourists to the slave dungeons of Elmina Castle in Ghana poses some interesting questions. The castle, which is one of the star attractions of Ghana's tourist trade, is viewed in different ways by the locals than by diasporic blacks. To African Americans, the castle is sacred ground: they want it to remain a cemetery for the slaves who died in the dungeon's inhuman conditions while waiting for the ships to transport them to the Americas. Ghanaians, on the other hand, want the castle restored, with good lighting and heating, so that it will be attractive to British, Dutch, and local tourists. In the end, the question is one of how the castle should be interpreted and also of the associated issue of power: who owns it?

Compared with the Jewish lobby, the African American lobby has had little effect on foreign policy issues in the United States. TransAfrica, the first legally mandated African American foreign policy lobby devoted exclusively to black diaspora issues outside the U.S., supported South African sanctions in 1986 and the retention of Rhodesian sanctions at the end of the 1970s. With these exceptions, few congressional foreign policy outcomes on African issues have been compatible with TransAfrica's policy positions.

Nonetheless, the last three decades have seen identification and connectedness grow between African Americans, Africans, and Caribbean blacks. Black studies, African studies, and Caribbean studies curricula are popular in a growing number of universities, colleges, and secondary schools. More of the previously hidden history of the African and African American peoples is being written and shared.

The Chinese diaspora is similar in some ways to the Jewish diaspora. According to Lin Qitan, the overseas Chinese migration happened in three stages: migration from inland to coastal areas in ancient times, migration to other regions of Southeast Asia in more recent times, and migration all over the world after World War II. The Chinese diaspora now spans 119 countries and regions worldwide.

Despite a continuing identification with Chinese culture in many diasporic communities, there is little sign that any but the most recent immigrants have a desire to return to China, Hong Kong, or Taiwan. Some Hong Kong Chinese have taken up a phantom residence in the diaspora, as a hedge against the mainland government turning oppressive. Some continue to do business in Hong Kong and China and may eventually return there for good, but many diasporic Chinese choose to remain in their adopted homelands. As opportunities for investment and economic development in China and other parts of the Pacific Rim remain outstanding, however, there are significant "pull factors" which draw diasporic Chinese back to their native homeland. By virtue of its size, history and culture, the People's Republic of China continues to have a profound impact on the diaspora's identity formation.

Assimilation of diasporic Chinese is always mixed, as it is for other diasporic groups. For example, Chinese people in Thailand vary considerably in their degree of Chinese ethnicity, and their "Thai-ness," depending on their place of residence, generation, class, religion, language, and gender. On the one side, national political socialization, Thai citizenship, and nation-building opportunities pull the diasporic Chinese towards assimilation. On the other side, global culture, trade flow, and transnational influences that include the economic growth of the People's Republic of China pull in the opposite direction.

THE DIASPORA AS TRANSNATIONAL STRUCTURE. New migration patterns imply new forms of migrant communities. Their experiences affect the perception both of national borders and geographical distance between people and groups. Migrants can maintain social and economic networks more easily than a few decades ago; their scope of action and social relations is transnational, and they constitute transnational non-territorial communities. In terms of belonging, however, they are not necessarily characterized by a transnational identity. These transnational communities may often be cemented by ethnic ties that go deeper than the formal membership of their members in the country in which they live. Thus, transnational communities are de-territorialized, but they nevertheless reproduce a traditional ethnic identity in a global world.

Transnationalism is the outcome of several interpenetrating complex factors: the globalization of capitalism, a revolution in communication and transportation technologies, decolonization and an expansion of human rights, and the growth of social networks that facilitate transnational migration patterns. Because transnationalism is a multifaceted, multi-local process, it has complicated consequences for power in both local and global communities.

Transnational social spaces, with their circular flows of people, goods, information, and symbols, provide immigrants and refugees with a third trajectory apart from assimilation and ethnic pluralism. Transnational groups often suffer from discrimination and xenophobia, as did the Turks in Germany. Informal networks of Turkish migrant families in Berlin present a similar picture: international labour migration has a profound impact on social change and the meaning attached to nationality and ethnicity, community and family.

The idea of a victim diaspora can be sustained in some cases: for example, the African slave trade, the Turkish mass deportation of Armenians. However, many diasporas have been characterized by some degree of voluntary emigration or a mix of forced and colonizing migration. Despite nationalist, culturalist, and return-home sentiments, the diaspora offers a possible alternative to nation-state loyalty. Increasingly, people live in international families that operate on the principle of networks rather than households. Among Caribbean immigrants to California, these networks are given form and content by women, mainly through a system of informal adoption (child-minding) that follows a long Caribbean tradition. With these women providing fixed nodes for childcare, other kin can work in a variety of locales.

Transnational families and childhoods are different from the "usual" experience of those not part of such diasporas. In some cases, chain migration results in adult family members coming first, leaving children behind to be cared for by relatives and friends in the home country. Later, children are sent for to join their parents. Ties to the home country may continue, with back-and-forth movements by children as well as adults. Children play an active role in sustaining transnational networks, both through their labour and how they link adults who share the tasks of parenting. By contrast, so-called "parachute children" are sent, unaccompanied, to live abroad, with the goal of taking long-term advantage of educational and economic opportunities, while their parents continue to live and work in the home country.

Migration of both kinds, whether one-way or back-and-forth, disrupts and reconfigures relationships between parents and children, alters definitions of children (their capabilities, their "proper places"), and challenges conventional Western assumptions about the nature of the child.

Migrant groups are, as William Butler Yeats said of the migrant Irish, communities "bound together by imaginative possessions." As transnationally mobile people evolve new roles and identities, host societies respond by trying to fit these people into often outdated categories. Peruvians of Japanese descent—Nikkei-Peruvians—provide an example of a community dispersed over different countries. Half of the 80,000 Nikkei-Peruvians live in Japan as contract workers, and the rest live in Peru and the U.S. Because of their Japanese blood, they are welcome as contract workers in Japan. Yet, although Nikkei Peruvians feel, behave, and are treated more like Japanese when in Lima, they feel, behave, and are treated more like Peruvians when in Japan. A result is the construction of a transnational ethnic identity that goes beyond bounded notions of nation, culture and ethnicity. This strategy of accommodation helps those "sojourners" who do not fit the traditional sense of fixed and mutually exclusive national, cultural, and ethnic boundaries.

DIASPORAS TO COME. Ethnic and national diasporas, as we have seen, can pose a threat to international peace and security. Several state-based established and incipient diasporas in Europe include the following: (1) the Albanians in Kosovo, Macedonia, Montenegro, and Greece; (2) the Germans in Russia, eastern Europe, and the central Asian States, principally Kazakhstan; (3) the Hungarians in Romania, Slovakia, and Vojvodina; (4) the Poles in Belarus, Lithuania, and Ukraine; (5) the Turks in Bulgaria; (6) Turkish labour migration to northwestern Europe; (7) the Russian diaspora that was created by the collapse of the USSR; and (8) migrant worker diasporas.

By studying diasporas we learn that ancestry is no less useful a category for understanding social organization than age or gender. The new electronic media make it possible to capitalize on this ancestral tie by building "virtual ethnic communities" that link diasporic groups with a common ancestry. National frontiers and physical distance need no longer pose barriers to regular and dense interactions. Russian Jews in Russia, Israel, the U.S. and elsewhere have created a worldwide community, for example, that relies on technological access and international travel.

The twenty-first century will likely see more of the inter-ethnic conflicts that were so common in the twentieth century. There will be more refugees but different ways of thinking about refugees and exile than in the past. Thinking about diasporas, displacement, and de-territorialization suggests traditional ideas about refugees and exile may be outdated. They only make sense if "home" is still there. In post-modernity, "there" is in doubt. (Where, after all, is Yugoslavia? The USSR? Czechoslovakia?) The future will hear more talk of displacement, diaspora, loss of home, homes away from home, roots and routes, and geographies of identity. We can only begin to imagine the transnational world that will come to life in people's imaginations.

CHAPTER FIVE

Mobility

Where migration is the movement of people in physical space, *mobility* (or *social mobility*) is the movement of people in social space. Just as "society" is an ideal or imaginary structure, so social space is an imaginary structure, a useful but invisible partitioning of the observable world.

An Overview

When we study social mobility, we study the movement of real people between imaginary locations: for example, between social classes, occupational statuses, or income levels. It is more difficult to say whether someone is a member of the working class than to say she is living in Toronto. One of the greatest difficulties in studying mobility, therefore, lies in knowing how to define and measure these imaginary locations.

Once we have established these imaginary categories of social space, the study of mobility is similar in many ways to the study of migration and diffusion. Imagine that we have succeeded in defining three categories in social space: the working class, middle class, and upper class. In studying mobility, we are interested in the flows between these locations and the *stock* of people who accumulate in each class because of these flows. As with diffusion, we are interested in the spread or coverage achieved by people who flow out of each location, and the rate at which they flow out. As with migration, we are interested in the total number of mobile people originating in each location, changes in the size of the stock of each location, the rate at which the stock turns over (i.e., enters and exits), and the degree that movements of people link locations.

This sounds abstract. More concretely, by studying mobility we want to learn about the size and composition of different social classes, and the links that tie these classes together. Some special features of mobility distinguish it from migration and bear special mention. Migration is horizontal movement in space; mobility is vertical movement. When we study mobile people, we are studying people who are moving "up" and "down," between what our society defines as better and worse social positions. Thus, we view *upward mobility* as opportunities for advancement. We are interested in studying the conditions under which more people or fewer people are upwardly mobile, and characteristics of the people who are most and least mobile. This tells us something about the openness of our society.

Second, just as there are many routes from (say) Toronto to Montreal, there are many channels of upward mobility. There is more than one way to move from junior executive to company president. However, some types of movement are impossible. For example, even the most diligent nurse cannot become a doctor simply by moving up within the profession of nursing itself. Retraining is required. In the military, even the most devoted sergeant (a non-commissioned officer) cannot become a lieutenant (a commissioned officer) without retraining. And even the hardest working hamburger flipper at McDonalds is unlikely to become CEO. There are observably well-trodden paths between some sets of positions and few (if any) observable paths between others. This is what we mean by *work force segmentation*. People are mobile within, not across, different channels of flow. Thus, we want to study the kinds of career paths that are open to people in different lines of work, with different starting conditions and different social characteristics. We are interested also in the conditions that make labour markets more segmented or less so.

Third, within channels of flow, people often have to wait for vacancies to open up before they can advance. This means that lineups or *queues* form. Often, the seniority principle, which is essentially a principle of "first come, first served," regulates entry into the best positions. In seniority systems, everyone is mobile and many move from bottom to top. That's what happens in a ticket line for a movie, for example, and it is what happens to commissioned officers in wartime. However, in some seniority systems, movement is slower than in other systems. Queues get longer and longer; the waiting time to promotion lengthens. So we want to study the conditions under which waiting times are shorter or longer, and whether people maintain or break the seniority rules. We are also interested in how people deal with waiting and queuing in a society where upward mobility is one chief aspect of what people consider personal "success."

So far, we have only spoken of mobile individuals. In fact, groups (such as families or ethnic groups) are socially mobile, too. With similar methods, we can study the mobility of business firms, nations, and empires. Social classes are especially important for studies of mobility. We are interested in the movement of people up the class ladder and, also, the change in class conditions compared to other classes: thus, class mobility. In Marxist theory, classes are historic actors. Their rise and fall is considered the engine of history.

The study of social mobility is the study of culturally meaningful changes in the human condition. As we already noted, individual mobility is how our culture measures "success," "openness" and "equal opportunity."

We call mobility across generations *intergenerational mobility*. We call mobility within a generation *intragenerational* or *career mobility*. We discuss both kinds of mobility in this chapter. When studying the mobile person (and his or her family), we are interested in the resources needed to become mobile, reasons for leaving one class and coming to another, the ease of assimilating economically and socially in a new class, and the myths and expectations that support social mobility.

EXCHANGE MOBILITY. *Exchange mobility* is mobility that requires the displacement of the occupant of a position. For example, there is only one Roman Catholic Pope or English monarch at a time. No one can enter these positions until the incumbents leave. In other organizations, the number of positions at a given level is greater than one, but limited. No one can become a judge on the Supreme Court, for example, until an office holder leaves his or her position. The British civil service, like many bureaucracies, works this way. There are only so many positions at any given level of the hierarchy. People occupying lower positions have to wait for a vacancy before advancing up the ladder. Even so, people can only advance single-file. The waiting time can be long, and longer for some than for others.

Mobility in most organizations is orderly and operates according to seniority. This tells us that we can use intragenerational mobility to reveal the hidden structure of an organization. Sociologist Harrison White (1970) invented the notion of *vacancy chains* to discuss this phenomenon. He studied the mobility of Episcopalian ministers through churches. He assumed that ministers move upwards over time, if they move at all. This fact makes it possible to detect what is "up": that is, what is the underlying hierarchical structure of the Episcopalian Church. By seeing which churches are *senders* and which are *receivers* of mobile ministers, he could figure out which churches are close in status to one another and which are distant, which are higher and which are lower. Then he could analyze the factors that determine a church's status.

White also studied the factors that determine the length of an average vacancy chain: that is, the number of moves that are set in motion by the creation of a single vacancy due to death or retirement. He studied the reasons why some years produce more chains and longer chains than other years. Typically, a longer chain starts higher in the church structure. Typically, it occurs during a period of organizational growth or stability, when all parishes still need ministers.

STRUCTURAL MOBILITY. *Structural mobility* is movement that does not require the displacement of an occupant of a position. It is mobility made possible by the creation of additional positions, typically through organizational or economic growth. In all industrial societies, upward and downward mobility is common within the (huge) middle class. Mobility into or out of the upper and lower classes is much less common (Heisz and Corak, 1996). That is because most job growth occurs within the middle class, the class that typically does white-collar work or owns businesses. As Lipset and Bendix show in a classic study of social mobility in industrial societies, the growth of the middle class determines a society's mobility rates, whatever that society's dominant culture or religion. The greater the rate at which economic development creates better jobs, the faster people move upward.

Where a society is industrializing rapidly, high mobility rates fill the newly created jobs and transform the class structure. With high rates of mobility, an agricultural society rapidly becomes a blue-collar (manufacturing) society, and a blue-collar society rapidly becomes a white-collar (service) society. How *long* the transformation takes will depend on (1) how *extreme* the starting conditions are, and (2) how *high* the rates of flow are from one class into another. Over time, even modest rates of flow affect the class structure.

Consider the results of a classic (1949) study by Glass and Hall of intergenerational social mobility in England and Wales. In this society, class inheritance is common. People are likely to remain in the class into which they are born. However, mobility is common, too. England after the Second World War was a fluid or open society. The middle class was the most common destination for all sons, whatever their class of origin. That was because, during and after the War, the middle class was growing more rapidly than any other class. However, we see little extreme movement (from rags to riches, or riches to rags) in this situation. The chances of "jumping" a class are slight, in this society and in other industrial societies that sociologists have investigated.

People born into the lowest class are especially likely to remain in their class of birth. Mathematicians would describe poverty as an "absorbing state"—a condition that, once entered, is impossible to leave. Sociologists have put forward various theories to explain this oft-noted fact. One common view that attributes poverty to faulty values and a lack of ambition finds little support in sociological research.

Three other explanations or models are more promising (Corcoran, 1995). First, the *resource model* proposes that parental resources consistently predict (and determine) children's adult attainments. Thus, poverty is due to parental lack of income and education, which predicts low educational aspirations and attainments, and low incomes, in children. Second, the *correlated disadvantage model* proposes that multiple disadvantages (for example, a broken family, few familial or community resources, or racial discrimination) compound problem of poverty. Finally, William Julius Wilson's *underclass model* proposes that the experiences of a poor labour market and a poor neighbourhood get children off to a slow start and burden them with low mobility as adults.

Like poverty, wealth is an absorbing state. Children inherit advantage just as they inherit disadvantage. The rich pass along to their children a good education, social skills, social connections, and property. It is truly odd when families lose their wealth.

Careers

As we mentioned in the introduction to this book, social mobility is harder to study than migration or diffusion because it obliges us to deal in imaginary, hard-to-define, and hard-to-measure categories like "social class." But in many instances, we are able in the study of social mobility to deal with real, defined, and measurable categories.

In studying intergenerational mobility, if we can agree that being a medical doctor is "better" or "higher status" than being (say) a car salesman—because it earns a higher average income and gains more respect on measures of job prestige—then we can say that a car salesman's daughter who became a medical doctor was upwardly mobile. Likewise, and conversely, we may be able to agree that a doctor's son who became (say) an auto mechanic was downwardly mobile. But we may have trouble agreeing that income and job prestige are suitable measures of a job's worth; indeed, it may be difficult to satisfy ourselves about the true standing of many professions, whatever their earning power. Consider the social worth of jobs like novelist, nurse, minister of religion, journalist, and high school teacher. Was the daughter of a car salesman who became a novelist or nurse upwardly mobile, downwardly mobile, or neither?

By comparison, the study of intragenerational or career mobility is often much simpler, if only because you don't have to grapple with ambiguous rating systems. A person who, as an auto mechanic, progresses from student to apprentice to licensed mechanic to auto shop owner, can reasonably be said to have had an upwardly mobile career. And that assessment is even easier for people who work in large, multi-level organizations, like armies or bureaucracies. A member of the armed forces who starts her career as a private, then progresses up the ranks to lieutenant, captain, major, colonel, and finally general can certainly be said to have been upwardly mobile in a career. And that is why the study of career mobility is much more rigorous and satisfying for sociologists than the study of inter-generational mobility. With career mobility, you can be much more certain about the kinds of conditions and personal characteristics that are associated with mobility and immobility, upward mobility and downward mobility.

The word "career" originates in words that mean "race course" and "carriage road." To say that a person has a *career*, then, implies he or she is rapidly moving toward a goal alongside, or in competition with, others.

Every career, like every horse or auto race, has a starting point. Starting from there, competitors move forward past road markers. Ideally, no one starts ahead of anyone else, and no one fails to pass a marker. Some competitors progress faster than others; one competitor "wins" the race, and others "place" or "show." Over an extended period, many competitors get to the finish line before leaving the track, though we do not consider them winners.

Though simplified, this depiction captures the essence of many careers, traditional and. Consider, for example, the careers of clerks in Great Britain's Lloyds Bank. In the nineteenth century, clerks' salaries were linked to their length of tenure. Clerks of varying seniority received widely varying salaries. Employees of lesser tenure might receive smaller salaries even if they held higher positions. By the late twentieth century, this had changed so that mobility and other rewards depended on rank and achievement. As banks grew, consolidated, and expanded their branch networks, the need for local job networks decreased. Higher levels of integration led to a wider division of labour and more competitive work environment. The male achievement-based career emerged as the entry of women created a new tier of employees within the clerical ranks.

Let's apply some formal concepts to this description. As the banking industry expanded, the number of clerical jobs increased. The occupational structure of banking differentiated, producing new jobs, so that people looking for a bank job could enter the industry at different levels. Men dominated some jobs, women others. Some required job candidates to possess a secondary educational degree, some a post-secondary degree. Within each of these *internal labour markets*, career progress was still largely predictable and based on seniority. However, advancement was less predictable than before. It was now largely based on achievement, in three senses.

ACHIEVEMENT VERSUS ASCRIPTION. First, with market differentiation, people with different credentials entered the industry at different job levels. Typically, men entered above women, and post-secondary graduates entered above less-educated candidates. Second, high achievers moved ahead farther and faster than ordinary, run-of-the-mill bank clerks. They might not pass all the customary road markers in the customary order, or at the customary time. Organizational growth led to more differentiation and more opportunities. High achievers could move about within an organization, gaining wider experience and exposure. Third, with the development of universalistic, or cross-organizational, credentials (such as educational degrees), high achievers could move from one organization to another, gaining additional experience and exposure in the industry at large but continually increasing their status and rewards.

Thus, career mobility increased through industrial growth and differentiation, and through the rise of achievement as a basis for ranking. Professions (such as medicine and law) are especially notable for these features, including their ability to control career entries, reward systems, and conditions of work. Note, however, that *ascription*—the assignment of status based on inheritance, not merit or achievement—never fully lost its importance as an ordering principle, nor did careers stop being time-dependent. Today, many careers are still gendered; we discuss career gendering and "glass ceilings" in a later section. Many employers continue to prefer candidates from particular ethnic or racial groups. All, increasingly, favour highly educated candidates over less educated ones. Though (in a sense) hiring by educational attainment is a way of rewarding achievement, education remains a largely ascribed characteristic. We largely inherit educational attainment, as we see in the next chapter, from our parents. So, ascription has scarcely disappeared.

Note, finally, the importance of persistence in career patterns. Over extended periods, people in careers remain in the same industries, occupations, and even jobs. "Rags to riches" aspirations abound, and people fulfill some; however, rapid and extreme ascent is the exception in mature industrial societies. This may due to the machinations of the highest-ranking "achievers": they have ensured that nothing can unseat them and people like them. It is only in societies *without* a stable government and economy—societies dominated by military juntas, black markets, and patron-client politics—that "rags to riches" stories are played out in real life.

Careers are highly patterned largely because of the workings of internal labour markets that impose a high degree of control over who enters, at what level, through what stages people will move, and at what rate. The result is that, even today, society sorts people into different types of careers, and their children into different neighbourhoods, schools, and marriages. By this means, we have maintained and transmitted inequality from one generation to the next, a topic we discuss at length later in the book.

CAREER LINES. *Career lines* have five elementary properties: *age*, *composition*, *continuity*, *channelling*, *ports of entry and exit*, and *career development*.

People enter the given career at similar ages and advance at similar (though not identical) rates. Between ages 18 to 30, their chances are structured, first, by differences in human capital and social psychological orientation. These determine, to a great degree, people's educational aspirations and achievements, and occupational aspirations. Gender also affects the access to career lines. Communities of origin and residence are the local opportunity structures within which people seek and find their first real jobs. Finally, life course events, in education, work, family, and otherwise, interact with contingencies to sort people into jobs with better and worse prospects.

Four major theories help us to understand the young adult's transition from school to the labour force. *Segmented labour market theory* notes the labour market is stratified, by that fact making entry and upward mobility difficult for employees with only a high school education. *Human capital theory* attributes the problems of new entrants to the labour force to deficiencies in their training that lessen their value to the hiring organization. *Signalling theory* refers to the employers' use of signs or signals to judge the potential worth and trainability of a young employee. Finally, *network theory* describes a method for obtaining employment based on the "word" of a friend or relative, who vouches for the quality of the potential employee.

A first job strongly predicts a later job, since it regulates access (through the internal labor market) to higher-level jobs. As time passes, people age and move up. Organizational level is largely age-dependent, and people at particular levels are the same ages. As time passes, people in organizations improve their status and income. By age 45, the incomes in most occupations plateau and income differences among occupations often become large.

A SERIES OF JOBS. Both in fact and belief, careers offer people a lifetime of jobs and status within, or sometimes across, organizations within an industry: so, continuity in a life course. Careers channel people from some specific positions into other specific positions, according to an organizational plan that reflects the dominant thinking about career development. The notion of "career development" implies a belief in the need to plan and to prepare a pool of candidates who will be suitable, in time, for high positions.

As we expect people to enter careers at particular levels, so we expect them to exit at particular levels, or though particular "ports." Typically, departure rates from a large hierarchical company decline as the level of already obtained achievement in the company increases. High-level, high-seniority people are less likely to leave voluntarily. Likewise, departure rates are lower in locations in the company with high promotion rates than in locations with low promotion rates. Thus, decisions to leave are dependent on internal career opportunities. People stay where the opportunities are best.

Seniority in the firm is much more important than age for departure decisions. Thus, a 45-year-old low-seniority worker is more likely to leave than a 45-year-old high-seniority worker, or even than a 60-year-old high-seniority worker. This suggests that turnover is related more to the build-up of firm-specific skills than to life-cycle considerations. Finally, women leave the organization for personal reasons more often than men, and less often for career reasons.

Different occupational groups and labour market segments have different career patterns (e.g., stages, ports of entry, and exits). This is due in large part to the organization's need to control labour, especially scarce and highly skilled labour, by promising future rewards, a practice we sometimes call *bureaucratic control*. This type of control combines two key elements: a mass of formal rules and procedures, and the promise of career rewards for conformity and effective performance. The career opportunity serves as an internalized source of control over behaviour. Looked at another way, career opportunities are the carrots and written rules the sticks of large organizations. Together, they ensure conformity and keep control in the hands of top management.

Bureaucratic control is most common in large offices that manage production, provide services, or manipulate information. The type of worker found in a bureaucracy is more highly educated than workers in many other organizations and possesses middle-class goals. Such a worker has learned to follow rules, both by formal schooling (at least through secondary school) and (often) by a middle-class upbringing. He or she also wants to get ahead. These goals persuade the worker to trade present conformity for future rewards.

THE IMPORTANCE OF PATHWAYS. Remember that a career is the promise of more than a job. It is the prospect of a series of increasingly desirable jobs. Research on organizations shows that it matters how employees arrive at a certain hierarchical level in an organization, and how fast they get there. The faster workers obtain their first promotion, the better are their chances for further promotions.

This observation accords with a "tournament model," which posits path dependence. Mobility early in one's career has a strong relationship with career ceiling, career floors, and promotion and demotion probabilities in each successive period. Said another way, it matters what path you take in your career, and not where you start. The paths we take, as much as our social origins and personal qualities, shape us all.

This becomes amply clear in studies of schools where they practice tracking or streaming. In subtle and complex ways, grade-weighting procedures belittle the achievements of lower-track students, reducing post-graduation opportunities. Tracking even changes students' IQ scores between eighth and tenth grades, after controlling for initial ability, sex, and social class. Tracking tends to differentiate the IQ scores of students in the higher track and homogenize scores in the lower one. Perhaps this is because teachers give their college-bound students more incentives for motivation, discipline, and achievement.

In college and university, the sorting of students into different programs with different curricula also influences later opportunities, by sending prospective employers different messages about the abilities of job candidates. Thus, a B.A. in philosophy sends a different message than a B.A. in physics or political science. In organizations, the sorting of workers into different authority levels amplifies the effects of postsecondary attainment on earnings. Graduates of preferred colleges earn more as well.

INSTITUTIONAL LINKAGES. The high school, postsecondary, and labour markets are linked over the life-course, and together shape the lifetime career. This connection is clearest in Japan, where schools and employers are highly responsive to each other. The Japanese institutional system reduces competition in the labour market by shifting the competition for jobs into and among schools. This creates a highly meritocratic system for allocating desirable jobs. Such institutional networks of schools and organizations differ from both economic markets and from personal networks, and have practical and theoretical implications for the relationship between education and work. In Japan, schools play a significant role in the student's job search. By contrast, Canadian and American schools are expected to provide training but not influence hiring.

Such *institutional linkages* are valuable to societies, employers, and employees. Economic theory warns about the inefficiencies of institutional linkages, but school-employer linkages can enhance incentives, the flow of information, and employment outcomes. The student's school-to-work transition is improved if schools make academic instruction vocationally relevant, employers base hiring on applicants' achievement in school, and we have appropriately designed and set up school-employer linkages.

We build institutional linkages on three expectations about the flow of labour: dependable supply, dependable skills, and dependable quality. At best, the school-workplace linkage can efficiently supply needed workers with the needed skills and verify their quality. In this way they support a reward system at work that is based on merit. What we need, first, is that high school guidance counsellors play a more active role as gatekeepers. They must act more vigorously to discourage students whose college plans are inappropriate—in effect, helping them to address unpleasant realities. Only in this way will employers come to trust available school information (e.g., grades) when hiring youth, and rely less on social networks or impressions gained during interviews. Doing so may also lead employers to respond to skill shortages by hiring skilled young workers rather than retraining the present work staff or lowering their expectations.

Thus, careers are job-related pathways over the life course. On the individual level, careers reflect differences (and similarities) in opportunities and human capital. On the corporate level, they reflect linkages within firms, across firms, and across institutions. As careers tie together life events, so they also tie together institutional activities.

DUAL LABOUR MARKETS. The market metaphor offers us a different way to view careers. It invites us to imagine a place where people meet to buy, sell, and bargain. A *job market* is an imaginary place where workers offer their services to employers with jobs to fill. However, not all jobs (or job-seekers) are in competition with one another.

Careers take place within submarkets or economic sectors, in which a segmentation of jobs and careers has occurred. *Dual labour markets*—primary and secondary—coexist within every region, province, and size of community. The primary labour market consists of jobs which offer good wages, chances to get ahead, and job security: it includes jobs like lawyer, plumber, and teacher. The secondary (or marginal) labour market consists of jobs that pay low wages, offer little chance to get ahead, and promise little job security: jobs like taxi driver, secretary, or bank teller.

People with different social traits, backgrounds, and skills often locate in different markets. For example, far more women and visible minorities have moved to the secondary labour market, and far more white men to the primary labour market, than could have occurred by chance. Within markets, we find submarkets that also contain different kinds of jobs and different kinds of people. The big difference between primary and secondary markets tends to blur important differences among jobs in the *same* market. For example, though both are in the primary labour market, few teachers feel they have the sort of benefits and opportunities that doctors do. And though both are in the secondary labour market, few bank tellers consider their work to be the same as that of taxi drivers.

We even find internal labour markets *within* occupations. Consider intercollegiate football and basketball coaches. Jobs within the core of this coaching market are more stable and people have greater chances for mobility. A pathway even leads from the top college jobs into the professional leagues. At the periphery of the market, coaches barely hold a job. Their prospects of moving to the "big time" are zero.

INTERNAL LABOUR MARKETS. From one standpoint, an internal labour market is an organizational process for allocating people with particular training and experiences to a particular sequence of positions. Internal labour markets aim at retaining employees with specific human assets. To reduce transaction costs resulting from turnovers, they design the exchange relations between employee and employer in such a way to ensure continuity. Employees are most committed to their organization when they are making the most progress in their careers. Younger, more educated workers who are not part of an internal labour market are the least satisfied with their career opportunities. Employees who are part of an internal labour market are more committed to their work and their organization than employees who are not.

In effect, an internal labour market is a social structure in which job histories and career lines are extremely predictable: no one gets from A to C without going through B; no one gets to D without going through A, B, and C first; and no one gets into A (therefore, B, C, or D) without satisfying certain entry requirements. Often, people are admitted to A with the expectation that most of them could, eventually, get to D.

Viewed from another perspective, an internal labour market is a self-contained labour entity based on favouritism and bureaucratic principles that is difficult for an outside worker to penetrate. This, as we will see, works against "outsiders" such as women, racial minorities, and the poor.

Internal labour markets are marked by their closure to external competition and by managerial discretion in promotion decisions. Research suggests the greatest concentration of such internal labour markets is found among male-dominated middle-management positions. Within such internal labour markets, experience counts for a great deal: sometimes, even more than education or expertise. Employers especially value on-the-job training and the acquisition of job-specific skills, and organizational loyalty. Other things being equal, *internal* markets gain and lose importance for careers inversely as *external* markets decrease and increase job creation.

Internal labour markets are similar in some respects to the dual labour markets discussed above. Both are exclusionary and offer their members more advantages than they offer non-members. Some labour markets are better than others. However, internal labour markets are likely to include a much wider variety of jobs, job skills, and job applicants, than are primary or secondary labour markets. In this respect, they are similar to the patron-client systems we discussed in an earlier chapter. Thought of another way, internal labour markets are vertically and, sometimes, horizontally integrated job sets.

STRUCTURED ADVANTAGE. Internal labour markets resemble what Ralph Turner called a "sponsored mobility" system in which people, once selected, are helped and guaranteed to get ahead. Education in this system is not so much a source of necessary skill as it is a mark of election to "the few." In countries where sponsored mobility is common (e.g., Japan, Germany, and traditionally Britain), jobs often require a specific type and level of education. Added educational qualifications do not enhance the competitive advantage of job applicants.

We find this educational "threshold" operating in countries with a strongly differentiated, standardized, and publicly recognized job-training system. In other countries, like Canada and the U.S., they constrain job competition less. Status and position are insecure. "The more education the better" is the rule guiding people in such undifferentiated job markets, though educational attainments may have no direct relevance to particular jobs. They differentiate this type of society hierarchically, though it is more open. We socially define school dropouts as unqualified for the labour market. Everyone else is in constant competition.

Much of the exclusiveness and inequality we associate with class relations can be derived from the theory of internal labour markets. Marxist theory may not need a class theory of how societies generate inequality within the labour market, since standard neoclassical economic theory seems consistent with Marx's own conception of the capitalist economy.

ETHNICITY AND PROTECTED MARKETS. Job markets that have perfected the exclusion of certain kinds of people on the basis of education will sometimes exclude them on the grounds of race, ethnicity, or gender, too. Think of the process of job-based racial inequality (or race-based employment) as a hiring queue in which minorities occupy the lower positions among workers ranked according to their desirability to employers.

Those at the head of the queue are first hired and last fired. Those at the tail, the least desirable, are last hired and first fired. Under these conditions, (1) the greater the difference between the two groups on the underlying (objective) determinants of employability, the greater the unemployment differential between them; (2) the less the variability of the disadvantaged group on the characteristics determining employability, the less the employment differential among them; and (3) the more depressed the economy, the greater the unemployment differential between advantaged and disadvantaged.

Economic stagnation and restructuring are impediments to progress toward equality, since employers often still use racial and ethnic queues in hiring. During economic contractions, minorities are more likely than whites to be laid off. Part of the explanation is the size of the minority group compared with the majority. The larger the minority, the greater the oversupply of workers. So, employers easily relegate a large minority to lower occupational standing.

In the American South, the larger the numbers of black men in the work force, the lower are their wages. Throughout the U.S., the larger the numbers of black men in the work force, the higher are the wages for whites (male and female) and black women. Racial queuing concentrates whites in better jobs. As increases in population increase the size of the job market, the best new jobs go disproportionately to white men. Thus, the labour force participation of white teenagers (ages 16 to 18) is both greater and more closely linked to family resources and local economic conditions than that of black teenagers.

Often, excluded minorities respond by creating protected markets. A protected market exists when consumers from an ethnic group uniformly obtain their goods and services from co-ethnics. Protected markets have contributed to the development of the professions and businesses of certain institutionally complete ethnic communities in Canada, such as the Jews and the Chinese.

Protected markets were ideal for ensuring the success of the Cuban entrepreneurial enclave in Dade County, Florida. The most important environmental conditions were (1) accessibility of suppliers, customers, and new markets; (2) ethnic economic control of an ethnically saturated internal labour market; (3) availability of capital and side investments; (4) availability of land; (5) social networks and living conditions similar to Cuba; and (6) government support. Within such conditions, excluded minorities can hope to have normal, or even better than normal, careers. Sometimes, they accomplish this at the expense of other minorities.

THE ROLE OF IMMIGRATION. Historically, the presence of lower-status blacks has enabled some white ethnics to move up the job queue and out of segregated occupations. Cities that had large and growing black populations had decreased occupational segregation for foreigners. Where many blacks were illiterate, levels of segregation for the foreign-born decreased. However, the numbers of foreign-born who were illiterate did not affect occupational segregation for the foreign-born during this period. Occupational segmentation especially affected African American women at the turn of the twentieth century. They were concentrated in the least desirable jobs.

As the topmost ethnic groups move up the labour queue, lower-ranking ethnic groups struggle to fill their place. The continuous recourse to new ethnic immigrants to fill the lowest-paying jobs has made ethnicity the crucial mechanism for ordering groups of people into distinct sets of jobs. As native-born whites vacated the labour market of New York City in the years after the Second World War, for example, new opportunities opened for newcomers to climb the economic totem pole. Since 1900, native-born white Americans (and particularly white males) have controlled generalized occupations to a high degree. Minority ethnic groups typically met much more success in business-related occupations with more specialized clienteles.

With the departure of native-born whites, New York's blacks consolidated their niche in public-sector jobs. However, these jobs required higher skills, more experience, and better credentials than most African Americans possessed. Simultaneously, their share of the remaining low-skilled jobs steadily eroded. Employers have found new immigrants to be more satisfactory for low-paying jobs than partly skilled African Americans. There, and in the unequal competition by higher-skilled blacks with native-born whites, the hopes of the partly disadvantaged and the requirements of jobs are persistently mismatched.

CONCLUDING COMMENTS. Careers take place within the boundaries of organizations. Thus, career opportunities change with changes in organizations: their number, size, structure (e.g., degree of inequality), division of labour, and so on.

Culturally determined preferences for, and perceptions of, certain kinds of people also shape them: men versus women, whites versus non-whites, immigrants versus native-borns. The unequal—many will say unfair—competitions for advancement between these different types of people take place in a cultural and organizational environment in which social legislation tries to regulate job discrimination. This structured competition goes on simultaneously within different sectors or niches: primary versus secondary, mainstream versus ethnic.

The common inclination in our culture to view careers as reflections of little more than the ambition and talent of people is surely misguided. Careers tell us at least as much about the culture, politics, and structuring of our society as they do about the individual people who are living these careers.

Downward Mobility

Downward mobility is the flow of people from positions of higher occupational status (also authority, income, prestige, and job security) to positions of lower status. From one standpoint, the study of downward mobility is simply the mirror image of the study of upward mobility. The things that make people upwardly mobile should be the same things that make people downwardly mobile, if we reverse the signs. Hence, if post-secondary education makes people *more* likely to be upwardly mobile, a failure to complete high school will presumably make people *less* likely to be upwardly mobile and more likely to be downwardly mobile. And the same can be said for a variety of other circumstances we discussed in the last section, especially the presence or absence of economic growth. Generally, a growing economy increases upward mobility, and a declining economy increases downward mobility.

Downward mobility has also interested sociologists for another reason. At least since the early twentieth century, political sociologists and political scientists have viewed downwardly mobile people as politically unpredictable and even regressive: for example, inclined to oppose progressive (i.e., redistributive) political policies. They have also tended to favour simplistic conservative policies, like the Ontario Progressive Conservatives' "Common Sense Revolution" in the 1990s, or the Tea Party's libertarian (i.e., small government) approach in the United States today. Both movements emphasize cuts in social spending and fewer social services in the interests of lower taxes and debt reduction. Even more importantly, the downwardly mobile have tended to hate and fear the poor, immigrants, Aboriginals, and others who seem strange to them and are demanding a place at the table. Downward mobility is a political force for destabilization in any society that is committed to social justice.

With this in mind, let's return to the beginning. People with a different social status than their parents are said to be upwardly or downwardly mobile. Many people are not mobile at all, but in industrial societies, most children are mobile when the economy is growing or declining (Lui, 2013). Though children tend to share their parents' social status, they also have the capacity to change that status (whether for better or worse), particularly when they are still relatively young adults.

DOWNWARDLY MOBILE ELITES. Downward mobility, or the loss of social standing, is sometimes easy to see. This is especially true of the downward mobility of elites in a society where elite people hold great power, compared to the mass of ordinary people. Writing about the former Soviet Union and present-day Russia, Kryshtanovskaia (2005) notes: "The elite are the social group that stands on the pinnacle of society. For this reason, having to leave its ranks always marks a fall in status. Sometimes this occurs abruptly, in the form of a fall from the top into political nonexistence, and other times it takes place smoothly and easily, by way of a gradual slide down from the top and a transfer to positions that are not of much importance but do afford some honour."

Departure from the elite is not always voluntary. Politicians have to retire for political reasons: the end of one's term of office, resignation by the head of the elite "in-group," hostility on the part of a superior, and so on. Because of the many privileges elite people enjoy, *excorporation*—or involuntary retirement from the elite—means more than formal dismissal; it is an effort to deprive the member of the elite of his power resources. The longer an elite official has been in his high position, the more resources he has at his disposal to resist removal, and the greater the amount of political capital he has accumulated. The result is always a struggle in which one political actor wins and another loses. In addition, for the members of the top elite, excorporation goes hand in hand with *excarceration*, or exit from the closed political space. This requires the person removed be re-socialized.

Complete excorporation means being forced out of elite positions, even including the loss of resources of power, which results in moving the person into the non-elite. The former elite may go on pension, be transferred to a low-level profession, or even be subjected to repression. Partial excorporation, by contrast, entails the loss of a portion of the person's political capital. In this case, the retired elite member may be able to retain a certain portion of the resources of power and capital that he acquired as part of the elite. This person, though no longer an official, still remains near to the elite or the ex-elite. *Decapitalization*, on the other hand, may deprive the member of the elite of his political capital, turning the official into an "empty suit," with a political vacuum around him. At its most extreme, removal may mean relegation to reserve status in zones of the ex-elite, from which he may be summoned in time. Being placed in reserve means a decline in the official's real status and the amount of his power.

In short, it is easy to see when a member of the elite is downwardly mobile through demotion, but far less easy to see when an ordinary person, outside a formal bureaucracy, is downwardly mobile.

DOWNWARD MOBILITY FOR ORDINARY PEOPLE. Because it is far harder to see and measure downward mobility in the general population, the topic of downward mobility often yields puzzling and sometimes complicated findings. Some researchers state conclusively that downward social mobility has harmful effects on people's mental and physical health and is associated with diminished living conditions. Other researchers find no such effects of downward social mobility; and some still assert that it is impossible to state conclusively what are the effects of downward social mobility, or even what downward mobility consists of.

When this happens, we are in the throes of a definitional debate—the kind of debate academic researchers thrive on. In order to make sense of the findings in this field, we need to clarify a few of the foundational debates in the field of social inequality and stratification. The first thing to note is that, if we are going to draw conclusions about upward and downward movement, we need to imagine an agreed-on hierarchy of social positions. This hierarchy can be constituted of different amounts of power, wealth, or social status, or all three.

In the Marxian conception of social class, the two main classes of interest are the capitalist and working classes; other classes—like the petit bourgeoisie and the landed aristocracy—are small and/or shrinking, at least in the original formulation of this model. So, in principle, intergenerational mobility out of the capitalist class into the working class can be viewed as downward mobility, in terms of power, wealth, and social status. However, over the course of the twentieth century, new classes arose that did not fit easily into this two-class model: for example, the managerial class. Also, the class of small business owner-managers and self-employed professionals increased in numbers dramatically.

This demanded a new formulation, which Max Weber provided. For Weber, there were more than two classes, and in a society, these classes were defined by *market position*. People can achieve a strong market position in several ways: for example, by owning the means of production (as Marx said), but also by controlling the means of production thanks to an important managerial or political position. People in the professions also have a strong market position, thanks to their high education and scarce skills whose paid use professional associations protect. Inherited wealth is a source of power and esteem, but so is earned wealth; and people can convert their power resources—wealth, authority, and prestige—freely into other power resources.

This realization led to a new focus on the power resources themselves and their interrelationship. The development of interest in *occupational prestige* as a focus of social-mobility research motivated researchers to examine educational attainment—the gateway (for many poor and middle-class people) into positions of wealth, authority, and esteem. Occupational prestige is well-predicted by income and average years of education associated with an occupation, and occupational prestige scores are stable over time and across industrial countries. In general, high-prestige occupations tended to be white-collar or non-manual. As a result, the intergenerational movement out of manual or blue-collar into non-manual or white-collar occupations can often be viewed as upward mobility.

This approach to social mobility was satisfactory as long as a majority of non-agricultural jobs were manual jobs in production or construction. As time went on and production jobs were shipped overseas or eliminated by automation, more and more of the workforce came to hold non-manual jobs. Some of these non-manual jobs, as in the past, earned a high income, required a high education, and enjoyed high prestige or repute in the community. Many, however, such as lower-level clerical and service jobs, earned little income, required little education, and did not enjoy high prestige or repute. Also, with the passage of time, even professional jobs (for example, teaching, nursing, law, and pharmacy) were "proletarianized": that is, made subject to more hierarchical control, less job autonomy, and lower earnings. It was no longer appropriate to assume that intergenerational movement out of manual work into non-manual work could be considered upward mobility, or that movement in the opposite direction (from non-manual to manual work) could be considered downward mobility. In terms of income and living standards, for example, it was far better to be a licensed electrician than a bank teller or retail salesperson.

Thus arose the classic problem in mobility analysis highlighted by Bland (1978) in his review of an article by Richardson (1977) about downward mobility. Bland notes that Richardson's discussion "only makes sense within the context of an assumption that, for practical purposes, we can treat all non-manual occupations as being in some sense 'higher' than all manual occupations." Though many or even most non-manual occupations enjoy higher social standing and prestige than do most manual occupations, this cannot be said of routine non-manual occupations in comparison with skilled manual occupations. As a result, many movements from manual to non-manual occupations may be status losses, not status gains. That is because, today, the relationship between manual/non-manual work and occupational prestige is problematic.

What this long-ago debate shows is that we can measure social mobility in several ways. Some ways are more precise and certain than others, because they are more easily quantifiable—for example, increases in average income, or movement between income quintiles—but they tell us little about other dimensions of status and power. Money doesn't always translate into power, authority, or prestige.

Some ways of measuring mobility are closer to lived experience: for example, using the reputational approach, which asks respondents to put families or people into prestige or status categories, of which a great many may exist in small, stable communities. However, this approach cannot be used in large or unstable communities, and reputation tells us little about income or power. Finally, approaches using socioeconomic status or occupational prestige are quantified but may have hard-to-interpret meanings, as we saw in the Richardson/Bland example above.

To the extent that we can measure mobility in an exact and persuasive way, what do we know about the causes and consequences of downward mobility? Researchers around the world have been trying to answer this question for half-a-century now, and have come to some striking conclusions.

First, people don't like downward mobility, and this is as true of high-status people as it is of middle- and lower-status people. Consider the following experiment by Burleigh and Meegan (2013): Students in a university course were asked to judge a hypothetical plan by which the grades for some would increase and the grades for others would remain the same, under two different conditions. In the so-called "peer-gets-ahead" condition, two students were of equal status before the program acted to differentiate them, and in the "inferior-catches-up" condition, the two students differed in status before the program acted to equalize them. A majority of students responded favourably to the program, with unanimous approval for the inferior-catches-up condition and modest approval for the peer-gets-ahead condition. High-status students were especially uncomfortable with the possibility that their status could decrease relative to some of their high-status peers in the peer-gets-ahead condition. Their objections used the language of social injustice, but they were averse to any situation that resulted in downward mobility.

Often, young people's educational decisions are intended to minimize the risk of downward mobility. Analyzing British data, Jaeger (2012) found that more than 90% of respondents were satisfied to attain their parents' social class position, and only a small group of people wanted to do otherwise. Those who opposed attaining their parents' social class position were characterized by low cognitive ability and a high incidence of behavioural problems in childhood, Jaeger reports.

The actual experience of downward mobility has a dramatic effect on people's political and social views. Dabalen et al. (2013), using a survey of 57,000 people from twenty-seven countries in eastern Europe and central Asia, found that intensive, persistent downward mobility increases support for income redistribution. A tendency to support income redistribution depends on not only how well-off one's parents were or how egalitarian was the society in which they grew up, but also the successes, failures, and hardships that shaped their lives.

Countries in eastern Europe and central Asia, under communism, were command economies in which wealth was extensively redistributed. The states provided education, housing, and health care services, subsidized basic consumer goods, and provided jobs in government or state-owned enterprises. However, with the breakdown of communist rule, these societies went through structural reforms that exposed their citizens to unprecedented economic shocks and hardships. Looser control over the market for jobs and commodities increased income inequality and unemployment rates. Many people not only lost their jobs, but also lost welfare benefits. A new elite class (mainly made up of new capitalists) and enlarged middle class emerged, but so did a socially deprived marginal class. The privatization of states' assets and increased income inequality exposed people to diverse and often-unwelcome mobility experiences. Not surprisingly, this increased their support for redistribution as a defence against downward mobility.

People's desire for redistribution—in effect, for a return to earlier ways—is a response to unemployment. As well, intensity of deprivation makes a difference:

for example, having insufficient or insecure food and lodging will count more than mere unemployment. Finally, the persistence of hardship also makes a difference. Long-term hardship does not make people more accepting of hardship; it makes them eager for change through redistribution

CAUSES AND CONSEQUENCES OF DOWNWARD MOBILITY. As we have seen, downward mobility, in its most extreme forms, is far from pleasant or interesting: it can be frightening, frustrating, discouraging, and angering. Consider the effects of the large-scale loss of job security in late twentieth-century America. Among the many upheavals in the United States in the second half of the last century, few were as significant to social mobility as the large-scale systematic loss of unionized manufacturing jobs. On this, Majka (1994) writes, "The result [was] a portrait of disrupted lives, family stress and coping, social service inadequacy, sub-employment, and downward mobility in a decade ironically celebrated as the boom years of the last quarter of the twentieth century."

Some social policy analysts have blamed the working poor for their own plight, the supposed result of low skills, low education, and low productivity. However, most of these people were hard workers whose education and skills were well-suited to jobs available in their communities. After the factories shut down, many of these workers sought and found the only jobs that were available to them in the service sector, as janitors, truck drivers, and security guards. Many who achieved re-employment went from secure, unionized jobs with a living wage to insecure, non-unionized jobs with low wages and no benefits. Many had to accept part-time schedules and intermittent employment, despite a prior history of steady, full-time work. Of all workers, women, blacks, and middle-aged men suffered the longest unemployment and largest income losses. In many communities, the jobs lost were never replaced with economic activity that required comparable skills or yielded comparable pay.

A recent work documenting downward mobility in the U.S.—more specifically, the gradual and continuing decline of opportunity—is George Packer's *The Unwinding: An Inner History of the New America* (2013). This book brilliantly documents the failure of dedication and persistence to yield economic benefits in a shrinking, unequal economy. A key earlier work on downward mobility, capturing the extent of this dilemma in broader ethnographic, more highly contextualized terms, is *Falling from Grace: The Experience of Downward Social Mobility in the American Middle Class*, by Katherine Newman (1988). This book analyzes the experiences of formerly secure middle-class Americans who suddenly lost their jobs and became downwardly mobile. This occurred in a variety of job domains; by no means was it restricted to blue-collar workers. Newman reports the real-life experiences of five groups of informants: (1) "de-layered" executives of large corporations, (2) the executives' families, (3) air-traffic controllers dismissed by President Reagan in the wake of a 1981 strike, (4) former operatives in Singer's flagship plant in Elizabeth, N.J., which closed in the early 1980s, and, finally, (5) divorced women who had previously shared their husbands' prosperous lifestyles. In each case, downward mobility turned these people's lives upside down.

The air-traffic controllers and the former operatives at Singer knew they were the victims of conditions beyond their control. All of them had friends or acquaintances who had suffered unemployment at one time or another, so no one blamed them personally, and members of these groups found social and moral support readily available. By contrast, former executives and their families belonged to networks of people who had never experienced a job loss. As a result, unemployed executives often found themselves isolated and labelled as deviants by friends as well as family. They were like the demoted elites we discussed earlier in the chapter, and they felt keenly alienated. Yet, these executives were so committed to a "culture of meritocracy"—so inclined to believe that achievements will reflect abilities—that they were unable to shake the feeling that they were to blame. As a group, the downwardly mobile executives therefore lost more self-esteem and suffered more family disruption than did any of the other groups Newman discusses. The only other group that was as disrupted and inclined to blame themselves were divorced women who grew up during the 1950s and had been socialized to think the fate of a marriage reflects the worth of the wife (Barley, 1990).

The air-traffic controllers and unemployed blue-collar workers from the Singer factory, whose lives were also disrupted, were shielded from self-blame by the collective nature of their plight. They may have felt like victims or crusaders, but they didn't feel like losers. That said, their lives were shaken up nonetheless, and even those who found new jobs had come to question their place in society (Bart, 1989).

Newman identifies "categorical fate" as a determinant of economic misfortune, where the job loss or drop in income "is attributed to his or her membership in a group (or social category) that is as a whole subject to victimization." As we have noted, recognizing categorical fate can help people preserve their self-esteem. In principle, blameless people who know they have been wronged or mistreated—for example, people who are victims of discrimination or bad management—are less given to self-blame. Yet there remains a tendency in our culture to "blame the victim"—to assume people get the fate they deserve, whether that fate is good or bad. This is part of the dominant ideology of our society that separates people into winners and losers, and glorifies the winners. As a result, a taint of blame—even self-blame—clings to even those who are, objectively speaking, the most blameless of unemployed and downwardly mobile people.

Partly for this reason job loss increases distress, though over time the effect wears off and is limited to non-employed men (Mandemakers, 2013). Evidence suggests that higher-educated men experience less distress following job loss than less-educated men. These educational differences in the impact of job loss become smaller over time and are mainly driven by re-employment chances. So, in the end, the unemployed executives Newman studied are more likely to land on their feet, and do so more quickly, than the unemployed factory and construction workers.

Other groups, besides the less educated, are especially vulnerable to the hard consequences of downward mobility. To show this, Janssen (2014) compared income mobility at the household level using tax data for Gothenburg, Sweden, from 1925 to 1994, focusing on three distinct eleven-year periods: 1925–36, 1947–58, and 1983–94. Taken as a whole, this was a period of enormous economic and social change. The first period came soon after the introduction of some minor but important measures, for example, a universal pension plan in 1913. During the second period, elements of the social insurance system were introduced, including a child allowance in 1948 and a sickness benefit system in 1955. The third period represented the full flowering of the welfare state, including the expansion of public child care and growing female labour force participation. The dual-earner household was then common and widely accepted.

In this context, incomes changed over time and income mobility was considerable during all three periods, with only one-third of all households immobile. There was a steady growth in average income in each period, with a majority of people experiencing growth in real income and only a minority experiencing sizable reductions.

In this growth scenario, two traditional poverty risks, associated with starting a family and with old age, lost much of their hold on people's incomes, For example, people were much less likely than in the past to become downwardly mobile economically when they became elderly. However, two new poverty risks arose, among young adults and immigrants. Young adults, in the face of limited job opportunities, were much more likely than in the past to suffer downward income mobility. Likewise, and for similar reasons, foreign-born households became much more likely to experience downward income mobility when starting a family, owing to this group's weak position in the labour market.

We have already noted some of the consequences of downward mobility, and there are others. They vary in type and intensity, but one can never say that they are trivial. For example, Lindstrom (2011) notes the associations between downward mobility, economic stress, and tobacco smoking. In the large sample he studied, 17.4% of men and 19.1% of women reported smoking tobacco. Smoking was found to be more prevalent among people with low occupational status, low social support, and economic distress. Upward social mobility was associated significantly with lower odds of smoking, but downward social mobility was associated significantly with higher odds of smoking. From this, the researchers concluded that downward social mobility and economic distress, whether in childhood or adulthood, are risk factors for tobacco smoking over the life-course.

Howe (2009) likewise examined the effect of social mobility on blood pressure among people aged 50 and 60 years. Using data from the Newcastle Thousand Families study, the researchers found that upward social mobility was associated with decreased blood pressure, but downward mobility was associated with increased blood pressure, compared to socially stable people. In particular, social mobility was significantly associated with high blood pressure at age 50.

Height is also affected by social mobility. Kryzanowska (2011) used a sample of 2,090 father and son pairs to study the extent of intra- and inter-generational social mobility over a forty-two-year period in a British cohort. Over this period, the mean height difference between the highest and lowest social class decreased from about four centimetres in the fathers' generation to about three centimetres in the sons' generations. Compared to the average height, downwardly mobile fathers were shorter by between 0.1 and 0.7 centimetres, but upwardly mobile fathers were taller by, on average, 0.6 to 1.7 centimetres. For sons, the downwardly mobile were on average 0.7 centimetres shorter and the upwardly mobile 0.8 centimetres taller. Inter-generationally, between 18% and 19% of sons were downwardly mobile; the downwardly mobile sons were shorter than average by about 0.9 centimetres, but the upwardly taller by between 0.6 and 1.2 centimetres.

Downward social mobility can even play a part in homicidal violence. Madfis (2014) notes that in the United States, middle-class white heterosexual men in their teenage years and in middle age commit mass murder—that is, the killing of at least three victims during a single episode at one or more closely related locations—in numbers disproportionately high relative to their share of the population. Using a variety of sources, Madfis notes the convergence of (1) white entitlement, (2) heterosexual masculinity issues, and (3) middle-class instability and downward mobility in the post-industrial economy as factors contributing to this trend. Madfis concludes that, for many mass killers, downward mobility undermines white heterosexual masculinity, leading to shame and anxiety and, ultimately, to acts of symbolic violence "to stave off subordinated masculinity."

THE ROLE OF GENDER. As we have seen, gender plays an important part in this story, and indeed, downward mobility operates differently for men and women. Bihagen (2007), for example, studied downward mobility from the so-called "Service I class," which is the most privileged class of employees within the EGP (Erikson–Goldthorpe–Portocarero) class schema, comprising higher-level professional, administrative and managerial employees. A substantial minority of position-holders within Service I originate in the working class, but they are especially likely to lose status in the face of adversity, particularly if they are women. In part, that is because these people tend to have a lower level of educational attainment than others in this class.

Additionally, women face the problem of combining family and working life. Women typically experience more problems in combining family obligations with working life in demanding jobs associated with autonomy and responsibility, as within the Service I class. Bihagen speculates that women from working class origins may be more prone to accept some downward mobility in order to solve this work–family conflict because they are less adverse to lower jobs or less able to avoid downward mobility. So they may reduce their work hours to solve the work–family conflict, or take a lower-status, less demanding job.

Dwyer (2004) reports a similar finding in data from the Panel Study of Income

Dynamics for 1983 to 1992. Her research shows that many workers voluntarily accept lower earnings to solve work-family conflicts. Others lose pay as they are pushed out of jobs or pulled to new jobs by non-pecuniary (e.g., family-related) factors they value more than pay. This may be especially true of women—and most especially mothers—in the labour force. Willingness to do this, in order to solve work-family conflicts, varies from one society to another, and it may be less common in European societies that are more committed to gender equality.

To assess this, Evertsson (2012) compares two welfare states with differing work and family strategies, Germany and Sweden, to study whether and how women's career interruptions influence their mobility in labour. Specifically, she compares women with continuous careers to those with discontinuous careers due to parental leave or homemaking, unemployment, or other reasons. A careful data analysis finds no significant relationship between a career interruption and upward occupational moves in Germany. However, in Sweden, the longer the duration of a family leave, the less likely is a woman's upward mobility to a higher position. Overall occupational mobility is higher in Sweden than in Germany, and since all almost women work for pay there, extended leaves have a more negative effect on career prospects than in Germany, where many new mothers drop out of the work force entirely. At the same time, in Germany unemployment can cause permanent harm, and the risk of downward mobility increases with increased unemployment and time out of the labour market.

THE IMMIGRANT EXPERIENCE OF DOWNWARD MOBILITY. Immigrants, like women, suffer a higher-than-average risk of downward mobility in most societies. This is especially true of new arrivals who were highly educated professionals in their country of origin; often, in their new country of residence, they are relegated to jobs requiring far less education and carrying less status. For some immigrants and refugees, downward mobility is temporary, but others may endure it all their lives and even pass the legacy on to their children (Gans, 2009).

The downward mobility that immigrants experience after coming to North America is not unique. Similar reactions, effects, and coping mechanisms are reported elsewhere. Different kinds of societies handle downward mobility and its effects differently, with some taking more notice than others of downward mobility among their newcomers, and taking measures to lessen its effects. For example, Canada, a country of high rates of immigration, pays a great deal of attention to the problems of immigrants and refugees. Canadian researchers Creese and Wiebe (2009) find that research points to a growing gap between immigrant and native-born outcomes in the labour market, despite continued efforts to recruit highly educated newcomers to the country. Sometimes, gender and gender inequality are to blame for poor immigrant integration. However, the problem is more general. Three-quarters of respondents report experiencing downward occupational mobility, landing in low skilled, low-wage, insecure forms of "survival employment" in Canada.

All immigrants face demands for "Canadian experience," "Canadian credentials," and "Canadian accents," though some sectors of the labour market are worse in this regard than others and women face particular difficulties. In the long run, though, women who invest in post-secondary education within Canada end up in better positions than men. Race and racism may also play a part. For instance, well-educated immigrants from sub-Saharan Africa face significant difficulties establishing themselves in the Greater Vancouver area. The majority are forced to take low-wage, low-skilled work well below the level they expected and, indeed, below the level of work they did at home before migrating. The situation is largely due to the refusal of Canadian employers and professional associations to recognize African educational credentials and work experience attained in Africa, but there are other factors as well. Governments tend to only fund short-term employment programs that yield low-wage employment. Many respondents also reported experiencing racism and/or sexism, with matters worsened by government's limited commitment to equity programs in employment, particularly where private employers are involved. As a result, many immigrants to Canada are downwardly mobile, at least for a time. Eventually, often within five to ten years, they recover their original occupational and earning position.

Similar problems arise in other societies of comparable economic development such as Sweden. Behtoui (2012) has investigated how children of immigrants from Turkey are integrated into Swedish society. He reports that descendants of Turkish immigrants are not socially or economically excluded and there is little risk that a distinct "underclass" will form in Sweden. However, the children of immigrants suffer something one may describe as "subordinate inclusion" nonetheless. In large part, the problem is educational. The educational level of the children of immigrants from Turkey is lower than that of children of natives. Social segregation also poses a problem. The immigrants and their children live in neighbourhoods and attend schools that are segregated in terms of class and immigrant background. Consequently, they develop segregated friendship networks during their school years. On the other hand, their parents' ambitions, high expectations, and extra efforts partly overcome the negative effects of such segregation.

Many immigrants in Sweden, as in Canada, consider themselves overqualified for their job—a problem much more often reported by immigrants than by native-born people. There is a definite wage gap between employed young people with immigrant as opposed to native-born backgrounds that cannot be explained by human capital and demographic variables. Put another way, despite similar educational attainment, the children of Turkish immigrants were not able to gain positions in the labour market on a par with Swedish-born children. This has second-order effects, including limited opportunities for informal relationships such as friendships, membership in informal groups, and marriage (Behtoui, 2012).

A great deal of research is concerned with the mental health consequences of immigration and immigrants' difficulties. For example, Das-Munshi et al. (2012)

report that changes in socioeconomic position in people who migrate may have adverse associations with mental health. Migrants to higher income countries who experienced downward mobility or underemployment were more likely to show common mental disorders, compared with migrants who were upwardly mobile or experienced no changes in their socioeconomic position.

Similar problems afflict immigrants from South America, Africa, and Asia. Margolis (1990) found that over a five-year period, as economic conditions in Brazil deteriorated, New York and other North American cities saw an influx of middle-class Brazilian immigrants. Although highly educated, most of these economic refugees had little knowledge of English and, often, no legal right to be here. As a result, the work available to them included menial service jobs cleaning houses, washing dishes, and bussing tables. Faced with the fact of their marginality, these immigrants developed various strategies to cope with their downward mobility and deprivation. Many of them coped by avoiding any deep identification with the work they do. Unlike many native-born workers, they did not invest themselves in their job, or think their job said anything about who they really were. Many viewed their coming to North America as temporary. If asked, they said they are concerned only with saving enough money to buy a home, land, or property back home in Brazil. Some are saving to return to school, others are planning to open a business; but few think they will stay.

Of course, such plans don't always work out as expected. People fail to save the amount they need and keep delaying their return to Brazil. Others return to Brazil but, after a while, return to North America, having become accustomed to North American standards of living. Yet they still tend, often for years or even decades, to imagine they will someday return to Brazil and settle there with a nest-egg earned in North America; and that means that they can view their menial job as temporary and tolerable.

Downward mobility is more or less tolerable depending on the expectations people hold and the degree they invest themselves in their situation. It seems likely that people who continue to think about a better future, and avoid blaming themselves for a meagre present, are the least likely to suffer long-term mental and physical decline as a result of their downward mobility.

Glass Ceilings

The *Oxford Dictionary of the Social Sciences* (2002) defines *glass ceiling* as "an unofficial and metaphorically invisible barrier to women's advancement at the highest levels of many career paths." Glass ceilings are interesting to us because they are barriers to flow. They are "the unseen, yet unbreachable barrier that keeps minorities and women from rising to the upper rungs of the corporate ladder, regardless of their qualifications or achievements" (Reich et al., 1995). In other words, invisible glass ceilings block the upward mobility of certain people and prevent them from entering the top jobs.

Groups that experience or complain about hitting a glass ceiling are groups that expect upward social mobility and may even deserve it, given their efforts and qualifications, but are prevented from achieving it. So, with the concept of glass ceiling, we are once again in the domain of a social phenomenon, like social structure and social class, that is invisible but is known by its effects. We know that women have hit a glass ceiling, for example, when they are underrepresented in judicial positions and the federal minister of justice says, without evidence, that the reason is because they aren't applying for judicial jobs because of their home responsibilities.

When we see people deflected from their upward trajectory for no obvious reason, we conclude that they have hit a glass ceiling. But to call the obstacle a glass ceiling is only to acknowledge its existence, not to identify what it is or how it works. It is often a cleverly disguised kind of sexism or gender discrimination; and in principle, we could talk about glass ceilings in connection with racism or homophobia or ageism just as meaningfully.

Until forty years ago, women were rarely considered for promotions in jobs outside of clerical or assembly-line work. Today, women receive promotions as often as men, and in a wide variety of careers, but occupy only a small number of society's most powerful positions. Many women who have attained jobs in middle-level positions find they are barred from top positions. This is not to say that all women end up in bad jobs and all men end up in good ones: both sexes occupy both good and bad jobs. However, data on the gender distribution across occupations and rankings shows men are much more likely to land the best jobs.

We can see this in the Fortune 500 ranking of the top U.S. public and private corporations based on revenue. In 2014, only twenty-four women held CEO positions in companies ranked on this list. That's less than 5% (Honda, 2014). And of those 24 women, only one was CEO of one of the top ten corporations on the list (Catalyst, 2014a). The situation is similar in Canada. Just over 5% of the CEOs in the top 500 Canadian companies are women (Catalyst, 2014b). Women make up almost half of the work force, but they hold only a little over one-third of all management positions and 23% of all senior-level positions, leaving the vast majority of senior management positions to be filled by men (Catalyst, 2014c). Note finally that 40% of Canadian companies have no women at all on their boards of directors (Catalyst, 2014d). It is easy to see that women are underrepresented in management positions in both Canada and the United States, despite their high degree of engagement in paid employment.

CONSEQUENCES OF THE GLASS CEILING. Jobs and promotions matter, to workers, employers, and corporations. Given the importance of work in peoples' lives, career advancement is often central to a person's self-esteem and well-being. Many people see their work as a way of demonstrating their competence and skills. Employers use hires and promotions to fill positions with the best available workers and to give their workers an incentive to work hard. Given this, the glass ceiling has harmful effects on both workers and employers, for it undermines both self-esteem and employee quality.

Many women who encounter the glass ceiling experience dissatisfaction with their job and employment prospects (O'Brien, 2013). In interviews, female workers employed in the municipal public sector said they felt barred from moving upward in their careers. This caused them to feel frustration, "disappointment in self and the organization, rejection, discouraged, de-motivated, dismissed, unheard, disrespected, undervalued, not appreciated, lonely, isolated, confused, sad, saddened, disheartened, defeated and at times angry" (O'Brien, 2013). As a result, many were reluctant to even express interest in moving to senior levels.

Some women expressed the desire to prove their knowledge or "build up [their] resume" by returning to school, but the presence of the glass ceiling caused many others to re-think their aspirations to move into positions with greater responsibility and authority. Some women sought out other jobs in other organizations to break through the glass ceiling. On the other hand, others still decided to "settle" (O'Brien, 2013) and remain in their dissatisfying current career. Not surprisingly, many women expressed resentment towards their male colleagues, whom they felt did not have to work as hard.

The glass ceiling can harm the way employees view their careers and their relationship with other workers. However, it also undermines the organization that limits the upward mobility of talented women. Companies that hire and promote more women gain a competitive edge by doing so. To assess this, Desvauc, Devillard-Hoellinger, and Meaney (2004) examined the performance of companies around the world and the number of women that hold top positions. They found that companies with three or more women in senior management scored higher on nine important organizational dimensions—capability, leadership, external orientation, accountability, motivation, coordination and control, innovation, direction, and work environment—than companies with no senior-level women. The same high-scoring companies also fared better financially, as indicated by their profitability levels.

Peni's (2014) examination of 500 firms lends support to this point. Peni examined the association between firm performance and the characteristics of the CEO of the company. Firms with women CEOs tend to financially outperform firms led by male CEOs, according to this research. Peni suggests that women's superior communication skills and ability to perform in group problem-solving are vital, profitable skills in management. Also, women's more cooperative leadership style may be more effective than men's competitive style.

Because the business world is dominated and controlled by men, women must demonstrate exceptional talent to achieve managerial positions. Thus, female executives are often more talented and devoted than male executives at the same level; in short, they have to be even better than men to get the same position. And that makes them especially fit for promotion.

TOKENISM. As Peni's study and others have suggested, gender diversity can play an important part in the success of large organizations. However, gender diversity in upper management must reach a critical mass to raise a firm's performance. When the number in upper management does not attain this critical mass, the women who are present remain tokens. This important insight is nearly forty years old, though many employers have continued to ignore it.

In 1977, Kanter (1977) pioneered the term "token" to refer to women's status as an organizational symbol or token in male-dominated organizations. Kanter noted that token employees of any kind are faced with three major problems: visibility, polarization, and assimilation. First, tokens are highly visible and are therefore faced with high performance pressures and singled out for their differences. Equally, their mistakes are highly visible, heavily reprimanded, and often attributed to the entire group they represent. This makes them less likely to take major risks and hinders their ability to perform in the workplace.

This suggests that gender diversity will only enhance a company's performance if the diversity is significantly large, a conclusion that has been supported by other research. For example, in a study of 151 German firms, Joecks et al. (2013) examined the link between gender diversity and corporate performance. They found a firm's performance is diminished when there is only a small number of women in the executive ranks, but that at very low levels of gender diversity, a small increase in diversity is actually associated with reduced firm performance. To outperform companies with completely male boards, a critical mass of women must be added. The study found that the critical mass was 30%: that is, 30% (or more) of the board members must be women to gain the advantages of diversity and outperform companies with lower percentages of women. Said another way, having three or more women on the board (assuming total board membership of ten directors) significantly increases a company's revenue, as compared to having zero, one, or two women on the board.

Torchia et al. (2011) come to similar conclusions in their analysis of 317 Norwegian firms. Here they find that the presence of a critical mass of women contributes importantly to firm innovation. Women are particularly valuable when they are involved in developing long-term strategies, implementing these strategies, and making follow-up decisions. Similarly, Konrad et al. (2008) suggest that three is the critical mass of women needed in the boardroom. Having three (or more) women on the board significantly increases a firm's ability to generate profits. But this happens only when gender diversity becomes "mainstream": that is, when the presence of women becomes normal and attention to gender-based differences drastically diminishes.

Breaking through the glass ceiling is not enough in itself; a critical mass of women is needed in higher management to gain the advantages of gender diversity. Why, then are women not better represented in the upper ranks of business and government?

SEGREGATION AND THE GLASS CEILING. Some researchers have proposed that women's underrepresentation in top jobs is due to a lack of education. This may have been true in the past, but in recent decades the number of women with bachelor's and graduate degrees has increased dramatically. In fact, women earned 52.7% of all Canadian university degrees (including bachelor's and higher degrees) in 2011 (Catalyst, 2014e). Yet despite their educational attainment, women still fall short of men in their occupational and income attainment.

Part of this is due to gender-based occupational segregation, the concentration of men and women in different jobs. Compared to their male counterparts, women are disproportionately segregated into jobs with short promotion ladders—jobs with few opportunities for raises and promotions. This is an international phenomenon, not limited to Canada. For example, Bihagen and Ohle (2007) studied data on 1.1 million workers to determine if women were barred from executive roles because they occupied so-called "dead-end" jobs. According to their data, 37% of men have dead end jobs compared to 53% of women. Further, the most common and least promising dead-end jobs are those related to personal care, such as day care, eldercare, and even nursing, teaching, social work, human resources, and public relations. Women hold 90% of all the personal care jobs, which is one reason why they are not promoted to higher status positions.

Women are also overrepresented at the lower levels in jobs with short promotion ladders. Take academia, for example. In universities and colleges, women hold a disproportionate share of contractual (non-tenure track) positions, compared to their male colleagues. In fact, more than half of full-time faculty members who are ineligible for tenure are women. Compared to full-time tenured appointments, non-tenure positions have low job security, pay, prestige, and virtually no opportunities for job advancement (Hart, 2011). Since resources are limited in non-tenured positions, non-tenured faculty members have difficulty gaining support for research or even office space. These limitations hinder their ability to show their skills and gain public recognition, further reducing their opportunities for advancement.

More generally, women's segregation into certain jobs limits their ability to show off their competence and skill. In business, comparatively few women are in "line" positions that involve profit-and-loss or revenue-generating opportunities. Currently, men hold around 90% of these line jobs in the United States and 89% in Canada (Berry and Franks, 2010). By contrast, women are two-and-a-half times more likely to hold "staff" positions (71%), such as human resources and public relations, than line positions (29%). These staff jobs offer fewer opportunities for workers to display their talents to their manager (Laff, 2007).

DISCRIMINATION AND GENDER STEREOTYPING. Here's a hypothesis about how discrimination may create the glass ceiling. The mass media depicts heroic white males as tough, assertive, rational, and independent; indeed, these are traditional requirements of the masculine role in North American culture. So, it is entirely possible that managers who are looking to hire (or promote) people with these qualities will look to white men first. They will not expect to find these qualities in women. As a result, women, perceived to be lacking these traditionally male characteristics, will be deemed less suitable for management. So, in decisions related to hiring and promotions, senior managers who hold these stereotypes will unconsciously exercise discrimination against women.

But does the data support this hypothesis? Consider Tyler and McCullough's (2009) study on the impact of stereotypes of hiring decisions. When presented with a resume containing traditionally male qualities, employers were 28% more likely to interview such a candidates. Further, when asked about hiring practices, interviewers stated that they believed that the best fit for management positions are male candidates who possess traditional male attributes. Decision-makers with such stereotypes in mind will unintentionally hinder women from attaining top jobs.

In medicine, too, the attributes perceived for successful performance in the field are consistent with male stereotypes (Burgess et al., 2012). Tenure criteria for instructors in medical schools include many more qualities commonly associated with male than female behaviours. Research finds little actual difference in the leadership effectiveness of men and women, but this perception still limits the ability of female applicants to attain a tenure-stream position.

The glass ceiling is even more shatterproof for women of colour. Oritz and Roscigno (2009) asked why African American women are underrepresented in senior executive positions. They concluded that black women are likely to experience higher levels of discrimination based on both their gender and race during hiring and promotion reviews, compared to white counterparts.

Women with children also bump up against the glass ceiling. Managers often ascribe negative attributes to women based on their family status and deem them less suitable for promotions to leadership roles. This is evident in Heilman and Okimoto's (2008) study of the impact of gender and parenthood on promotions. In promotion decisions, mothers generally are viewed more negatively than women without children. Mothers are perceived as less committed, less ambitious, and less dependable employees than non-mothers and thus less suitable for upper-level management. Fathers, on the other hand, are evidently not disadvantaged by their status as parents and do not garner as many negative reactions.

ORGANIZATIONAL CHARACTERISTICS. Popular depictions of upper management include images of men chatting over beers (or martinis) after work and during rounds of golf. Engagement in the social and cultural aspects of a firm increases a person's visibility and connection with upper managers, thereby heightening one's chances of promotion. Women are traditionally excluded from such "boys' clubs," diminishing their prospects. According to a survey by Sabattini and Dinolfo (2010), exclusion from social contact with male executives is one of women's biggest impediments to career advancement. Building relationships with superiors was identified as the most crucial aspect for gaining advancement to an executive position. The researchers identified two important factors in gaining a promotion:

female candidates (1) must be visible to male decision-makers, and (2) must make male executives aware of their work performance.

On these matters, consider the following study by Purcell (2012) on the impact of cultural capital in large organizations. In the firm examined by Purcell, women make up 80% of the bottom tier but only 20% of the top tier of employees. Purcell attributes this disparity to a gendered inequality in cultural capital; this refers to the cultural knowledge and practices that reproduce inequality in organizations and in society as a whole. The cultural capital in this organization centres largely on knowledge about sports and a willingness to drink, and thus is masculine and male-dominated.

Informal outings allow employees to interact and connect with executives, increasing their visibility. All employees acknowledge the importance of engaging in these outings, in order to advance. Women in this organization were not actively excluded from such informal outings among male executives, where this cultural capital was most useful. However, many of them said they didn't like the style and tone of these outings, which they described as "too insular, too male, and too mean" (Purcell, 2012).

According to Callahan and Tomaszewski (2007), boys' clubs are well established in many large organizations. Women who exclude themselves, or feel excluded from, this informal male culture may form their own communities in response. Some women are also concerned about socializing with men outside work, fearing they will be the subjects of malicious gossip, however unwarranted. For whatever reason, the absence of women from these boys' clubs hinders career advancement in the long run, as it reduces their personal visibility and opportunities to build relationships with important men.

THE GLASS ESCALATOR. So far, we have examined why women hit a glass ceiling that prevents them from entering the top jobs. It is also important to look at factors in the workplace that privilege men, even in female-dominated jobs.

In 1992, Williams coined the term "the glass escalator" to refer to the hidden advantages men receive in predominantly female professions, such as nursing, teaching, and social work. For one thing, men in both male- and female-dominated jobs are often assumed to be more competent and better leaders and so get to ride the glass escalator into higher-paying, higher-status jobs. Some may experience gender discrimination when they participate in female-dominated occupations, but this discrimination generally *aids* their employment and promotional prospects.

The glass escalator is still present in certain occupations today. Buhr's (2011) analysis of Canadian male nurses supports the view that such a glass escalator exists. Using data from the 2005 National Survey of Work and Health, Buhr found that male nurses were overrepresented in the higher income bracket among nurses. As well, male nurses were more likely to be in supervisory positions than female nurses. However, the glass escalator phenomenon does not apply to all men. Racialized, homosexual, and working-class class men are less likely to benefit from the glass escalator than their white, heterosexual, middle-class counterparts (Williams, 2013).

Consider a study conducted by Wingfield (2009) on black male nurses. While white male nurses were often mistaken for doctors, black male nurses were often mistaken for orderlies and janitors. Black male nurses were viewed as less skillful and their leadership abilities as more menacing, compared to white male nurses. The skills of black men in women-dominated jobs are particularly unrecognized because of cultural notions that stereotype black men as more violent than white men. As a result, black male nurses do not share the same gendered benefits as their white male colleagues. Rather, they often encounter discrimination, which hinders their career development.

Homosexual men are also excluded from the glass escalator unless they act in a "heterosexual manner." In research on homosexual teachers, Connell (2012) finds gay men are pressured into hiding their sexuality. They often have to alter their manner of dress, mannerisms, and behaviours to satisfy heterosexual male norms. From this, it is evident that the glass escalator privileges only men who are heterosexual.

CLOSING REMARKS. While women have made great strides in the workplace, they still bump their heads on a glass ceiling. More women today manage to get into top management, but women are still over-represented in low-level jobs and face particular barriers when trying to move up. Men, on the other hand, may end up taking the glass escalator and more easily move into higher-level jobs when they compete with women in women-dominant organizations. Like women, though, racialized and homosexual men do not reap the gendered benefits. It is evident that the North American workplace is still organized for the benefit of white, heterosexual men. All others are likely to encounter the glass ceiling in their efforts to achieve upward mobility.

CHAPTER SIX

Renewal Processes

Renewal processes are processes that add and subtract units to an existing stock of units. This sounds complicated but it isn't; we are all familiar with a wide range of *renewal processes*.

An Overview

Imagine water pouring into a kitchen sink from a faucet above the sink and, at the same time, draining out the bottom of the sink. The most important thing to understand here is that the size and composition of the stock is entirely determined by the rates of entry and exit of units. So, if water is running into the sink *faster* than it is draining out, the water level will overflow the sink. If water is running into the sink *slower* than it is draining out, the level of water in the sink will continually get lower. Finally, if water is running into the sink *at the same rate* as it is draining out, the level of the water will stay steady and unchanging. Likewise, if we start with ice-cold water in the sink and let hot water gush into it, the temperature of the water in the sink at any moment will mainly be determined by the rate at which hot water is entering and cold water is leaving the system.

As this example shows, a renewal process is all about the relative rates of change in the inputs and outputs of a system. Now, the same principles apply to a human population—say, the population of Canada. If Canada's birth rate is the same as its death rate (and there is no immigration), the population will remain steady in size and composition. If the birth rate is *lower* than the death rate—as it is today—the population of Canada will become gradually smaller and finally disappear, unless there is immigration into the country to prevent this from happening. And in fact, Canada depends on such immigration, without which the population of Canada would indeed disappear—i.e., drop to zero—in several centuries.

Interestingly, when birth and death rates are equal, the population will achieve a stable, unchanging age structure. If the birth and death rates are both equally *high*, the result will be a young population, with a low average age and a high proportion of people in childhood and early adulthood. If the birth and death rates are both equally *low*, the result will be an old population with a high average age and a high proportion of people in late adulthood and old age. And contrary to what you might think, birth rates are especially influential. A low birth rate, far more than improved life expectancies at (say) ages 70, 80, and 90, creates a relatively elderly population like Canada's, with an average age of 40 or 45 years.

Immigration rates are also very important in determining a population's age structure. In a population with *low* birth and death rates that are stable (or unchanging), *high* immigration rates have an enormous impact on the age structure. Immigrants to Canada and other economically developed countries tend to be young adults, ready to produce lots of children. Similarly, within Canada, young, fertile people tend to migrate from traditional, rural regions to urban regions, and from less prosperous to more prosperous provinces. The newcomers are more often than not from high-fertility cultures, and by coming to Canadian cities and reproducing, they influence the age structure of different parts of a country. These are the forces of immigration, both international and internal, that keep the populations of Toronto and Vancouver relatively young, and the populations of St. John's and Regina relatively old.

Toronto and Vancouver, the recipients of both higher-than-average natural growth and immigration, do not simply stay young, they also renew themselves. These cities are often transit stops or jumping-off points for people on the move to somewhere else. Said another way, people who move to Toronto or Vancouver from a foreign country, or even another part of Canada, are more likely to move to somewhere else than people who move to St. John's or Saskatoon from a foreign country or another part of Canada. That is not because Toronto and Vancouver are less welcoming than, say, St. John's or Saskatoon. Rather, the kinds of people who move to Toronto and Vancouver from elsewhere are more likely to be movers than stayers: they are people who are looking for opportunities for upward mobility. And by coming to Toronto and Vancouver, they gain opportunities for further advancement that they will not find in similar abundance in St. John's or Regina.

Now, the same kinds of things we have said about water in a sink, and about the population of Toronto or Vancouver, can be said about any human organization. All human organizations grow, shrink, and renew themselves through processes of recruitment (births) and retirement (deaths). In most organizations, people start at (i.e., are recruited into) the bottom and, over time, as they age, they work their way up the authority and reward ladder. Eventually, they finish their career and retire. In the context of formal organizations, we can view the lateral transfer-in of outsiders at middle and upper levels as similar to foreign immigration: these newcomers come with already established histories and records of achievement, at adult ages.

Like all human populations, formal organizations have age structures and age-related problems: for example, they may have a troublesome ratio of older staff to younger staff, meaning an aging workforce. They may have size problems; for example, they may be too small to compete effectively or too big for their available resources. And they may also have renewal problems: for example, they may change too quickly to achieve a stable identity or too slowly to adapt to a rapidly changing environment. Renewal is an inevitable but often troubled process in every human population and organization. As we will see in the sections that follow, issues of population renewal—including birth and death, and also issues of illness and recovery, adversity and survival, disability and adaptation—face all human societies. Indeed, they face all human beings.

From a population standpoint, renewal is the cleansing and rejuvenating effect of birth and death. For an individual human being, birth and death are end-points; only the part in-between—a person's lifetime—is subject to any control. Many people strive to renew themselves physically and psychologically over their lifetime, some with more success than others. But in the end, all people are the victims of their own history and mortality. So, most people experience renewal—the space between birth and death—by waiting, a topic we also discuss below.

POPULATIONS AND BIRTHS. The single most important fact about societies is that they are made up of people: collections of human beings. Human beings are flesh and blood, they need food, and they occupy space. Since in every important sense, people possess materiality, we need to say something about ourselves as material beings.

A sociologist may begin with the observation that people live in *populations*. Populations are nothing more than stocks or inventories of people. We could interest ourselves in other kinds of populations—populations of cars, birds, memories, beliefs, or pop tunes, to pick just a few items at random—but in general, social scientists are interested in populations of people. More specifically, they are interested in the processes or flows that create and maintain populations, or even increase their size. These flow processes—population inputs and outputs—affect the size and composition of the population stock or inventory.

As we noted above, the flows fall into two main categories: *inflows* and *outflows*. Inflows typically occur through birth or in-migration, while outflows typically occur through death or emigration. In organizations and other social structures, such inflows are typically called *entries* or *recruitments*, while the outflows are typically called *exits* or *retirements*. In every population, there is turnover, through continued entries and exits. The remaining stock constituted by these inflows and outflows gets older—ages—between the time it enters and exits; so, every population is characterized by an age structure or age composition. In a population with a high rate of births (or entries), old stock is rare, compared to new stock.

The population stock ages over time. In most societies, stock as it ages advances up a hierarchy of rights and responsibilities, with older stock gaining authority, respect, and even power. This is typical where high birth rates and high death rates make old stock especially rare. In societies or social structures with low birth rates and low death rates, where old stock is common, age brings fewer such benefits and youth earns a higher premium.

What takes place between entry and exit can be viewed in various ways, depending on one's perspective. As mentioned, it can be viewed as *aging*: a measure of the length of time an item has been in the inventory. Or it can be viewed as *advancement*: a measure of the status that is gained through the mere passage of time. Finally, from the standpoint of physical decline and death (or departure), it can be viewed as *waiting*. In the sections that follow we discuss aging, decline, waiting, and death. But populations that survive renew themselves, and we will also discuss *renewal*.

There is a field of social science called *demography* that studies human populations; many sociologists are familiar with demography and some even contribute to research in that field. The questions that demographers or demographically informed sociologists will likely ask include the following: First, does it matter socially whether a human population is large or small? Second, does it matter socially whether a population is densely concentrated in space—that is, if the population is crowded? Third, does the make-up or composition of a population (for example, its age structure, ratio of men to women, or mixture of skills) matter? Fourth, does it matter whether the population is mainly healthy or unhealthy, and whether the lifespan is short or long? And fifth, related to this, does it matter whether people pass through the population quickly or slowly?

The answer to all these questions is "Yes, it matters." So we need to consider the significance of these population features: how and why they serve as important indicators of the material conditions of social life. We also need to ask whether changes in the population lead to, or result from, changes in other societal processes: for example, the diffusion of ideas or wealth. Here again, the answer is "Yes, they do."

Population size is important in itself, for several reasons. First, a large population puts more pressure on the natural environment than a small population does. Second, a large population is likely to innovate—to invent new technologies and develop new ways of producing food and wealth—or else break into smaller populations. Large populations, especially large, rapidly growing populations, require the systematic production of food and food surpluses. There are no hunter-gatherer societies with large populations. The observed connection between population size and food production, as the first demographer, Thomas Malthus, explained, is due to a close connection between population increase (which he said was always exponential) and food increase (which he said takes place on a linear scale). We will say more about this shortly.

Second, large populations are often dense or crowded, and usually they live in cities. So when the world's human population became large, as it did in the last few hundred years, it also became mainly urban. Urban communities, housed vertically in tall buildings, can hold many more people than rural communities; and this vertical increase results in more crowding. Urban life is a different experience than rural life. As humanity grew in size, transient hunter-gatherer lifestyles gave way to settled agricultural lifestyles, then to urban industrial and post-industrial lifestyles. The connections between population size, location, and type of economic production are not accidental; but they are too complex to discuss thoroughly in a few sentences.

Third, large, dense populations invent new social and economic roles, or as

Durkheim said, they divide the labor of society in specialized ways. Productive tasks are broken into smaller, detailed tasks that require training. Increasingly, social roles are distinguished not only by age and sex but also by other characteristics associated with skill, aptitude, and interest. And within any set of social roles, the population composition makes a difference. For example, it makes a difference whether a population of 20,000 people is composed of 95% men or only 50% men. The first (95% men) is typical of a frontier town—say, a mining or mill town—with many single transient young men who often behave in disorderly ways. The second (50% men) is typical of a settled family community that includes children and old people. Here, disorder poses much less of a problem.

Sex ratio makes a difference, and so does age composition. It makes a difference whether the population is "young," where half the population is under the age of 15; or "old," where half the population is over the age of 45. A young population demands a good deal of spending on education; an old population needs pensions and health care. Other things being equal, a young population is unruly, creative in certain kinds of ways, and up-to-date with the latest technology; an old population is more sedate, rule-abiding, and conservative. As a result, politics and popular culture vary between younger and older societies.

The health and longevity of a population also affect how a society works. A healthy long-lived population is likely to contain a higher level of *human capital*: skills gained through lengthy education and on-the-job experience. Other things being equal, this human capital will contribute to higher productivity and increased prosperity. As well, leaving aside immigration, a healthy, longer-living society will have a lower rate of population turnover. As a result, people will develop stronger loyalties to the community. And with population stability, the social networks on which people rely for information and support will remain intact for longer periods.

At the same time, an older, longer-living society will rely more on immigration to provide needed population renewal by way of new skills and human capital that community is unable to provide for itself. So, population turnover has both a positive and negative effect: on the downside, it continuously undermines traditional culture and existing social networks. But on the upside, it continuously reinvigorates the culture and introduces new social elements that enrich our social networks through diversity. In Canada, which is demographically an aged and aging society, this turnover is especially important since many of the people who immigrate are young parents of young families.

DEMOGRAPHIC TRANSITION. During the last three centuries, much of the world has undergone what scholars call a *demographic transition*. High mortality rates and high fertility have been replaced by low mortality and low fertility rates, giving rise to periods of robust population growth. This was first observed in Europe, where mortality rates fell dramatically as industrialization took hold in the nineteenth century. As fertility rates remained more or less the same initially, the

European population quadrupled itself between 1700 and 1900 (Blue and Espenshade, 2011). By the mid-twentieth century, fertility rates started to fall to "replacement" levels and Europe thus became the first region of the world to complete the demographic transition.

Interestingly, the demographic transition occurred at a much faster pace in the developing world. In India, Mexico, and Kenya, for instance, life expectancy rose by approximately ten years during the 1950s and 1960s. With no accompanying decline in fertility, many of these countries experienced shockingly rapid population growth in the latter half of the twentieth century. Within a couple of decades, fertility rates did decline, and many developing countries now have fertility rates which are at or near the replacement level (Blue and Espenshade, 2011).

Governments around the world, most particularly in the developing world, have sought to exercise control over the process of demographic transition. As Feng, Cai, and Gu (2012) argue, countries like India and China devoted a large amount of resources to shortening the time it takes for fertility rates to decrease to replacement levels. In China, the one-child policy was enacted in 1980 to achieve these aims, while in India, forced sterilization programs were imposed in the mid-1970s.

Demographic trends can change a population's age structure and spark dramatic shifts in the relationship between generations. In general, efforts by older people to dominate young people create resistance and even sabotage at home, school, and work. When older people become more numerous, as with the aging of the Baby Boomers, the younger generation can be expected to devise more subtle tactics of resistance.

ARE THERE TOO MANY PEOPLE? Questions about population that keep re-surfacing include: *Are there (or will there soon be) too many people on earth? If so, how many are too many? And what must we do to keep the world's population from reaching this figure?* From one perspective, these questions are worthy of consideration and a great deal of data exists that is relevant to them. Scherbov, Lutz, and Sanderson (2011) predict that total world population will likely reach eight billion sometime between 2024 and 2033. Given the fact that total world population was just 2.5 billion in 1950, questions about the speed with which our planet is approaching a "limit" seem appropriate (An and Liu, 2010). When one considers just how quickly the world is aging as well, the aforementioned questions seem all the more urgent. Scherbov, Lutz, and Sanderson (2011) predict that one-third of the world's population will likely be over the age of 60 before the twenty-first century ends. It is a well-known fact that the need to support an ever-older population poses many problems. There might come a time, in the not so distant future, where the whole world collectively has to deal with these problems together. Simply ignoring questions of population growth and our planet's ability to support it seem unwise.

Viewed from another angle, however, these questions make little sense. They are like the questions *Does Amazon earn too big a profit?* or *Is the audience for the Super Bowl too big?* And like those questions, this global population question invites us to ask additional questions like *Too big for what?* and *Under what conditions may it be too big?*

A way of looking at things we will not address here in detail but that is worth thinking about takes as its starting point the total mass of living matter the earth can support. The well-known science fiction and science writer Isaac Asimov (1971), who was a biochemist by profession, set out the issue in the following way. The total amount of living matter is limited by two factors: the amount of sunlight that reaches the planet's surface, and the efficiency of photosynthesis. Because only so much sunlight reaches the surface, and photosynthesis is capable of using only a certain fraction of that energy in enabling plants to build up complex organic molecules (proteins, lipids, and carbohydrates) out of simple components (water, carbon dioxide, and other elements and compounds necessary in relatively small quantities), the total amount of plant life has a ceiling.

Animals are capable of converting only a certain fraction (the figure usually cited is one-tenth) of the plant food they eat into their own living tissue, and this is why the mass of living matter represented by plants is so much greater than that of animals. Therefore the Earth can support only so much animal life, and the more people there are, the less there will be of all other animals (tigers, lions, butterflies, and so on). Humans make up a greater percentage of total living matter than any other single animal species ever has before in the Earth's history, and in theory an ecosystem could be constructed that is made up of nothing but a form of plant life (probably algae) capable of conversion to human food with maximum efficiency and minimum wastage, and human beings themselves. So the question isn't necessarily *How many people can the Earth support?* but, rather, *How little biodiversity are we willing to endure?*

Limiting himself in his book of the same title to the more modest question *How Many People Can the Earth Support?* population expert Joel Cohen (1995) argues that our "population time bomb" question cannot be answered as posed. The Earth can support many more people than currently live on it, but it supports them with more or less ease under different conditions. Cohen notes several factors that determine when more or fewer people are feasible:

- *Equality of well-being.* With more equal sharing of resources, Earth can support many more people than it does today.
- *Technological development.* With more time to prepare technologically for their arrival, Earth can support many more people.
- *Political institutions.* With governments that are more honest, effective and peaceful, Earth can support many more people. (But more people may limit our liberty and political participation.)
- *Economic institutions.* With safer, better organized work, and healthier, better educated workers, Earth can support many more people.

- *Demographic arrangements.* With a higher death rate and shorter life span, Earth can support many more people. (Also, with better child care arrangements, to allow more women to work.)
- *Level of well-being.* If we can tolerate a lower level of material well-being, Earth can support many more people than today.
- *Environmental conditions.* If we can tolerate more physical and biological degradation of the environment, Earth can support many more people.
- *What range of variation?* If we can tolerate more fluctuation in death rates and material conditions, Earth can support many more people.
- *What risk of catastrophe?* If we can tolerate more uncertainty about the occurrence and outcome of disasters—famines, epidemics, wars, and so on—Earth can support many more people.

Two things are to be noted about this list of questions and answers. First, we cannot bank on changes occurring—for example, more equality, better government, or new technology—that will make Earth able to support many more people. Second, most of us will be unwilling to give up many of our "goods"—things like material prosperity, long life, political liberty, and a low-risk future—merely to have more people on Earth.

Putting these two observations together, Cohen is telling us the world is not a "population bomb" if we can adjust the Earth to accommodate more people, and adjust ourselves to doing without things we like and value. If we cannot or will not make these changes, then there are limits to how many people the Earth can support and the world *is* a population bomb.

Waiting

Waiting, in a certain sense, has the same relation to flows as does the glass ceiling we discussed early. It is not a type of flow, but rather, a barrier to flow or, at best, a delay of flow.

Many things can make us wait for the next opportunity to move, whether in traffic or in a career; but this section will talk mainly about the experience of waiting and what can be done to improve that experience. Unlike glass ceilings, which can be eliminated through gender-equal social policy-making, waiting can never be fully eliminated; and that means we all need to learn how to wait better. Just as we have to learn how to flow to our best advantage (in migration and mobility), we also have to learn how to wait to our best advantage. And here, social planners can provide better and worse waiting experiences for us, though few have seemingly spent time thinking about this problem.

Given a fixed supply of goods and services, more people means more scarcity for all. At best, it means a longer wait until people get what they want: longer waiting lines for food, gasoline, information, and other valued commodities. A branch of mathematics called *queuing theory* is the mathematical study of waiting lines. More concretely, queuing theory is concerned with creating models that predict queue lengths and waiting times as a function of the rate of arrivals (i.e., "system births"), the number of servers available, and the average serving time, assuming a random arrival of customers and more or less flawless assignment of customers to one or more servers. At worst, it means that people never get what they want—that the line is too long to bother with, or that by the time a resource is available it is too late to be of any use.

Similar thoughts apply to the topic of migration, which we discussed earlier. Consider how people wait to be granted a visa to enter a country, how they wait to become a citizen, and how the lure of citizenship can be used to make people wait for opportunities and advantages that they, as immigrants, are lacking.

Considered part of operations research, models of waiting are extremely useful in making business decisions about the allocation of resources. Obviously, the modeling process has to make assumptions about how quickly people need to be served, how long people are willing to tolerate a wait before leaving, and how quickly servers can reliably and responsibly perform their assigned task. And in the domain of health care, to choose an important example, such assumptions are extremely problematic. Health care involves matters of life and death: people left to wait too long may get sicker or even die. From the political standpoint, people left to wait too long for health service may demand a change of government, or at least, a change in the government's budget priorities.

At the same time, it is obvious that no system, however benevolent or rich, can ever provide instantaneous service, especially since arrivals and demands for service are essentially random. To provide instantaneous service would mean a huge number of servers standing around waiting for customers for a huge proportion of their time; and while that service model may work at McDonalds, where serving people are relatively poorly skilled and poorly paid, it will not work well in the health care system, where serving people—doctors, nurses, and technicians—are highly skilled and highly paid. So the question facing health care systems is how to provide care that is expert and timely though not instantaneous. Because sick people are often in pain and fearful about their physical condition, we have to consider how to make people feel as though the service they are getting is as expert and timely as they can possibly hope for, so that they will feel safe relying on such a system.

Though the comments that follow are concerned with queuing for health care, similar principles apply to all human services, and especially services that are provided by highly paid personnel such as lawyers, dentists, professors, architects, and so on. In a service economy like Canada's, a great deal of work is of this kind—that is, concerned with expert and timely service, hence concerned with the willingness of clients to queue and wait. But this topic is especially pressing in the health domain, because here (as mentioned) queuing and waiting are visibly matters of life and death. These days, every Canadian is concerned about health issues and health care. Every free dollar in the provincial budgets is earmarked for new health expenditures (perhaps that is an exaggeration, but not far off.) And one of the biggest popular concerns is *wait time*. It will be worth our while to understand what waiting is and why people have such a problem with it.

According to a dictionary of synonyms, "to wait" is to tarry, linger, postpone, take it easy, dally, idle, and trifle; also, to expect, look for, watch for, and keep a sharp look-out for something. This all sounds pleasant and benign. By contrast, "to not wait" is to hurry, quicken, urge, spur, whip, goad, and lose no time. But this linguistic analysis doesn't answer the question. Why is waiting such a problem, especially in health care?

Let's consider the opposite of waiting. We know that people don't like waiting, because life is speedy and waits for no one. It is full of rapid, sudden, impatient turns of event: full of flows and overflows of people, information, ideas, inventions, and capital. Much of social life—especially government—is concerned with removing the barriers to these flows. Obstacles, delays, and waiting are problems for most people, most of the time. Time is of the essence. A penny saved is a penny earned. As well, questions about the legitimacy of the wait, the fairness of selection for service, and the quality of service once obtained also colour people's behaviour and perceptions. Waiting times and waiting lines (or queues) become sources of irritation.

Yet we spend much of our life waiting. To adjust, we have created social arrangements like waiting rooms, queue etiquette, and call waiting. There is even a class of workers called "waiters" and "waitresses"—or "wait staff"—whose job it is to linger, bide their time, and keep a sharp look-out for the wishes of their customers. Interestingly, to fill the job of waiting is not to take it easy, dally, idle, or trifle. A classic study by Karasek and Theorell (1990) shows that people who wait on tables for a living, because of their high volume of work and low level of control over customers, are especially likely to develop hypertension and heart disease.

Waiting is expected and endured in society today, but many questions remain to be answered: for example, how long are people willing to wait, under various circumstances? Are there circumstances under which waiting may harm a person's mental and physical health? Is there anything we can do to make waiting briefer or, at least, make it seem briefer? This issue has at least two elements, both worth sociological exploration: (1) What causes long waiting times? and (2) What causes people to be upset about long waiting times?

First, long waiting times are caused by too many customers and too few servers, too slow service or too slow allocation of customers to servers. (This is true whether we are thinking about medical care or buying tickets for a movie.) As sociologists we may study what drives up the number of customers for a medical procedure, what limits the number of servers, and whether the procedures for (say) allocating patients to doctors or doctors to operating rooms are unnecessarily slow. This is the "demography of waiting." Viewed from another perspective, it could be called the "economics of waiting," and if we factor in the issue of power and social inequality—the possibility that some people push to the front of the line—it becomes the "politics of waiting."

There will never be enough money to eliminate all waiting. So we must also consider the factors that cause people to get *upset* about waiting, and ask how we can minimize their upset. Many things upset people waiting for significant medical care: they may include pain, danger, fear of death, interrupted daily life, a sense of unfair treatment, uncertainty about outcomes, and so on. In problematic circumstances, enhanced emotional responses and situational awareness increase the "density" of experience in a certain length of time, so time appears to be elapsing faster. Said another way: stress and the resulting hyperawareness make wait times feel even longer than they truly are. This suggests that the perception of wait times is influenced most by circumstance (Flaherty et al., 2005). As well, many things shape people's willingness and ability to "be patient" while waiting. Likely, there are cultural and religious differences, maybe even age and gender differences that play a role. Perhaps we could call this the "anthropology of waiting."

Also, there is the "psychology of waiting." Some people are, by virtue of their personality, impatient, edgy, high-strung, and extremely sensitive to the slow passage of time. Others are calmer, more docile, and—well, patient. Psychological research has been carried out on how social comparison affects people's willingness to wait. Fifty years ago, Leon Festinger found that people are more willing to wait with people who are similarly miserable, than they are with people who are cheerier than them. This exemplifies a principle we will see repeated below: namely, that people are happier when they are equal to or better off than their comparison group.

An interesting cross-national finding shows, however, that not everyone picks the same comparison group when waiting. Observations of waiting lines in different countries have shown that Americans judge their position by how far they are from the *front* of the line. In a slow-moving line, they spend a great deal of time feeling discontented. By contrast, Japanese people judge their position by how far they are from the *back* of the line. In a slow-moving line, they spend a great deal of time feeling pleased that so many people are even worse off than they are.

Finally, there is even a "biochemistry of waiting." A research team led by Dr. Gregory S. Berns used MRI technology to image the brain while people waited to have a painful procedure. It found that of the thirty-two volunteers who agreed to have a series of shocks to the foot, some of them dreaded each shock so much that they repeatedly chose to have an earlier, higher-voltage jolt so they could get it over with more quickly. These people, labeled *extreme dreaders*, showed greater activity in a brain region related to both pain and attention. The findings show that dread arises not from simple fear, but from the brain's tendency to focus on the unpleasant event. They suggest that extreme dreaders could ease their anxiety by finding a distraction, such as meditation, exercise, or some other activity, to take their minds off the anticipated event (*Science*, May 5, 2006).

So far, sociologists have devoted little effort to studying waiting. There has been sociologically interesting research, in medicine, marketing, psychology, and elsewhere, on various issues related to waiting. Consider some of the findings from medicine. Patients awaiting coronary artery bypass surgery feel doubt, physical limitation, anxiety about chest pains, fear of the operation, and dissatisfaction with the care offered to them. Typically, they feel more frightened if their pains increase while waiting (Fitzsimons et al., 2003). Patients waiting for a lung transplant feel tension about "having to wear a beeper" and "fear the transplant will come too late." The longer patients are on the waiting list, the more anxiety and depression they experience (Vermeulen et al., 2005).

Among patients waiting for cataract surgery, those who wait less than their maximum acceptable waiting time ("MAWT") are retrospectively more satisfied with their wait than patients who wait more than their MAWT (Conner-Spady et al., 2004). Patients' experience depends on their medical condition. Patients awaiting varicose vein surgery or hernia repair experience little physical, psychological or social suffering because of the delay, and few worsen significantly. However, patients awaiting an operation for breast cancer often suffer intensely, and complications are more likely to occur (Oudhoff et al., 2004).

Patients waiting for coronary artery bypass graft surgery react in different ways, depending on their sex. Despite similar heart rates and blood pressure levels, men suffer much less anxiety during the wait than women (Parry, 2004). On the other hand, female patients waiting for the results of diagnostic testing in a breast clinic experience no change in their state of mind. Waiting does not worsen their anxiety, depression, doubt, or confusion (Poole et al., 1999). Patients visiting the emergency department of a hospital experience the wait in different ways, depending on their beliefs. Those who think they have a voice in the triage process view the selection as fairer and the wait as shorter than those who feel they have no voice in the triage. As well, patients kept busy and told how long they can expect to wait are more satisfied with waiting (Naumann and Miles, 2001).

Patients making a second or later visit to an eye clinic are typically less satisfied with their wait than first-time patients. Patients who come with someone else feel the wait to be much longer than patients who come on their own (Barlow, 2002). Patients waiting for an injection of nuclear materials and waiting to be scanned underestimate the waiting time before injection but overestimate the waiting time before scanning. Patients who receive information about the reasons for delay are significantly more satisfied with their wait (DeMan et al., 2005).

The point here is that waiting is entirely subjective. We tend to view time as an absolute, but nowhere is the phrase "Time flies when you're having fun"—and the implication that it drags when you're not—more applicable. Patients prefer to see a doctor for assessment soon after going on a waiting list, to make contact and receive some coping advice. What patients like about the early contact are mainly "non-specific" parts such as reduced isolation and increased understanding (Westbrook, 1995). Among patients at an emergency department, the size and direction of the difference between perceived service and expected service affects satisfaction most. Patients are least satisfied when waiting times are longer than expected; satisfied when waiting times are equal to expectations; and highly satisfied when waiting times are shorter than expected (Thompson and Yarnold, 1995).

Differences in actual waiting time may not matter much at all. After a heart attack, waiting times for coronary surgery or angioplasty are much longer and rates of intervention much lower in Canada than the U.S. However, even though Canadians are more symptomatic than Americans, the differences in overall quality of life are trivial, return to work rates are similar, and patient satisfaction is not dramatically different between the two countries (Mark et al., 1994).

Research also shows that simple interventions can play an important part in easing the common anxieties people feel while waiting. For example, doctors can lessen the negative effects of long waiting times by spending more time with their patients (Feddock et al., 2005). Patients who are kept busy in the waiting room are less likely to be dissatisfied (Dansky and Miles, 1997). Patients who are "taught" while they wait in a clinic to see the doctor are more satisfied with their clinic experience than patients who are not taught or given any other activity (Oermann, 2003). Couples feel less anxiety if they receive cognitive behavioral therapy (CBT) to help them deal with the wait. CBT lessens "waiting stress" and stimulates discussion and awareness (Tarabusi, Volpe, and Facchinetti, 2004). Patients on a waiting list for cardiac catheterization feel less anxiety if a nurse gives them detailed information or an educational session within two weeks of being placed on the waiting list (Harkness et al., 2003).

Most important, perhaps, satisfaction levels in emergency rooms are higher when patients receive information about how long they can expect to wait to see a doctor. Their satisfaction levels rise again when timing expectations are confirmed (Licata and McPhail, 1993). Giving patients information, expressing concern, and managing waiting time perceptions and expectations may do more to improve patient satisfaction than decreasing actual waiting time (Thompson et al., 1996).

Waiting also affects the treatment of substance abuse. Addicts seeking treatment often report being on a waitlist as a problem. It becomes a barrier to treatment, and surprises many who expect instantaneous referrals. The longer the wait, the less likely patients are to start treatment. Patients question the willingness and ability of the system to do any good, or alternatively they "stay clean" during the wait time and then feel they no longer need treatment. Either way, the wait time is detrimental, especially since most patients feel an extreme urgency to start treatment right away. The motivating factor to seek help is often a personal crisis of some sort, and if the opportunity is not seized while it's fresh in mind, committing to treatment becomes less likely. Having said that, there have been no consistent findings connecting wait times and outcomes of treatment. Patients have reported higher levels of success if the wait time is filled with participation in self-help groups, suggesting that how the time is spent is highly relevant (Redko et al., 2006). If the wait time cannot be reduced, or the system made no more efficient, simply organizing the wait time differently may make a considerable difference.

Some of the findings from psychology and market research suggest better ways to organize waiting, for medical assistance or otherwise. For example, the redesign of a service may not only change the actual waiting time but also the *sensed* waiting time, making the customer feel she has waited a shorter time. The result is more customer satisfaction (Luo et al., 2004). In voice-to-voice interactions via telephone, playing music, especially music the customer likes, lessens the sense of waiting and increases satisfaction (Whiting and Donthus, 2006).

Music can manipulate experiences of waiting time, and satisfaction with waiting. In particular, slow-tempo music produces a significantly better emotional response—more satisfaction and relaxation—than fast-tempo music (Oakes, 2003). A customer's willingness to accept delay is related to the assigned causes for delay. Various stress-reduction mechanisms may include giving customers advance notice of expected waiting time, speeding up pre-process waiting time, and publicly admitting customers' rights to quick service (Nie, 2000). Frequent positive feedback on the estimate of the remaining waiting time can improve customer satisfaction with waiting.

Customer frustration with waiting increases when servers do not process customers fairly and justly. Waiting in a single queue causes less stress than waiting in multiple queues. However, dividing customers into service classes and serving them through express and regular lanes also reduces customer stress (Kocas, 2000). Whenever customers must wait, they react best to a provider-not-at-fault explanation; however, providing no explanation whatsoever leads to more positive reactions than a provider-at-fault explanation (Groth and Gilliland, 2006).

To summarize, the literature on waiting shows an increasing consensus on the topic. In studies of waiting in situations that range from students in queues to patients waiting in emergency rooms, the findings are similar. In general, no one enjoys waiting. In the long run, most patients who have to wait for surgery or a medical appointment suffer no harmful physical or mental effects as long as they are chosen according to a maximum acceptable waiting time. These results show that patients are satisfied when perceived performance meets or exceeds patient expectations. This confirms Maister's (2006) proposition about successful management consulting, that satisfaction equals perception minus expectation. Said another way: we are highly satisfied if we get more or better service than we had expected.

In turn, this means that we can solve the waiting problem by lowering people's expectations or raising their sense of pleasure in the waiting experience. Repeatedly, researchers find that they can ease much of the agitation associated with waiting by simple things such as playing soft music, providing low-cost educational items in waiting rooms (for example, pamphlets and magazines), and telling patients or customers the reason for any delay, as well as assuring them that they remain a priority. When patients must wait longer than expected before seeing a physician, doctors can offset dissatisfaction by spending a reasonable amount of time with those patients when they finally do see them. In short, simple techniques can ease much of the discomfort associated with waiting.

It seems the perception of being cured is at least as important as the cure itself. This reminds us of Voltaire's statement: "The art of medicine consists in amusing the patient while nature cures the disease." In a general sense, we need to help find ways to "amuse the patient." We can call this a "sociology of waiting." Additionally, there is the possibility of organizing the process of waiting more effectively, so there could be supportive "waiting communities." Perhaps here, issues of trust, integration and communication are important. Ideally, these "waiting communities" will help people structure and understand their "careers in waiting." Kathy Charmaz's excellent study, *Good Days, Bad Days*, hints at some of this.

Waiting, as we have seen, is easier when people are aware of their position in the queue, know how fast the queue is moving, and understand the reasons for delays. We do not know if communication with other people-in-waiting or past people-in-waiting may be helpful. For example, are there specific things that family members or community organizations could do to make the waiting process less upsetting? Surely, there must be evidence that could help to answer these questions, however tentatively, drawn from the wide variety of situations that involve waiting, delays, setbacks, and other frustrating uncertainties.

When visiting the emergency room, people often claim the wait times as the largest aspect of their negative experience. Quality of care is a close second (Wellstood et al., 2005). Perhaps a joint solution is possible, wherein the staff communicates with patients more regularly by providing them with time estimates and updates.

Case management of waiting situations may help solve the problem. For example, every person in a queue could be given a case manager to sympathetically answer questions, provide information, and liaise with the relevant medical personnel. Court systems increasingly use such case managers to ensure that cases move smoothly from one stage to the next. These caseworkers may not supply personal counseling, but they do provide an ongoing overview for the client. Perhaps such a social arrangement will solve the waiting problem for people with prolonged or chronic medical problems as well. This will not speed up the illness or the cure, but for many, even most, sick people on the conveyor belt headed for wellness, it will create the perception of moving toward a cure. In the midst of a social life characterized by flows, it will provide a sense of forward movement, and a feeling that people are working to remove the barriers to these flows. Humans will be there to rationalize, explain, and excuse the inevitable obstacles, delays, and waiting periods.

If this happens, then people will not only *be* cared for by the health-care system—they will finally *feel* cared for. This will increase their satisfaction with health care and reduce the sense of endless waiting.

Family Supports in the Face of Adversity

The flows we discuss in this chapter—births, deaths, and renewal—typically take place in a family context. Historically, people have relied on families to reproduce the membership of society and protect them against problems resulting from poverty, injury, and physical decline. Therefore, it is appropriate to examine the institution of the family and ask about the conditions under which it best performs this important social function. Viewed from the standpoint of flows, we can think of families as dams that slow the rapid progress of life from birth to death, thus increasing human longevity. We can also think of families as institutions responsible for the constant renewal of society, in the face of unceasing death, disability, and other hardship. Families provide us with important practical and emotional support, and this is especially important when we are ill or infirm.

Marriage is a health-enhancing institution—especially for men—and the social integration associated with it benefits people's health. In this context, family life could be seen as the pre-eminent surviving form of social life and social integration in a society where more and more people are "bowling alone." The question of interest, then, is how, when, and why does social integration improve people's health? Specifically, why do marriage and family life improve people's chances of health and survival? Even more specifically, what is it that families do that promotes good health and prevents new illness, aids in the recovery from acute illness, or contributes to preserving as-good-as-can-be-expected health for people with chronic health problems or disabilities?

WHAT CONDITIONS PROMOTE GOOD/BAD HEALTH? If you survey the literature on health, and (for that matter) consult lay wisdom on the topic, it becomes immediately clear that we know what social situations promote good health or bad. All things being equal, poverty and discomfort are bad for your health, while wealth and comfort are good. In addition, neglect, abuse, conflict, stress, inequality, low status, and lack of control are bad for your health; while attention, kindness, peace, absence of stress, consideration, and support are good. (There is some disagreement about the health consequences of lower status, however, with Schieman et. al [2006] finding that high-status jobs can also produce unhealthy stress consequences.)

The question then becomes: Are sick people more likely to satisfy their needs at home or in a formal health care setting—for example, in a hospital or long-term recovery institution? Is family care, under specifiable conditions, as good as, or even better than, professional care?

At first glance, one might suppose family care would be best. After all, families are supposed to provide attention, kindness, peace, absence of stress, consideration, and support. That is our normative understanding of "family." Unlike hospitals and other formal organizations, families may not always be efficient, but they are supposed to be loving and attentive. Sometimes, hospitals and other health institutions may boast more wealth and better facilities, but even this cannot be guaranteed. An underfunded hospital may be less comfortable than the average family home.

On the other hand, sociologists know that families often fail to live up to popular expectations. Many people in many families report experiencing neglect, abuse, conflict, stress, inequality, low status, and lack of control. This is especially true of children and the aged, and often more true of women than men—wives compared to husbands, mothers compared to fathers, sisters compared to brothers. The Canadian Incidence Study of Reported Child Abuse and Neglect reports that in 2003, an estimated 235,315 child maltreatment investigations were conducted in Canada. This corresponds to an estimated 38.33 investigations per thousand children. Just under half of these reports were substantiated by the investigating child welfare worker. It's fair to say that only *some* families provide what sick people need to get well, and *some* members are more likely to get it than others.

Some families are more egalitarian than others. Others are more prone to conflict. Finally, some are more cohesive and adaptable than others. This means than some families routinely produce more stress than other families, and some are more able to change under conditions that require them to provide care to a sick person.

COSTS OF CAREGIVING TO A FAMILY. Even the least conflictual, most egalitarian, cohesive, and adaptable families may pay an enormous price when called on to provide extended care to a family member. Family caregivers have to provide practical (instrumental) and emotional help of varied kinds, depending on the illness or disability. Doing so will often use up much leisure time and may eat into hours otherwise used for paid work or sleep. The costs of care may include foregone income, the price of various medicines and treatments, and the cost of hiring people to do household jobs (e.g., cooking, cleaning, shopping, babysitting) that previously were done by the primary caregiver.

Sometimes, caregivers may have to reduce their work responsibilities, change to part-time work, or even give up paid work. When they keep a full-time job, employers may treat them differently, the way they sometimes shunt new mothers onto a "mommy track"—that is, a career path intended for women who prioritize family responsibilities ahead of job responsibilities. As well, all family members will find that their usual expectations about life, especially family life, are violated by the need to provide in-home care. Meals may become less regular, housecleaning more perfunctory, school and career accomplishments (and goals) less ambitious.

In these respects, the primary caregiver is most likely to suffer from violated expectations. Here, highly educated, ambitious caregivers are the most likely of all to experience severe dislocation, and will need to think hard about ways to adjust their plans to the new circumstances. Typically, these primary caregivers are women: wives, mothers, and daughters. The research reports a high frequency of depression and burnout among such women. The research literature also reports a change in family relationships. Sometimes, the caregiver assumes a parental relationship with the spouse to whom he or she is providing care. This disrupts the earlier marital relationship, distorting authority relations and sex life, as well as the division of labor. Marital quality and perceptions of inequity in the relationship are related to caregiver burnout. A study conducted among intimate partners of cancer and multiple sclerosis (MS) patients found that higher perceptions of inequity are strongly accompanied with higher emotional exhaustion and depersonalization in the caregiver, as well lower feelings of personal accomplishment (Ybema et al., 2002).

Children are asked to take on extra household duties as secondary caregivers, and this will have a negative effect on their education and development. Such children may also suffer from neglect, or at least feel neglected by the primary caregiver. This problem is especially problematic when the sick family member is a sibling; the feeling of neglect then is compounded by existing (ordinary) feelings of sibling rivalry in the household.

Under what conditions are families able to adjust to these new demands in ways that minimize the unavoidable costs of caring for a sick family member at home? As we said earlier, some families are more egalitarian, some more conflictual, and some more cohesive and adaptable than others. The general principle here is simple: families that bring a history of unresolved problems to caregiving will fare badly. Likewise, so will families that have no experience with collective problem solving, open discussion, or flexibility in the face of changing circumstances. Said another way, the caregiving experience will bring out both the best and worst in families. It is unlikely that, when faced with significant caregiving responsibilities, well-functioning families will become pathologically careless, abusive, or stressed. On the other hand, it is unlikely that poorly functioning families faced with significant caregiving responsibilities will become attentive, kind, peaceful, considerate, and sympathetic.

FAMILY STRUCTURES. In attempting to determine how families can improve or maintain the health of an ill family member, it is necessary to distinguish between *family structures* and *family processes*. It is also necessary to recognize that families offer two types of support, instrumental and emotional. Family structures are related to instrumental support, while family processes are related to emotional support.

Certain structural elements of a family can either aid or hinder a patient's recovery, such as marital status, the patient's age, or the gender of the family caregiver. In a study of open-heart surgery, Carmody (2004) studied patient recovery patterns in relation to age, gender, family environment, and occupational differences, and concluded the family environment was one of the most significant factors affecting the recovery of the patient after surgery. Another study of patients who had had coronary artery bypass surgery, carried out by Okkonen and Vanhanen (2006), found that patients living alone reported more chest pain after surgery than those living with someone. They linked low family support to depressive symptoms, anxiety, and hopelessness, factors that reduce a patient's quality of life. They also reported that in general, female patients and patients with lower vocational education were in poorer health whether they lived alone or not.

Since female family members are the ones who do most of the caregiving for ill family members, the relationship between the patient and the female caregiver is of more importance than ties to other male family members. Sharon Mann's (1998) interviews with fifty adolescents in active medical treatment for cancer found that "perceived maternal conflict was associated with psychological distress [while] conflict with fathers, siblings, and best friends was not associated with distress." It is more important, then, for patients to have a strong relationship with the female members of the family than with the men if a healthy outcome is to be expected.

Multiple environmental factors may well work in tandem, resulting in systemic poor health. Through interviews with the maternal caregivers for children with traumatic brain injury (TBI), Keenan (2006) found that multiple environmental factors put children at risk for poor developmental outcomes, including living in single-parent families, living below the poverty level, or having low social capital. Naar-King's (2006) study of caregivers for children with HIV/AIDS had several unique predictors of low compliance with medication. Caregivers were rarely the biological parents, but were more often extended family, adoptive parents, and foster parents. Low adherence was predicted in part by caregiver substance abuse and positive HIV status. Substance abuse in the caregiver was in turn predicted by high family conflict, stressful life events, and low satisfaction with the medical team.

A study of family support for schizophrenic patients by Garcia et al. (2006) explored the impact of support on patients' compliance with medication. High familial instrumental support predicted higher medication usage. Lopez et al. (2004) examined the role of families in contributing to or preventing relapse in schizophrenic episodes. There was a racial component to this study, comparing Anglo-American and Mexican-American families. In Anglo-American families, high criticism and high attribution of control resulted in a higher likelihood of relapse. In Mexican-American families, low family warmth and low family contact had a similar result. What is important to take from this study is that cultural differences can have an effect on which types of caregiving are effective. Note, too, that many families have trouble dealing with a member who is depressed or anxious and sometimes try to conceal the fact that someone they know has this disease.

There is, however, no simple answer as to which kinds of families work better because the age-specific needs of each patient must be taken into account. Cohen et al.'s (2004) study of diabetic children found that their glycemic control depended in part on the family structure and in part on the degree of adaptability within the family. Younger children had higher control when their families were low in adaptability (possibly because they needed structure and order at that stage of their lives) while adolescents had poorer control in such families (possibly because they needed more independence and autonomy).

It becomes clear after extended analysis of the existing literature that care is best provided in multiple-caregiver, financially stable families with high contact and low conflict. It is also best for the patient to have a healthy relationship with his or her female family members.

POSITIVE FAMILY PROCESSES. There is a lot of research suggesting that entry into marriage can positively or negatively influence health, depending on relationship quality and the length of the relationship. As well, there is research linking one's spouse as a social network member to the ability to access medical care.

Committed marriages can do people a lot of mental and physical good, though bad ones can do them much harm. Best of all, most of the time people can choose the people they want to join in close relations, and can act to improve their relationship if it starts to produce unhealthy results.

Other things being equal, married people are healthier and happier than unmarried people. Compared with married people, separated, divorced, and unattached people are, on average, less happy, less healthy, more disturbed, and run a higher risk of early death (Keyfitz, 1988). Cohabiting people are typically less stable and satisfied than married people, though people in long-term committed cohabiting relations are happier and better off than unattached people.

High divorce rates in North America may cause people to be more skeptical about marriage, but most people still marry, and the institution continues to provide strong benefits for those people. Indeed, research has found the benefits of marriage for some groups have actually increased over the past several decades. For instance, unmarried middle-aged men are now about one-third likelier than married men to die in any given year from causes ranging from cancer to respiratory disease to suicide (Jaffe, Dena, Manor, Eisenbach, and Neumark, 2007).

Findings such as these show the strong associations that consistently link marriage and health. But the link between marriage and health is mediated by the quality of the relationship—that is, how a couple gets along. The higher the quality of the relationship, the stronger is its positive effect on health.

Because a good marriage produces happiness and health, we can gauge the quality of a marriage from the partners' mental and physical health. In fact, we may be able to make a better guess about the quality of a marriage by looking at the health of the people in it than by listening to what the same people tell us about their marriage. However, marital stressors are related to both mental and physiological problems (Kiecolt-Glaser and Newton, 2001). The cause-and-effect relationship goes both ways: for example, psychiatric symptoms can lead to marital difficulties, or marital difficulties can aggravate psychiatric symptoms. People in unhappy marriages often show signs of psychological difficulty. The symptoms include a weaker will to live, less life satisfaction, and reported poorer health, compared with people in happy marriages (Shek, 1995).

Marriage quality affects the mental health of wives more than it affects that of husbands (Horowitz, McLaughlin, and White, 1998). Women tend to respond in a more directly emotional manner to adverse marital experiences. Under conditions of stress, men tend to act out—to drink or act violently, for example; while under the same conditions, women are likelier to suffer depression—that is, to drive the anxiety inward. A happy marriage can improve every part of a person's life, including health and parenting skills, especially if the mother is satisfied with the marriage (Feldman, Fisher, and Seitel, 1997). But a bad marriage is far worse, especially for women, than singlehood or divorce.

A good marriage is especially important to people who are sick, weak, or vulnerable in other ways. For example, pregnant women benefit from being in a good marriage with a kind and understanding partner. The quality of the attachment between a pregnant woman and her partner increases the woman's sense of well-being (Zachariah, 1996). Intimacy gives both partners health protection within a stable and caring family environment. Intimacy may also promote coping strategies in dealing with stressful life events (Ren, 1997).

Recent studies have shown the positive effects of marriage are not only found among married heterosexual couples, but also among gay and lesbian married couples (Wienke and Hill, 2009). Many people cannot handle stress all by themselves. A partner or family can provide support during difficult times.

The likeliest explanation for the link between marriage and health is that a good marriage provides economic and emotional support. Emotional stability in turn strengthens the immune system, making partners more able to avoid or recover from illness. It also increases the will to live and promotes prudence and self-care. As well, marriage provides economic support. Married people who live together can pool their funds to avoid economic hardship. This increases their access to health care and also permits them to focus on healthy lifestyles. These two factors are likely the best explanation for the good health of people in good marriages.

Structural elements of the family are vital to recovery, but the processes that occur within the family are just as important, and perhaps even more so. A positive family environment aids in the psychosocial recovery of the care-receiver, which improves quality of life by guarding against depression and aiding in the social reintegration of the patient, thus leading to better long-term adjustment. To achieve this environment, open communication, positive attitudes, high levels of support and warmth, and high family cohesion and adaptability are necessary. Cohesion reflects the degree of help, commitment, and support that family members are willing to provide for one another. Committed relationships are necessary to pull through illnesses that have a lasting impact, such as cognitive disorders or degenerative diseases.

Adaptability is fundamental because family structures and routines will need to change around the ill family member and families need effective problem solving skills to deal with the upheaval caused by a major illness. Honda and Kagawa-Singer (2006) illustrate the correlation between a strong family support network and patterns of colorectal cancer screening adherence among Japanese Americans. It was found that screening adherence depended to a significant degree on levels of emotional family support and the presence of cohesion in terms of effectively enforcing standard family norms.

A good family environment for spouses results in high marital satisfaction, which also predicts good caregiving. A study of coronary artery bypass surgery patients by Elizur and Hirsh (1999) examined the effect of social, personal, and marital resources on psychosocial recuperation, finding that only marital resources had a significant positive effect and that marital adaptability was a major resource that contributed towards recovery. A study by Matthews et al. (2006) on recipients of coronary artery bypass surgery examined the effect of pre-surgical spousal attributes on post-surgery psychological well-being. Results showed that lower marital satisfaction on the patient's part predicted higher depression. The authors noted the study was important because depressive symptoms could increase the risk of future myocardial infarctions and morbidity.

The most supportive families are those that are cohesive, low in conflict and control, and have low emphasis on intellectual or cultural topics and religion. These are the findings of a study of bone marrow transplant survivors carried out by Molassiotis et al. (1997). The authors found that a good family environment corresponded directly and significantly with better psychosocial adjustment. Interestingly, it was also found that families of bone marrow transplant survivors were in general more cohesive and lower in conflict than the control families, who had no illness in the family. This implies that illness and caregiving may cause families to function better, but is not a finding replicated in other studies. Families that function well caregive well, and vice versa.

The role of family support on the functional status, depression status, and social status of stroke victims was examined in a study by Tsouna-Hadjis et al. (2000). A high level of support was found to lower rates of depression even after controlling for stroke severity, and different types of family support affected different domains. Instrumental support was most important in raising functional and social status, while emotional support raised the subject's depressive status.

The ability to secure employment is the strongest contributor to an adult TBI patient's quality of life, according to Webb et al. (1995). If a patient does not have a job and cannot afford to pay for health care, his or her health will naturally suffer. Instrumental family support is vital in the job-search process and it also improves quality of life by increasing functional independence. For children with TBI, employment is not a viable option. A study of pediatric TBI done by Wade et al. (2001) found that lower distress following TBI (but not, curiously, orthopedic injuries) was associated with the use of humour. Making the situation funny is probably related to acceptance, which is associated with lower burden and distress.

For patients at the other end of the spectrum, different health outcomes are expected. Horvath et al. conducted a study of caregivers to patients with progressive dementia, such as Alzheimer's disease. The researchers found that family support was key to preventing instances of home injury, a major concern in this patient group. Family support was defined as an acceptance and ability to make role changes, teaching and role modeling from professionals, and long-standing values and family traditions.

NEGATIVE FAMILY PROCESSES. Just as good family dynamics can improve rehabilitation, poor dynamics can have a negative effect on the subject's health, ranging from non-compliance with medications to a higher likelihood of relapse. A poorly functioning family is one that has high conflict, low warmth, and poor cohesion and adaptability. A study by Gerson et al. (2006) examining Irritable Bowel Syndrome (IBS) and predictors for IBS activity asked patients a series of questions regarding their relationships with significant others, their beliefs about what was causing their symptoms, and their personal assessment of their quality of life. The results showed that more severe symptoms were common in relationships characterized by a high level of conflict and that relationships with low levels of conflict and higher levels of support yielded less severe symptoms.

Negative attitudes towards the care-receiver, the surgery (or surgeon), or the prescribed medication can also have a profound effect on health. Resentment, guilt, or the feeling the patient is responsible for and in control of his or her illness may exacerbate the patient's condition. Naar-King et al.'s (2006) study of children with HIV/AIDS found that caregivers' negative outcome expectancies were a major predictor of adherence to medication, and Matthews et al.'s (2006) study of heart surgery patients revealed that high pre-surgical neuroticism in the spouse was correlated with higher patient depression.

Negative attitudes often take the form of *expressed emotion*. Expressed emotion (EE) is the level of emotion expressed by the family of someone with an illness. Typical characteristics are emotional over-involvement, hostility, and criticism. High levels of expressed emotion are considered detrimental and predict a poorer outcome. Looking at families with high expressed emotion, Ivanovic and Bebbington (1994) found that schizophrenic relapse was ten times more likely than in families with low EE. However, an often-overlooked positive aspect of expressed emotion is family warmth. The authors found that a low relapse rate was associated with a high degree of warmth in fathers and *any* degree of warmth shown by mothers. It's important to note the gender gap in this case. It took a much higher degree of warmth from fathers than mothers to evoke a positive response. Perhaps this is because mothers are more effective at expressing warmth, or perhaps it is because children are more accustomed to receiving warmth from their mothers than their fathers. The matter has not been explored in depth, but the impact of gender on caregiving effectiveness must not be understated, especially considering the majority of caregivers are adult women.

Studies done in the Netherlands by Wassenberg et al. (2004) and in Australia by Anderson (2006) show that for children with TBI, improved health outcomes were largely determined by the family's psychosocial characteristics. Wassenberg's study showed that high pre-injury psychosocial adversity and low pre-injury adaptive functioning significantly predicted a greater number of inattention errors when testing for attention-deficit/hyperactivity disorders (SADHD, ADHD). Anderson's study concluded that children in families with low pre-injury adaptive skills and who are coping poorly with the aftermath of the injury are at greatest risk of long-term impairment. In contrast to the Molassiotis study mentioned above, this research shows that it is important for the family to be cohesive and flexible before a crisis arises. It is unlikely that a traumatic event like an injury will bring a family together and turn them into quality caregivers.

Last, but not least, how the family reacts with the world outside can also have an effect on health. Carroll et al. (2005) investigated the complaints made by users of pediatric emergency services. It was discovered that visits by white children resulted in a complaint rate more than five times higher than visits by African American children. Programs that use complaints in quality control and risk management efforts may thus unintentionally exclude segments of the population. Perhaps there is truth in the old adage, "The squeaky wheel gets the grease." A family that voices its discontent is more likely to receive better care and be in better health than a passive family. And, according to Carroll's study, being white doesn't hurt either.

FAMILY FUNCTIONING MAKES A DIFFERENCE. Regardless of the type of illness, whether physical or mental/cognitive, positive family dynamics and environment have a positive effect on quality of life and health outcomes and negative family dynamics and environment have a negative effect. A study by Buchanan (2004) showed that therapy designed to improve the quality of communication and relationships between caregivers and dementia patients in their families succeeded in reducing symptoms of depression and frustration among the caregivers, as well as in reducing frustration levels among patients. Family characteristics in these cases were instrumental in affecting the caregiver's mental health and this in turn affected the patient's quality of life. This pattern was visible across illnesses.

Even in deteriorative cognitive illnesses, levels of family functioning and the type of family environment continue to have an effect despite the patient's decline. Graham and Basset (2006) give us a comprehensive review of the interaction process between caregiver and Alzheimer's patient in the informal family setting. They show that part of an effective care process is having a high level of adaptability in the caregiver-patient relationship, enabling the reconstruction and renegotiation of the patient's continually evolving self. The benefits of this adaptability process were not undermined by cognitive disability. The essentials of quality caregiving remained the same, despite differences in the patient's mental condition.

The caregiving process and the challenges associated with it seem to be the same no matter what the illness is. A study by Stetz and Brown (2004) compared physical and psychosocial health in families caring for people with AIDS and cancer. Twenty-six caregivers of people with either cancer or AIDS were given a questionnaire that addressed measures of depression and grief, stress symptoms, demands of caregiving, quality of personal relationships, and quality of life and health status. The results showed no significant differences between either caregiving group. The researchers propose that support delivered to caregivers must emphasize a more inclusive approach as opposed to a disease-specific perspective in order to increase the depth and breadth of services provided to families undertaking these services.

Families do make a difference in the caregiving process. The quality of care is affected by dynamics in the family such as level of cohesion, adaptability, and communication and family environment. These measures affect the quality of care and quality of life for both caregivers and care receivers across illnesses, whether physical, cognitive, or mental (on this, see for example, Farrell and Barnes, 1993).

On the question of whether home care is better for patients than institutionalized care, the evidence is not entirely conclusive, though there are distinct advantages to home care. Perhaps both caregiving settings can be equally effective so long as the patients' needs are being met physically as well as emotionally and psychosocially. But there may well be something unique to good families that cannot be replicated in an institutional setting.

Accidents and Opportunities

Everyone is born and everyone dies; but within that general framework, people have a wide variety of experiences. As we have seen, families play an important—indeed, essential—role in protecting and helping their members against adversity. In that sense, families help people to prolong and improve their lives, as well as allowing them to reproduce new generations. Husbands are especially important for their wives' health, and, to an even greater degree, wives are important for their husbands' (and children's) health.

Not everyone, however, is able to form a conjugal family, because not everyone has the same opportunity to do so. Let us spend some time considering one particular factor that limits people's ability to form a family: catastrophic physical injury. This is only one example, but we may be able to generalize from this case to other factors—for example, to other physical and social disabilities—that impede people's opportunities to form families and, in that way, to survive.

Consider the results of TBI, a condition that has significant documented impacts on dating, mating, and marriage. Traumatic (or acquired) brain injury is commonly the result of an accidental fall or motor vehicle accident, though it is also common in sports injuries, assault, and domestic violence. Researchers commonly map the following eight dimensions of decline after traumatic brain injury: decline in social competence, intimacy, behavioural, maturity/independence, neurophysiological, mood, and executive and non-executive functions.

All severe illnesses and injuries, including TBI, affect social relationships, especially if the results are chronic, disabling, and long-lasting. Even in the best of circumstances, such injuries force couples and families to rethink their activities. The mass of evidence shows that severe injuries put severe stress on relationships and lessen the likelihood that people will enter or remain in close relations. Here we will focus on women who have suffered TBI; the social and marital consequences are probably similar but less extreme for men. We begin by considering the factors that influence a general likelihood of dating, mating, and marrying.

FACTORS INFLUENCING MARRIAGEABILITY. In general, women leave home, marry, and have children at a younger age than men. Their chances of marrying are determined by the chances of meeting a suitable mate, which means people are affected by the size and composition of their social network. People tend to mate and associate with one another based on the principle of *homogamy*. That is, they are more likely to mate with others who have similar personal characteristics, including political attitudes, lifestyle values, personality, appearance, or ethnicity.

Age, social class, and religious homogamy are strong factors in mate selection. People of a similar age, social class status, and religious background are typically considered attractive partners. According to exchange theory, the stability of any relationship is characterized by a dyadic exchange of costs and benefits. In a model of social exchange, one seeks a mate who brings a set of assets and liabilities comparable to one's own. Similarly, it is disadvantageous for a person to stay in a relationship in which the costs outweigh the benefits.

The importance of educational homogamy—the tendency to select a partner with a similar educational background in marriage—has increased in Canada over the last three decades. This means that people with above-average educational attainment (for example, a postsecondary education) are likely to seek a partner with a comparable education. People are also becoming less likely to marry partners with significantly less education.

IMPACT OF MENTAL DISABILITY ON DATING, MATING, AND MARRIAGE. For some victims of TBI, the greatest resulting disability will lie in the realm of psychosocial functioning. People with significant injuries are likely to spend less time in social settings where non-injured people spend time—for example, workplaces, public places, and schools. They are likely to spend more time in private places (home) or public places where other injured people spend time (for example, hospitals and doctors' offices). They also spend more time alone, so they are less exposed to other people and hence to potential mates. They meet fewer people altogether and meet a higher-than-average number of injured people. Their interactions with non-injured people will be more difficult and interaction with other injured people easier.

For adolescents with disabilities, relationship concerns may be even more acute because they may have limited opportunities to develop dating skills or to even think of themselves as potential dating partners. This may be due to both the characteristics of their disability or illness and the messages they receive from others (for example, parents, teachers, peers) that discourage dating and sexuality for people with disabilities. Although there has been an ideological shift toward recognition of sexual autonomy for people with an intellectual disability, people with an intellectual disability continue to encounter social and cultural barriers to sexual expression.

A study by Healy et al. (2009) assessed the sexual knowledge, experiences, and aspirations of individuals with an intellectual disability. Family attitudes were found to be influential in the views of the respondents. Negative responses by family members towards the sexuality of those with an intellectual disability led to similar attitudes within the individuals, who were then less likely to receive education about sexuality and engage in discussion on the topic. This created a barrier toward their independence, as they had inadequate knowledge about their own sexuality and sexual expression.

The study also examined the individuals' perceptions of impediments they faced in achieving sexual autonomy. The subjects in the study had all received some form of sexual education, and individuals in both the over-18 and under-18 groups had similar aspirations of relationships and marriage. However, even though they had an understanding of their sexual rights, they still perceived social and cultural barriers that prevented them from achieving sexual autonomy. Provision of sex education and promotion of positive attitudes toward sexual expression are critical for sexual independence.

These findings were consistent with previous research on the topic. Howland and Rintala (2001) interviewed women aged 22 to 69 with various disabling conditions. Themes emerging from their stories showed that the timing of the onset of the disability, and the response to that disability by family, friends, and society in general, were critical influences on their dating behavior. Likewise, in a study by Wiegerink et al. (2006) of adolescents and young adults with cerebral palsy, the adolescents in question said that sexuality was an important aspect of their lives, but that they experienced difficulties developing a sexual relationship. Factors associated with this difficulty included psychological maladjustment, inadequate self-efficacy, and low sexual self-esteem; these all undermined the development of social and sexual relationships for disabled young adults.

Similar findings are reported in studies of other physical and cognitive disabilities. For example, Milligan (2004), reporting on romantic relationship satisfaction among men and women living with spinal cord injury, found that over two-thirds of participants were not dating or involved in an intimate relationship. All interviewees shared the view that negotiating intimacy post-injury is a venture fraught with challenges imposed by physical injury and disability. Three major challenges were identified: sexual difficulties, accessibility and mobility issues, and negative societal attitudes. Self-acceptance and improved communication skills were identified as important assets for achieving relationship satisfaction.

Social stigma often hinders disabled people who are inclined to seek dates and mates. Strohmer et al. (1984) report that many people are unable to imagine social or sexual relationships with disabled people, who are thought to be significantly unlike other humans. As with other types of prejudice, this prejudice responds well to increased familiarity. The researchers find that increased contact with people with a disability, younger age, and higher levels of education were the best predictors of more favourable attitudes towards people with a disability. Even so, social distance is often maintained. For adults with disabilities, acceptance comes more readily when they are perceived as fellow employees or casual friends than when they are viewed as potential dating or marriage partners.

Many people continue to feel uncomfortable about sexual activity among the disabled. As a result, dating and mating are less common among people who are physically or mentally disabled. Disabled people are more likely than others to report dissatisfaction with dating frequency, as well as to perceive constraints on attracting partners, societal barriers to dating, and communication problems.

Because stereotypes, stigma, and traditional attitudes persist around dating and mating with disabled people, the people who date and mate disabled people tend to be unusual, even exceptional. Partners of disabled people are more likely to be described as having nurturing qualities than the partners of non-disabled people, and less likely to be described as intelligent, sociable, or athletic. In general, significantly injured people will typically gain less education and less occupational success than non-injured people. Therefore, they will be less similar to and less attractive to highly educated, successful people, and this will reduce the likelihood they will be sought out for dates or marriage.

Mental illness also reduces the likelihood of marriage, especially when the patients have a past diagnosis of a mental illness compounded by perceived danger to others. Some types of mental illness promote early marriage, but people with severe mental illness or cognitive deficiencies are less likely to marry. If they do marry, they are more likely to divorce, after which their chances of remarriage are low. A survey of 1,600 respondents found that people's perceptions they are unable or unlikely to marry are associated with lower income, less education, illness, or a caregiving responsibility (Crompton, 2005).

Psychological balance has also been proved to be important for marital stability. Women with a diagnosed mental disorder are 2.5 times more likely to divorce than women without the diagnosis. Prior psychiatric disorders are also found to increase chances of divorce. Women, in particular, are at a great disadvantage. A 1998 survey found that women lost 48 million of years of marriage, whereas men lost only 23 million years of marriage because of a divorce or separation due to a prior psychiatric disorder (Kessler et al., 1998).

OBSERVATIONS ABOUT TRAUMATIC BRAIN INJURY. For the reasons suggested above, traumatic brain injury can have deep and lasting social outcomes for those who experience it. TBI victims often suffer from neurobehavioral disability—a combination of cognitive, behavioral, and emotional problems. Common complaints include memory damage, disinhibited behavior, lack of motivation, mood swings, personality changes, communication problems, and denial of deficits. Many brain-injured people continue throughout life to need much supervision and attention. These problems put a huge strain on caregivers and make it difficult for TBI victims to keep and expand their social network. TBI victims may also have reduced communication abilities, sexual dysfunction, and poor social integration, all of which lessen the chance of forming a deep and lasting intimate relationship.

The extent of long-term disability and resulting social-interactional problems depends largely on the severity of the traumatic injury. Definitions of mild head injury are more controversial and less definite. Mildly injured patients offer suffer from post-concussional syndrome, a disorder whose symptoms include somatic complaints (headache, fatigue, and dizziness), cognitive complaints (poor concentration and memory), and emotional complaints (irritability, depression, and anxiety). These symptoms resolve within a few weeks, and some studies have found no long-term weaknesses. However, some studies have found evidence of lasting cognitive and emotional damages even after mild injury, although to a lesser extent than after severe injury.

Even mild TBI (MTBI) can have marked effects on people's lives. This was obvious in a study that compared (1) people who had not been injured in a car accident nor had an MTBI; (2) those who *had* been injured in an accident but did not have an MTBI; and (3) those who had an MTBI with altered consciousness. Compared with uninjured "control" participants, MTBI patients experienced greater likelihood of depression and of post-concussional syndrome. MTBI also was associated with problems seeing and walking. Similarly, the MTBI group had poorer psychosocial outcomes, including an increased likelihood of self-reported disability, under-employment, low income, and marital problems.

Whereas TBI is diagnosed by extensive loss of consciousness, MTBI can result even if none occurred. As a result, individuals may not realize how badly they are injured until side-effects make themselves known. Studies have shown that people suffering from MTBI may develop a profound and lasting "loss of self." Laundau and Hissett (2008) found that victims of MTBI experienced changes in self-image, increases in self-doubt, and decreased confidence following their injury. They felt a diminished role in their family or partnership. This led to feeling disconnected with others. Long-term symptoms were likely to cause disintegration of family relationships. The physical and psychological pain surrounding MTBI can lead to personality changes, as well as exacerbating previously resolved addictions and disorders. All these factors lead to higher incidence of relationships breaking down and subsequent separation or divorce.

EFFECTS ON PSYCHOSOCIAL FUNCTIONING. For reasons suggested above, most existing studies point in the same direction: marriage is rare among TBI victims.

In addition, couples in which a spouse suffered a TBI during the marriage are put under much stress and are found to be more susceptible to marital breakdown. People who have suffered TBI may also have poor social outcomes because of communication difficulties, lack of insight into social situations, and apathy. Research finds that TBI victims are less socially integrated than the general population. They may also experience sexual dysfunction, which further lowers the likelihood of a romance that leads to marriage.

First, there is a problem of reduced social insight. Compared with the control group, TBI patients often show increased apathy, withdrawal, and communication difficulties. They may also have difficulty recognizing facial and vocal expression and commit more social gaffes. Impaired social perception is a problem often reported following traumatic brain injury. TBI victims may also show deficits in using social cues to make interpersonal judgments—also, poorer insight into their deficits, compared with healthy volunteers.

Second, communication skills are likely to be impaired. Those who had suffered a head injury are less correct in language use and speech delivery. They also have poor conversational skills, and are passive and disinterested when talked to, an attribute which is likely to discourage conversation. Marsh and Knight (1991) speculate patients suffer poor social integration due in part to their subnormal communication skills. Other victims also perform significantly worse in social interaction tasks, because of deficits in word fluency. As a result, TBI victims are likely to suffer poorer social interaction and interaction to the community. In one study, TBI patients were compared to a corresponding group with a limb fracture (Oddy and Humphrey, 1980). Those with head trauma had fewer social outings, fewer friends, and fewer social visits paid to them. Doljanac and Larson (2005) report that, in the U.S., intellectually disabled people are less likely to either meet or talk on the phone with friends or neighbors than people in other identified disability groups. TBI often results in a long-term increase in social isolation, producing high rates of depression, psychomotor slowness, and loneliness.

Not surprisingly, brain injury and impaired social interaction are connected to the development of sexual problems. The problems facing brain-injured subject include decreases in sex drive and frequency of sexual activity, and a decreased ability to satisfy one's partner, stay aroused, reach climax, or enjoy sex (Ponsford, 2003). No wonder that, in another study, a quarter of the subjects hadn't had sexual intercourse since their injury and another quarter reported decreased sexual activity.

Some TBI patients display inappropriate social behavior: for example, though aware of social norms of intimacy, they are unaware they are violating those norms. The embarrassment typically associated with such behavior was elicited in these patients only when their self-monitoring increased after viewing videos of themselves. Often, people with intellectual disability show poor overall knowledge of sexuality, especially in the areas of sexually transmitted infections, sexual health, safer sex practices, legal issues, and contraception.

Several other conditions share social characteristics and outcomes similar to TBI, such as poor communication and social skills, large amounts of dependence on caregivers, great needs for supervision, and so on. Three of these comparable conditions are intellectual disability, autism, and stroke. Research on the social and marital status of people with these disabilities also finds poor levels of social interaction than in the general population.

PROBABILITIES OF MARRIAGE FOR SURVIVORS. The marriage rate of these groups—those who suffered TBI as well as those who have comparable mental difficulties—is much lower than that of the general population. Research has found that people with severe TBI have a low chance of marriage, high rates of marital breakdown, and a variety of psychosocial problems. The chances of marriage after suffering a severe TBI are significantly lessened.

Note, however, that *severe* brain injury is different from *mild* brain injury in the extent of its social and psychological effects. People with severe brain injury are much more likely than people with mild brain injury to be viewed as bringing significant liabilities to a relationship, because of their continuing need for care, supervision, and understanding. Thus, even the probabilities of extended co-habitation (and subsequent support obligations) are lessened by a severe brain injury.

Studies also suggest that marriages are more volatile in people with TBI, which points to a high turnover rate. For example, Wood and Yurdakul (1997) found that 49% of adults divorced their partner during the five to eight years following TBI. The same study also found that having children in the relationship did not lessen the chances of leaving, though in other circumstances children are a factor in keeping troubled marriages intact.

Mood swings and unpredictable behaviour on the part of TBI patients were a statistically significant factor in placing a strain on the relationship between two partners, contributing to the relationship breakdown (Kreutzer, 2007; Wood, 2005). In another study, of thirty-eight patients who were single pre-injury, only eleven (29%) had married in the subsequent seventeen years (Wood and Rutherford, 2006).

A study of forty-five male soldiers recently returned from military deployment in Iraq found that individual trauma negatively impacts relationship satisfaction in military couples. The resulting stress resulted in the disintegration of intimate relationships. Trauma symptoms, particularly sleep problems, dissociation, and severe sexual problems, predicted lower marital/relationship satisfaction for both soldiers and their female partners (Nelson et al., 2007).

Family members of victims of TBI go through different experiences depending on their relationship to the patient. Partners experience more stress than parents and score higher on depression scales, while parental stress is greater when afflicted children are living at home. Children in families with TBI patients encounter difficulties as well, as they must now compete with the affected parent or sibling for the attention of the caregiver (Verhaeghe, Defloor, and Grypdonck, 2004).

Not the severity but the nature of the injuries determines the stress experienced by family members. The victim's personality, behavioural, emotional, and intellectual problems show a strong correlation with the extent to which family members experience pressure, anxiety, and feelings of depression. Even ten to fifteen years after the injury, the primary physical problems are less stressful than the psychological effects, some of which only appear after the passage of a considerable amount of time. Young families with several children and little social support, or who have pre-existing financial, psychiatric, and/or medical problems, are the most vulnerable (Verhaeghe, Defloor, and Grypdonck, 2004).

CONCLUSIONS. Marriage rates of TBI patients, and others with similar impairments, are much lower than those of the overall population. Young people with intellectual and developmental disabilities face many issues related to dating and sexual intimacy, such as unwanted pregnancies, sexually transmitted diseases (STDs), and possibilities of abuse, assault, and negligence. For these reasons, the parents of intellectually disabled children may try to limit their children's intimate activities.

Only about 10% of severely brain-injured adult women are married, as compared to 60% of adult Canadian women overall. In other words, severely brain-injured women are only one-sixth as likely to get married. This may be an underestimate, because of the fact that relationships involving brain-injured patients don't tend to last as long. Still, traumatic brain injury lessens a woman's likelihood of ever marrying by an enormous amount. And if such a woman does marry, there is a strong chance she will marry someone with less-than-average education and a lower-than-average income, because her mating "marketability" is lower than average. Her marriage will likely also be shorter-lived and more likely to end in separation or divorce. If she cohabits instead of marrying, chances the relationship will be short-lived are even greater.

Death, Bereavement, and Renewal

Death is the final chapter in a person's life, though not the final chapter in the lives of institutions and organizations. That is because institutions and organizations, unlike individual people, can renew themselves with new, living members.

For individuals, however, the loss of a life companion may be the most distressing event in any person's life. *Bereavement* can describe the state brought about by any number of losses: that of a child, a parent, a friend, or even a national icon. Literature suggests that the loss of a child can bring about the most intense grief reactions of all (Alam et al., 2012). However, this section will focus on the loss of a spouse. It is a clear example of a loss that demands restructuring of one's life, as well as having far-reaching consequences for well-being.

Bereavement is also associated with psychological disturbances that may include depression, hallucinations, insomnia, and depression. The risk of suicide, too, is also heightened by the sudden onset of widowhood, with younger widows being the most likely to commit suicide. There is no clear consensus on whether an expected death is easier to cope with than a sudden death. Some researchers suggest that with widowhood comes an increased likelihood of mortality, though this relationship has yet to be concretely supported. Finally, the loss of a spouse may be especially shocking for young widows, who are less likely to have a peer group of widows for support. This unnaturally early event may also force a premature adjustment of roles. For example, young widows may find themselves taking on the new and unwelcome role of a single parent. Children in the household often aggravate the stressors associated with premature widowhood and forced role change.

The loss of a spouse is often associated with physiological impairment, including lowered immunity and harmful neuro-endocrine changes. These changes make widows more susceptible to viruses and other illnesses. Because of heightened stress, bereavement is associated with increased cardiovascular risk, especially during the first few weeks after the onset of widowhood. Psychological stress is widely understood to trigger cardiovascular problems including hypertension, heart attacks, and strokes. Conjugal bereavement is also linked to major changes in diet and even malnutrition. Following the death of a spouse, widows are prone to change their eating habits. In part, this reflects a loss of companionship: as wives they once enjoyed cooking for their spouse, but as widows they no longer took pleasure in cooking.

Many of these problems are short-lived. In fact, most health problems associated with bereavement are not long-lasting, and only a minority of bereaved spouses experience long-lasting health problems. In general, younger widows (and the widows of younger husbands) are more likely than average to experience poor health during bereavement. There is no clear consensus about whether (male) widowers' health suffers more than (female) widows' health during bereavement. However, men tend to suffer from bereavement more intensely than women, as measured by declines in their quality of health.

Health declines during bereavement may also depend on prior marital quality. Where the marriage was good, the loss of a supportive spouse is likely to cause increased grief symptoms in the surviving spouse. Loss of a spouse following a poor relationship, however, is less likely to lead to health concerns, since there was slight support to begin with. Other studies suggest the time of bereavement may be an opportunity for widows to make positive health changes. Widowhood is at first stressful, but some women experience long-term benefits afterward, the result, for example, of changing their health routine or joining a gym.

As noted, the stress of widowhood affects mental as well as physical health. A study of life-event stressors linked to mental health found that widows in the first year of bereavement tend to experience a threefold increase in their risk of mental distress. For example, hallucinations are a common psychological problem among the bereaved. In a Welsh study of widows, half had hallucinations of a dead spouse. Sleep disturbances are also common during bereavement. The prevalence of grief-related insomnia is also gendered, and insomnia is more common in widows than widowers.

Depression is common among the bereaved. Research shows that widows are more likely to suffer from depression than continuously married women. Problems of depression in widowhood include "depressed mood, crying, sleep trouble, loss of appetite, weight loss, fatigue, difficulty concentrating, slowing of thought processes, loss of interest, poor memory, hopelessness, hallucinations, and wishes to be dead, in descending order of magnitude" (Clayton, 1974, summarized by Windolz, Marmar and Horowitz, 1985).

Some studies suggest widowed men are at a higher risk of depression than widowed women, but that men recover faster. The intensity of grief also varies by gender. In general, women report higher levels of grief than do men one month after the death. One explanation proposed by researchers is that each gender experiences different strains in bereavement, and these strains structure the experience of depression. For example, among women, widowhood is often associated with poverty, so depression is partly a result of financial constraints. A loss of income or social support increases the likelihood of depression for both men and women.

Widowhood often leads to depression, and it may also lead to substance abuse: for example, self-medication using alcohol or pills. Other widows respond to depression by committing suicide. In the first six months, bereaved people are four times more likely to die of suicide than people who are not widowed. Also, among younger people, especially young men, suicide is a common cause of death, compared to natural causes.

One of the founders of sociology, Émile Durkheim, noted in 1897 that unattached people, including widowed, divorced, and single people, run an especially high risk of suicide. This fact still holds true today in North America. Widowed women are more than twice as likely to commit suicide as married women, and five times more likely to commit suicide than married men. Younger widows are especially at risk; specifically, women aged 25 to 34 are more than three times more likely to commit suicide than married women of the same age.

Perhaps the most important relationship that widows experience following the death of a spouse is the relationship with themselves. This new relationship includes their self-perception, confidence in parenting, and resilience, as well as feelings of belonging to a new community. But these transitions are hard to make, especially for older people. It may be for that reason that widows are more likely than other women of the same age and health status to die shortly after their spouse's death—the so-called "widowhood effect." Widows are also more likely than married women to encounter health problems, and, accordingly, are also more likely to consult doctors.

It is not hard to think of reasons widows and widowers may want to commit suicide following bereavement. Marital status is thought to have a "protective" effect on spouses, because of increased financial stability, reduced stress, enhanced friendships with others, a decreased likelihood of engaging in risky behavior such as excessive drinking, and improved health-seeking behavior, such as seeing a doctor when sick.

The loss of a spouse has clear negative effects. When looking at seniors specifically, spousal bereavement is directly correlated with a greater risk of institutionalization and co-residence. The risk is highest directly after the loss, lessening over time as grief, with its many consequences for physical and mental health, fades into acceptance (Strohschein, 2011). Physical relocation or not, a new set of habits and daily routines must be adopted after the loss of someone so intimately involved in one's life.

Now let us turn our attention to the plight of a particular group of widows—military widows—to give the topic more specificity, and to show how bereavement can change into renewal.

STUDIES OF MILITARY BEREAVEMENT. Military life, as everyone knows, is demanding and highly structured. It also places unique demands on marriages. As a report by the National Center on Family Homelessness notes: "Serving in the military is more than an individual occupation; it also has a culture of shared beliefs, practices and experiences. The impact of deployments and reintegration military marriages and children are a part of the shared sacrifice that comes with military service. Frequent moves, non-traditional work hours, and long absences of the deployed parents are common among military families. Families must live with constant worries about the safety of their war fighter" (Houston et al., 2009).

Some of the stresses experienced by military spouses and children are a direct result of the stressful nature of military work experienced by their partners. Long absences from home on combat deployment significantly raise the risk of alcohol dependence, a risk factor in family conflict and violence after the partner's return. As well, military families are also severely stressed by injury and disability resulting from combat.

Another aspect of the military life is what the report characterizes as a "role reversal when members are away on tours of duty, with the spouse taking up the slack at home. This tends to leave the member feeling that he or she is no longer part of the family structure and can only be alleviated if spouses are willing to give up some of the control they had while the member was away."

Given the heavy demands placed on military personnel and their closest kin, some sociologists have called the military a "greedy institution." Such an institution demands that its members put the organization's needs and priorities ahead of their own or those of their families. Not surprisingly, the overlapping demands placed on people by family and the military create tensions between the two, and stress for members of both. As a greedy institution, the military makes it hard for families to fulfill the physical and emotional needs of their members.

Insufficient practical support for military families results in stress for all the family members, and especially for military spouses. It is said the spouse who lives with a serviceperson, lives with the military. Practically speaking, being a military spouse not only affects one's work at home; it also has negative impacts on paid employment and earning abilities. There is a measurable loss in income for military spouses, owing in part to the temporary, mobile, and unpredictable nature of their work-lives.

What's more, military families are aware of this. Most military spouses think the fact their spouse belongs to the military negatively impacts their own employment opportunities. Of the many reasons cited for this, frequent moves stood out as most important. As well, many respondents noted the hardships associated with caring for children in the frequent absence of their spouse. Many felt like single parents. The challenges of meeting child-care costs were also problematic, since most of these couples had moved away from relatives who could offer free help.

Many spouses feel stigmatized when they try to find employment, since some employers are reluctant to hire military spouses on a short-term basis. Frequent relocation plays the largest part in limiting the employability and earning capacity of military spouses. Besides, transfer is stressful. A typical military family reportedly moves every two to three years, and these moves affect the family in many negative ways, both practical and emotional. Besides uprooting spouses from their paid jobs, homes, friends, and neighbourhoods, they also uproot children from their schools and regular routines. Indeed, most literature on military spouses highlights the negative effects of relocation. In sociological terms, military relocation is *tied migration* for a serviceperson's spouse.

Most military spouses are women, and for them, the penalties are even heavier. They suffer significant problems in finding appropriate work at an adequate level of pay after moving. Considering that the most cited reason for military spouses seeking employment is financial need, this is a substantial problem (Castaneda, 2008). In locales where the military employs a large fraction of the working population, women typically have fewer opportunities, especially if the available non-military jobs are male-dominated. When asked how the military could help with the employment issues, the most common response from spouses involved child care. It was not only too expensive, but was not readily available for part-time or evening work (Castaneda, 2008). Finding paid work is complicated by the fact that the military often expects army wives to play an active role as unpaid volunteers in the organizations and activities of the military community, to a degree that varies by their husband's rank.

Besides practical costs of being a military spouse, there are also psychological costs. Research shows that military spouses experience many types of stress, especially around their spouse's deployment. These include the stress of potential deployment, actual deployment, and the risk of spousal death, as well as the challenge of spending extended periods on their own.

During the pre-deployment phase, the most stressful problem is a feeling the family's life is "on hold," awaiting whatever lies ahead. During deployment, the most significant stresses centre on fear for the partner's safety and well-being. As well, spouses suffered from the loneliness and anxiety of waiting, and overwhelming feelings of burden that attend the increase in family responsibilities, especially child care. Increasingly, spouses have been able to stay in touch with their partners by mobile phone, texting, and email, and to some degree this (and keeping busy) helps them avoid feeling overcome by loneliness and longing. Finally, with the return of spouses from active duty, the period of post-deployment brings its own stresses, in the form of adjustment. Each of these stages demands sacrifices by military spouses. To cope, spouses rely on a strong support system made up of friends and relatives who offer practical as well as emotional support.

Combat experience has an adverse effect on marital relations. Military service tends to produce stress and antisocial behaviour. In turn, the antisocial behaviour decreases marital quality and increases the risk of divorce.

Inevitably, some soldiers die in combat. In previous decades the dominant organizational response was to provide concrete and practical help to bereaved families. The American military now assigns a casualty assistance officer (CAO) whose duties include arranging for funeral and memorial services, counseling services, and running the errands necessary following the death of a serviceperson. But such support is often available only briefly, and mostly for families who live on base.

For families, the personal grief that follows a military loss is often overwhelming. The death of a loved one in military service causes suffering and intense feelings of denial, remorse, bewilderment, anger, frustration, and deep sadness. While all family members need support (both practical and emotional), some need it more than others. For spouses, the severity of the loss and grief depends on various things. The duration and quality of the spousal relationship, and the presence of children, are the most important. Also important is whether the spouse has access to a support network of family and friends.

Even with a support network, it is a tall order to make sense of one's loss. Bereaved partners whose spouses die prematurely or "preventably" often find it the most difficult to accept, as it feels unjust that the deceased was not given the opportunity to accomplish all that he or she wished to in life. When a person is older, or has neglected his or her health, it is more common for the surviving spouse to assign the deceased partner a modicum of blame (Carr, 2009). Nor is this necessarily a bad thing, as it serves as that elusive explanation for loss that many people crave, and may contribute to closure. With military deaths, it is often the institution that is blamed by the surviving spouse, something that can be problematic as that institution remains a major part of their personal identity.

Where longitudinal data are available, we find the most frequent pattern of grieving features a stable, low level of depression and—eventually—a steady recovery of resilience. The spouses who are most resilient after a partner's death have the most access to social support and other coping resources. Some widows are better able than others to benefit from such support. For example, widows with high self-esteem place a premium on emotional help, but widows with lower self-esteem value instrumental help more highly.

RECOVERING FROM DEATH AND BEREAVEMENT. For most military widows, the loss of a spouse means a change in roles, relationships, and lifestyles. Our personal identities are closely tied to the roles we play and the social scripts we follow. Like all people, these widows enter and leave roles throughout life, and so enter and leave identities as well. But what is most striking about widows, and especially military widows, is the extensiveness and rapidity of the change that is required. They are obliged to build a new life and a new self, unexpectedly and immediately.

Changing or leaving a role sometimes means leaving a community, which can have a profound effect on identity. Consider Helen Ebaugh, a sociologist who became interested in identity shifting when she ended her life as a nun in a convent to become an academic sociologist. In her book *Becoming an Ex: The Process of Role Exit* (1992), Ebaugh reminds us that the shift to important new roles can be difficult and stressful, especially when it occurs suddenly as the result of unwanted changes. This kind of sudden shift, known as *role exit*, may result in social dislocation and a sudden need to learn and practice new social roles. Ebaugh notes that a normal process of social transition—out of one role and into another—typically involves four stages, which she names "first doubts," "seeking alternatives," "turning points," and "creating the 'ex'-role."

But not every case is "normal." When the army wife loses a spouse in combat, she is suddenly thrust into widowhood; she is robbed of the first two or three of Ebaugh's stages and must immediately begin to re-imagine her life in the new role of "ex-wife" or "widow." Ebaugh notes the ease or difficulty of role exit depends on a variety of factors. These include the voluntariness and irreversibility of the shift, the centrality of the role being exited to the individual's identity, the length of time the individual has assumed the role, the amount of control the individual has over the process, whether role exit is being experienced by the individual alone or as part of a group, whether it involves a single exit or multiple exits, the degree of institutionalization of the role, and the degree of awareness of an impending exit.

For military widows, the sudden loss of a spouse in combat is involuntary and irreversible, and the role that is lost—that of spouse—is vitally central, especially if the couple has been together for many years and has children. The widowed spouse is likely to feel that she has little control over subsequent events, largely because the entire process is so sudden and unexpected. She is likely to feel alone in her "exit" from marriage, and the exit may entail changes of residence, domestic work activities, paid work activities, social activities, and contacts with friends. The army wife may receive help from friends and military administrators, but much of the transition will be new and unassisted, and far from familiar.

There are a great many aspects to the exit from any social role. Many of the changes set in motion are unintended and, sometimes, even unconscious. In the case of the widowed army wife, sudden changes may also include moving one's housing off base, moving the children to another school in another city, taking up or resuming a career, finding new social supports, and developing new social contacts. In effect, widowhood will mean building a new social world, almost overnight. So, the shift from military spouse to military widow can be dramatic, stressful, and painful, especially when it happens suddenly.

Yet, from the standpoint of flows, the passage from spouse to widow, and the shift in lifestyle, identity, community, and social status that accompany it, are all part of individual and collective renewal. Death brings an end to one life yet, through the personal renewal of those left behind, may also mark a new beginning.

All living things—including people and the relationships, groups, families, and organizations that people form—die. Often death results in new relationships, groups, families, and organizations. When we say the Roman Empire declined and fell, we do not mean the portion of the world inhabited by Romans disappeared from the face of the earth, much less from human history. We mean that people re-organized themselves into new groupings, with new loyalties, lifestyles, and identities, like the military spouses. All social organizations renew themselves in this way, through death, birth, migration, and re-commitment.

AFTERWORD
Conclusions and Recapitulations

In this book, we have looked at a variety of flows: flows of information, support, capital, and people. On the surface, these flows and the problems associated with them are different. Beneath the surface, they are similar, and if we wish, we can develop a common vocabulary to describe these flows and frame similar questions about them.

A Vocabulary of Flows

In developing such a vocabulary, we find that we can translate useful insights from one area of flow to another. Such translation requires learning a new conceptual language, and admittedly that's a bit of a nuisance. So we ask the reader's patience in exploring these at first new but then quite obvious ideas.

Every flow has a *source*, or *point of origin*. Here, we find the starting point of a *stream* of information, support, capital, people, or other fluid. Any origin can give rise to more than one stream. Likewise, any stream can have more than one origin, in the sense that smaller streams come together to form a larger one. Every stream has measurable characteristics. They include length, volume, and rate of flow.

Consider a few simple illustrations.

The *length* of a river is the distance from the river's origin to the place where the river empties into a lake or ocean. By comparison, the length of a rumour stream is the total number of people who hear the rumour as it travels from its origin to its last recipient. The length of a migration stream may be either the geographic distance, or the number of intervening locations, between the point of origin and the final destination.

The *volume* of a river is the average distance from one bank of the river to another multiplied by the average depth of the water. That's a static measure of how much water you'll find within a specific section of a river at a specific split-second in time. Start the clock ticking, and you can measure *flow volume*: the amount of water that passes by a given point on a river bank over a set amount of time. The flow volume of a rumour stream is the number of people who are hearing the rumour at any given moment. The flow volume of a migration stream is the number of people who are flowing at any given point in time from a point of origin past a particular milestone and then on toward their final destination. (For instance, in measuring illegal immigration into the United States, flow volume might be measured as the number of migrants crossing the border each night.)

The *rate of flow* of a river is closely related to flow volume, and is the rate (or speed) at which an average unit of water passes a fixed point on the river bank. The rate of flow of a rumour is the number of new people who receive the rumour, per unit of time. The rate of flow of migrants is the number of people who come from a source to a specific destination, per unit of time.

All streams flow through *channels.* Rivers flow through visible carved-out hollows in the ground. Rumours flow through social networks that are visible through regular patterns of social exchange and interaction. Migrants flow through channels that are sometimes less visible, involving social networks and opportunity queues. Where the channels are less than perfectly visible, we infer their existence from our observations of regular, patterned flows.

Sometimes, rivers and streams *flood*, meaning that they overflow their banks and leave their customary channels. In terms of the flows we are studying, floods are sudden increases in the stream dimensions—the length, volume, and/or rate of flow—that cause the stream to spill out of its usual channel. This means, for example, that a flooding rumour moves faster, reaches more people, and travels outside of the usual social networks. A flood of migrants—for example, a sudden surge of refugees from a war-torn country—moves faster, arrives at a wider variety of destinations, and makes use of more varied pathways, than would otherwise be the case.

Occasionally, rivers and streams are diverted or stopped by a *dam*, which is a barrier to their flow. On one side of the dam, this prevents the further spread of water; on the other side, it creates a build-up of water volume. The damming of a rumour stream means the censorship or prevention of further flow. More often, damming is a result of lack of contact between social networks that contain the rumour and social networks that do not. The damming of a migration stream may result from the refusal of destination-states to accept inflow, or the refusal of origin-states to permit outflow. This has happened to many refugee groups over the centuries.

Where the damming of a stream occurs, a common result is the creation of a *backwater*. This is a pool of stagnant (i.e., non-moving) water that is not renewed either by inflow or outflow. Rumour backwaters are created through the formation of cliques and other segregated social groupings. Migration backwaters are created by the interruption of free movement from origin to destination. Typically, backwaters have different social and cultural properties than fast-moving streams.

Every stream passes by, or through, a large number of locations. Ultimately, the stream reaches a destination that is, often, a *delta*. A river delta is that place where a stream flows into a larger body of water, typically a lake or ocean. A rumour delta is a social state, where a rumour has become "common knowledge" as a result of the confluence of many rumour streams. A migration delta is a geographic location where many streams of migrants have converged, as for example in a multi-immigrant city like Toronto, or a multi-immigrant country like Canada. Beyond the delta, in the "lake" itself, the rumour streams (or migrant streams) are no longer distinguishable. A high degree of mixing and loss of differentiation occurs beyond the point at which the river empties into its destination body of water.

What we have done here represents the merest beginning of an effort to re-think and re-name the flows around us. Conceivably, such re-naming will permit new kinds of measurements, comparisons, and theories. And that is precisely the point. Without this, we are likely to continue failing to ask—and answer—a great many interesting sociological questions with theoretically and practically important answers.

Questions Unasked—and Unanswered

As will become clear below, however briefly, we can use this vocabulary to frame common questions for a variety of flows: questions that have to do with the conditions under which damming or flooding occur, or the conditions under which flows speed up, slow down, grow more or less voluminous. Some flows are harder than others to capture in this vocabulary because they have fewer common markers. For instance, it is harder to conceptualize social mobility than migration. That is because migration has obvious reference to a limited number of locations in the real world: Canada, Toronto, Cuba, wherever. Social mobility does not.

As we have also seen, it is harder to conceptualize the flows of capital, influence, or power than the flows of rumour or gossip. A rumour or piece of gossip has a clear narrative boundary: it is about someone and something particular. Capital, influence, and power are, as the social theorist Talcott Parsons said, generalized media of exchange. They can be, and are, about anything.

The study of flows opens our eyes to enormous gaps that exist in sociology at the present time. All of the topics we have discussed have certain features in common. They all involve location changes over time, as well as processes of change in a social system and processes of change of a social system. From this standpoint, we realize that what we call "social structure" is a set of frozen change processes. Time is the backdrop for studying both change and structure.

But even as we acknowledge these facts, we must ask ourselves: What do we really know about the timing of everyday flows? Consider some of the many things we don't know. First, how long does it take for an average rumour to pass through a town, for a fad or fashion to die out, for a secret to be exposed, for clients of a patron to form alliances, or migrant families to assimilate? We don't know.

Nor do we know how long it takes for gossip to travel among friends, a person to find a mate, a jury to decide a murder case, or a qualified manager to reach the "top" of a hierarchy. We don't know the half-life of a clique, a job search, a spy network, or a household chain migration. We don't know the age structure of various flow processes, whether they be one hundred home-repair websites or a hundred social support networks in Manitoba, to pick two examples entirely at random.

Here are some simpler things we still don't know: Under what conditions does it take half as much time as usual for a rumour to pass through a town, a fad or fashion to die out, or a secret to be exposed? We don't know how to speed up the completion of a job search, the discovery of a spy network, or the building of a social-support network. Nor do we know how to double the rate of renewal of belief systems or lists of best-selling books or information technology networks.

Sociology lacks the answers to such important, obvious, and basic questions about the world we live in. Imagine if dentists knew as little about teeth, or farmers as little about their crops, as sociologists know about social processes. This ignorance suggests sociology has been on the wrong track. That's a big problem, and to solve it we would first have to agree on its causes and then work out a way of moving toward a solution. But at this point there are few agreed-on research strategies, few agreed-on research priorities.

Only one thing is clear. The study of flows tells us we must start rethinking sociology, from the bottom up.

Acknowledgments

I want to begin by thanking David Stover for encouraging the preparation and publication of this book, and for editing the manuscript with his usual expert insight. I expect this will be the start of a new, long collaboration with Rock's Mills Press, and with David Stover.

Many people helped me revise this manuscript, which originated in the last moments of the twentieth century and took a long time to gestate. First, thanks go to my amazing undergraduate student assistants at the University of Toronto. Sally Chiang researched and wrote a draft of the section on glass ceilings, and edited the section on gossip. Sylvia Urbanik, Sabrina Apitz-Grossman, and Seungchul (Timmy) Shin each updated and revised a variety of sections. Master's student Andreea Mogosanu helped to find a large number of missing references and offered useful suggestions for improvement. Doctoral student Laura Upenieks read the entire manuscript and also suggested improvements. Finally, my friend and colleague Jack Veugelers read the manuscript and offered a global critique, which I took into serious account when revising this manuscript.

It is in the nature of scholarship that no book ever has the last word on a topic and no version of a book is ever the last possible version. The world is always changing, and so are the ideas we bring to studying it. My own ideas about the world and about sociology have continued to change since I started this book. Indeed, working on this book played a part in changing those ideas, and the book shows the marks of a shift in my own thinking. That said, I have tried to provide a clear, consistent picture of what I consider a powerful approach to understanding the social world. I thank everyone who has helped me do this.

Thanks go finally to Andrey Markov (1856–1922), after whom is named the "Markov chain," a mathematical model that has proved useful in studying flow processes. What is interesting about the Markov chain is that it lacks a memory: in a Markov-type flow, the next move depends only on a mover's current position and not on the sequence of moves that preceded it. This "memorylessness"—the so-called Markov property—greatly simplifies the modeling of real-world flows. It also forces us to ask ourselves about the role of memory in social affairs and personal lives, and, therefore, about culture and human agency.

I dedicate this book to Harrison White, who inspired so many of us at Harvard in the late 1960s; and to the group of students who surrounded him then: a group that included my friends Joel Cohen, Bonnie Erickson, Mark Granovetter, Nancy Howell, Joel Levine, Jim Rosenbaum, and Barry Wellman, among others. This book reflects some of what I learned from them.

References

Acosta-Belén, E., & Santiago, C.E. (2006). *Puerto Ricans in the United States: A contemporary portrait.* Boulder, CO: Lynne Rienner Publishers.

Adler, A.B., Bartone, P.T., & Vaitkus, M.A. (1995). *Family Stress and Adaptation During a U.S. Army Europe Peacekeeping Deployment.* U.S. Army Medical Research Unit, Europe. USAMRU-E Technical Report 95-1.

Adler, P.A. & Adler, P. (1995). Dynamics of inclusion and exclusion in preadolescent cliques. *Social Psychology, Quarterly. 58*(3), 145-162.

Agid, O., Shapira, B. Zislin, J., Ritsner, M., Hanin, B., Murad, H., Troudart, T., Bloch, M., Heresco-Levy, U., & Lerer, B. (1999). Environment and vulnerability to major psychiatric illness: A case control study of early parental loss in major depression, bipolar disorder, and schizophrenia. *Molecular Psychiatry, 4,* 163-172.

Aitken, A. (2009). Online support following a death in the Armed Forces. *Bereavement Care 28* (3), 29-30.

Al-Ali, N., Black, R., & Koser, K. (2001). Refugees and transnationalism: the experience of Bosnians and Eritreans in Europe. *Journal of Ethnic and Migration Studies 27*(4), 615-634.

Alam, R., Barrera, M., D'Agostino, N., Nicholas, D. B., & Schneiderman, G. (2012). Bereavement experiences of mothers and fathers over time after the death of a child due to cancer. *Death Studies, 36*(1), 1-22.

Allport, G.W., & Postman, L. (1947). *The psychology of rumor.* Oxford, England: Henry Holt.

Alvesson, M. (1990). On the popularity of organizational culture. *Acta Sociologica, 33*(1), 31-49. doi: 10.1177/000169939003300103.

An, L., & Liu, J. (2010). Long-term effects of family planning and other determinants of fertility on population and environment: Agent-based modeling evidence from Wolong Nature Reserve, China. *Population and Environment, 31*(6), 417-459.

Anderson, C. J., & Vogel, L.C. (2003). Domain-specific satisfaction in adults with pediatric-onset spinal cord injuries. *Spinal Cord: The Official Journal of the International Medical Society of Paraplegia, 41*(12), 684-91

Anderson, J.G, Jay, S.J., Perry, J., & Anderson, M.M. (1990). Diffusion of computer applications among physicians: A quasi-experimental study. *Clinical Sociology Review, 8,* 116-127.

Anderson, V.A. et al. (2006). Understanding predictors of functional recovery and outcome 30 months following early childhood head injury. *Neuropsychology, 20*(1), 42-57.

Anderson, V., Catroppa, C., Morse, S., Haritou, F., & Rosenfeld, J. (2001). Outcome from mild head injury in young children: A prospective study. *Journal of Clinical and Experimental Neuropsychology, 23,* 705-717.

Angeles, V.S.M. (2011). The Middle East and the Philippines: Transnational linkages, labor migration and the remaking of Philippine Islam. *Comparative Islamic Studies, 7(1/2),* 157.

Antonelli, C. (1990). Induced adoption and externalities in the regional diffusion of information technology. *Regional Studies, 24*(1), 31-40.

Applewhile, L.W., & Segal, D.R. (1990). Telephone use by peacekeeping troops in the Sinai. *Armed Forces and Society, 17*(1), 117-126.

Arango-Lasprilla J.C., Ketchum J.M., Dezfulian T., Kreutzer S.J., O'neil-Pirozzi T.M., Hammond F., & Jha A. (2008). Predictors of marital stability 2 years following traumatic brain injury. *Brain Injury, 22*(7–8), 565–574.

Arnett, J.J., & Jensen, L.A. (1994). Socialization and risk behavior in two countries: Denmark and the United States. *Youth and Society, 26*(1), 3-22.

Arnett, J.J., Offer, D., & Fine, A. (1997). Reckless driving in adolescence: "State" and "trait" factors. *Accident Analysis and Prevention 29*(1), 57-63.

Asimov, I. (1971). *The Stars in Their Courses.* New York: Doubleday.

Attewell, P. (1992). Technology diffusion and organizational learning: The case of business computing. *Organization Science 3*(1), 1-19.

Attias-Donfut, C. (2013). Migration, retirement and transnationalism in the Mediterranean region. *Ageing in the Mediterranean*, 173.

Australian Institute of Health and Welfare. (2003). People with an intellectual or early onset disability in Australia. *Journal of Intellectual and Developmental Disability, 28*, 79-83.

Ausubel, J.H. (1991). Rat-race dynamics and crazy companies: The diffusion of technologies and social behaviour. *Technological Forecasting and Social Change, 39*(1-2), 11-22.

Avasthi, A. (2010). Preserve and strengthen family to promote mental health. *Indian Journal of Psychiatry, 52*(2), 113.

Bakirtzief, Z. (1996). Obstacles to compliance with treatment for Hansen's disease. *Cadernos de Saúde Pública, 12*(4), 497-505.

Ball, J. F. (1976). Widow's grief: The impact of age and mode of death. *OMEGA, 7*(4), 307-333.

Barcus, H. (2004). Urban-rural migration in the USA: An analysis of residential satisfaction. *Regional Studies, 38*(6), 643-657.

Barkay, T. (2013). When business and community meet: A case study of Coca-Cola. *Critical Sociology 39*(2), 277-293.

Barlow G.L. (2002). Auditing hospital queuing. *Managerial Auditing Journal, 17*, 397–403.

Bartone, P.T., & Ender, M.F. (1994). Organizational responses to death in the military. *Death Studies, 18*, 25-39.

Baumeister, R. F., Zhang L., & Vohs, K.D. (2004). Gossip as cultural learning. *Review of General Psychology, 8*(2), 111–121.

Becher, T., & Trowler, P. (2001). *Academic Tribes and Territories: Intellectual Enquiry and the Culture of Disciplines.* (2nd ed.) Buckingham: Open University Press.

Beder, J. (2007). War, death, and bereavement: How we can help. In A.E. Dell Orto and P.W. Power (eds.), *The Psychological and Social Impact of Illness and Disability.* (5th ed.) New York: Springer Publishing Corporation.

Beer, J.S., John, O.P., Scabini, D., & Knight, R.T. (2006). Orbitofrontal cortex and social behavior: Integrating self-monitoring and emotion-cognition interactions. *Journal of Cognitive Neuroscience. 18*(6), 871-879

Behtoui, A. (2013). Incorporation of children of immigrants: The case of descendants of immigrants from Turkey in Sweden. *Ethnic and Racial Studies, 36*(12), 2141-2159.

Belgrave, F. Z., & Lewis, D. M. (1994). The role of social support in compliance and other health behaviors for African Americans with chronic illnesses. *Journal of Health and Social Policy, 5*(3-4), 55-68.

Bell, D.B., Tiggle, R.B., & Scarville, J. (1991). Army family research program: Select preliminary findings on army family support during Operation Desert Shield. *U.S. Army Research Institute for the Behavioral and Social Sciences*, U.S. Army Research Institute.

Ben-Sira, Z. (1983). Loss, stress, and readjustment: The structure of coping with bereavement and disability. *Social Science and Medicine, 17*(21), 1619-1632.

Benedeck, D.M., & Ursano, R.J. (2006). Mass violent death and military communities: Domains of response in military operations, disaster, and terrorism. In E.K. Rynearson (ed.), *Violent Death: Resilience and Intervention Beyond the Crisis.* New York, NY, US: Routledge/Taylor and Francis Group.

Bennett, D.L. (2009). *The bereaved parent experience over time.* Doctoral Dissertation, Faculty of Social Work, University of Calgary.

Bernstein, D.M. (1999). Recovery from mild head injury. *Brain Injury, 13*, 151-72.

Berry, P., & Franks, T.J. (2010).Women in the world of corporate business: Looking at the glass ceiling. *Contemporary Issues in Education Research, 3*(2), 1-10.

Betancourt, J. R., Carrillo, J. E., & Green, A. R. (1999). Hypertension in multicultural and minority populations: Link in communication to compliance. *Hypertension Reports, 1*(6), 482-488.

Betcherman, G. (1990). Computer technology, work and society. *Canadian Journal of Sociology/Cahiers canadiens de sociologie, 15*(2), 195-201.

Bian, Y. (1994). Guanxi and the allocation of urban jobs in China. *The China Quarterly, 140*, 971-999.

Bian, Y., & Ang, S. (1997). Guanxi networks and job mobility in China and Singapore. *Social Forces, 75*(3), 981-1005.

Biddix, J.P. & Park, H.W. (2008). Online networks of student protest: The case of the living wage campaign. *New Media & Society, 10*(6), 871-891.

Biegel, D. E., & Schulz, R. (1999). Caregiving and caregiver interventions in aging and mental illness. *Family Relations, 48*, 345-354.

Bihagen, E. (2007). Class origin effects on downward career mobility in Sweden, 1982–2001. *Acta Sociologica, 50*(4), 415–430

Bihagen, E., & Ohls, M. (2006). The glass ceiling–where is it? Women's and men's career prospects in the private vs. the public sector in Sweden 1979–2000. *The Sociological Review 54*(1), 20-47.

Bihagen, E., & Ohls, M. (2007). Are women over-represented in dead-end jobs? A Swedish study using empirically derived measures of dead-end jobs. *Social Indicators Research, 84*(2), 159-177.

Bird, S. E. (1996). CJ's revenge: Media, folklore, and the cultural construction of AIDS. *Critical Studies in Mass Communication*, 44-58

Birkinshaw, J., & Mol, M. (2006). How management innovation happens. *Sloan Management Review, 47*(4).

Bixler, R.P., Taylor, P.L. (2012). Toward a community of innovation in community-based natural resource management: Insights from open source software. *Human Organization 71*(3), 234-243.

Black, N. (2013). When have violent civil conflicts spread? Introducing a dataset of substate conflict contagion. *Journal of Peace Research 50*(6), 751-759.

Blais M.C, & Boisvert J. (2005). Psychological and marital adjustment in couples following a traumatic brain injury (TBI): A critical review. *Brain Injury, 19*(14), 1223–1235.

Blais, M.C., & Boisvert, J. (2007). Psychological adjustment and marital satisfaction following head injury: Which critical personal characteristics should both partners develop? *Brain Injury, 21*(4), 357-372.

Bland, R. (1978). Comment. *The British Journal of Sociology, 29*(3), 372-375.

Blee, K.M. (2008). *Women of the Klan: Racism and gender in the 1920s.* United States: University of California Press.

Blue, L., & Espenshade, T. (2011). Population momentum across the demographic transition. *Population and Development Review, 37*(4), 721-747.

Blume, S.S. (2013). Medical innovations: Their diffusion, adoption and critical interrogation. *Sociology Compass, 7*(9), 726-737.

Bobkowski, P., & Smith, J. (2013). Social media divide: Characteristics of emerging adults who do not use social network websites. *Media, Culture and Society, 35*(6), 771-781.

Bocker, A. (1994). Chain migration over legally closed borders: settled immigrants as bridgeheads and gatekeepers. *Netherlands Journal of Social Sciences, 30*(2), 87-106

Bonanno, G.A., Wortman, C.B., Lehman, D.R., Tweed, R.G., Haring, M., Sonnega, J., Carr, D., & Nesse, R.M. (2002). Resilience to loss and chronic grief: A prospective study from preloss to 18-months postloss. *Journal of Personality and Social Psychology 83*(5), 1150-1164.

Bono, J.E., & Ilies, R. (2006). Charisma, positive emotions and mood contagion. *The Leadership Quarterly, 17*, 317–334.

Booth, Bradford. (2003). Contextual effects of military presence on women's earnings. *Armed Forces and Society, 30*(1), 25-52.

Borstein, J.A. (2001). *Tripping over colossal heads: settlement patterns and population development in the upland Olmec heartland.* Doctoral dissertation. Pennsylvania State University.

Botwin, M., Buss, D.M., & Shackelford, T.K. (1997). Personality and mate preferences: Five factors in mate selection and marital satisfaction. *Journal of Personality, 65*, 107-136.

Bouchard, M.M. (2010). *Geographic mobility and employment: An investigation of tied migration issues among employed military spouses.* Doctoral dissertation. Dissertation Abstracts International, 70(12-A), 4753.

Boucher, L., Renvall, M. J., & Jackson, J. E. (1996). Cognitively impaired spouses as primary caregivers for demented elderly people. *Journal of the American Geriatrics Society, 44*(7), 828-831.

Bourdais, C., & Lapierre-Adamcyk, E. (2004). Changes in conjugal life in Canada: Is cohabitation progressively replacing marriage? *Journal of Marriage and Family, 66*, 929–942.

Bovenkerk, F. (1981). Why returnees generally do not turn out to be 'agents of change': The case of Suriname. *Nieuwe West-Indische Gids/New West Indian Guide*, 154-173.

Boxman, E.A., De Graaf, P.M., and Flap, H.D. (1991). The impact of social and human capital on the income attainment of Dutch managers. *Social networks, 13*(1), 51-73.

Boyle, P.J., Feng, Z., & Raab, G.M. (2011). Does widowhood increase mortality risk? Testing for selection effects by comparing causes of spousal death. *Epidemiology, 1*, 1-5.

Bracy, C.A., & Douglas, J.M. (2005). Marital dyad perceptions of injured partners' communication following severe traumatic brain injury. *Brain Impairment, 6*(1), 1-12

Brant, M. (2006). No child left behind: More than 1,200 U.S. kids have lost a parent in Iraq or Afghanistan. How the Pentagon is helping them cope. *Newsweek, 147*(18), 32.

Breton, R. (1964). Institutional completeness of ethnic communities and the personal relations of immigrants. *American Journal of Sociology, 70*(2), 193-205.

Brettell, C.B., & Hollifield, J.F. (eds.) (2000). *Migration theory: Talking across the disciplines.* New York: Routledge.

Brinton, M.C., & Kariya, T. (1998). Institutional embeddedness in Japanese labor markets. In Brinton, M.C., & Nee, V. (Eds.), *The New Institutionalism in Sociology* (pp.181-207). United States: Stanford University Press.

Brodu, J. (1990). A rumour of drought. *Communications, 52*, 85-97

Brosius, H., & Weimann, G. (1991). The contagiousness of mass-mediated terrorism. *European Journal of Communication, 6*(1), 63-75.

Brown, A. J. (2005). The Germans of Germany and the Germans of Kazakhstan: A Eurasian Volk in the twilight of diaspora. *Europe-Asia Studies, 57*(4), 625-634.

Brown, J., Sorrell, J.H., McClaren, J., & Creswell, J.W. (2006). Waiting for a liver transplant. *Qualitative Health Research, 16*, 119-136

Brown, L. A., Jorge A. B., & Goetz, A. R. (1988). Policy aspects of development and individual mobility: Migration and circulation from Ecuador's rural Sierra. *Economic Geography*, 147-170.

Broxton, T., Interian, Y., Vaver, J., & Wattenhofer, M. (2013). Catching a viral video. *Journal of Intelligent Information Systems, 40*, 241–259.

Brubaker, R. (1998). Migrations of ethnic unmixing in the "New Europe". *International Migration Review*, 1047-1065.

Brubaker, R. (2001). The return of assimilation? Changing perspectives on immigration and its sequels in France, Germany, and the United States. *Ethnic and Racial Studies, 24*(4), 531-548.

Buchanan, J.A. (2004). *Generalization of the effects of a cognitive-behavioural intervention for family caregivers of individuals with dementia.* Doctoral dissertation. Dissertation Abstracts International, 65(2-B).

Buhr, K. J. (2011). Is there a glass escalator for male nurses in Canada? *Nursing Leadership, 24*(3), 86-100.

Burgess, D., Joseph, A., van Ryn, M., & Carnes, M. (2012). Does stereotype threat affect women in academic medicine? *Journal of Academic Medicine, 87*(1), 506-512.

Burgess, Z., & Tharenou, P. (2002). Women board directors: Characteristics of the few. *Journal of Business Ethics, 37*(1), 39-49.

Burleigh, T.J., & Meegan, D.V. (2013). Keeping up with the Joneses affects perceptions of distributive justice. *Social Justice Research, 26*, 120–131

Burmeister, L.L. (1990). State, industrialization, and agricultural policy in Korea. *Development and Change 21*(2), 197-223.

Burnam, M.A., Meredith, L.S., Sherbourne, C.D., Burciaga Valdez, R., & Vernez, G. (1992). Army families and soldier readiness. *RAND Corporation.* Santa Monica, CA.

Burrell, L.M., Adams, G.A., Durand, D.B., & Castro, C.A. (2006). The impact of military lifestyle demands on well-being, army, and family outcomes. *Armed Forces and Society, 33*(1), 43-58.

Burridge, A.C., Williams, W.H., Yates, P.J., Harris, A., & Ward, C. (2007). Spousal relationship satisfaction following acquired brain injury: The role of insight and socio-emotional skill. *Neuropsychological Rehabilitation, 17*(1), 95-105.

Burruss, G.W., & Giblin, M.J. (2014). Modeling isomorphism on policing innovation: The role of institutional pressures in adopting community-oriented policing. *Crime and Delinquency, 60*(3), 331-355.

Byrne, D. (1971). *The Attraction Paradigm.* New York: Academic Press.

Cadwallader, M.T. (1992). *Migration and Residential Mobility: Macro and Micro Approaches.* Madison: University of Wisconsin Press.

Callahan, J.L., & Tomaszewski, L. (2007). Navigating the good ol' boys club: women, marginality, and communities of practice in a military non-profit organization. *Studies in Continuing Education, 29*(3), 259-276.

Callede, J. (1993). Basque Pelota in the European space: Towards a sociological use of the notions of sporting evolution and diffusion. *International Review for the Sociology of Sport, 28*(2-3), 223-243.

Campana, A., & Ratelle, J. (2014). A political sociology approach to the diffusion of conflict from Chechnya to Dagestan and Ingushetia. *Studies in Conflict and Terrorism, 37*(2), 115-134.

Campbell, C.L. (2000). Adult children of fathers Missing in Action (MIA): An examination of emotional distress, grief, and family hardiness. *Family Relations 49*(3), 267-276.

Carley, K. (1989). The value of cognitive foundations for dynamic social theory. *The Journal of Mathematical Sociology, 14*, 171-208

Carley, K. (1990). Structural constraints on communication: The diffusion of the homomorphic signal analysis technique through scientific fields. *The Journal of Mathematical Sociology 15*(3-4), 207-246.

Carmody, D.B. (2001). Open-heart surgery: The toll it takes on people's lives. *Southern Sociological Society.*

Carr, D. (2009). Who's to blame? Perceived responsibility for spousal death and psychological distress among older widowed persons. *Journal of Health and Social Behavior, 50*(3), 359-75.

Carre, P.A. (1993). Uncertain development: Diffusion of the telephone in France before 1914. *RESEAUX: The French Journal of Communication, 1*(2), 245-260.

Carrington, W. J., & De Lima, P. J. F. (1996). The impact of 1970s repatriates from Africa on the Portuguese labor market. *Industrial and Labor Relations Review*, 330-347.

Carroll, K. N. et al. (2005). Characteristics of families that complain following pediatric emergency visits. *Ambulatory Pediatrics, 5*(6), 326-331

Castaneda, L., & Harrell, M. (2008). Military spouse employment. *Armed Forces and Society, 34*(3), 389-412.

Castaneda, L. W., & Harrell. M .C. (2008). Military spouse employment: A grounded theory approach to experiences and perceptions. *Armed Forces and Society, 34*(3), 389-412

Catalyst. (2014d). *2013 Catalyst Census: Financial Post 500 Women Board Directors*. Retrieved June 22, 2013 from catalyst.org/knowledge/2013-catalyst-census-financial-post-500-women-board-directors.

Catalyst. (2014c). *Statistical Overview of Women in the Workplace*. Retrieved June 22, 2014 from http://www.catalyst.org/knowledge/statistical-overview-women-workplace.

Catalyst. (2014b). *Women CEOs and Heads of the Financial Post 500*. Retrieved June 23, 2014 from catalyst.org/knowledge/women-ceos-and-heads-financial-post-500.

Catalyst. (2014a). *Women CEOs of the Fortune 1000*. Retrieved June 23, 2014 from http://catalyst.org/knowledge/women-ceos-fortune-1000.

Catroppa, C., & Anderson, V. (2002). Recovery in memory function in the first year following TBI in children. *Brain Injury, 16*, 369-84.

Cattelani, R., Lombardi, F., Brianti, R., & Mazzuchi, A. (1998). Traumatic brain injury in childhood: Intellectual, behavioural and social outcome into adulthood. *Brain Injury, 12*, 283-96.

Cawkill, P. (2010). Death in the Armed Forces: Casualty notification and bereavement support in the UK Military. *Bereavement Care, 28*(2), 25-30.

Centers for Disease Control and Prevention, Department of Health and Human Services (US), National Center for Health Statistics. (2002, July). *Cohabitation, Marriage, Divorce and Remarriage in the United States, Vital and Health Statistics, Series 23, Number 22.*

Chambre, S. M. (2001). Parallel power structures, invisible careers, and the changing nature of. *Women, Philanthropy, and Civil Society, 18*, 169.

Champion, A. (1998). Population distribution in developed countries: has counter-urbanization stopped? *Population Distribution and Migration*, 66-83.

Chan, H., Chor, C., Ling, W., Kwok-Chu Wong, G., Chi-Ping Ng, S., & Poon, W. (2005). Long-term disability in the local population 2 years after mild head injury: Prospective cohort study. *Surgical Practice, 9*, 8-11.

Chan, J. (2007). Carers' perspective on respite for persons with acquired brain injury. *International journal of rehabilitation research/Internationale Zeitschrift fur Rehabilitationsforschung, 30*(2), 137-46.

Chan, T. W., & Boliver, V. (2013) The grandparents effect in social mobility: Evidence from British birth cohort studies. *American Sociological Review, 78*(4), 662–678.

Chandra, A., Lara-Cinisomo, S., Jaycox, L. H., Tanielian, T., Burns, R. M., Ruder, T., & Han, B. (2010). Children on the homefront: The experience of children from military families. *Pediatrics 125*(1), 16-25.

Chandra, V. P. (1997). Remigration: Return of the prodigals-An analysis of the impact of the cycles of migration and remigration on caste mobility. *International Migration Review*, 162-170.

Chang, K. A., & Groves, J. M. (1995). Redefining service: Empowerment and control in the Filipina maid community in Hong Kong. In Sautman, B. (ed.), *Racial identities in East Asia* (pp. 496-534). Hong Kong: HKUST.

Chang, K. A., & Ling, L. (2000). Filipina domestic workers in Hong Kong. *Gender and Global Restructuring: Sightings, Sites and Resistances, 2*, 27.

Chapman, R. J. K. (1990). Information diffusions: Reconciling scientific knowledge and public policy. *Prometheus, 8*(2), 240-256.

Charlton, R., Sheahan, K., Smith, G., & Campbell, I. (2001). Spousal bereavement: Implications for health. *Family Practice, 18*(6), 614-618.

Cheek, C. (2010). Passing over: Identity transition in widows. *International Journal of Aging and Human Development, 70*(4), 345-364.

Chen, J. (2013). Does global fertility and cultural transition affect human development? The neglected role of the demographic transition. *Social Indicators Research, 113*(3), 941-971.

Chen, M., Xu, C., & Wang, R. (2007). Key natural impacting factors of China's human population distribution. *Population Environment, 28*(1), 187-200.

Chen, P., & Wilmoth, J. M. (2004). The effects of residential mobility on ADL and IADL limitations among the very old living in the community. *The Journals of Gerontology Series B: Psychological Sciences and Social Sciences, 59*(3), S164-S172.

Choi, N. G. (1996). Older persons who move: Reasons and health consequences. *Journal of Applied Gerontology, 15*(3), 325-344.

Chorev, N. (2012). Changing global norms through reactive diffusion: The case of intellectual property protection of AIDS drugs. *American Sociological Review, 77*(5), 831-853.

Clark, W. A. V., & Onaka, J. L. (1983). Life cycle and housing adjustment as explanations of residential mobility. *Urban Studies, 20*(1), 47-57.

Clarke, M. (2007). Kinship, propriety and assisted reproduction in the Middle East. *Anthropology of the Middle East, 2*(1), 70-88.

Cliff, C., & First, A. (2013). Testing for contagion/diffusion of terrorism in state dyads. *Studies in Conflict and Terrorism, 36*(4), 292-314.

Coates, J. (2004). *Women, men, and language: A sociolinguistic account of gender differences in language*. Canada: Pearson Education.

Cohen, D. M., Lumley, M. A., Naar-King, S., Partridge, T., & Cakan, N. (2004). Child behavior problems and family functioning as predictors of adherence and glycemic control in economically disadvantaged children with Type 1 Diabetes: A prospective study. *Journal of Pediatric Psychology, 29*, 171-84.

Cohen, J., & Segal, M. A. (2009). Veterans, the Vietnam era, and marital dissolution. *Armed Forces and Society, 36*(1), 19-37.

Cohen, J. E. (1995). *How many people can the Earth support?* New York: Norton.

Cohen, J. A., Goodman, R. F., Campbell, C. L., Carroll, B., & Campagna, H. (2009). Military children: The sometimes orphans of war. In S. M. Freeman, B. A. Moore, and A. Freeman (eds.), *Living and surviving in harm's way: A psychological treatment handbook for pre- and post-deployment of military personnel* (pp. 395-416). New York: Routledge.

Colantonio, A., Ratcliff, G., Chase, S., Kelsey, S., Escobar, M. & Vernich, L. (2004). Long term outcomes after moderate to severe traumatic brain injury. *Disability and Rehabilitation, 26*(5), 253-261.

Cole, J. M., & Scrivener, H. (2013). Short term effects of gossip behavior on self-esteem. *Psychology, 32*, 252–260.

Coleman, J. S., Katz, E., & Menzel, H. (1966). *Medical innovation: A diffusion study*. Indianapolis: Bobbs-Merrill Company.

Collins, M. D., & Frey, J. H. (1992). Drunken driving and informal social control: The case of peer intervention. *Deviant Behavior, 13*(1), 73-87.

Comerford, V. E., Geffen, G. M., May, C., Medland, S. E., & Geffen, L. B. (2002). A rapid screen of the severity of mild Traumatic Brain Injury. *Journal of Clinical and Experimental Neuropsychology, 24*, 409-19.

Connell, C. (2012). Dangerous disclosures. *Sexuality Research & Social Policy*, 9(2), 168-177.

Connell, R. (2006). Glass ceilings or gendered institutions? Mapping the gender regimes of public sector worksites. *Public Administration Review*, *66*(6), 837-849.

Conner-Spady, B., Estey, A., Arnett, G., Ness, K., McGurran, J., Bear, R., Noseworthy, T., & Steering Committee of Western Canada Waiting List Project. (2005). Determinants of patient and surgeon perspectives on maximum acceptable waiting times for hip and knee arthroplasty. *Journal of Health Services Research and Policy, 10*(2), 84-90.

Connor-Spady, B. L., Sanmugasunderam, S., Courtright, P., McGurran, J.J., Noseworthy, T. W., & the Steering Committee of the Western Canada Waiting List Project. (2004). Determinants of patient satisfaction with cataract surgery and length of time on the waiting list. *British Journal of Ophthalmology, 88*(10), 1305-1309.

Cooke, T. J., & Speirs, K. (2005). Migration and employment among the civilian spouses of military personnel. *Social Science Quarterly, 86*(2), 343-355.

Cooney Jr., R. T. (2003). Moving with the military: Race, class, and gender differences in the employment consequences of tied migration. *Dissertation Abstracts International, A: The Humanities and Social Sciences, 64*(6), 2261.

Corcoran, M. (1995). Rags to rags: Poverty and mobility in the United States. *Annual Review of Sociology, 21*, 237-267

Cornelius, W. A. (2005). Controlling 'unwanted' immigration: Lessons from the United States, 1993–2004. *Journal of Ethnic and Migration Studies, 31*, 775-794.

Correa, T. (2014). Bottom-up technology transmission within families: Exploring how youths influence their parents' digital media use with dyadic data. *Journal of Communication, 64*(1), 103-124.

Correll, T. C. (2008). 'You Know about Needle Boy, Right?': Variation in rumors and legends about attacks with HIV-Infected Needles. *Western Folklore*, 59-100.

Coser, L. A. (1974). *Greedy Institutions: Patterns of Undivided Commitment*. New York: Free Press.

Coulter, R., Ham, M., & Feijten, P. (2012). Partner (dis)agreement on moving desires and the subsequent moving behaviour of couples. *Population, Space and Place, 18*(1), 16-30.

Cowgill, D. O. (1978). Residential segregation by age in American metropolitan areas. *Journal of Gerontology, 33*(3), 446-453.

Crawford, M. (1995). *Talking difference: On gender and language, Volume 7*. Canada: Sage.

Creese, G., & Wiebe, B. (2012). 'Survival employment': Gender and deskilling among African immigrants in Canada. *International Migration, 50*(5), 56-76

Crompton, S. (2005). Always the bridesmaid: People who don't expect to marry. *Canadian Social Trends, 77*, 2-8.

Cross, J. L., & Lin, N. (eds.). (2008). Access to social capital and status attainment in the United States: Racial/ethnic and gender differences. In *Social Capital: An International Research Program*. Oxford: Oxford Scholarship Online.

Cuba, L., & Hummon, D. M. (1993). Constructing a sense of home: Place affiliation and migration across the life cycle. *Sociological Forum, 8*(4), 547-572.

Curry, E. M. (2006). Long term effects of traumatic brain injury as perceived by parental and spousal caregivers: A mixed methods study. Doctoral dissertation. University of Nebraska – Lincoln.

Dabalen, A., Parinduri, R., & Paul, S. (2013). The effects of the intensity, timing, and persistence of personal history of mobility on support for redistribution. Policy Research Working Paper Series, The World Bank.

Damousi, J. (1999). *The labour of loss: Mourning, memory, and wartime bereavement in Australia*. New York, NY: Cambridge University Press.

Danaei, G., et al. (2009). The preventable causes of death in the United States: Comparative risk assessment of dietary, lifestyle, and metabolic risk factors. *PLoS Medicine, 6*(4).

Dansky, K. H., & Miles, J. (1997). Patient satisfaction with ambulatory healthcare services: Waiting time and filling time. *Hospital and Health Services Administration, 42*, 165-77.

Das-Munshi, J., Das-Munshi, G., Leavey, S., Stansfeld, A., & Prince, M.J. (2012). Migration, social mobility and common mental disorders: Critical review of the literature and meta-analysis. *Ethnicity and Health, 17*(1-2), 17-53

David, P. A., & Sanderson, W. C. (1990). Cohort parity analysis and fertility transition dynamics: Reconstructing historical trends in fertility control from a single census. *Population Studies, 44*(3), 421-445.

Davis, G. F., & Greve, H. R. (1997). Corporate elite networks and governance changes in the 1980s. *American Journal of Sociology, 103*(1), 1-37.

De Bruyna, A., & Lilienb, G. L. (2008). A multi-stage model of word-of-mouth influence through viral marketing. *International Journal of Research in Marketing, 25*, 151-163.

De Man, S., Vlerick, P., Gemmel, P., De Bondt, P., Matthys, D., & Dierckx, R. A. (2005). Impact of waiting on the perception of service quality in nuclear medicine. *Nuclear Medicine Communications, 26*(6), 541-547.

De Tona, C. 'I remember when years ago in Italy': Nine Italian women in Dublin tell the diaspora. *Women's Studies International Forum, 27*(4), 315-334.

DeLoach, C. P. (1994). Attitudes toward disability: Impact on sexual development and forging of intimate relationships. *Journal of Applied Rehabilitation Counseling, Special Issue: Sexuality and disability: Dimensions of human intimacy and rehabilitation counseling practice, 25*(1), 18-25

Dennett, A., & Stillwell, J. (2008). Population 'turnover' and 'churn': Enhancing understanding of internal migration in Britain through measures of stability. *Population Trends, 134*, 24-41.

Desvaux, G., Devillard-Hoellinger, S., & Meaney, M. (2008). A business case for women. *The McKinsey Quarterly*.

Diederen, P. J. M., Kemp, R. P. M., Muysken, J., & De Wit, G. R. (1991). Diffusion of process technology in Dutch banking. *Technological Forecasting and Social Change, 39*(1-2), 201-219.

Difonzo, N., & Bordia, P. (2007). Rumor, gossip and urban legends. *Diogenes, 213*, 19-35.

Dimiceli, E. E., Steinhardt, M. A., & Smith, S. E. (2010). Stressful experiences, coping strategies, and predictors of health-related outcomes among wives of deployed military servicemen. *Armed Forces and Society, 36*(2), 351-373.

Doljanac, R., & Larson, S. A. (2005). *Social activities of non-institutionalized adults in the NHIS-D: Gender, age and disability differences.* DD Data Brief, Research and Training Center on Community Living, Institute on Community Integration (UCEDD), University of Minnesota, 7(2).

Dominguez-Folgueras, M., & Castro-Martin, T. (2013). Cohabitation in Spain: No longer a marginal path to family formation. *Journal of Marriage and Family, 75*(2), 422-437.

Donnelly, J. P., Donnelly, K., & Grohman, K. K. (2005). A multi-perspective concept mapping study of problems associated with traumatic brain injury. *Brain Injury, 19*(13), 1077-1085.

Donovan, J. E. (1993). Young adult drinking-driving: Behavioral and psychosocial correlates. *Journal of Studies on Alcohol and Drugs, 54*(5), 600.

Dowling, G. R., & Walsh, P. K. (1990). Describing the new product adoption behaviour of countries using a new product growth model. *Behavioral Science, 35*(4), 269-280.

Downs, A. (2005). *Still stuck in traffic: coping with peak-hour traffic congestion.* Washington, DC: Brookings Institution Press.

Dratva, Julia, et al. (2010). Impact of road traffic noise annoyance on health-related quality of life: results from a population-based study. *Quality of Life Research, 19*(1), 37-46.

Dreby, J. (2009). Gender and Transnational Gossip. *Qualitative Sociology, 32*, 33–52.

Drentea, P. (1998). Consequences of women's formal and informal job search methods for employment in female-dominated jobs. *Gender and Society, 12*(3), 321-338.

Drucker, E. (1990). Epidemic in the war zone: AIDS and community survival in New York City. *International Journal of Health Services, 20*(4), 601-615.

Drummet, A. R., Coleman, M., & Cable, S. (2003). Military families under stress: Implication for family life education. *Family Relations, 52*(3), 279-287.

Dunbar, R. (2004). Gossip in Evolutionary Perspective. *Review of General Psychology, 8*(2), 100-110.

Durant, Doris B., Cindy L. Larison, and Florence R. Rosenberg. (1994). *In-Depth Analysis of the Survey of Army Families II (1991-1992), Volume 2: Thematic Analysis of Spouses' Comments.*

Dustmann, C., Bentolila, S., & Faini, R. (1996). Return migration: the European experience. *Economic Policy*, 213-250.

Dustmann, C. (2003). Return migration, wage differentials, and the optimal migration duration. *European Economic Review 47*(2), 353-369.

Dutton, W. H. (2013). The social shaping of digital research. *International Journal of Social Research Methodology, 16*(3), 177-195.

Dwyer, R. E. (2004). Downward earnings mobility after voluntary employer exits. *Work and Occupations, 31*(1), 111-139.

Eaton, D. K., et al. (2012). Youth risk behavior surveillance: United States, 2011. *Morbidity and Mortality Weekly Report, Surveillance summaries, 61*(4), 1-162.

Eaton, J., & Kortum, S. (1996). Trade in ideas: Patenting and productivity in the OECD. *Journal of International Economics, 40*(3), 251-278.

Ebaugh, H. R. F. (1992). *Becoming an ex: The process of role exit.* Chicago: University of Chicago Press.

Edwards, Gemma. (2014). Infections innovations? The diffusion of tactical innovation in social movement networks, the case of suffragette militancy. *Social Movement Studies, 13*(1), 48-69.

Ellers, G. M. (2004). Improving patient satisfaction with waiting time. *Journal of American College Health, 53*(1), 41-43.

Elizur, Y., & Hirsh, E. (1999). Psychosocial adjustment and mental health two months after coronary artery bypass surgery: A multisystemic analysis of patients' resources. *Journal of Behavioral Medicine, 22*, 157-177.

Ellis, D. (2008). *Off to war: Voices of soldiers' children.* Toronto: Groundwood Books.

Ender, M. G. (1995). G.I. phone home: The use of telecommunications by the soldiers of Operation Just Cause. *Armed Forces and Society, 21*(3), 435-453

Ender, M. G., & Hermsen, J. M. (1996). Working with the bereaved: U.S. Army experiences with nontraditional families. *Death Studies, 20*(6), 557-575.

Eran-Jona, M. (2011). Married to the military: Military-family relations in the Israel defense forces. *Armed Forces and Society, 37*(1), 19-41.

Escobedo, L. G., Chorba, T. L., & Waxweiler, R. (1995). Patterns of alcohol use and the risk of drinking and driving among US high school students. *American Journal of Public Health, 85*(7), 976-978.

Evertsson, M., & Grunow, D. (2012). Women's work interruptions and career prospects in Germany and Sweden. *International Journal of Sociology and Social Policy, 32*(9/10), 561-575.

Fairchild, C. (2014). *Number of Fortune 500 women CEOs reaches historic high.* Retrieved June 23rd, 2014 from http://fortune.com/2014/06/03/number-of-fortune-500-women-ceos-reaches-historic-high/.

Fan, C. C. (2004). Out to the city and back to the village: The experiences and contributions of rural women migrating from Sichuan and Anhui. In A. M. Gaetano & T. Jacka (eds.), *On the move: Women and rural-to-urban migration in contemporary China*, (pp. 177-206). New York: Columbia University Press.

Fanning, B. (ed.). (2007). *Immigration and social change in the Republic of Ireland.* Manchester: Manchester University Press.

Farley, S. D., Timme, D. R., & Hart, J. (2010). On coffee talk and break-room chatter: Perceptions of women who gossip in the workplace. *Journal of Social Psychology, 150*, 361–368.

Farrell, M. P., & Barnes, G. M. (1993). Family systems and social support: A test of the effects of cohesion and adaptability on the functioning of parents and adolescents. *Journal of Marriage and the Family, 55*(1), 119-132.

Fawcett, J.T. (1989). Networks, linkages, and migration systems. *International Migration Review*, 671-680.

Feddock, C. A., Hoellein, A. R., Griffith, C. H., Wilson, J. F., Bowerman, J. L., Becker, N. S., & Caudill, T. S. (2005). Can physicians improve patient satisfaction with long waiting times? *Evaluation and the Health Professions, 28*(1), 40-52.

Feinberg, M., Willer, R., Stellar, J., and Keltner, D. (2012). The virtues of gossip: Reputational information sharing as prosocial behavior. *Journal of Personality and Social Psychology, 102*(5), 1015-1030.

Feldman-Bianco, B. (1992). Multiple layers of time and space: The construction of class, ethnicity, and nationalism among Portuguese immigrants. *Annals of the New York Academy of Sciences, 645*(1), 145-174.

Feliciano, C. (2005). Educational selectivity in US immigration: How do immigrants compare to those left behind? *Demography, 42*(1), 131-152.

Feng W., Cai Y., & Gu, B. (2012). Population, policy, and politics: How will history judge China's one child policy. *Population and Development Review, 38* (Supplement), 115-129.

Fernandez, J. J., & Lutter, M. (2013). Supranational cultural norms, domestic value orientations and the diffusions of same-sex union rights in Europe, 1988-2009. *International Sociology, 28*(1), 102-120.

Ferraro, K.F. (1994). Physician resistance to innovations: The case of contract medicine. *Sociological Focus, 26*(2), 109-131.

Finkel, L. B., Kelley, M. L., & Ashby, J. (2003). Geographic mobility, family, and maternal variables as related to the psychological adjustment of military children. *Military Medicine, 168*(12), 1019-1024.

Finnie, R. (1999). Inter-provincial migration in Canada: A longitudinal analysis of movers and stayers and the associated income dynamics. *Canadian Journal of Regional Science, 22*(3), 227-262.

Finseraas, H. (2012). Poverty, ethnic minorities among the poor, and preferences for redistribution in European regions. *Journal of European Social Policy, 22*(2), 164–180.

Fischer, C. S. (1992). *America calling: A social history of the telephone to 1940.* Berkeley, CA: University of California Press.

Flaherty, M. G., Freidin, B., & Sautu, R. (2005). Variation in the perceived passage of time: A cross-national study. *Social Psychology Quarterly, 68*(4), 400-410.

Flap, H., & Boxman, E. (1999). Getting a job as a manager. In Leenders, R. Th. A. J., & Gabbay, S. M. (eds.), *Corporate social capital and liability* (pp. 197-216). New York: Springer.

Forthofer, M.S., et al. (1996). The effects of psychiatric disorder on the probability and timing of first marriage. *Journal of Health and Social Behaviour, 37,* 121-132.

Frank, R. G., & Gertler, P. (1991). Mental health and marital stability. *International Journal of Law and Psychiatry, 14,* 377-366.

Freeman, S. M., Moore, B. A., & Freeman, A. (eds.). (2009). *Living and surviving in harm's way: A psychological treatment handbook for pre- and post-deployment of military.* New York: Routledge.

Friedberg, A. (2006). An uncivilized argument. *Foreign Affairs, 85,* 59-60.

Friedlander, D., Schellekens, J., & Ben-Moshe, E. (1991). The transition from high to low marital fertility: Cultural or socioeconomic determinants. *Economic Development and Cultural Change, 39*(2), 331-351.

Frobisher, C., Lancashire, E. R, Winter, D. L., Jenkinson, G. J., Butler, J., Iacono, T., & Leighton, D. (2004). The assessment of sexual knowledge in people with intellectual disability. *Journal of Intellectual and Developmental Disability, 29*(4), 350-365.

Gajduschek, G. (2003). Bureaucracy: Is it efficient? Is it not? Is that the question: Uncertainty reduction: An ignored element of bureaucratic rationality. *Administration and Society, 34*(6), 700-723.

Gal, Reuven, & Wyatt, T. C. (1990). *Legitimacy and commitment in the military.* Westport, CT: Greenwood Press.

Gandrud, C. (2013). The diffusion of financial supervisory governance ideas. *Review of International Political Economy, 20*(4), 881-916.

Gans-Morse, J., Mazzuca, S., & Nichter, S. (2014). Varieties of clientelism: Machine politics during elections. *American Journal of Political Science, 58*(2), 415-432.

Gans, H. J. (2009). First generation decline: downward mobility among refugees and immigrants, *Ethnic and Racial Studies, 32*(9), 1658-1670.

Gärling, T., & Steg, L. (eds.). (2007). *Threats from car traffic to the quality of urban life: Problems, causes, and solutions.* Oxford: Elsevier.

Gaster, B. (1990). Assimilation of scientific change: The introduction of molecular genetics into biology textbooks. *Social Studies of Science, 20*(3), 431-454.

Gay, M. (1982). The adjustment of parents to wartime bereavement. *Series in Clinical and Community Psychology: Stress and Anxiety, 8,* 243-247.

Gee, G. C., & Takeuchi, D. T. (2004). Traffic stress, vehicular burden and well-being: A multilevel analysis. *Social Science and Medicine, 59*(2), 405-414.

Gerlough, D. L., and Huber, M. J. (1975). *Traffic flow theory: a monograph.* Transportation Research Board, National Research Council, Washington, D.C.

Geroski, P. A. (2000). Models of technology diffusion. *Research Policy, 29,* 603–625.

Gerson, M., et al. (2006). An international study of Irritable Bowel Syndrome: Family relationships and mind-body attributions. *Social Science and Medicine, 62* (11), 2838-2847.

Gerstel, N. (1988). Divorce and kin ties: The importance of gender. *Journal of Marriage and the Family, 50*(1), 209-219.

Gill, C., & Krieger, H. (1992). The diffusion of participation in new information technology in Europe: Survey results. *Economic and Industrial Democracy, 13*(3), 331-358.

Gimbel, C., & Booth, A. (1994). Why does military combat experience adversely affect marital relations. *Journal of Marriage and the Family, 56,* 691-703.

Glazer, I. M., & Ras, W. A. (1994). On aggression, human rights, and hegemonic discourse: The case of a murder for family honor in Israel. *Sex Roles, 30*(3-4), 269-288.

Gmelch, G., & Gmelch, S. B. (1995). Gender and migration: The readjustment of women migrants in Barbados, Ireland, and Newfoundland. *Human Organization, 54*(4), 470-473.

Goetz, A. M. (2007). Manoeuvring past clientelism: Institutions and incentives to generate constituencies in support of governance reforms. *Commonwealth and Comparative Politics, 45*(4), 403-424.

Goldhaber, M. K., Houts, P. S., & DiSabella, R. (1983). Moving after the crisis: A prospective study of Three Mile Island area population mobility. *Environment and Behavior, 15*(1), 93-120.

Goldstein, S. B., & Johnson, V. A. (1997). Stigma by association: Perceptions of the dating partners of college students with physical disabilities. *Basic and Applied Social Psychology, 19*(4), 495-504

Golledge, R. G. (1997). *Spatial behavior: A geographic perspective.* New York: Guilford Press.

Golub, A., Elliott, L., & Brownstein, H. H. (2013). The opiate pain reliever epidemic among U.S. arrestees 2000-2010: Regional and demographic variations. *Journal of Ethnicity in Substance Abuse, 12*(1), 1-29.

Gonzalez-Bailon, S., Borge-Holthoefer, J., & Moreno, Y. (2013). Broadcasters and hidden influentials in online protest diffusion. *American Behavioral Scientist, 57*(7), 943-965.

Gordon, J. L., et al. (2006). Positive family environment predicts improvement in symptoms and social functioning among adolescents at imminent risk for onset of psychosis. *Schizophrenia Research, 81*, 269-275.

Gordon, P. A., & Tschopp, M. K. (2004). Dating Considerations for Adolescents with Disabilities. In Bowman, C. A., & Jaeger, P. T (eds.), *A guide to high school success for students with disabilities*, pp. 70-82. Westport, CT: Greenwood Press.

Gosling, J., & Oddy, M. (1999). Rearranged marriages: marital relationships after head injury. *Brain Injury, 13*, 785-96.

Goss, J. (1995). 'We Know Who You Are and We Know Where You Live': The Instrumental Rationality of Geodemographic Systems. *Economic Geography*, 171-198.

Graham, J. E., & Basset, R. (2006). Reciprocal relations: The recognition and co-construction of caring with Alzheimer's Disease. *Journal of Aging Studies, 20*(4).

Granovetter, M. S. (1973). The strength of weak ties. *American Journal of Sociology, 78*(6), 1360-1380.

Greenhill, B. (2010). The company you keep: International socialization and the diffusion of human rights norms. *International Studies Quarterly, 54*, 127-145.

Grella, C. E. (1990). Irreconcilable differences: Women defining class after divorce and downward mobility. *Gender and Society, 4*(1), 41-55.

Griffiths, E. (2013). Race, space and the spread of violence across the city. *Social Problems, 60*(4), 491-512.

Grimes, G. A., Hough, M. G., Mazur, E., & Signorella, M. L. (2010). Older adults' knowledge of internet hazards. *Educational Gerontology, 36*, 173–192.

Groth, M. and Gilliland, S. W. (2006), Having to wait for service: Customer reactions to delays in service delivery. *Applied Psychology: An International Review, 55*, 107–129.

Groves, J. M., & Chang, K. A. (1999). Romancing resistance and resisting romance: Ethnography and the construction of power in the Filipina domestic worker community in Hong Kong. *Journal of Contemporary Ethnography, 28*(3), 235-265.

Gubanski, J. (2004). Comparative criminal justice. *Crime, Law and Social Change, 41*(1), 15-32.

Gulati, G. J., & Williams, C. B. (2013). Social media and campaign 2012: Developments and trends for Facebook adoption. *Social Science Computer Review, 31*(5), 577-588.

Guo, S. (2013). Economic integration of recent Chinese immigrants in Canada's second-tier cities: The triple glass effect and immigrants' downward mobility. *Canadian Ethnic Studies, 3*, 95-115.

Gutmann, M. P., & Watkins, S. C. (1990). Socio-economic differences in fertility control. Is there an early warning system at the village level? *European Journal of Population, 6*(1), 69-101.

Haight, F. A. (1963). *Mathematical theories of traffic flow.* New York: Academic Press.

Hall, I., Strydom, A., Richards, M., Hardy, R., Bernal, J., & Wadsworth, M. (2005). Social outcomes in adulthood of children with intellectual impairment: Evidence from a birth cohort. *Journal of Intellectual Disability Research, 49*, 171-82.

Hall, K., & Bucholtz, M. (eds.). (2012). *Gender articulated: Language and the socially constructed self.* New York: Routledge.

Hansen, M. N. (1997). 'Sosiale nettverk, rekrutteringskanaler og lønn i det norske arbeidsmarkedet' [Social networks, recruitment channels, and wages in the Norwegian labour market]. *Tidsskrift for samfunnsforskning, 38*, 171-195.

Hanser, A. (2002). Youth job searches in urban China: The use of social connections in a changing labor market. In Gold, T., Guthrie, D., & Wank, D. (eds.), *Social Connections in China: Institutions, culture, and the changing nature of Guanxi* (pp. 137-162). United Kingdom: Cambridge University Press.

Harkness, K., Morrow, L., Smith, K., Kiczula, M., & Arthur, H. M. (2003). The effect of early education on patient anxiety while waiting for elective cardiac catheterization. *European Journal of Cardiovascular Nursing, 2*(2), 113-121

Harrell, M. C. (2001). Army officers' spouses: Have the white gloves been mothballed? *Armed Forces and Society, 28*(1), 55-75

Hart, J. (2011). Non-tenure track women faculty: Opening the door. *The Journal of the Professoriate, 4*(1), 96-124.

Hart, M. (2006). Possibility of avoiding discrimination: Considering compliance and liability. *Connecticut Law Review, 39*(4), 1621.

Haslip-Viera, G., de Montellano, B. O., & Barbour, W. (1997). Robbing Native American cultures: Van Sertima's Afrocentricity and the Olmec. *Current Anthropology, 38*(3), 419-441.

Hastings, R. P., & Brown, T. (2002). Behavior problems of children with autism, parental self-efficacy, and mental health. *American Journal on Mental Retardation, 107*(3), 222-232.

Hatcher, A. M. (2013). From the Internet to the streets: Occupy Wall Street, the Internet, and activism. Doctoral dissertation, ProQuest, Ann Arbor MI, 2013. AAI1537772.

Hatfield, E., Traupmann, J., Sprecher, S., Utne, M., & Hay, J. (1985). Equity and intimate relationships: Research. In Ickes, W. (ed.), *Compatible and incompatible relationships*. New York: Springer-Verlag.

Hawkins, H. C., & Michael, M. (2007). Long-term population-based marriage rates among adult survivors of childhood cancer in Britain. *International Journal of Cancer, 121*(4), 846-55.

Hazelrigg, L. E., & Hardy, M. A. (1995). Older adult migration to the Sunbelt assessing income and related characteristics of recent migrants. *Research on Aging, 17*(2), 209-234.

Hazen, A., & Ehiri, J. E. (2006). Road traffic injuries: Hidden epidemic in less developed countries. *Journal of the National Medical Association, 98*(1), 73.

Healy, E., McGuire, B. E., Evans, D.S., & Carley, S. N. (2009). Sexuality and personal relationships for people with an intellectual disability. Part I: service-user perspectives. *Journal of Intellectual Disability Research, 53*, 905-912.

Heilman, M. E. (2001). Description and prescription: How gender stereotypes prevent women's ascent up the organizational ladder. *Journal of Social Issues, 57*(4), 657-674.

Heilman, M., & Okimoto, T. (2008). Motherhood: a potential source of bias in employment decisions. *The Journal of Applied Psychology, 93*(1), 189-198.

Helbing, D., et al. (2001). Self-organizing pedestrian movement. *Environment and Planning, 28*(3), 361-384.

Hemenway, D., & Solnick, S. J. (1993). Fuzzy dice, dream cars, and indecent gestures: Correlates of driver behavior? *Accident Analysis and Prevention, 25*(2), 161-170.

Herzog, H. (2004). Family-Military relations in Israel as a gendered social mechanism. *Armed Forces and Society, 31*(1), 5-30.

Hingson, R., et al. (2002). Age of drinking onset, driving after drinking, and involvement in alcohol related motor-vehicle crashes. *Accident Analysis and Prevention, 34*(1), 85-92.

Hobday, M. (1994). Technological learning in Singapore: a test case of leapfrogging. *The Journal of Development Studies, 30*(4), 831-858.

Hobfoll, S. E., Spielberger, C. D., Bteznitz, S., Figley, C., Folkman, S., Lepper, B., Green, D., Meichenbaum, Milgram, N. A., Sandier, I., Sarason, I., & van der Kolk, B. (1991). War-related stress: Addressing the stress of war and other traumatic events. *American Psychologist, 46(8)*, 848-855.

Hobsbawm, E. (1962). *The age of revolution: Europe, 1789–1848*. New York: Vintage.

Hodson, R., Martin, A. W., Lopez, S. H., & Roscigno, V. J. (2012). Rules don't apply: Kafka's insights on bureaucracy. *Organization, 20*(2), 256-278.

Hodson, R., Roscigno, V. J., Martin, A., & Lopez, S. H. (2013). The ascension of Kafkaesque bureaucracy in private sector organizations. *Human Relations, 66*(9), 1248-1273.

Hodson, R. (1990). Symposium: Dispelling the Japanese mystique? Quality circles: Are they America's future? *Contemporary Sociology, 19*(6), 792-795.

Hogan, P. F.,& Seifert, R. F. (2010). Marriage and the military: Evidence that those who serve marry earlier and divorce earlier. *Armed Forces and Society, 36*(3), 420-438.

Hogan, T. D., & Steinnes, D. N. (1996). Arizona sunbirds and Minnesota snowbirds: Two species of the elderly seasonal migrant genus. *Journal of Economic and Social Measurement, 22*(2), 129-139.

Hogan, T. D., & Steinnes, D. N. (1993). Elderly migration to the Sunbelt: Seasonal versus permanent. *Journal of Applied Gerontology, 12*(2), 246-260.

Holmes-Eber, P. (1997). Migration, urbanization, and women's kin networks in Tunis. *Journal of Comparative Family Studies*, 54-72.

Holtgraves, T. (2001). Politeness. In W. P. Robinson and H. Giles (eds.), *The new handbook of language and social psychology* (pp. 341–355). West Sussex: Wiley.

Honda, K., & Kagawa-Singer, M. (2006). Cognitive mediators linking social support networks to colorectal cancer screening adherence. *Journal of Behavioural Medicine, 39*(5).

Hoofien, D., Vakil, E., & Donovick, P. J. (2001). Traumatic brain injury (TBI) 10-20 years later: A comprehensive outcome study of psychiatric symptomatology, cognitive abilities and psychosocial functioning. *Brain Injury, 15*(3), 189-209.

Horvath, K. J., et al. (2005). Caregiver competence to prevent home injury to the care recipient with dementia. *Rehabilitation Nursing: the official journal of the Association of Rehabilitation Nurses, 30*(5), 189-196.

Hosch, H. M., Barrientos, G. A., Fierro, C., Ramirez, J. I., Pelaez, M. P., Cedillos, A. M., & Perez, Y. (1995). Predicting adherence to medications by Hispanics with schizophrenia. *Hispanic Journal of Behavioral Sciences, 17*(3), 320-333.

Hou, F., & Myles, J. (2007). The changing role of education in the marriage market: Assortative marriage in Canada and the United States since the 1970s. *Statistics Canada – Analytical Studies Branch Research Paper Series.*

Houston, T. K., Cooper, L. A., and Ford, D. E. (2002). Internet support groups for depression: A 1-year prospective cohort study. *The American Journal of Psychiatry, 159*(12), 2062-8.

Hout, W. (2007). Development under Patrimonial Conditions: Suriname's State Oil Company as a Development Agent. *Journal of Development Studies, 43*(8), 1331-1350.

Hovinen, G. R. (1995). Heritage issues in urban tourism: An assessment of new trends in Lancaster County. *Tourism Management, 16*(5), 381-388.

Howe, N. L., Mann, K. D., & Pearce, M. S. (2013). The effects of social mobility on blood pressure at ages 50 and 60 years–in the Newcastle Thousands Families Study. *Journal of Epidemiological Community Health, 67*(Supplement 1), A1–A84

Howland, C. A., Rintala, D. H. (2001). TI: Dating behaviors of women with physical disabilities. *Sexuality and Disability, 19*(1), 41-70.

Howlin, P., & Mawhood, L. (2000). Autism and developmental receptive language disorder – a follow-up comparison in early adult life. II: Social, behavioural, and psychiatric outcomes. *Journal of Child Psychology and Psychiatry, 41*, 561-78.

Hsueh, Y., & Anderton, D. L. (1990). Temporal dimensions of the fertility transition: An age-period cohort analysis of frontier fertility. *Sociological Perspectives, 33*(4), 447-464.

Huang, F. (2013). Globalisation of sport: The NBA's diffusion in China. *International Journal of the History of Sport, 30*(3), 267-284.

Huang, R., & Sun, X. (2014). Weibo network, information diffusion and implications for collective action in China. *Information, Communication and Society, 17*(1), 86-104.

Hughes, A. (2007). Geographies of exchange and circulation: Flows and networks of knowledgeable capitalism. *Progress in Human Geography, 31*, 527-535.

Hunter-King, E. J. (1993). Long-term effects on children of a parent missing in wartime. In Whiteman Kaslow, F. (ed.), *The Military Family in Peace and War*. New York: Springer.

Hutchison, J., & Brown, A. (eds.). (2001). *Organising labour in globalising Asia*. New York: Psychology Press.

Iecovich, E. (2008). Caregiving burden, community services, and quality of life of primary caregivers of frail elderly persons. *The Journal of Applied Gerontology, 27*(3), 309-330.

Innes, M., & Sheptycki, J. (2004). From detection to disruption: Intelligence and the changing logic of police crime control in the United Kingdom. *International Criminal Justice Review, 14*, 1-24.

Innes, M., & Sheptycki, J. W. E. (2004). From detection to disruption: Intelligence and genes, and languages. *American Anthropologist, 105*(3), 501-514.
Innis, H. (1950). *Empire and communications*. Oxford: Oxford University Press.
Ivanovic, M., Vuletic, Z., & Bebbington, P. (1994). Expressed emotion in the families of patients with schizophrenia and its influence on the course of illness. *Social Psychiatry and Psychiatric Epidemiology, 29*, 61-65.
Jaeger, M. M., & Holm, A. (2012). Conformists or rebels? Relative risk aversion, educational decisions and social class reproduction. *Rationality and Society, 24*(2), 221–253.
James, J. (2013). The diffusion of IT in the historical context of innovations from developed countries. *Social Indicators Research, 111*(1), 175-184.
Jansson, B. (2014). Intragenerational income mobility in Gothenburg, Sweden, 1925-94: Before, during and after the rise of the welfare state. *Australian Economic History Review, 54*(1), 14-36.
Jo, H. (2003). Basic life resources and marital status of people with disabilities in the United States and Korea. *Dissertation Abstracts International, 64-03A*, 1077.
Joecks, J., Pull, K., & Vetter, K. (2013). Gender diversity in the boardroom and firm performance: What exactly constitutes a 'critical mass?'. *Journal of Business Ethics, 118*(1), 61-72.
Johnson, S. K. (2009). Do you feel what I feel? Mood contagion and leadership outcomes. *The Leadership Quarterly, 20*, 814–827.
Johnson, M. B. (1990). The holistic paradigm in nursing: The diffusion of an innovation. *Research in Nursing and Health, 13*(2), 129-139.
Johnson, P., Wood, G., Brewster, C., & Brookes, M. (2009). The rise of post-bureaucracy: theorists' fancy or organizational praxis?. *International Sociology, 24*(1), 37-61.
Jones, D. (2003). Kinship and deep history: Exploring connections between culture areas, knowledgeable capitalism. *Progress in Human Geography, 31*(4), 527-535.
Josserand, E., Teo, S., & Clegg, S. (2006). From bureaucratic to post-bureaucratic: The difficulties of transition. *Journal of Organizational Change Management, 19*(1), 54-64.
Juby, H., & Le Bourdais, C. (2005). Families in Transition. *Expert Roundtable on Challenges for Canadian Families, Social Development Canada.*
Jung, J.J. (2014). Measuring trustworthiness of information diffusion by risk discovery process in social networking services. *Quality and Quantity, 48*(3), 1325-1336.
Junger, M., West, R., & Timman, R. (2001). Crime and risky behavior in traffic: An example of cross-situational consistency. *Journal of Research in Crime and Delinquency, 38*(4), 439-459.
Kalleberg, A.L., & Mastekaasa, A. (2001). Satisfied Movers, Committed Stayers The Impact of Job Mobility on Work Attitudes in Norway. *Work and Occupations, 28*(2), 183-209.
Kamann, D. F., & Nijkamp, P. T. (1991). Technogenesis: Origins and diffusion in a turbulent environment. *Technological Forecasting and Social Change, 39*(1-2), 45-66.
Kanter, R. M. (1977). *Men and women of the corporation*. New York: Basic Books.
Karasek, R., & Theorell, T. (1990). *Healthy work: Stress, productivity, and the reconstruction of working life*. New York: Basic Books
Kaslow, F. (2004). Death of one's partner: The anticipation and the reality. *Professional Psychology: Research and Practice, 35*(3), 227-233.
Keefe, J. H. (1991). Do unions influence the diffusion of technology? *Industrial and Labor Relations Review, 44*(2), 261-274.
Keenan, H. T., et al. (2006). Longitudinal follow-up of families and young children with traumatic brain injury. *Pediatrics, 117*(4), 1291-1297.
Keller, M. C., Thiessen, D., & Young, R. K. (1996). Mate Assortment in Dating and Married Couples. *Personality and Individual Differences, 21*, 217-221.
Kelly, E., Ammons, S., Chermack, K., & Moen, P. (2010). Gendered challenge, gendered response: Confronting the ideal worker norm in white-collar organization. *Gender and Society, 24*(3), 281-303.
Kelly, R. M., Hale, M. M., & Burgess, J. (1991). Gender and managerial/leadership styles: A comparison of Arizona public administrators. *Women and Politics, 11*(2), 19-39.
Kessler, R. C., Walters, E. S., & Forthofer, M. S. (1998). the social consequences of psychiatric disorders, III: Probability of marital stability. *American Journal of Psychiatry, 155*, 1092-1096.
Khan, M. A. (2003). Factors associated with oral contraceptive discontinuation in rural Bangladesh. *Health Policy and Planning, 18*(1), 101-108.
Kildea, G. (1977). Colonialism. *American Anthropologist, New Series, 79*(2), 506-507.

Kilduff, M., & Tsai, W. (2003). *Social networks and organizations.* Thousand Oaks, CA: Sage.

King, R. (1993). *Mass migrations in Europe: the legacy and the future.* London: Belhaven Press.

Klonoff, H., Clark, C., & Klonoff, P. S. (1993). Long-term outcome of head injuries: A 23 year follow up study of children with head injuries. *Journal of Neurology, Neurosurgery, and Psychiatry, 56*, 410-15.

Klonoff, P. S., Watt, L. M., Dawson, L. K., Henderson, S. W., Gehrels, J., & Wethe, J. V. (2006). Outcomes 1-7 years after comprehensive milieu-oriented neuro-rehabilitation: The role of pre-injury status. *Brain Injury, 20*(6), 601-612.

Kobayashi, R., Murata, T., & Yoshinaga, K. (1992). A Follow-up study of 201 children with autism in Kyushu and Yamaguchi areas, Japan. *Journal of Austism and Developmental Disorders, 22*, 395-411.

Kocas, C. (2000). On the psychological cost of waiting in queues. *Dissertation Abstracts International, 63-06A*, 2307.

Koller, H., Richardson, S. A., & Katz, M. (1988). Marriage in a young mentally retarded population. *Journal of Mental Deficiency Research, 32*, 93-102.

Kolsto, P. (1996). The new Russian diaspora: an identity of its own? Possible identity trajectories for Russians in the former Soviet republic. *Ethnic and Racial Studies, 19*(3), 609-639.

Konrad, A., & Kramer, V. (2008). Critical mass: The impact of three of more women on corporate boards. *Organizational Dynamics, 37*(3), 145-164.

Kotler, P. (1989). From mass marketing to mass customization. *Strategy and Leadership, 17*(5), 10-47.

Kreuter, M., Dahllof, A. G., Gudjonsson, G., Sullivan, M., & Siosteen, A. (1998). Sexual adjustment and its predictors after traumatic brain injury. *Brain Injury, 12*, 349-368.

Kreutzer, J. S., Marwitz, J. H., Hsu, N., Williams, K., & Riddick, A. (2007). Marital stability after brain injury: An investigation and analysis. *NeuroRehabilitation*, 22(1), 53-59.

Kriel, R. L., Krach, L. I., Bergland, M. M., & Panser, L. A. (1988). Severe adolescent head injury: Implications for transition into adult life. *Pediatric Neurology, 4*, 337-341.

Krinsky, J., & Crossley, N. (2014). Social movements and social networks: Introduction. *Social Movement Studies, 13*(1), 1-21.

Kryshtanovskaia, O. V. (2005). Has-beens: Trends of downward mobility of the Russian elite. *Sociological Research, 44*(2), 7–54.

Krzyzanowska, M., & Mascie-Taylor, C. G. (2011). Intra- and intergenerational social mobility in relation to height, weight and body mass index in a British national cohort. *Journal of Biosocial Science, 43*, 611–618.

Kubey, R. W., & Peluso, T. (1990). Emotional response as a cause of interpersonal news diffusion: The case of the space shuttle tragedy. *Journal of Broadcasting and Electronic Media, 34*(1), 69-76.

Laff, M. (2007). The invisible wall: Most observers are discouraged about the progress women have made in reaching the executive level. *Training and Development, 61*(3), 32-39.

Laff, M. (2014). *The invisible wall: Workplace barriers and self-image hinder women's leadership advancement.* Retrieved on June 22nd, 2014 from http://www.rowan.edu/open/centers/womensNetwork/documents/InvisibleWall0307.pdf.

Lainer-Vos, D. (2010). Diaspora-homeland relations as a framework to examine nation-building processes. *Sociology Compass, 4*(10), 894-908.

Lakhani, H. (1994). The socioeconomic benefits to military families of home-basing of Armed Forces. *Armed Forces and Society, 21*(1), 113-128.

Lamberg, L. (2004). When military parents are sent to war, children left behind need ample support. *JAMA, 292*, 13.

Landau J., & Hissett, J. (2008). Mild Traumatic Brain Injury: Impact on identity and ambiguous loss in the family. *Families, Systems, and Health, 26*(1), 69-85.

Lapp, C. A., Taft, L. B., Tollefson, T., Hoepner, A., Moore, K., & Divyak, K. (2010). Stress and coping on the home front: Guard and reserve spouses searching for a new normal. *Journal of Family Nursing, 16*(1), 45-67.

Larson, J. A. (2013). Social movements and tactical choice. *Sociology Compass, 7*(10), 866-879.

Larson, S. A., Doljanac, R., & Lakin, K. C. (2005). United States living arrangements of people with intellectual and/or developmental disabilities in 1995. *Journal of Intellectual and Developmental Disability, 30*(4), 248-251.

Lee, S., Cho, E., Grodstein, F., Kawachi, I., Hu, F. B., & Colditz, G. A. (2005). Effects of marital transitions on changes in dietary and other health behaviours in US women. *International Journal of Epidemiology, 34*(1), 69-78.
Lee, R. (2003). The demographic transition: Three centuries of fundamental change. *Journal of Economic Perspectives, 17*(4), 167-190.
Leonetti, D., & Chabot-Hanowell, B. (2011). The foundation of kinship: Households. *Human Nature, 22*(1), 16-40.
Levin, H. S., Song, J., Ewing-Cobbs, L., Chapman, S. B., & Mendelsohn, D. (2001). Word fluency in relation to severity of closed head injury, associated frontal brain lesions, and age at injury in children. *Neuropsychologia, 39*, 122-31.
Levy, Y. (2009). An unbearable price: War casualties and warring democracies. *International Journal of Politics, Culture and Society, 22*, 69-82.
Liben-Nowell, D., & Kleinberg, J. (2008). Tracing information flow on a global scale using Internet Chain-Letter Data. *Proceedings of the National Academy of Sciences of the United States of America, 105*(12), 4633-4638.
Light, R., McCleary, C., Asarnow, R., Satz, P., Lewis, R., & Zaucha, K. (1998). Mild closed-head injury in children and adolescents: Behavior problems and academic outcomes. *Journal of Consulting and Clinical Psychology, 66*, 1023-29.
Lim, H. (2013). The diffusion and transmission of cricket among European, Indigenous and Migrant communities in the British Straits settlements and Malay States during the late eighteenth and nineteenth century, 1786-1899. *International Journal of the History of Sport, 30*(3), 210-231.
Limpawattana, P., Theeranut, A., Chindaprasirt, J., Sawanyawisuth, K., & Pimporm, J. (2013) Caregivers burden of older adults with chronic illnesses in the community: A cross-sectional study. *Journal of Community Health, 38*(1), 40-45.
Lin, S., & Chen, S. (2013). Innovation attributes and pedagogical quality: A concretization of joint theories on course management systems acceptance. *Quality and Quantity, 47*(4), 2309-2317.
Lindstrom, D. P. (1996). Economic opportunity in Mexico and return migration from the United States. *Demography, 33*(3), 357-374.
Lindstrom, M., Modén, B., & Rosvall, M. (2013). A life-course perspective on economic stress and tobacco smoking: a population-based study. *Addiction, 108*, 1305–1314.
Link, B. G., et al. (1987). The social rejection of former mental patients: Understanding why labels matter. *American Journal of Sociology, 92*(6), 1461-1500.
Lipset, S. M. (1988). American exceptionalism reaffirmed. *International Review of Sociology, 2*(3), 25-69.
Llambias-Wolff, J. (1993). The voluntary repatriation process of Chilean exiles. *International Migration, 31*(4), 579-599.
Longino, C. F., & Biggar, J. C. (1981). The impact of retirement migration on the South. *The Gerontologist, 21*(3), 283-290.
Lopez, S. R., et al. (2004). Ethnicity, expressed emotion, attributions, and course of schizophrenia: Family warmth matters. *Journal of Abnormal Psychology, 113*, 428-39.
Losinger, W. C. (2010). Notes regarding the 2006 survey of active duty spouses. *Armed Forces and Society, 36*(3), 558-570.
Lovås, G. G. (1994). Modeling and simulation of pedestrian traffic flow. *Transportation Research Part B: Methodological, 28*(6), 429-443.
Lowe, M. E., & McClement, S. E. (2010). Spousal bereavement: The lived experience of young Canadian widows. *Omega, 62*(2), 127-148.
Lu, M. (1998). Analyzing migration decision making: relationships between residential satisfaction, mobility intentions, and moving behavior. *Environment and Planning, 30*(8), 1-473.
Lui, C. K., Chung, P. J., Wallace, S. P., & Aneshensel, C. S. (2013). Social status attainment during the transition to adulthood. *Journal of Youth and Adolescence, 43*(7), 1134-1150.
Luis, C. A., & Mittenberg, W. (2002). Mood and anxiety disorders following pediatric Traumatic Brain Injury: A prospective study. *Journal of Clinical and Experimental Neuropsychology, 24*, 270-79.
MacDonald, J. S., & MacDonald, L. D. (1964). Chain migration ethnic neighborhood formation and social networks. *The Milbank Memorial Fund Quarterly*, 82-97
Mackett, R. L., & Edwards, M. (1998). The impact of new urban public transport systems: will the expectations be met? *Transportation Research, Part A: Policy and Practice 32*(4), 231-245.

Madfis, E. (2014). Triple entitlement and homicidal anger: An exploration of the intersectional identities of American mass murderers. *Men and Masculinities, 17*(1), 67-86.

Maegaard, M., Jensen, T. J., Kristiansen, T., & Joergensen, J. N. (2013). Diffusion of language change: Accommodation to a moving target. *Journal of Sociolinguistics, 17*(1), 3-36.

Mah, L., Arnold, M. C., & Grafman, J. (2004). Impairment of social perception associated with lesions of the prefrontal cortex. *The American Journal of Psychiatry, 161*(7), 1247-55.

Majka, L. C. (1992). Review of from middle income to poor: Downward mobility among displaced steelworkers. *American Journal of Sociology, 98*(3), 690-692

Major, A. (2013). Transnational state formation and the global politics of austerity. *Sociological Theory, 31*(1), 24-48.

Mandemakers, J. J., & Monden, C. W. S. (2013) Does the effect of job loss on psychological distress differ by educational level? *Work, Employment and Society, 27*(1), 73–93.

Mann, S., & Miller, D. (1998). Social support, social conflict, and adjustment among adolescents with cancer. *Journal of Pediatric Psychology, 23*(2).

Mao, H., Chen, C., & Hsieh, T. (2009). The relationship between bureaucracy and workplace friendship. *Social Behaviour and Personality, 37*(2), 255-266.

Marchant, K. H., & Medway, F. K. (1987). Adjustment and achievement associated with mobility in military families. *Psychology in the Schools, 24*(3), 289-294.

Mark, D. B., et al. (1994). Use of medical resources and quality of life after acute myocardial infarction in Canada and the United States. *New England Journal of Medicine, 331*(17), 1130ff.

Marsh, N. V., & Knight, R. G. (1991). Behavioral assessment of social competence following severe head injury. *Journal of Clinical and Experimental Neuropsychology, 13*, 729-40.

Marsh, N. V., Knight, R. G., & Hamish P. D. G. (1990). Long-term psychosocial adjustment following very severe closed head injury. *Neuropsychology, 4*, 13-27.

Marsh, N. V. (1991). Relationship between cognitive deficits and social skill after head injury. *Neuropsychology, 5*, 107-17.

Marshall, B. (1992). 'Migration' into Germany: Asylum seekers and ethnic Germans. *German Politics, 1*(1), 124-134.

Martin, L. G. (1990). Changing intergenerational family relations in East Asia. *Annals of the American Academy of Political and Social Science 510*(1), 102-114.

Martin, M. (1991). Communication and social forms: The development of the telephone, 1876-1920. *Antipode, 23*(3), 307-333.

Martin, P. L. (1994). Nine options to reduce unwanted immigration. In Cornelius, W. A., Martin, P. L., & Hollifield, J. F. (eds.), *Controlling immigration: A global perspective.* Stanford: Stanford University Press.

Mason, J. (2004). Managing kinship over long distances: The significance of "The Visit". *Social Policy and Society, 3*(4), 421-429.

Massey, D. S. (1987). Understanding Mexican migration to the United States. *American Journal of Sociology, 92*(6), 1372-1403.

Massey, D. S., & Espinosa, K. E. (1997). What's driving Mexico-US migration? A theoretical, empirical, and policy analysis. *American Journal of Sociology, 102*(4), 939-999.

Massie, D. L., Campbell, K. L., & Williams, A. F. (1995). Traffic accident involvement rates by driver age and gender. *Accident Analysis and Prevention, 27*(1), 73-87.

Masson, F., Maurette, P., Salmi, L. R., Dartigues, J. F., Vecsey, J., Destaillats, J. M., & Erny, P. (1996). Prevalence of impairments 5 years after a head injury, and their relationship with disabilities and outcome. *Brain Injury, 10*, 487-97.

Matthews, K. A., et al. (2006). Does who you marry matter for your health? Influence of patients' and spouses' personality of their partners' psychological well-being following coronary artery bypass surgery. *Journal of Personality and Social Psychology, 91*, 255-67.

Matthys, C. (2013). Domestic servants and diffusion of fertility control in Flanders, 1830-1930. *The History of the Family, 18*(4), 456-480.

May, A. D. (1990). *Traffic flow fundamentals.* Englewood Cliffs, NJ: Prentice Hall.

McAndrew, F. T., Bell, E. K., and Garcia, C. M. (2007). Who do we tell and whom do we tell on? Gossip as a strategy for status enhancement. *Journal of Applied Social Psychology, 37*(7), 1562–1577.

McClendon, M. J., Smyth, K. A., & Neundorfer, M. M. (2006). Long-term-care placement and survival of persons with Alzheimer's Disease. *Gerontology: Series B: Psychological Sciences and Social Sciences, 61B*(4).

McCormick, B. J., & Tate, R. B. (2006). Uncertainty, symptom distress, anxiety, and functional status in patients waiting for coronary artery bypass surgery. *Heart and Lung, 35*(1), 34-45.

McDaniel, S. A., Gazso, A., & Um, S. (2013). Generationing relations in challenging times: Americans and Canadians in mid-life in the Great Recession. *Current Sociology*, doi:10.1177/0011392113475806.

McDonald K. L., Putallaz, M., Grimes, C. L., Kupersmidt, J. B., & Coie, J. D. (2007). Girl talk: Gossip, friendship, and sociometric status. *Merrill-Palmer Quarterly, 53*(3), 381-411.

Mcdonald, S., & Flanagan, S. (2004). Social perception deficits after Traumatic Brain Injury: Interaction between emotion recognition, mentalizing ability, and social communication. *Neuropsychology, 18*, 572-79.

McGowan, F. (2014). Regulating innovation: European responses to shale gas development. *Environmental Politics, 23*(1), 41-58.

McKain, J. L. (1973). Relocation in the military: Alienation and family problems. *Journal of Marriage and the Family, 35*(2), 205-209.

Mckinlay, A., Dalrymple-Alford, J. C., Horwood, L. J., & Fergusson, D. M. (2002). Long term psychosocial outcomes after mild head injury in early childhood. *Journal of Neurology, Neurosurgery, and Psychiatry, 73*, 281-288.

McPherson, M., Smith-Lovin, L., & Cook, J. M. (2001). Birds of a feather: Homophily in social networks. *Annual Review of Sociology, 27*, 415-444.

Mead, N., MacDonald, W., Bower, P., Lovell, K., Richards, D., Roberts, C., & Bucknall, A. (2005). The clinical effectiveness of guided self-help versus waiting-list control in the management of anxiety and depression: A randomized controlled trial. *Psychological Medicine, 35*(11), 1633-1643.

Mearsheimer, J., & Walt, S. (2006). Unrestricted access. *Foreign Affairs, 85*, 57-58.

Meichenbaum, D. (1995). Disasters, stress and cognition. In Hobfoll, S. E., & De Vries, M. W. (eds.), *Extreme stress and communities: Impact and intervention*, pp. 33-61. Amsterdam: Springer.

Meier, A., Galinsky, M. J., & Rounds, K. A. (1996). Telephone support groups for caregivers of persons with AIDS. *Social Work with Groups, 18*(1), 99-108.

Milders, M., Fuchs, S., & Crawford, J. R. (2003). Neurological impairments and changes in emotional and social behaviour following severe traumatic brain injury. *Journal of Clinical and Experimental Neuropsychology, 25*, 157-172.

Miller, D. E. (1992). 'Snakes in the greens' and rumor in the innercity. *Social Science Journal, 29*(4), 381-393.

Milligan, M. S. (2004). TI: Forging intimate relationships following spinal cord injury: An investigation of individual factors. *Dissertation Abstracts International Section A: Humanities and Social Sciences, 65*(1-A), 69.

Mitchell, B. A. (2006). *The boomerang age: Transitions to adulthood in families.* Piscataway, NJ: Transaction Publishers.

Mitrani, V. B., & Czaja, S. J. (2000). Family-based therapy for dementia caregivers: clinical observations. *Aging and Mental Health, 4*(3), 200-209.

Miyares, I.M., et al. (2003). The interrupted circle: Truncated transnationalism and the Salvadoran experience. *Journal of Latin American Geography, 2*(1), 74-86.

Molassiotis, A., van den Akker, O. B. A., & Boughton, B. J. (1997). Perceived social support, family environment and psychosocial recovery in bone marrow transplant long-term survivors. *Social Science and Medicine, 44*, 317-25.

Momsen, J. H. (ed.). (1993). *Women and change in the Caribbean: A pan-Caribbean perspective.* Bloomington, IN: Indiana University Press.

Motlova, L., et al. (2006). Relapse prevention in schizophrenia: Does group family psychoeducation matter? One year prospective follow-up field study. *International Journal of Pyschiatry in Clinical Practice, 10*, 38-44.

Mowen, J. C., Licata, W., & McPhail, J. (1993). Waiting in the emergency room: How to improve patient satisfaction. *Journal of Health Care Marketing, 13*(2), 26-33.

Naar-King, S., et al. (2006). Psychosocial factors and treatment adherence in paediatric HIV/AIDS. *AIDS Care, 18*, 621-8.

Naess, H., Waje-Andreassen, U., Thomassen, L., Nyland, H., & Myhr, K. (2006). Health-related quality of life among young adults with ischemic stroke on long-term follow-up. *Stroke, 37*, 1232-1236.

Nah, S., Saxton, G. D. (2013). Modeling the adoption and use of social media by non-profit organizations. *New Media and Society, 15*(2), 294-313.

National Center on Family Homelessness. (n.d.). Understanding the experience of military families and their returning war fighters: Military literature and resource review.

National Defence. (1998, October). Moving forward – A strategic plan for quality of life improvements in the Canadian Forces: Chapter V – The Military Family. *SCONDVA – Quality of Life Report Tabled in the House of Commons.*

Nauck, B. (2009). Patterns of exchange in kinship systems in Germany, Russia, and the People's Republic of China. *Journal of Comparative Family Studies, 40*(2), 255-278.

Naumann, S., & Miles, J. A. (2001). Managing waiting patients' perceptions: the role of process control. *Journal of Management in Medicine, 15*(4-5), 376-386.

Nelson, B. S., Goff, N., Crow, J. R., Reisbig, A. M. J., & Hamilton, S. (2007). The impact of individual trauma symptoms of deployed soldiers on relationship satisfaction. *Journal of Family Psychology, 21*(3), 344 –353.

Nepstad, S. E. (2013). Nonviolent civil resistance and social movements. *Sociology Compass 7*(7), 590-598.

Newell, S., & Clark, P. (1990). The importance of extra-organizational networks in the diffusion and appropriation of new technologies: The role of professional associations in the United States and Britain. *Knowledge, 12*(2), 199-212.

Newman, K. S. (1988). *Falling from grace: The experience of downward mobility in the American middle class.* New York: Free Press.

Nie, W. (2000). Waiting: integrating social and psychological perspectives in operations management. *Omega, 28*(6), 611-629.

Nielsen, R. K. (2013). Mundane internet tools, the risk of exclusion and reflexive movements – Occupy Wall Street and political uses of digital networked technologies. *The Sociological Quarterly, 54*(2), 173-177.

Northcott, J. (1986). *Microelectronics in industry: Promise and performance.* London: Policy Studies Institute.

Northcott, J., & Walling, A. (1988). *The impact of microelectronics: Diffusion, benefits and problems in British industry.* London: Policy Studies Institute.

Northcott, J., Christie, I., & Walling, A. (1990). *Information technology and management awareness: Advanced information technologies.* London: Her Majesty's Stationery Office.

O'Brien, K. E., et al. (2008). A meta-analytic investigation of gender differences in mentoring. *Journal of Management,* doi:10.1177/0149206308331861

O'Brien, T. L. (2006, March 19). Why do so few women reach the top of big law firms? *The New York Times,* p. B1.

O'Brien, D. H. (2013). *Women in the public sector who experience feelings of bumping their heads on the glass ceiling: a grounded theory study.* Dissertation, Capella University.

O'Callaghan, E. M. (2010). *A study of longitudinal gender differences in faculty promotion and rank attainment at a research university: Toward an understanding of the glass ceiling* (Unpublished doctoral dissertation). University of Wisconsin-Madison.

Oakes, S. (2003). Musical tempo and waiting perceptions. *Psychology and Marketing, 20*(8), 685-705.

Obinger, H., Schmitt, C., & Starke, P. (2013). Policy diffusion and policy transfer in comparative welfare state research. *Social Policy and Administration, 47*(1), 111-129.

Oddy, M., & Humphrey, M. (1980). Social recovery during the year following severe head injury. *Journal of Neurology, Neurosurgery, and Psychiatry, 43*, 798-202.

Oddy, M., Coughlan, T., Tyerman, A., & Jenkins, D. (1985). Social adjustment after closed head injury: a further follow-up seven years after injury. *Journal of Neurology, Neurosurgery, and Psychiatry, 48*, 564-68.

Odero, W., Garner, P., & Zwi, A. (1997). Road traffic injuries in developing countries: a comprehensive review of epidemiological studies. *Tropical Medicine and International Health, 2*(5), 445-460.

Oermann, M. H. (2003). Effects of educational intervention in waiting room on patient satisfaction. *Journal of Ambulatory Care Management, 26*(2), 150-158.

Ogawa, N., & Retherford, R. D. (1993). Care of the elderly in Japan: Changing norms and expectations. *Journal of Marriage and the Family, 55*(3), 585-597.

Oh, I. (2012). From nationalist diaspora to transnational diaspora: The evolution of identity crisis among the Korean-Japanese. *Journal of Ethnic and Migration Studies,* 38(4), 651-669.

Okkonen, E., & Vanhanen, H. (2006). Family support, living alone, and subjective health of a patient in connection with a coronary artery bypass surgery. *Heart and Lung, 35*(4), 234-244.

Orthner, D. K., & Rose, R. (2005). *Deployment and separation adjustment.* Army Family Deployment Report. The University of North Carolina at Chapel Hill.

Ortiz, S. Y., & Roscigno, V. J. (2009). Discrimination, women, and work: Processes and variations by race and class. *The Sociological Quarterly, 50*(2), 336-359.

Osterman, P. (1993). How common is workplace-transformation and who adopts it. *Industrial and Labour Relations Review, 47*(2), 173-188.

Oudhoff, J. P., Timmermans, D. R., Bijnen, A. B., & Van der Wal, G. (2004). Waiting for elective general surgery: physical, psychological and social consequences. *ANZ Journal of Surgery, 74*(5), 361-367.

Packer, G. (2013). *The unwinding: An inner history of the new America.* New York: Farrar, Straus and Giroux.

Padden, D. L., Connors, R. A., & Agazio, J. G. (2011). Stress, coping, and well-being in military spouses during deployment separation. *Western Journal of Nursing Research, 33*(1), 247-267.

Palmer, C. (2008). A theory of risk and resilience factors in military families. *Military Psychology, 20*(3), 205-217.

Paniak, C. E., Shore, D. L., Rourke, B. P., Finlayson, M. A. J., & Moustacalis, E. (1992). Long-term vocational functioning after severe closed head injury: A controlled study. *Archives of Clinical Neuropsychology, 7*(6).

Park, J. (2008). A profile of the Canadian forces. *Perspectives, Statistics Canada Catalog no.75-001-X,* pages 17-30,

Parrenas, R. S., & Siu, L. (ed.). (2007). *Asian diasporas: New conceptions, new formations.* Stanford: Stanford University Press

Parrenas, R. S. (2001). *Servants of globalization: Women, migration, and domestic work.* Stanford: Stanford University Press

Parrenas, R. S. (2005). *Children of global migration: Transnational families and gendered woes.* Stanford: Stanford University Press

Parry, M. J. E. (2004). Physiologic and psychological responses of men and women waiting for coronary artery bypass graft surgery. *Masters Abstracts International, 39*(3), 830.

Parsons, T. (1951). Illnesss and the role of the physician: A sociological perspective. *American Journal of Orthopsychiatry, 21*(3), 452-460.

Pasura, D. (2011). A fractured transnational diaspora: The case of Zimbabweans in Britain . *International Migration, 50*(1), 143-161.

Patterson, O. (1994). Ecumenical America: Global culture and the American cosmos. *World Policy Journal,* 103-117.

Payne, D. M., Warner, J. T., & Little, R. D. (1992). Tied migration and return on human capital: The case of military wives. *Social Science Quarterly, 73*(2), 324-339.

Pegram T. (2010). Diffusion across political systems: The global spread of national human rights institutions. *Human Rights Quarterly, 32*(3), 729-760.

Peirce, W. S. (1991). Innovation and diffusion in the 'Single Europe': Institutional structure and industrial prospects for the European communities. *Technological Forecasting and Social Change, 39*(1-2), 35-44.

Pendery, D. (2008). Identity development and cultural production in the Chinese diaspora to the United States, 1850-2004: New perspectives. *Asian Ethnicity, 9*(3), 201-218.

Peni, E. (2014). CEO and chairperson characteristics and firm performance. *Journal of Management & Governance 18*(1), 185-205.

Peni, E., & Vähämaa, S. (2010). Female executives and earnings management. *Managerial Finance, 36*(7), 629-645.

Pentikäinen, O., & Trier, T. (2004). Between integration and resettlement: The Meskhetian Turks. *ECMI Working Papers.*

Pentland, L., Todd, J. A., & Anderson, V. (1998). The Impact of Head Injury Severity on Planning Ability in Adolescence: A Functional Analysis. *Neuropsychological Rehabilitation, 8*, 301-317.

Perez, P. A., & McDonough, P. M. (2008). Understanding Latina and Latino college choice: A social capital and chain migration analysis. *Journal of Hispanic Higher Education*, 7(3), 249-265.

Perlesz, A., & O'Loughlan, M. (1998). Changes in stress and burden in families seeking therapy following traumatic brain injury: A follow up study. *International Journal of Rehabilitation Research, 21*, 339-54.

Peters, K., & Kashima, Y. (2007). From social talk to social action: shaping the social triad with emotion sharing. *Journal of Personality and Social Psychology, 93*, 780–797.

Pfammatter, M., Junghan, U. M., & Brenner, H. D. (2006). Efficacy of psychological therapy in schizophrenia: Conclusions from meta-analyses. *Schizophrenia Bulletin, 32*.

Phelps, J. E., Lewis, R., Mobilio, L., Perry, D., & Raman, N. (2004). Viral marketing or electronic word-of-mouth advertising: Examining consumer responses and motivations to pass along email. *Journal of Advertising Research, 44*(4), 333-348.

Philips, J. F. (1978). Continued use of contraception among Philippine family planning acceptors: A multivariate analysis. *Studies in Family Planning*, 182-192.

Pierotti, R. S. (2013). Increasing rejection of intimate partner violence: Evidence of global cultural diffusion. *American Sociological Review*, 78(2), 240-265.

Pilkington, H. (1998). *Migration, displacement, and identity in post-Soviet Russia.* New York, NY: Routledge.

Pitschel-Walz, G., et al. (2001). The effect of family interventions on relapse and rehospitalization in schizophrenia: A meta-analysis. *Schizophrenia Bulletin, 27*, 73-92.

Plympton, T. J., & Hibbard, J. H. (1991). AIDS prevention: Application of health education principles to different subcultures. *International Quarterly of Community Health Education, 12*(1), 51-58.

Ponic, P., Varcoe, C., Davies, L., Ford-Gilboe, M., Wuest, J., & Hammerton, J. (2011). Leaving ≠ moving: Housing patterns of women who have left an abusive partner. *Violence Against Women, 17*(12), 1576-1600.

Ponsford, J. (2003). Sexual changes associated with traumatic brain injury. *Neuropsychological Rehabilitation, 13*, 275-89.

Ponzetti, J. J., jr. (ed.). (2003). *International encyclopedia of marriage and family*, 2nd ed. New York: Macmillan.

Poole, K., Hood, K., Davis, B. D., Monypenny, I. J., Sweetland, H., Webster, D. J. T., Lyons, K., & Mansel, R. E. (1999). Psychological distress associated with waiting for results of diagnostic investigations for breast disease. *Breast, 8*(6), 334-338.

Poster, M. (2008). Global media and culture. *New Literary History, 39*(3), 685-703,763.

Program for Appropriate Technology in Health (PATH). (1989). Summary of findings from oral contraceptive focus group discussions. Report to USAID/Cairo. Washington, D.C.: PATH.

Purcell, D., MacArthur, K. R., & Samblanet, S. (2010). Gender and the glass ceiling at work. *Sociology Compass, 4*(9), 705-717.

Purcell, D. (2012). Baseball, beer, and Bulgari: Examining cultural capital and gender inequality in a retail fashion corporation. *Journal of Contemporary Ethnography, 42*(3), 291-319.

Purcell, K., Elias, P., & Wilton, N. (2006). *Looking through the glass ceiling: a detailed investigation of the factors that contribute to gendered career inequalities.* Warwick, England: IER.

Radel, R., Sarrazin, P., Legrain, P., & Wild, T. C. (2010). Social contagion of motivation between teacher and student: Analyzing underlying processes. *Journal of Educational Psychology, 102*(3), 577–587.

Ramirez, G., et al. (2006). Family support predicts psychiatric medication usage among Mexican American individuals with schizophrenia. *Social Psychiatry and Psychiatric Epidemiology, 41*, 624-31.

Ranson, G. (2005). No longer 'One of the Boys': Negotiations with motherhood, as prospect or reality among women in engineering. *The Canadian Review of Sociology and Anthropology, 42*(2), 145-166.

Rapoport, M., McCauley, S., Levin, H., Song, J., & Feinstein, A. (2002). The role of injury severity in neurobehavioral outcome 3 months after Traumatic Brain Injury. *Neuropsychiatry, Neuropsychology, and Behavioral Neurology, 15*, 123-132.

Ravenstein, E. G. (1885). The laws of migration. *Journal of the Statistical Society of London, 48*(2), 167–235.

Ravenstein, E. G. (1889). The laws of migration. *Journal of the Royal Statistical Society, 52*(2), 241–305.

Ray, K. (2000). Repatriation and de-territorialization: Meskhetian Turks' conception of home. *Journal of Refugee Studies, 13*(4), 391-414.

Reardon, K. K., & Richardson, J. L. (1991). The important role of mass media in the diffusion of accurate information about AIDS. *Journal of Homosexuality, 21*(1-2), 63-75.
Redelmeier, D. A., & Tibshirani, R. J. (1997). Association between cellular-telephone calls and motor vehicle collisions. *New England Journal of Medicine, 336*(7), 453-458.
Redko, C., Rapp, R. C., & Carlson, R. G. (2006). Waiting time as a barrier to treatment entry: Perceptions of substance users. *Journal of Drug Issues, 36*(4), 831-852.
Reher, D. S. (2004). The demographic transition revisited as a global process. *Population, Space and Place, 10*(1), 19–41.
Reisman, A. S. (2003). *The psychological effects of ambiguous grief: Adult children of killed-in-action and missing-in-action servicemen from the Vietnam War*. Doctoral dissertation. Ann Arbor, MI: University of Michigan.
Renard, J. (1991). LSD tattoo transfers: Rumor from North America to France. *Folklore Forum, 24*(2), 3-26.
Reyneri, E. (1998). The mass legalization of migrants in Italy: Permanent or temporary emergence from the underground economy? *South European Society and Politics, 3*(3), 83-104.
Rhoades, R. E. (1978). Intra-European return migration and rural development: Lessons from the Spanish case. *Human Organization*, 37(2), 136-147.
Richardson, C. J. (1977). The problem of downward mobility. *British Journal of Sociology, 3*, 301-320.
Richter, M. (2004). Contextualizing gender and migration: Galician immigration to Switzerland. *International Migration Review, 38*(1), 263-286.
Rintala, D. H., Howland, C. A., Nosek, M. A., Bennett, J. L., Young, M. E., Foley, C. C., Rossi, C. D., & Chanpong, G. (1997). Dating issues for women with physical disabilities. *Sexuality and Disability, 15*(4), 219-42.
Robinson, J. P., Lee, C. W. (2014). Society's (virtually) time-free transition into the digital age. *Social Indicators Research, 117*(3), 939-965.
Robolis, S., & Xideas, E. (1996). The economic determinants of Greek return migration to the Islands of the East Aegean. *International Migration, 34*(2), 297-319.
Rodriguez, S. (2013). Making sense of social change: Observing collective action in networked cultures. *Sociology Compass, 7*(12), 1053-1064.
Rogers, P., Knetsch, W., & De Lestapis, B. (1985). *Microelectronics in industry: An international comparison: Britain, Germany, France (No. 635).* London: Policy Studies Institute.
Roscoe, P. B. (1990). The bow and spreadnet: Ecological origins of hunting technology. *American Anthropologist, 92*(3), 691.
Rose, J., & Rennie, M. (2007). Managing the risks associated with sexual activity. In Walker-Hirsch, L. (ed.), *The facts of life . . . and more: Sexuality and intimacy for people with intellectual disabilities*, pp. 193-221. Baltimore, MD: Paul H. Brookes Publishing.
Rosegger, G. (1991). Diffusion through interim cooperation. *Technological Forecasting and Social Change, 39*(1-2), 81-101.
Roseman, C. C. (1971). Migration as a spatial and temporal process, *Annals of the Association of American Geographers, 61*(3), 589-598.
Rosen, L., Durand, D., Westhuis, D. J., & Teitelbaum, J. (1996). Marital adjustment of army spouses one year after Operation Desert Storm. *Journal of Applied Social Psychology, 25*(8), 677-692.
Rosen, L., Durand, D., Teitelbaum, J., & Westhuis, D. J. (1993). Stressors, stress mediators, and emotional well-being among spouses of soldiers deployed to the Persian Gulf during Operation Desert Shield/Storm. *Journal of Applied Social Psychology, 23*(19), 1587-1593.
Rosenberg, M. M., & Jedwab, J. (1992). Institutional completeness, ethnic organizational style and the role of the state: The Jewish, Italian and Greek communities of Montreal. *Canadian Review of Sociology, 29*(3), 266-287.
Ross, D. (2006). The mind-set matters. *Foreign Affairs, 85*, 60-61.
Rubin, S. S., Malkinson, R., & Witztum, E. (1999). The pervasive impact of war-related loss and bereavement in Israel. *International Journal of Group Tensions, 28*(1).
Russell, P., Sudhakar, S., et al. (2004). Family intervention and acquisition of adaptive behaviour among intellectually disabled children. *Journal of Learning Disabilities, 8*, 383-395.
Ryan, B., & Gross, C. (1943). The diffusion of hybrid seed corn in two Iowa communities. *Rural Sociology, 8*, 15-24.

Ryan, G. A., Legge, M., & Rosman, D. (1998). Age related changes in drivers' crash risk and crash type. *Accident Analysis and Prevention, 30*(3), 379-387.

Sabattini, L., & Crosby, F. (2008). Overcoming resistance.: Structures and attitudes. In Thomas, K. M. (ed.), *Diversity Resistance in Organizations*, pp. 273-302. New York: Taylor & Francis.

Sabattini, L., & Crosby, F. J. (2009). Ceilings and walls: Work-life and "family-friendly" policies. In Barreto, M., Ryan, M. K., Schmitt, M. T. (eds.), *The glass ceiling in the 21st century: Understanding barriers to gender equality*, pp. 201-223. Washington, D.C.: American Psychological Association.

Sabattini, L., & Dinolfo, S. (2010). *Unwritten rules: Why doing a good job might not be enough.* Retrieved June 25th, 2014 from http://www.cpa2biz.com/Content/media/PRODUCER_CONTENT/Newsletters/Articles_2010/Career/UnwrittenRules.jsp.

Sadoh, A. E., Sadoh, W. E., Fawole, A. O., Oladimeji, A., & Sotiloye, O. (2009). Attitude of health care workers to patients and colleagues infected with human immunodeficiency virus. *Journal of Social Aspects of HIV/AIDS, 6*(1), 17-23.

Safran, W. (2005). The Jewish diaspora in a comparative and theoretical perspective. *Israel Studies, 10*(1), 36-60.

Safran, W. (1991). Diasporas in modern societies: Myths of homeland and return. *Diaspora: A Journal of Transnational Studies, 1*(1), 83-99.

Sanua, V. D. (1983). War bereavement in Israel. *Mainstream, 29*(3), 23-27.

Sarmento Jr., K. M., Tomita, S., & Kos, A. O. (2005). The problem of waiting lines for otorhinolaryngology surgeries in public services. *Brazilian Journal of Otorhinolaryngology*, 71(3), 256-262.

Satz, P., Zaucha, K., Light, R., McCleary, C., Asarnow, R., & Becker, D. (1997). Mild head injury in children and adolescents: A review of studies (1970-1995). *Psychological Bulletin, 122*, 107-131.

Scanlon, J., et al. (1985). Coping with the media in disasters: Some predictable problems. *Public Administration Review*, 123-133.

Scanlon, T. J. (1977). Post-disaster rumor chains: A case study. *Mass Emergencies, 2*(126), 22-27.

Schaake, K., Burgers, J., & Mulder, C. H. (2010). Ethnicity at the individual and neighborhood level as an explanation for moving out of the neighborhood. *Population Research and Policy Review, 29*(4), 593-608.

Scheff, T. J. (2003). Shame in self and society. *Symbolic Interaction, 26*(2), 239-262.

Scheirer, M. A. (1990). The life cycle of an innovation: Adoption versus discontinuation of the fluoride mouth rinse program in schools. *Journal of Health and Social Behavior, 31*(2), 203-215.

Scherbov, S., Lutz, W., & Sanderson, W. (2011). The uncertain timing of reaching 8 billion, peak world population, and other demographic milestones. *Population and Development Review, 37*(3), 571-578.

Schmitt, C. & Obinger, H. (2013). Spatial interdependencies and welfare state generosity in Western democracies. *Journal of European Social Policy, 23*(2), 119-133.

Schneiberg, M. (2013). Movements as political conditions for diffusion: Anti-corporate movements and the spread of cooperative forms in American capitalism. *Organization Studies, 34*(5-6), 653-682.

Schoen, R., & Canudas-Romo, V. (2005). Timing effects on first marriage: Twentieth-century experience in England and Wales and the USA. *Population Studies, 59*(2), 135-146.

Schwarz, B., Trommsdorff, G., Kim, U., & Park, Y. (2006). Intergenerational support: Psychological and cultural analyses of Korean and German women. *Sociology, 54*(2), 315-340.

Sciortino, G. (2004). Immigration in a Mediterranean welfare state: The Italian experience in comparative perspective. *Journal of Comparative Policy Analysis: Research and Practice* 6(2), 111-129.

Scott, D. L. (2010). War-related deaths in the family. In Scott, D. L (ed.), *Helping bereaved children: A handbook for practitioners*. New York: Guilford Press.

Segal, M. W. (1986). The military and family as greedy institutions. *Armed Forces and Society 13*(1), 9-38.

Sells, M. A. (1996). *The bridge betrayed: Religion and genocide in Bosnia, Vol. 11*. Berkeley, CA: University of California Press.

Servais, L. (2006). Sexual health care in persons with intellectual disabilities. *Sexual Health Care in Persons with Intellectual Disabilities, Mental Retardation and Developmental Disabilities Research Reviews, 12*(1), 48-56.

Settzer, M. M., Shattuck, P., Abbeduto, L., & Greenberg, J. S. (2004). Trajectory of development in adolescents and adults with autism. *Mental Retardation and Developmental Disabilities Research Reviews, 10*, 234-47.

Sharma, B. R., et al. (2001). Road-traffic accidents: A demographic and topographic analysis. *Medicine, Science and the Law, 41*(3), 266-274.

Sheffer, G. (1998). The Israeli diaspora: Yordim (emigrants) are the authentic diaspora. In Massil, S. (Ed.), *The Jewish Yearbook*, pp. 19-31. London: Wallentine Mitchell.

Sheth, J. N., Sisodia, R. S., & Sharma, A. (2000). The antecedents and consequences of customer-centric marketing. *Journal of the Academy of Marketing Science, 28*(1), 55-66.

Shibutani T. (1966). *Improvised news: A sociological study of rumor.* Indianapolis: Bobbs-Merrill.

Shiff, O. (1994). The integrative function of early American Zionism. *Journal of Israeli History, 15*(1), 1-16.

Shifman L. (2011). An anatomy of a YouTube meme. *New Media & Society, 14*(2), 187 –203.

Shin, E. H., & Chin, S. K. (1989). Social affinity among top managerial executives of large corporations in Korea. *Sociological Forum, 4*(1), 3-26.

Short, J. R., & Pinet-Peralta, L. M. (2010). No accident: Traffic and pedestrians in the modern city. *Mobilities, 5*(1), 41-59.

Sikkink, K., Kim, H. J. (2013). The justice cascade: The origins and effectiveness of prosecutions of human rights violations. *Annual Review of Law and Social Science, 9*, 269-285.

Silverberg, G. (1991). Adoption and diffusion of technology as a collective evolutionary process. *Technological Forecasting and Social Change, 39*(1-2), 67-80.

Simon, R. J., & Brettell, C. B. (1986). *International migration: the female experience.* Totowa, NJ: Rowman & Allanheld.

Smallman-Raynor, M. R., & Cliff, A. D. (1990). Acquired immune deficiency syndrome (AIDS): Literature, geographical origins and global patterns. *Progress in Human Geography, 14*(2), 157-213.

Snijders, C., Zijdeman, R., & Und Kritnik, A. (2004). Reputation and Internet auctions: eBay and beyond. *Proquest, 26*, 158-184.

Söderlund, N., & Zwi, A. B. (1995). Traffic-related mortality in industrialized and less developed countries. *Bulletin of the World Health Organization 73*(2), 175.

Solove, D. J. (2007). *The future of reputation: Gossip, rumor, and privacy on the Internet.* New Haven, CT: Yale University Press.

Sorensen, et al. (2002). How effective are interventions with caregivers? An updated meta-analysis. *The Gerontologist, 42*(3), 356-372.

Soule, S. A. (1997). The student divestment movement in the United States and tactical diffusion: The shantytown protest. *Social Forces, 75*(3), 855-882.

Sperling, M. R. (2004). The consequences of uncontrolled epilepsy. *CNS Spectrums, 9*(2), 98-109.

Statistics Canada. (2002). Changing conjugal life in Canada. General Social Survey: Cycle 15.

Statistics Canada. (2006). Report on the demographic situation in Canada 2003 and 2004. Demography Division.

Statistics Canada. (2007). Marriages. *The Daily.* Accessed November 1, 2007, at http://www.statcan.ca/Daily/English/070117/d070117a.htm.

Steen, J. M., & Asaro, M. R. (2006). *Military widow: A survival guide.* Annapolis, MD: Naval Institute Press.

Stern, M. J., & Rookey, B. D. (2013). The politics of new media, space and race: A sociospatial analysis of the 2008 presidential election. *New Media and Society, 15*(4), 519-540.

Stetz, K. M., & Brown, M. (2004). Physical and psychosocial health in family caregiving: A comparison of AIDS and cancer caregivers. *Public Health Nursing, 21*(6).

Stillwell, J. H. C., & Stillwell, P. (1997). *National traumatic brain injury study.* Warwick: University of Warwick.

Stinchcombe, A. L. (1975). A Parsonian theory of traffic accidents. *Sociological Inquiry, 45*(1), 27-30.

Stokes, S. C. (2005). Perverse accountability: A formal model of machine politics with evidence from Argentina. *American Political Science Review, 99*(3), 315-325.

Stone, R., Cafferata, G. L., & Sangl, J. (1987). Caregivers of the frail elderly: A national profile. *The Gerontologist, 27*(5), 616-626.

Strang, D. (1990). From dependency to sovereignty: An event history analysis of decolonization 1870-1987. *American Sociological Review, 55*(6), 846-860.

Strang, D. (1991). Adding social structure to diffusion models: An event history framework. *Sociological Methods and Research, 19*(3), 324-353.

Straub, D. W. (1994). The effect of culture on IT diffusion: E-mail and fax in Japan and the U.S. *Information Systems Research, 5*(1), 23-47.

Strohmer, D. C., Grand, S. A., Purcell, M. J. (1984). Attitudes toward persons with a disability: An examination of demographic factors, social context, and specific disability. *Rehabilitation Psychology, 29*(3), 131-145.

Strohschein, L. (2011). Spousal bereavement as a triggering mechanism for a loss of residential independence among Canadian seniors. *Research on Aging, 33*(5), 576-597.

Surr, Claire Alice (2006). Preservation of self in people with dementia living in residential care: A socio-biographical approach. *Social Science and Medicine, 62*(7).

Swan, J. A., & Newell, S. (1995). The role of professional associations in technology diffusion. *Organization Studies, 16*(5), 847-874.

Szoc, R., & Seboda, B. L. (1987). Follow-up study of family factors critical to the retention of naval personnel. *Organizational Effectiveness Research Programs Office of Naval Research.*

Szwarcberg, M. (2013). The microfoundations of political clientelism: Lessons from the Argentine case. *Latin American Research Review, 48*(2), 32-54.

Tang, F., & Lee, Y. (2011). Social support networks and expectations for aging in place and moving. *Research on Aging, 33*(4), 444-464.

Tarabusi, M., Volpe, A., & Facchinetti, F. (2004). Psychological group support attenuates distress of waiting in couples scheduled for assisted reproduction. *Journal of Psychosomatic Obstetrical Gynaecology, 25*(3-4), 273 – 279.

Tate, R. L., & Broe, G. A. (1999). Psychosocial adjustment after traumatic brain injury: What are the important variables? *Psychological Medicine, 29*, 713-25

Teague, P., Roche, B., & Hann, D. (2012). The diffusion of alternative dispute resolution practices in Ireland. *Economic and Industrial Democracy, 33*(4), 581-604.

Teasell, R. W., McRae, M. P., & Finestone, H. M. (2000). Social issues in the rehabilitation of younger stroke patients. *Archives of Physical Medicine and Rehabilitation, 81*, 205-209.

Teitelbaum, M. S. (1989). Skeptical noises about the immigration multiplier. *International Migration Review*, 893-899.

Tejerina, B., Perugorria, I., Benski, T., & Langman, L. (2013). From indignation to occupation: A new wave of global mobilization. *Current Sociology, 61*(4), 377-392.

Tepperman, L., & Marsden, L. (1985). The migrant wife: the worst of all worlds. *Journal of Business Ethics, 4*, 205-213.

Tepperman, L., & Meredith, N. (2015). *Waiting to happen: Accidental injuries in Canada.* Don Mills, ON: Oxford University Press.

Tepperman, L. (1985a). Musical chairs: the occupational experience of migrants to Alberta, 1976-80. *Social Indicators Research, 16*, 51-67.

Thomas, S. A. (2007). Lies, damn lies, and rumors: An analysis of collective efficacy, rumors, and fear in the wake of Katrina. *Sociological Spectrum, 27*, 679–703.

Thomas, J. K., Ladewig, H., McIntosh, W. A. (1990). The adoption of integrated pest management practices among Texas cotton growers. *Rural Sociology, 55*(3), 395-410.

Thompson, D. A., & Yarnold, P. R. (1995). Relating patient satisfaction to waiting time perceptions and expectations: The disconfirmation paradigm. *Academic Emergency Medicine: Official Journal of the Society for Academic Emergency Medicine, 2*(12), 1057-1062.

Thompson, D. A., Yarnold, P. R., Williams, D. R., & Adams, S. L. (1996). Effects of actual waiting time, perceived waiting time, information delivery, and expressive quality on patient satisfaction in the emergency department. *Annals of Emergency Medicine 28*(6), 657-665.

Thompson, M. D., & Irby, J. W., jr. (2003). Recovery from mild head injury in pediatric populations. *Seminars in Pediatric Neurology, 10*, 130-39.

Thomsen, I. V. (1989). Do young patients have worse outcomes after severe blunt head trauma? *Brain Injury, 3*, 157-162.

Tominaga, K. (1991). A theory of modernization and social change of the non-Western societies: Toward a generalization from Japan's experiences. *International Review of Sociology 3* (new series), 95-120.

Torchia, M., Calabro, A., & Huse, M. (2011). Women directors on corporate boards: From tokenism to critical mass. *Journal of Business Ethics, 102*(2), 299-317.

Townes, M. (2012). The spread of TCP/IP: How the Internet became the Internet. *Millennium: Journal of International Studies, 41*(1), 43-64.

Trachtman, L. E. Spirek, M. M., Sparks, G.G., & Stohl, C. (1991). Factors affecting the adoption of a new technology. *Bulletin of Science, Technology and Society, 11*(6), 338-345.

Trachtman, L. E., Spirek, M. M., Sparks, G. G., Stohl, C., & Trampusch, C. (2014). Why preferences and institutions change: A systematic process analysis of credit rating in Germany. *European Journal of Political Research, 53*(2), 328-344.

Tremayne, M. (2014). Anatomy of protest in the digital era: A network analysis of Twitter and Occupy Wall Street. *Social Movement Studies, 13*(1), 110-126.

Trottier, D. A., Potter, L. S., Taylor, B. A., & Glover, L. H. (1993). User characteristics and oral contraceptive compliance in Egypt. *Studies in family planning, 25*(5), 284-292.

Tsakanikos, E., Bouras, N., Sturmey, P., & Holt, G. (2006). Psychiatric co-morbidity and gender differences in intellectual disability. *Journal of Intellectual Disability Research, 50*(8), 582-587.

Tsouna-Hadjis, E., et al. (2000). First-stroke recovery process: The role of family social support. *Archives of Physical Medicine and Rehabilitation, 81*, 881-887.

Turner, M. M., Mazur, M. A., Wendel, N., & Wilmslow, R. (2003). Relational ruin or social glue? The joint effect of relationship type and gossip valence on liking, trust, and expertise. *Communication Monographs, 70*, 129–141.

Turner, R. H. (1994). Rumor as intensified information seeking: Earthquake rumors in China and the United States. In Dynes, R. R., & Tierney, K. J. (eds.), *Disasters, collective behavior, and social organization*, pp. 244-256. Newark, DE: University of Delaware Press.

Turrisi, R., Wiersma, K. A., & Hughes, K. K. (2000). Binge-drinking-related consequences in college students: Role of drinking beliefs and mother–teen communications. *Psychology of Addictive Behaviors, 14*(4), 342.

Turrittin, J.S. (1976). Networks and mobility: The case of West Indian domestics from Montserrat. *Canadian Review of Sociology, 13*(3), 305-320.

Tyler, J., & McCullough, J. (2009). Violating prescriptive stereotypes on job resumes: A self-presentational perspective. *Management Communication Quarterly, 23*(2), 272-287.

Ursano, R. J. (1996). *Emotional aftermath of the Persian Gulf war: Veterans, families, communities, and nations*. Washington, D.C.: American Psychiatric Press.

Van Naarden Braun, K. (2003). A multi-dimensional approach to the epidemiology of developmental disabilities: From school-age to young adulthood. *Dissertation Abstracts International, 64*(10B), 4893.

Van Vranken, E. W., Jellen, L. K., Knudson, K. H. M., Marlow, D. H., & Segal, M. W. (1984). The impact of deployment separation on army families. *U.S. Army Medical Research and Development Command.*

Van, Sertima. I. (1976). *They came before Columbus*. New York: Random House.

Vanderploeg, R. D., Curtiss, G., Duchnick, J. J., Luis, C. A. (2003). Demographic, medical, and psychiatric factors in work and marital status after mild head injury. *Journal of Head Trauma Rehabilitation, 18*(2), 148-163.

Vanderploeg, R. D., Curtiss, G., Luis, C. A., & Salazar, A. M. (2007). Long-term morbidities following self-reported mild traumatic brain injury. *Journal of Clinical and Experimental Neuropsychology, 29*(6), 585-598.

Vaughan, D. (1983). Uncoupling: The social construction of divorce. In Robboy, H., & Clark, C. (eds.), *Social interaction*, pp. 405-422. New York: St. Martin's Press.

Vega, W. A. (1990). Hispanic families in the 1980s: A decade of research. *Journal of Marriage and the Family, 52*(4), 1015-1024.

Verhaeghe, S., Defloor, T., & Grypdonck, M. (2004). Stress and coping among families of patients with traumatic brain injury: A review of the literature. *Journal of Clinical Nursing, 14*, 1004–1012.

Verhaeghe, P. P., & Tampubolon, G. (2012). Individual social capital, neighbourhood deprivation, and self-rated health in England. *Social science and medicine, 75*(2), 349-357.

Vermeulen, K. M., Bosma, O. H., Bij, Wv., Koeter, G. H., & Tenvergert, E. M., (2005). Stress, psychological distress, and coping in patients on the waiting list for lung transplantation: an exploratory study. *Transplant International, 18*(8), 954-959.

Vertovec, S. (2006). Is circular migration the way forward in global policy? *Around the Globe, 3*(2), 38-44.

Victor, J. S. (1989). A rumor-panic about a dangerous satanic cult in western New York. *New York Folklore, 15*, 23-49.

Wade, S. L., et al. (2001). The relationship of caregiver coping to family outcomes during the initial year following pediatric traumatic injury. *Journal of Consulting and Clinical Psychology, 69*(3), 406-415.

Wagenaar, A. C., & Toomey, T. L. (2002). Effects of minimum drinking age laws: Review and analyses of the literature from 1960 to 2000. *Journal of Studies on Alcohol and Drugs, 14*, 206.

Waldorf, B. S. (2009). Is human capital accumulation a self-propelling process? Comparing educational attainment levels of movers and stayers. *The Annals of Regional Science, 43*(2), 323-344.

Wallerstein, J. S., & Kelly, J. B. (2008). *Surviving the breakup: How children and parents cope with divorce.* New York: Basic Books.

Walton, J. K. (1994). *Fish and chips, and the British working class, 1870-1940.* London: Bloomsbury.

Wang, C., Quddus, M. A., & Ison, S. . (2009). Impact of traffic congestion on road accidents: A spatial analysis of the M25 motorway in England. *Accident Analysis and Prevention, 41*(4), 798-808.

Wassenberg, R., et al. (2004). Sustained attention in children and adolescents after traumatic brain injury: Relation to severity of injury, adaptive functioning, ADHD and social background. *Brain Injury, 18*(8), 751-764.

Waters, J. L. (2002). Flexible families? 'Astronaut' households and the experiences of lone mothers in Vancouver, British Columbia. *Social and Cultural Geography, 3*(2), 117-134.

Waters, J. L. (2005). Transnational family strategies and education in the contemporary Chinese diaspora. *Global Networks, 5*(4), 359-377.

Waters, M. C., & Jiménez, T. R. (2005). Assessing immigrant assimilation: New empirical and theoretical challenges. *Annual Review of Sociology*, 105-125.

Watkins, S. C., & Danzi, A. D. (1995). Women's gossip and social change: Childbirth and fertility control among Italian and Jewish women in the United States, 1920-1940. *Gender and Society, 9*(4), 469-490.

Webb, C. R., Wrigley, M., Yoels, W., & Fine, P. R. (1995). Explaining quality of life for persons with traumatic brain injuries 2 years after injury. *Archives of Physical Medicine and Rehabilitation, 76*(12), 1113-1119.

Weber, E. G., & Weber, D. K. (2005). Geographic relocation frequency, resiliency, and military adolescent behaviour. *Military Medicine, 170*, 638–642.

Webster, T. L. (2005). Adaptation processes for elderly care recipients and their caregivers in the context of a medicalized home environment. *Dissertation Abstracts International, 65*(8-A).

Wechsler, H., et al. (1998). Changes in binge drinking and related problems among American college students between 1993 and 1997. Results of the Harvard School of Public Health College Alcohol Study. *Journal of American College Health, 47*(2), 57-68.

Wegener, B. (1991). Job mobility and social ties: Social resources, prior job, and status attainment. *American Sociological Review*, 60-71.

Weinberg, N., Schmale, J., Uken, J., & Wessel, K. (1996). Online help: Cancer patients participate in an online support group. *Health and Social Work, 21*(1), 24-29.

Weiner, A. B. (1977). Review of 'Trobriand Cricket': An ingenious response to colonialism. *American Anthropologist, 79*, 506-507.

Weiner, E. C. (1990). The threat to the legitimacy of war. In Wyatt, T. C., & Gal, R. (eds.) *Legitimacy and commitment in the military*, pp. 97-116. Westport, CT: Greenwood Press.

Weiner, M. (1982). International migration and development: Indians in the Persian Gulf. *Population and Development Review*, 1-36.

Wejnert, B. (2013). Reflections on the impact of globalization: Diffusion, equality and opportunities. *Research in Political Sociology, 21*, 255-261.

Wells, T., Sandefur, G. D., & Hogan, D. P. (2003). What happens after the high school years among young persons with disabilities? *Social Forces, 82*, 803-832.

Wellstood, K., Wilson, K., & Eyles, J. (2005). 'Unless you went in with your head under your arm': Patient perceptions of emergency room visits. *Social Science and Medicine, 61*(11), 2363-2373.

Wenhong, L., Liberatore, M. J., Nydick, R. L., Chung, Q.B., & Sloane, E. (2004). Impact of process change on customer perception of waiting time: A field study. *Omega, 32*(1), 77-83

Westbrook, D. (1995). Patient and therapist views of different waiting list procedures. *Behavioural and Cognitive Psychotherapy, 23*(2), 169-175.

Westphal, J. D., Gulati, R., & Shortell, S. M. (1997). Customization or conformity? An institutional and network perspective on the content and consequences of TQM adoption. *Administrative Science Quarterly, 42*(2), 366–394.

Wheeler, A. R., & Stone, R. A. T. (2010). Exploring stress and coping strategies among National Guard spouses during times of deployment: A research note. *Armed Forces and Society, 36*(3), 545-557.

Whetten-Goldstein, K., et al. (2000). Civil liability, criminal law, and other policies and alcohol-related motor vehicle fatalities in the United States: 1984–1995. *Accident Analysis and Prevention 32*(6), 723-733.

White, H. (1970). *Chains of opportunity: System models of mobility in organizations*. Cambridge, MA: Harvard University Press.

Whiting, A., et al. (2006). Managing voice-to-voice encounters: Reducing the agony of being put on hold. *Journal of Service Research, 8*, 234-244.

Whitnall, L., McMillan, T. M., Murray, G. D., & Teasdale, G. M. (2006). Disability in young people and adults after head injury: 5-7 year follow up of a prospective cohort study. *Journal of Neurology, Neurosurgery, and Psychiatry, 77*, 640-645.

Wickham-Crowley, T. (2014). Two 'waves' of guerrilla-movement organizing in Latin America, 1956-1990. *Comparative Studies in Society and History, 56*(1), 215-242.

Wicks, L. A. (1996). Ethnicity and psychotherapy with HIV-infected patients: Three case studies. *Journal of Social Distress and the Homeless, 5*(1), 67-82.

Wiegerink, D. J. H. G., Roebroeck, M. E., Donkervoort, M., Stam, H. J., & Cohen-Kettenis, P. T. (2006). Social and sexual relationships of adolescents and young adults with cerebral palsy: A review. *Clinical Rehabilitation, 20*(12), 1023-1031.

Williams, A. F., Lund, A. K., & Preusser, D. F. (1986). Drinking and driving among high school students. *Substance Use and Misuse, 21*(6), 643-655.

Williams, C. (2013). The glass escalator, revisited: Gender inequality in neoliberal times. *Gender and Society, 27*(5), 609-629.

Williams, C. L. (1992). The glass escalator: Hidden advantages for men in the "female" professions. *Social Problems*, 253-267.

Williams, J. C. (2003). Beyond the glass ceiling: The maternal wall as a barrier to gender equality. *Thomas Jefferson Law Review, 26* (1).

Wilson, D. S., Wilczynski, C., Wells, A., & Weiser, L. (2002). Gossip and other aspects of language as group-level adaptations. In Heyes, C., & Huber, L. (eds.), *The evolution of cognition*, pp. 347–365. Cambridge, MA: MIT Press.

Wilson, T. D. (1998). Weak ties, strong ties: Network principles in Mexican migration. *Human Organization, 57*(4), 394-403.

Wingfield, A. H. (2007). The modern mammy and the angry black man: African American professionals' experiences with gendered racism in the workplace. *Race, Gender and Class*, 196-212.

Wingfield, A. H. (2009). Racializing the glass escalator: Reconsidering men's experiences with women's work. *Gender and Society, 23*(1), 5-26.

Wodak, R. (ed.). (1997). *Gender and discourse*. Thousand Oaks, CA: Sage.

Wood, R. L., & Yurdakul, L.K. (1997). Change in relationship status following traumatic brain injury. *Brain Injury, 11*, 491-502.

Wood, R. L., & Rutherford, N. A. (2006). Psychosocial adjustment 17 years after severe brain injury. *Journal of Neurology, Neurosurgery, and Psychiatry, 77*, 71-73.

Wood, R. L., Liossi, C., & Wood. L. (2005). The impact of head injury neurobehavioural sequelae on personal relationships: Preliminary findings. *Brain Injury, 19*, 845-51.

Wood, S., Scarville, J., & Gravino, K. S. (1995). Waiting wives: Separation and reunion among army wives. *Armed Forces and Society, 21*(2), 217-236.

Woodill, G. (1992). Controlling the sexuality of developmentally disabled persons: Historical perspectives. *Journal on Developmental Disabilities, 1*(1), 1-14.

Wright, K. M., Burrell, L. M., Schroeder E. D., & Thomas, J. L. (2006). Military spouses: Coping with the fear and reality of service member injury and death. In Castro, C. A., Adler, A. B., & Britt, T. W. (eds.), *Military life: The psychology of serving in peace and combat*. Westport, CT: Praeger.

Yap, M., & Konrad, A. M. (2009). Gender and racial differentials in promotions: Is there a sticky floor, a mid-level bottleneck, or a glass ceiling? *Industrial Relations, 40*, 593-619.

Ybema, J. F, Kuijer, R. G., Hagedoorn, M., & Buunk, B. P. (2002). Caregiver burnout among intimate partners of patients with a severe illness: An equity perspective. *Personal Relationships, 9*, 73-88.

Yoon, B. L. (1992). Reverse brain drain in South Korea: State-led model. *Studies in Comparative International Development, 27*(1), 4-26.

Yu, B. (2008). *Chain migration explained: The power of the immigration multiplier*. El Paso, TX: LFB Scholarly Publishing.

Zador, P. L., Krawchuk, S. A., & Voas, R. B. (2000). Alcohol-related relative risk of driver fatalities and driver involvement in fatal crashes in relation to driver age and gender: An update using 1996 data. *Journal of Studies on Alcohol and Drugs 61*(3), 387.

Zapf, W. (1991). The role of innovations in modernization theory. *International Review of Sociology, 3* (new series), 83-94.

Zevelev, I. (1996). Russia and the Russian diasporas. *Post-Soviet Affairs, 12*(3), 265-284.

Zhang, Z., & Zhang, Z. (2009). An interplay model for rumour spreading and emergency development. *Physica A, 388*, 4159–4166.

Zheng, W. (1998). Trends in marriage patterns in Canada. *Policy Options*, 3-6.

Zink, T., et al. (2003). Cohort, period, and aging effects: A qualitative study of older women's reasons for remaining in abusive relationships. *Violence Against Women*, 9(12), 1429-1441.

Zipf, G. K. (1946). The P1 P2/D Hypothesis: On the intercity movement of persons. *American Sociological Review, 11*, 677.

Zipf, G. K. (1949). *Human behavior and the principle of least effort: An introduction to human ecology*. Cambridge, MA: Addison-Wesley.

Zippay, A. (1990). The limits of intimates: Social networks and economic status among displaced industrial workers. *Journal of Applied Social Sciences, 15*(1), 75-95.

Zippay, A. (2001). Roles of social capital in reclaiming human capital: A longitudinal study of occupational mobility among displaced steelworkers. *Journal of Sociology and Social Welfare, 28*, 99.

Index